TEACHER'S GUIDE

SIDE by SIDE Plus

BOOK 3

Life Skills, Standards, & Test Prep

Steven J. Molinsky
Bill Bliss

Contributing Authors

Sarah Lynn
Mary Ann Perry

with

John Kopec

PEARSON
Longman

D1133747

Correlation and Placement Key

Side by Side Plus correlates with the following standards-based curriculum levels and assessment system score ranges:

	Side by Side Plus 1	Side by Side Plus 2	Side by Side Plus 3	Side by Side Plus 4
NRS (National Reporting System) Educational Functioning Level	Low Beginning	High Beginning	Low Intermediate	High Intermediate
CASAS (Comprehensive Adult Student Assessment System)	181–190	191–200	201–210	211–220
BEST Plus (Basic English Skills Test)	401–417	418–438	439–472	473–506
BEST Oral Interview	16–28	29–41	42–50	51–57
BEST Literacy	8–35	36–46	47–53	54–65

For correlations to other major curriculum frameworks, please visit: www.pearsonlongman.com/sidebysideplus

**Side by Side Plus 3
Teacher's Guide**

Copyright © 2009 by Prentice Hall Regents
Addison Wesley Longman, Inc.
A Pearson Education Company.
All rights reserved.
No part of this publication may be reproduced,
stored in a retrieval system, or transmitted
in any form or by any means, electronic, mechanical,
photocopying, recording, or otherwise,
without the prior permission of the publisher.

Pearson Education, 10 Bank Street, White Plains, NY 10606

Editorial director: *Pam Fishman*
Vice president, director of design and production: *Rhea Banker*
Director of electronic production: *Aliza Greenblatt*
Director of manufacturing: *Patrice Fraccio*
Senior manufacturing manager: *Edith Pullman*
Director of marketing: *Oliva Fernandez*
Production editor: *Diane Cipollone*
Digital layout specialists: *Warren Fischbach, Lisa Ghiozzi, Paula Williams, Wendy Wolf*
Text composition: *TSI Graphics*
Interior design: *Wendy Wolf*
Interior art: *Judy A. Wolf*
Cover design: *Wanda España, Wee Design Group; Warren Fischbach*
Cover art: *Richard E. Hill*

The authors gratefully acknowledge the contribution
of Tina Carver in the development of the original
Side by Side program.

Pearsonlongman on the Web
Pearsonlongman.com offers online resources for teachers and students.
Access our Companion Websites, our online catalog, and our local offices around the world.
Visit us at **pearsonlongman.com**.

ISBN 978-0-13-240217-0; 0-13-240217-3

Printed in the United States of America
3 4 5 6 7 8 9 10 – V3NL – 18 17 16 15 14

CONTENTS

Guide to Life Skills, Standards, & Test Prep Features

Side by Side has helped over 25 million students worldwide persist and succeed as language learners. Now, in this special edition for adult learners in standards-based programs, *Side by Side Plus* builds students' general language proficiency *and* helps them apply these skills for success meeting the needs of daily life and work.

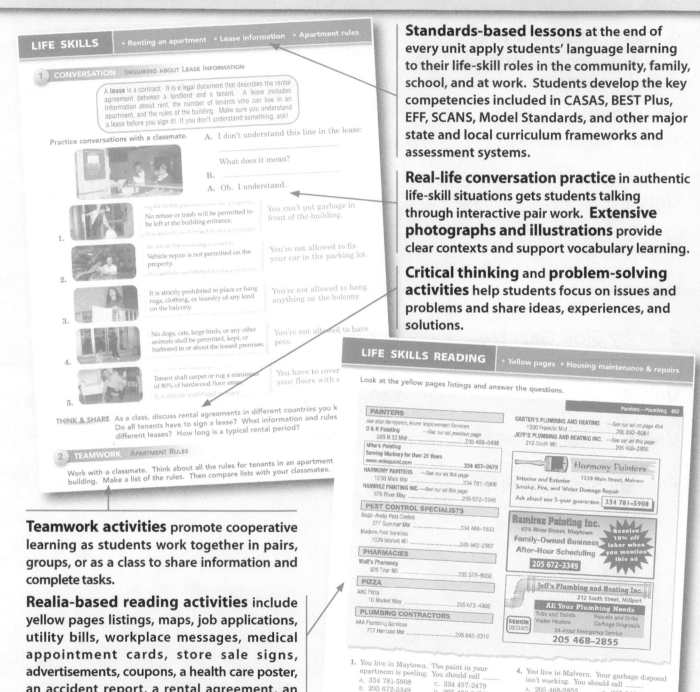

Standards-based lessons at the end of every unit apply students' language learning to their life-skill roles in the community, family, school, and at work. Students develop the key competencies included in CASAS, BEST Plus, EFF, SCANS, Model Standards, and other major state and local curriculum frameworks and assessment systems.

Real-life conversation practice in authentic life-skill situations gets students talking through interactive pair work. **Extensive photographs and illustrations** provide clear contexts and support vocabulary learning.

Critical thinking and **problem-solving activities** help students focus on issues and problems and share ideas, experiences, and solutions.

Teamwork activities promote cooperative learning as students work together in pairs, groups, or as a class to share information and complete tasks.

Realia-based reading activities include yellow pages listings, maps, job applications, utility bills, workplace messages, medical appointment cards, store sale signs, advertisements, coupons, a health care poster, an accident report, a rental agreement, an apartment building notice, an employee manual, and a medical history form.

Life skills writing activities include lists, notes, personal information forms, employment application forms, a cover letter, and a resume.

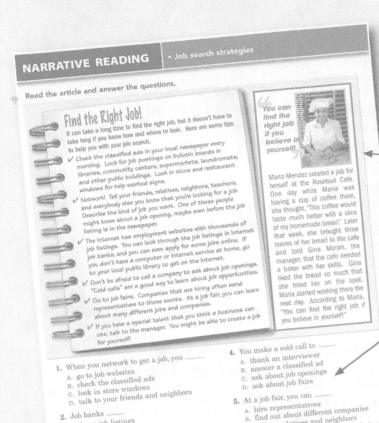

Read the article and answer the questions.

Find the Right Job!

It can take a long time to find the right job, but it doesn't have to take long if you know how and where to look. Here are some tips to help you with your job search.

✓ Check the classified ads in your local newspaper every morning. Look for job postings on bulletin boards in libraries, community centers, supermarkets, laundromats, and other public buildings. Look in store and restaurant windows for help wanted signs.

✓ Network! Tell your friends, relatives, neighbors, teachers, and everybody else you know that you're looking for a job. Describe the kind of job you want. One of these people might know about a job opening, maybe even before the job listing is in the newspaper.

✓ The Internet has employment websites with thousands of job listings. You can look through the job listings in Internet job banks, and you can even apply for some jobs online. If you don't have a computer or Internet service at home, go to your local public library to get on the Internet.

✓ Don't be afraid to call a company to ask about job openings. "Cold calls" are a good way to learn about job opportunities.

✓ Go to job fairs. Companies that are hiring often send representatives to these events. At a job fair, you can learn about many different jobs and companies.

✓ If you have a special talent that you think a business can use, talk to the manager. You might be able to create a job for yourself!

"You can find the right job if you believe in yourself!"

Maria Mendez created a job for herself at the Rosebud Cafe. One day while Maria was having a cup of coffee there, she thought, "This coffee would taste much better with a slice of my homemade bread." Later that week, she brought three loaves of her bread to the cafe and told Gina Moran, the manager, that the cafe needed a baker with her skills. Gina liked the bread so much that she hired her on the spot. Maria started working there the next day. According to Maria, "You can find the right job if you believe in yourself!"

1. When you network to get a job, you _____.
   A. go to job websites
   B. check the classified ads
   C. look in store windows
   D. talk to your friends and neighbors

2. Job banks _____.
   A. have job listings
   B. give money
   C. are on bulletin boards
   D. are in public buildings

3. If you want to get on the Internet, you can go to _____.
   A. a job fair
   B. a job bank
   C. the library
   D. the Rosebud Cafe

4. You make a cold call to _____.
   A. thank an interviewer
   B. answer a classified ad
   C. ask about job openings
   D. ask about job fairs

5. At a job fair, you can _____.
   A. hire representatives
   B. find out about different companies
   C. talk to relatives and neighbors
   D. look in windows for help wanted signs

6. The Rosebud Cafe hired Maria Mendez because _____.
   A. they were looking for a baker
   B. she answered their ad
   C. she saw Gina Moran's help
   D. she created a job for herself

Narrative reading passages offer practice with simple magazine articles on topics such as job search strategies, identity theft, small talk at work, and career advancement. **Academic lessons** in school textbook formats prepare students for success in continuing education through subject-matter content including government, history, and health.

Reading comprehension exercises in multiple-choice formats help students prepare for the reading section of standardized tests.

Choose the correct answer.

1. Samantha got a raise, and now her _____ is higher.
   A. report
   B. elevator
   C. boss
   D. salary

2. I went to the doctor for an examination. She gave me _____.
   A. a presentation
   B. the flu
   C. an injection
   D. X-rays

3. Let's go _____ on the river this weekend!
   A. kayaking
   B. camping
   C. hiking
   D. bowling

4. Did you watch the president's _____ about world problems on television last night?
   A. course
   B. speech
   C. inventory
   D. term paper

Look at Wanda's job application form. Choose the correct answer.

9. Wanda worked as a receptionist _____.
   A. in Detroit
   B. for two and a half years
   C. in 2008
   D. at the Brandon Corporation

10. Wanda hasn't _____ in a long time.
   A. sorted mail
   B. typed reports
   C. taken messages
   D. filed documents

5. I didn't understand the present perfect tense, but my teacher _____ it very well.
   A. examined
   B. complained
   C. explained
   D. expressed

6. What _____ are you applying for?
   A. employer
   B. position
   C. skills
   D. reference

7. I saw a _____ for a receptionist on the bulletin board in the library.
   A. job posting
   B. job bank
   C. representative
   D. job fair

8. I made _____ to the Randall Company and asked about job openings.
   A. a network
   B. a job listing
   C. an opportunity
   D. a cold call

Date	Name & Address of Employer	Position	Reason for Leaving
From: 7/05 To: present	Brandon Corporation 1100 First Ave., Detroit, MI	office assistant	want to learn new skills
Duties: type reports, file documents, sort mail			
From: 2/05 To: 8/07	Tech-World Corporation 599 Tyler St., Chicago, IL	receptionist	returned to school
Duties: answered the telephone, took messages, and greeted clients			

SKILLS CHECK

Words:
☐ classified ads
☐ cold call
☐ dates of employment
☐ education history
☐ employer
☐ employment application
☐ employment history
☐ help wanted sign
☐ job bank
☐ job fair
☐ job listing
☐ job opening
☐ job posting
☐ job search
☐ personal information
☐ position
☐ reference
☐ representative
☐ salary
☐ skills
☐ apply for
☐ complete
☐ fill in
☐ hire
☐ network

I can ask & answer:
☐ Have you ever seen it?
   Yes, I have. I saw it last year.
☐ Have you gone to the bank yet?
   Yes, I have.
   No, I haven't.
☐ I've driven for many years.
☐ I've already gone there.
☐ I've never been on television.

I can:
☐ identify employment application procedures
☐ apply for a job
☐ describe job search strategies

I can express satisfaction:
☐ It was excellent/very good/wonderful/great/fantastic/terrific/phenomenal/awesome.

I can write:
☐ a list of things I've done
☐ employment history on a job application form

I can write about:
☐ experiences in the place where I live

50d

Check-up tests allow a quick assessment of student achievement and help prepare students for the kinds of test items found on standardized tests.

More complete **Achievement Tests** for each unit, including listening test items, are available as reproducible masters and printable disk files in the Teacher's Guide with Multilevel Activity & Achievement Test Book and CD-ROM. They are also available in the companion Activity & Test Prep Workbook.

Vocabulary checklists and **language skill checklists** help students review words they have learned, keep track of the skills they are developing, and identify vocabulary and skills they need to continue to work on. These lists promote student persistence as students assess their own skills and check off all the ways they are succeeding as language learners.

Guide to Multilevel Resources

The *Side by Side Plus Teacher's Guides* provide valuable resources for effective multilevel instruction. Easy-to-use strategies help teachers preview and pre-drill lesson objectives for students who need extra preparation. Hundreds of dynamic expansion activities offer reinforcement and enrichment for students at three different ability-levels:

- *Below-level* students who need extra support and some re-teaching of skills and content to master basic objectives;
- *At-level* students who are performing well in class and can benefit from reinforcement;
- *Above-level* students who want and deserve opportunities for enrichment and greater challenge.

Getting Ready sections are ideal lesson-planning tools. They provide a careful sequence of instructional steps teachers can use during the warm-up, preview, and initial presentation stages of a lesson—especially helpful for *below-level* students who need careful preparation for a lesson's new vocabulary, grammar, topics, functions, or language skills.

The Getting Ready section is an "on-ramp" that allows students to get up to speed with lesson content so that they comprehend the lesson and master its learning objectives.

Text Pages 14–15: How Did Marty Break His Leg?

FOCUS

- Review: Past Continuous Tense

CLOSE UP

RULE: The past continuous tense is commonly used to show a past activity that was in progress when another event happened.

EXAMPLES: He **broke** his leg while he **was snowboarding**.
She **sprained** her ankle while she **was playing** volleyball.

GETTING READY

1. Use your own visuals or *Side by Side* Picture Cards for verbs to review the past continuous tense.

   a. Hold up visuals and ask students questions in the past continuous tense. For example:

      (*Side by Side* Picture Card 44)
      A. What were they doing last night?
      B. They were playing cards.

      (*Side by Side* Picture Card 36)
      A. What was she doing last night?
      B. She was reading.

   b. Hold up visuals and have pairs of students ask and answer, using the past continuous tense.

2. Review the irregular past forms of the following verbs: *lose–lost, cut–cut, fall–fell, get–got, hurt–hurt.*

   a. Write the following verbs on the board:

cut	hurt
fall	lost
get	

   b. Call on students to pantomime actions with those verbs and have the class tell what the person just *did*.

INTRODUCING THE MODEL

1. Have students look at the model illustration.
2. Set the scene: "Two people are talking about Marty's accident."
3. Present the model.
4. Full-Class Repetition.
5. Ask students if they have any questions. Check understanding of the word *snowboard*.
6. Group Choral Repetition.
7. Choral Conversation.
8. Call on one or two pairs of students to present the dialog.

   (For additional practice, do Choral Conversation in small groups or by rows.)

SIDE BY SIDE EXERCISES

Examples

1. A. How did Greta sprain her ankle?
   B. She sprained it while she was playing volleyball.
   A. That's too bad!
2. A. How did Larry lose his wallet?
   B. He lost it while he was hiking in the woods.
   A. That's too bad!

52   UNIT 2

---

vi

Multilevel Expansion Activities include games, tasks, brainstorming, discussion, movement, drawing, miming, and role playing—all designed to reinforce and enrich instruction in a way that is stimulating, creative, and fun! Activity levels are indicated through a three-star system:

⭐ **One-star activities** are designed for *below-level* students. These activities typically present students with a single task, such as listening for particular vocabulary words or grammar, repeating words or phrases, or pantomiming actions. These activities are highly structured with very defined answers. Often the direction of input is from the teacher, rather than the student.

⭐⭐ **Two-star activities** are for *at-level* students. These activities usually present dual tasks—such as categorizing while taking dictation, listening to a partial sentence and completing it, or speaking and finding a student with a matching line. These are moderately structured activities, with some open answers and room for interpretation. They can be teacher-directed or student-directed, so these activities require that students have some control of language and some independence.

⭐⭐⭐ **Three-star activities** are for *above-level* students. These activities often include several steps and multiple language tasks, such as role plays, discussions, debates, and creative writing based on lesson themes. These activities are highly unstructured, with much room for student input, interpretation, and control. Since most input comes from students, these activities require mastery of vocabulary and student independence.

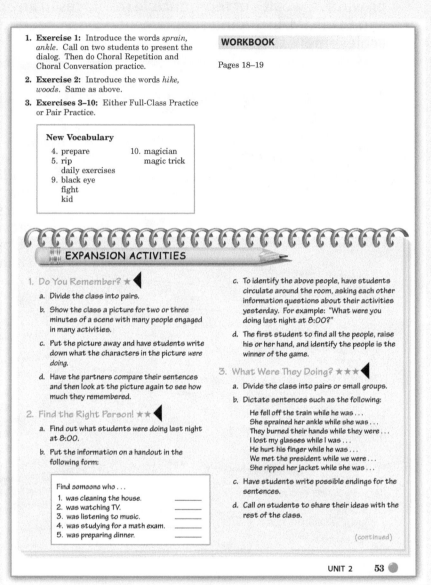

Here's an at-a-glance summary of how **Side by Side Plus Teacher's Guides** expansion activities are differentiated by the nature of the tasks, their structure, and the extent of teacher/student input.

	⭐ Below-level	⭐⭐ At-level	⭐⭐⭐ Above-level
Tasks	Single task	Dual tasks	Multi-tasks
Structure	Highly structured	Moderately structured	Less structured/Unstructured
Input	Teacher-directed	Teacher-directed/Student-directed	Student-directed

Guide to Multilevel Activity & Achievement Test Book and CD-ROM

This Teacher's Guide is part of an **all-in-one teacher support package** that provides a wealth of reproducible resources in an accompanying printed volume and CD-ROM, including supplemental worksheets, activity masters, and unit achievement tests.

UNIT 1
Multilevel Grammar Worksheet

Student's Name _____
Date _____

A. Choose the correct word. ★

1. (I practice   I'm practicing) the violin whenever I can.
2. Naomi is busy. (She cleans   She's cleaning) her garage.
3. Luis (isn't   doesn't) like to swim. He (isn't   doesn't) a very good swimmer.
4. They (aren't   don't) very good dancers. They (aren't   don't) dance very often.
5. She's calling (her   its) brother in Detroit. She calls (her   him) every Sunday.
6. We're visiting (are   our) next-door neighbors. We visit (us   them) very often.

B. Complete the sentences. Write the correct form of the verb, and choose the correct word in parentheses. ★★

| paint | play | talk | watch | write |

1. My sister is very busy today. She's _____ (her   us) living room.
2. My husband likes to _____ the news on TV. He _____ (him   it) every evening.
3. I'm at home today. I'm _____ poetry. I _____ poetry whenever (it ...
4. Mr. and Mrs. Martinez are _____ cards with (them   their) friends ...
   They _____ cards with (her   them) every weekend.
5. We're on the phone. We're _____ to (are   our) daughter in De...
   We _____ to (her   him) every weekend. Sometimes (we   sh...
   (us   her), and sometimes (we   she) calls (us   her).

C. Complete the sentences any way you wish. ★★★

1. My children _____ now. _____ every ni...
2. My sister _____ today. _____
3. Mr. and Mrs. Wong _____ their grandchildren. _____
4. I'm busy today. _____ I _____
5. We don't like to _____ because _____ very go...

Side by Side Plus Book 3
Unit 1 Multilevel Grammar Worksheet

© 2009
Dupli...

Present Continuous Tense,
Simple Present Tense, Pronouns,
Possessive Adjectives

Multilevel Grammar Worksheets

contain a variety of word-choice, fill-in, and sentence-completion exercises providing differentiated practice for below-level, at-level, and above-level students on each reproducible page.

UNIT 1
Multilevel Vocabulary Worksheet

Student's Name _____
Date _____

A. Choose the correct word. ★

1. Herman's stove doesn't work. He's (composing   complaining) to the landlord.
2. My sister loves to play music. She's an excellent (violinist   athlete).
3. What's his (weight   height)? He's six feet two inches.
4. What's her marital status? She's (widowed   a natural-born citizen).
5. He's a victim of identity theft. Someone (bribed   stole) his wallet.
6. Make sure the information on your pay (stub   amount) is correct.
7. Very few people live in Wyoming. It has a small (population   representative).
8. There are nine (senators   justices) on the Supreme Court.
9. The President is the head of the (executive   legislative) branch of government.
10. The President (elects   appoints) members of the Cabinet.

B. Complete the sentences. ★★

The United States has three _____ ¹ of government. The _____ ² branch makes the laws and has the power to declare _____ ³. There are two _____ and 435 _____ ⁵. The _____ ⁴ from each state _____ ⁶ branch enforces the _____ ⁷. The _____ ⁸, the _____ ⁹, and the Cabinet are part of this branch. The _____ ¹⁰ branch interprets or _____ ¹¹ the laws.

C. Change these words to agent nouns and write them in the correct column. ★★★
   Agent nouns end in -er, -r, -double consonant +er, -or, and -ist.

act	journal	reception	sing	teach
dance	manage	senate	skate	translate
drive	paint	shop	ski	type
instruct	program	shred	swim	violin

paint**er**	danc**er**	program**mer**	act**or**	journal**ist**

Side by Side Plus Book 3
Unit 1 Multilevel Vocabulary Worksheet

© 2009 Pearson Education, Inc.
Duplication for classroom use is permitted.

Multilevel Vocabulary Worksheets

also offer three levels of differentiated practice through a variety of word-choice, sentence-completion, cloze-reading, and language arts exercises on each page.

Student's Name _____

Date _____

UNIT 6
Life Skills Worksheet 23

Reading the Yellow Pages

Read the yellow pages and write the correct telephone number.

HARDWARE
Contractor's Discount Hardware .... (254) 889–1327
21 Baker Carl
Economy Hardware – see our ad this page .... (254) 298–9911
24 High Clif

HARDWOOD
Southern Hardwood Supply .... (254) 536–9121
52 Essex Clif
Top Floor Hardwoods – see our ad this page .... (254) 889–7745
201 Elm Carl

HEATING CONTRACTORS
Ajax Air Conditioning & Heating .... (254) 889–6162
167 Washington Carl
Holmes Heating Corp – see our ad this page .... (254) 536–2113
52 Lakeview Burl

Economy Hardware
All bathroom and kitchen
plumbing fixtures

Open 5:00 AM – 6:00 PM every day
24 High Street, Clifton (254) 298–9911

Top Floor Hardwoods
Supply
Installation
Repair
201 Elm Avenue, Carlton (254) 889–7745

HOLMES HEATING CORP
HEATING & PLUMBING
24 HOUR EMERGENCY SERVICE
52 LAKEVIEW ROAD, BURLINGTON
254 536–2113

1. You're looking for a new kitchen sink and bathtub.

   You should call (254) _____-_____.

2. Your air conditioning just broke.

   You should call (254) _____-_____.

3. You are a contractor in Clifton. You need to order some building materials.

   You should call (254) _____-_____.

4. It's 10:00 at night. A pipe broke and is leaking all over the floor.

   You should call (254) _____-_____.

5. Your wood floor is broken. You need someone to come to your ... fix it.

   You should call (254) _____-_____.

© 2009
Duplica...

Side by Side Plus Book 3
Unit 6 Life Skills Worksheet 23

Life Skills Worksheets provide realia-based reading and writing activities including forms, maps, bank deposit and withdrawal slips, checks, checkbook registers, yellow pages listings, advertisements, coupons, templates for resumes and cover letters, a paycheck and pay stub, and a job performance evaluation.

UNIT 9
Life Skills Worksheet 37

Student's Name _____

Date _____

Sale Prices

Read the advertisement and answer the questions.

JAMESON'S DEPARTMENT STORE
Once-a-Year Sale

Men's Suits
40% off
NOW $96–$168
Were $160–$280

60% Savings on Women's Dresses
Orig. $90–$160
Reduced to $36–$64

Men's Clancy Sports Jackets
Buy one, get one half price
Reg. $80–$150

Women's Blouses
2 for $45 or 3 for $60
(original $29.99–$36.99)

Men's Dress Shirts
2 for $55 or $29.99 each

Women's Skirts
Half Price!
Reg. $50–$70
Sale $25–$35

1. The sale price for a $200 men's suit is $_____.

2. If you buy two Clancy men's sports jackets with an original price of $90 each, you pay $_____.

3. With the sale price, you save $_____ on a $90 women's dress.

4. If you buy one men's dress shirt, you pay $_____.

5. If you buy four men's dress shirts, you pay $_____.

6. When you buy a women's skirt with a regular price of $60, the sale price is $_____.

7. When you buy three women's blouses, you pay $_____ for each one.

8. If you buy a men's suit on sale for $168, you save $_____.

Side by Side Plus Book 3
Unit 9 Life Skills Worksheet 37

© 2009 Pearson Education, Inc.
Duplication for classroom use is permitted.

Student's Name _____
Date _____

A. IMMIGRATION AROUND THE WORLD

Read the first article on text page 33 and answer the questions.

1. More than 145 million immigrants
   _____
   A. live outside
   B. move to be with family members
   C. live in urban neighborhoods
   D. leave their countries

2. _____ are examples of natural disasters.
   A. Political problems
   B. Bad living conditions
   C. Floods and earthquakes
   D. Wars

3. The main idea of paragraph 1 is immigrants _____.
   A. are everywhere
   B. have economic problems
   C. have political problems
   D. move for many different reasons

4. According to paragraph 2, many immigrants move from _____.
   A. North Africa to Western Europe
   B. Asia to Africa
   C. Latin America to Asia
   D. Western Europe to Eastern Europe

5. _____ has a larger percentage of immigrants than New York.
   A. Los Angeles
   B. Saudi Arabia
   C. Athens
   D. Rome

6. In Saudi Arabia _____ is native born.
   A. 10% of the population
   B. 40% of the population
   C. 50% of the population
   D. 90% of the population

7. The author refers to Esquilino as a *historic* neighborhood because _____.
   A. it's an urban neighborhood
   B. it has many Chinese immigrants
   C. it has a long history
   D. it has many schools that teach history

8. According to this article, in New York _____
   A. the schools teach 140 languages
   B. 40% of the people were born in a foreign country
   C. 50% of the children are foreign born
   D. there are fewer immigrants than in Los Angeles

9. According to this article, _____.
   A. most immigrants are from Asia
   B. most immigrants live far from the city
   C. immigration changes neighborhoods
   D. most immigrants in Los Angeles are children

10. Immigrants probably move to urban neighborhoods because _____
    A. urban neighborhood
    B. urban neighborhood
    C. urban neighborhood
    D. urban neighborhood

B. IMMIGRATION IN OUR CLASS: A SURVEY

Take a class survey. What countries are the students in your c___
did they and their families come to the United States?

© 200_
Dupli___

Gazette Worksheets provide practice with reading comprehension, vocabulary, idioms, and interpretation of charts and graphs, fully coordinated with the magazine-style Gazette sections in the *Side by Side Plus* student book. The bonus Gazette Audio CD that is included with the student book offers entertaining radio program-style recordings of key Gazette features. Students will enjoy listening along as they read the text and do the activities included in the Gazette worksheets. Use these resources to encourage students to extend their language-learning through self-study—building a bridge between the classroom and the home.

Activity Masters include ready-to-use word cards, graphics, charts, and activity sheets for the multilevel activities and games suggested throughout the *Side by Side Plus 3* Teacher's Guide.

| UNIT 4 | Information Gap: Employment History | ACTIVITY MASTER 26 |

Julie's Employment History A

Employer Name: **Kay's Clothing**
Supervisor's Name: **Peter Chen**   Phone Number: **(480) 525-1829**
Position: **store manager**   Date Worked: From _____ To **present**
Duties: **organize schedules, take inventory, make sales orders**   Salary: _____
Reason For Leaving: _____

Employer Name: **Pinter's Department Store**
Supervisor's Name: **Liz Spock**   Phone Number: **(602) 737-2837**
Position: _____   Date Worked: From **10/30/06** To **9/7/08**
Duties: _____   Salary: **$9/Hour**
Reason For Leaving: **left for a better job**

- -

How much does Julie make in her current job?
When did Julie start her current job?
What's her reason for leaving her current job?

What was her previous job?
What were her job duties?

Julie's Employment History B

Employer Name: **Kay's Clothing**
Supervisor's Name: **Peter Chen**   Phone Number: **(480) 525-1829**
Position: _____   Date Worked: From **9/15/08** To **present**
Duties: _____   Salary: **$11/Hour**
Reason For Leaving: **want more responsibility**

Employer Name: **Pinter's Department Store**
Supervisor's Name: **Liz Spock**   Phone Number: **(602) 737-2837**
Position: **salesperson and cashier**   Date Worked: From **10/30/06** To _____
Duties: **operate cash register, greet customers, help customers**   Salary: _____
Reason For Leaving: _____

What's Julie's current job?
What are her job duties?
When did Julie leave her last job?

How much did Julie make at her last job?
What was her reason for leaving her last job?

Name _____

Date _____ **Class** _____

1

A PERSONAL INFORMATION FORM

Name: (1) _____

Address: (2) _____

City: (3) _____ State: (4) _____ Zip Code: (5) _____

Social Security Number: (6) _____ Country of Origin: (7) _____

Telephone: (8) _____ E-mail: (9) _____ Date of Birth: (10) _____

Height: (11) _____ Eye Color: (12) _____ Hair Color: (13) _____ Marital Status: (14) _____

Family Members in Household (Name—Relationship):

(15) _____

Look at the information. Choose the correct line on the form.

1. 11/14/88
   - Ⓐ Line 5
   - Ⓑ Line 6
   - Ⓒ Line 8
   - Ⓓ Line 10

2. 224-67-8139
   - Ⓐ Line 5
   - Ⓑ Line 6
   - Ⓒ Line 8
   - Ⓓ Line 10

3. Mexico
   - Ⓐ Line 3
   - Ⓑ Line 4
   - Ⓒ Line 7
   - Ⓓ Line 10

4. 1263 Main St.
   - Ⓐ Line 2
   - Ⓑ Line 7
   - Ⓒ Line 9
   - Ⓓ Line 15

5. 5'9"
   - Ⓐ Line 5
   - Ⓑ Line 6
   - Ⓒ Line 10
   - Ⓓ Line 11

6. married
   - Ⓐ Line 7
   - Ⓑ Line 12
   - Ⓒ Line 14
   - Ⓓ Line 15

7. FL
   - Ⓐ Line 3
   - Ⓑ Line 4
   - Ⓒ Line 5
   - Ⓓ Line 14

8. blue
   - Ⓐ Line 11
   - Ⓑ Line 12
   - Ⓒ Line 13
   - Ⓓ Line 14

9. (305) 965-4213
   - Ⓐ Line 5
   - Ⓑ Line 6
   - Ⓒ Line 8
   - Ⓓ Line 9

10. Alma Suarez—wife
    - Ⓐ Line 1
    - Ⓑ Line 2
    - Ⓒ Line 14
    - Ⓓ Line 15

11. Miami
    - Ⓐ Line 3
    - Ⓑ Line 4
    - Ⓒ Line 5
    - Ⓓ Line 9

12. cjs24@msl.co
    - Ⓐ Line 2
    - Ⓑ Line 3
    - Ⓒ Line 8
    - Ⓓ Line 9

1 Ⓐ Ⓑ Ⓒ Ⓓ   7 Ⓐ Ⓑ Ⓒ Ⓓ   10 Ⓐ Ⓑ Ⓒ Ⓓ
2 Ⓐ Ⓑ Ⓒ Ⓓ   5 Ⓐ Ⓑ Ⓒ Ⓓ   8 Ⓐ Ⓑ Ⓒ Ⓓ   11 Ⓐ Ⓑ Ⓒ Ⓓ
3 Ⓐ Ⓑ Ⓒ Ⓓ   6 Ⓐ Ⓑ Ⓒ Ⓓ   9 Ⓐ Ⓑ Ⓒ Ⓓ   12 Ⓐ Ⓑ Ⓒ

Go to the next

Side by Side Plus Book 3
Unit 1 Achievement Test (Page 1 of 4)

© 2009 Pearson Educa
Duplication for classro

Unit Achievement Tests assess student progress and prepare students for the types of standardized tests and performance assessments used by many instructional programs. The tests include multiple-choice questions that assess vocabulary, grammar, reading, and listening skills; writing assessments that can be evaluated with a standardized scoring rubric and be collected in portfolios of students' work; and speaking performance assessments designed to stimulate face-to-face interactions between students.

SIDE BY SIDE PLUS
Learner Assessment Record

BOOK 3 UNIT 1

Student's Name _____

Course _____

_____ Teacher _____ I.D. Number _____

Date _____

Score: _____

Test Sections & Scoring Guidelines/Rubrics:

A–E. MULTIPLE-CHOICE QUESTIONS
Personal Information Form
Grammar in Context: Small Talk at Work
Cloze Reading: Grading Systems
Reading: The Education System
Listening Assessment: An Automated Message

F. WRITING ASSESSMENT: A Personal Information Form
For each of the following lines on the form: correct x **2** points
Score **1** if completed correctly.
Score **0** if incorrect or missing.

Name: _____
Address/City/State/Zip Code: _____
Social Security Number: _____
Country of Origin: _____
Telephone: _____
E-mail (Don't score) _____
Date of Birth: _____
Height: _____
Eye Color/Hair Color: _____
Marital Status: _____
Family Members in Household: _____

_____ (80)

G. SPEAKING ASSESSMENT
Score _separately_ the student's ability to ask and answer the questions based on appropriateness, grammatical correctness, and comprehensibility:
Score **5** (Excellent), **4** (Good), **3** (Fair), **2** (Poor), or **1** (Unsatisfactory)

Asking the Questions: _____
Answering the Questions: _____

_____ (10)

_____ (10)

TOTAL SCORE: _____ (100)

Side by Side Plus Book 3
Unit 1 Learner Progress Evaluation

© 2009 Pearson Education, Inc.
Duplication for classroom use is permitted.

Learner Assessment Records are designed for easy scoring and documentation of student performance on the tests. The forms contain scoring rubrics for all multiple-choice questions, writing assessments, and speaking assessments. Each test is scored on a 100-point scale, providing a consistent means to evaluate student achievement of topics, vocabulary, grammar, and listening, speaking, reading, and writing skills. The Learner Assessment Records can serve as documentation of student progress during the course of the instructional program.

The Multilevel Activity & Achievement Test CD-ROM organizes all the reproducible resources in a set of convenient folders designed for easy access and flexible use. All resources can be accessed both by their type and by their unit. Instructors can therefore easily find the reproducibles they need to make lesson-planning quick and efficient.

INTRODUCTION

Side by Side Plus is a standards-based and grammar-based English language program for adult and young-adult learners. The program builds students' general language proficiency and prepares them for their life-skill roles in the community, family, school, and at work.

Side by Side Plus offers four levels of instruction: Low Beginning (Book 1), High Beginning (Book 2), Low Intermediate (Book 3), and High Intermediate (Book 4). For students at the Pre-Beginning level, the *Foundations* program offers literacy and basic English instruction to prepare students for future success and an easy transition to *Side by Side Plus* Book 1. For additional vocabulary enrichment, the *Word by Word* Picture Dictionary and its multilevel workbooks correlate with all levels of *Side by Side Plus*.

Program Components and Key Features

STUDENT BOOKS

The *Side by Side Plus* Student Books provide all-skills practice through a standards-based and grammar-based curriculum that integrates vocabulary, life skills, grammar, and communication.

- **Picture dictionary lessons** introduce unit vocabulary in a clear, easy-to-use format.

- The **guided conversation methodology** integrates grammar, vocabulary, and topics through real-life communication practice that is student-centered, interactive, and fun.

- **Standards-based lessons** in each unit develop the competencies included in CASAS, BEST Plus, EFF, SCANS, Model Standards, and other major curriculum frameworks and assessment systems.

- **Teamwork, critical thinking, and community tasks** promote cooperative learning, problem-solving, and civics connections.

- **Diverse reading and writing activities** include realia, narrative readings, and journal-writing to develop skills for daily life, self-expression, and academic advancement.

- **Built-in assessment** in each unit includes a check-up test and vocabulary and skill checklists enabling students to assess their progress.

- **Gazette magazine sections** promote learner persistence through high-interest material that students can use in class or on their own, building a bridge between the classroom and the home.

- A **Bonus Gazette Audio CD** included with each student book offers entertaining radio program-style recordings of Gazette activities.

ACTIVITY & TEST PREP WORKBOOKS

- **All-skills activities** reinforce learning objectives in the Student Books.

- **GrammarRaps** motivate learners and promote language mastery through entertaining practice with rhythm, stress, and intonation.

- **Unit Achievement Tests** assess student progress and prepare students for standardized tests.

TEACHER'S GUIDES

The *Side by Side Plus* Teacher's Guides offer complete tools for lesson planning and instruction.

- **Step-by-step instructions** in a clear and easy-to-use format help new and experienced teachers use the text with students at a wide range of levels.

- **Hundreds of multilevel expansion activities** include games, tasks, brainstorming, discussion, movement, drawing, miming, and role-playing.

- **Life-skills teaching strategies** promote effective standards-based instruction, including cooperative learning, critical thinking, problem solving, and civics connections.

- **Concise grammar rules and explanations** are provided for convenient teacher reference.

- **Complete answer keys** are included for all activities in the student book and workbook.

MULTILEVEL ACTIVITY & ACHIEVEMENT TEST BOOKS AND CD-ROMS

A book of reproducibles and a CD-ROM are included with each Teacher's Guide. These instructional resources help with lesson planning by providing ready-to-use activity masters, supplemental worksheets, and student assessment materials.

- **Multilevel Grammar and Vocabulary Worksheets** offer differentiated practice for below-level, at-level, and above-level students on each reproducible page.
- **Life Skills Worksheets** provide real-life reading and writing practice including forms, maps, bank deposit and withdrawal slips, checks, checkbook registers, yellow pages listings, advertisements, coupons, templates for resumes and cover letters, a paycheck and pay stub, and a job performance evaluation.
- **Gazette Worksheets** provide practice with reading comprehension, vocabulary, idioms, and interpretation of charts and graphs, fully coordinated with the magazine-style Gazette sections in the Student Book.
- **Activity Masters** include word cards, graphics, charts, and activity sheets for the multilevel activities and games suggested in the Teacher's Guide.
- **Tests** include periodic check-up tests and unit achievement tests for the assessment of student progress.

PICTURE CARDS

Picture Cards illustrating key concepts and vocabulary items are designed for introduction of new material, for review, for enrichment, and for role-playing activities. (See pages 455–457 of this Teacher's Guide for a helpful triple listing of the Picture Cards: numerically, alphabetically, and by category.)

AUDIO PROGRAM

In addition to the Bonus Gazette Audio CD included with each Student Book, *Side by Side Plus* offers comprehensive audio supplements on audio CDs and audio cassettes.

- **Complete Student Book audios** offer comprehensive language practice in the classroom, in the language laboratory, and at home. Through their highly interactive format, the audios serve as a student's speaking partner, making conversation practice possible even when the student is studying alone. The audios contain all unit vocabulary practice, all conversation models and exercises, listening exercises, pronunciation practice, and reading selections.
- **Workbook audios** contain listening and pronunciation exercises along with GrammarRaps for entertaining practice with rhythm, stress, and intonation.

MULTIMEDIA PROGRAMS

Side by Side Plus Levels 1 and 2 are complemented by innovative multimedia materials for self-study, distance learning, and computer and language laboratories.

- **Side by Side TV** videos (DVD and VHS) offer entertaining language practice through comedy, interviews, and music.
- **Side by Side Interactive** multimedia software provides interactive self-paced practice through award-winning easy-to-use technology. (CD-ROM, network, and installable versions are available.)
- **Side by Side Interactive Activity Workbooks** offer a variety of activities for users of the videos or the multimedia software, with complete answer keys for self-study.

UNIT OPENING PAGES

The opening page of each unit provides a listing of the grammatical structures and topics that are treated in the unit. A Vocabulary Preview depicts some of the key vocabulary words that students will encounter within the unit. Some teachers may wish to present and practice these words before beginning the unit. Other teachers may prefer to wait until the words occur in the particular lesson in which they are introduced.

GUIDED CONVERSATION LESSONS

The *guided conversation* is the core learning device that integrates grammar, vocabulary, and topics and serves as the springboard for the all-skills language practice and life-skills practice that follows.

Grammatical Paradigms

A new grammatical structure appears first in the form of a grammatical paradigm, or "grammar box"—a simple schema of the structure. (Grammar boxes are in a light blue tint.) These paradigms are meant to be a reference point for students as they proceed through a lesson's conversational activities. While these paradigms highlight the structures being taught, they are not intended to be goals in themselves. Students are not expected to memorize or parrot back these rules. Rather, we want students to take part in conversations that show they can *use* these rules correctly.

Model Guided Conversations

Model conversations serve as the vehicles for introducing new grammatical structures and communicative uses of English. Because the model becomes the basis for all the exercises that follow, it is essential that students be given sufficient practice with it before proceeding with the lesson.

Side by Side Exercises

In the numbered exercises that follow the model, students pair up and work "side by side," placing new content into the given conversational framework. These exercises

form the core learning activity of each conversation lesson.

LANGUAGE EXERCISES AND ACTIVITIES

The initial lessons in each unit develop students' general language proficiency through a research-based grammatical sequence, a communicative approach, and all-skills language-learning activities.

- **Short structured stories** offer enjoyable reading practice that simultaneously reinforces the grammatical and thematic focus of each unit.
- **Reading *Check-Up*** exercises provide focused practice in reading comprehension.
- **Listening** activities enable students to develop their aural comprehension skills.
- **Pronunciation** exercises provide models of authentic pronunciation and opportunities for student listening and speaking practice.
- **How to Say It!** activities help students develop key communication strategies.
- **Talk About It!** and **Think About It!** activities stimulate free conversation practice through classroom discussion of interesting topics.
- **Role Play, Interactions,** and **Interview** activities provide opportunities for dynamic classroom interaction.
- **On Your Own** and **How About You?** activities invite students to apply lesson content to their own lives and experiences and to share opinions in class. Through these activities, students bring to the classroom new content based on their interests, their backgrounds, and their imaginations.
- **In Your Own Words** activities provide topics and themes for student compositions and classroom discussions in which students write about their friends, families, homes, schools, and themselves.
- *Side by Side* **Journal** activities prompt students to write about things that are meaningful to them.
- **Grammar Focus** sections contain grammar charts and accompanying exercises for useful reference and focused practice with the structures in each unit.

LIFE SKILLS EXERCISES AND ACTIVITIES

Standards-based lessons in the "yellow pages" at the end of every unit apply students' language learning to their life-skill roles in the community, family, school, and at work.

- **Real-life conversation practice** in authentic life-skill situations gets students talking through interactive pair work. Extensive photographs provide clear contexts and support vocabulary learning.

- **Teamwork activities** promote cooperative learning as students work together in pairs, in groups, or as a class to share information and complete tasks.

- **Critical thinking** and **problem-solving activities** help students focus on issues and problems and share ideas and solutions.

- **Realia-based reading activities** include an accident report, a letter to parents from a school principal, a school campus map, a job application, a resume, a cover letter, a new employee manual, lease terms in a rental agreement, utility bills, a letter to tenants, yellow pages listings, workplace notes and messages, medical appointment cards, a medical history form, a chart with preventive care guidelines, public health department information, store advertisements, and product coupons.

- **Narrative reading passages** offer practice with simple newspaper and magazine articles on high-interest topics such as preventing identity theft, job search strategies, small talk at work, and career advancement. Follow-up reading comprehension exercises in multiple-choice formats help students prepare for the reading section of standardized tests.

- **Academic lessons** provide content-based reading practice in the formats of subject-matter textbooks to prepare students for success when they continue their education beyond English instruction. Academic topics include U.S. government, U.S. history, health, and nutrition.

- **Community tasks** introduce basic civics topics related to community life and help students connect to community information and services.

- **Life skills writing activities** include filling out forms, writing notes to a child's teacher, filling out a job application, preparing a resume and cover letter, and completing a workplace self-evaluation questionnaire.

ASSESSMENT

The final page of each unit provides built-in resources for assessment of student progress.

- **Check-up tests** allow a quick assessment of student achievement and help prepare students for the kinds of test items and answer sheets found on standardized tests.

- **Vocabulary checklists** and **language skill checklists** help students review words they have learned, keep track of the skills they are developing, and identify vocabulary and skills they need to continue to work on.

For more comprehensive assessment, unit achievement tests are provided in multiple formats for programs' convenience: as text pages in the Activity & Test Prep Workbooks, and as reproducibles and downloadable files in the Multilevel Activity & Achievement Test Book and CD-ROM included with this Teacher's Guide.

SIDE BY SIDE GAZETTE

Gazette "magazine-style" sections that occur periodically throughout the Student Book review and expand the language and themes of preceding units.

- **Feature Articles** cover interesting topics such as immigration around the world, "24/7" work schedules, the Olympics, and marriage traditions and customs.

- **Fact Files** present interesting information about the world and offer students valuable practice interpreting data in charts, tables, and lists.

- **Interviews** offer students an in-depth look into people's lives.

- **Fun with Idioms** sections introduce students to common idiomatic expressions.

- **Around the World** photo essays introduce cross-cultural topics and stimulate sharing of cultural information in the classroom.

- **We've Got Mail!** sections provide clear, simple explanations of key grammatical structures through an entertaining advice-column format.

- **Global Exchange** activities give students experience with online communication.

- **Authentic Listening** activities offer students practice with real-life listening comprehension tasks.
- **What Are They Saying?** cartoons stimulate class discussion and role playing.

SUPPORT AND REFERENCE SECTIONS

- A **Scope and Sequence Chart** highlights the language skills and life skills in each unit and correlates unit objectives to curriculum

standards and assessment systems including CASAS, BEST Plus, EFF, SCANS, and other major state and local frameworks.

- An **Appendix** contains Listening Scripts, a Vocabulary List, and a list of Past Tense Irregular Verbs.
- A three-part **Index** enables users to locate all course content by skill, by topic, and by grammar.
- A **Map of the United States** is provided as a convenient reference tool.

Format of the Teacher's Guide

UNIT OVERVIEW

The Unit Overview provides the following:
- Functional and grammatical highlights of the unit
- A listing of new vocabulary and expressions

UNIT OPENING PAGE

The Teacher's Guide offers suggestions for presenting and practicing the words depicted in the Vocabulary Preview. This preview is optional. Some teachers may wish to introduce the words before beginning the unit. Other teachers may choose to wait until the words first occur in a specific lesson.

STEP-BY-STEP LESSON GUIDE

Conversation Lessons

Included for each conversation lesson are the following:
- **FOCUS:** the grammatical and topical focus of the lesson
- **CLOSE UP:** short grammar explanations accompanied by examples from the lesson
- **GETTING READY:** suggestions for introducing the new concepts in the lesson
- **INTRODUCING THE MODEL:** steps for introducing model conversations
- **SIDE BY SIDE EXERCISES:** suggestions for practicing the exercises, as well as a listing of new vocabulary
- **LANGUAGE NOTES, CULTURE NOTES,** and **PRONUNCIATION NOTES**

- **WORKBOOK:** page references for exercises in the Activity & Test Prep Workbook that correspond to the particular lesson
- **EXPANSION ACTIVITIES:** optional multilevel activities for review and reinforcement of the content of the lesson

Short Structured Stories

Included for each reading lesson are the following:
- **FOCUS** of the story
- **NEW VOCABULARY** contained in the story
- **READING THE STORY:** an optional preliminary preview stage before students begin to read the selection, along with suggestions for presenting the story and questions to check students' comprehension
- **READING CHECK-UP:** answer keys for the reading comprehension exercises
- **READING EXTENSION:** additional questions and activities that provide further skill reinforcement based on the story

Other Language Skills Lessons

Included for other language skills lessons are the following:
- **LISTENING** scripts and answer keys for the listening exercises
- Strategies for actively involving students in the *How to Say It!, How About You?, On Your Own, In Your Own Words, Role Play, Interactions, Interview, Talk About It!, Think About It!, Pronunciation,* and *Side by Side Journal* activities
- **GRAMMAR FOCUS** answer keys

Life Skills Lessons (The "Yellow Pages")

Included for the life skills lessons are the following:

- **LIFE SKILLS CONVERSATION ACTIVITIES:** step-by-step instructions for previewing the conversation's context using the accompanying photo or graphic and for having students practice conversations in pairs, including multilevel variations for students of different ability-levels

- **TEAMWORK ACTIVITIES:** strategies for using these activities to promote cooperative learning and enhance students' abilities to work as members of a team

- **CRITICAL THINKING AND PROBLEM-SOLVING:** suggestions for posing the issues and problems presented in the lesson and for encouraging students to share ideas and solutions

- **COMMUNITY CONNECTIONS:** suggestions for relating lesson topics to community life and for helping students connect to community information and services

- **LIFE SKILLS WRITING ACTIVITIES:** strategies for previewing the writing tasks and instructions for how students should complete them, including multilevel variations

- **LIFE SKILLS READING:** strategies for previewing the reading, checking students' reading comprehension, discussing the reading in class, and extending the reading through any recommended follow-up activities

- **LIFE SKILLS ENRICHMENT:** instructions for using the life skills worksheets to offer students real-life reading and writing practice with forms, maps, bank deposit and withdrawal slips, checks, checkbook registers, yellow pages listings, advertisements, coupons, resumes and cover letters, a paycheck and pay stub, and a job performance evaluation

- **EXPANSION ACTIVITIES:** optional multilevel activities for review and reinforcement of each life skills lesson

ASSESSMENT

Included for each unit's assessment page are the following:

- **ANSWER KEY** for the unit's Check-Up Test

- **SKILLS CHECK:** strategies for using the vocabulary and language skills checklists to activate classroom practice and encourage student self-evaluation of skills and progress

- **EXPANSION ACTIVITIES:** optional multilevel activities and games for motivating review and reinforcement of the unit's vocabulary, expressions, and topics

SIDE BY SIDE GAZETTE

Included for the *Side by Side* Gazette pages are the following:

- Strategies for introducing, practicing, and expanding upon the *Feature Articles, Fact Files, Interviews, Fun with Idioms, Around the World, We've Got Mail!, Global Exchange, Listening,* and *What Are They Saying?* sections of the Gazette.

RESOURCES IN THE APPENDIX

The Appendix to this Teacher's Guide includes the following:

- Activity Workbook Answer Key & Listening Scripts

- Unit Achievement Tests Answer Key & Listening Scripts

- *Side by Side* Picture Cards lists (numerical, alphabetical, and by categories)

- Glossary of all vocabulary and expressions in the Student Book

General Teaching Strategies

VOCABULARY PREVIEW

You may wish to introduce the words in the Vocabulary Preview before beginning the unit, or you may choose to wait until they first occur in a specific lesson. If you choose to introduce them at this point, the Teacher's Guide offers these suggestions:

1. Have students look at the illustrations and identify the words they already know.

2. Present the vocabulary. Say each word and have the class repeat it chorally and individually. Check students' understanding and pronunciation of the words.

3. Practice the vocabulary as a class, in pairs, or in small groups. Have students cover the word list and look at the pictures. Practice the words by saying a word and having students tell the number of the illustration and/or giving the number of the illustration and having students say the word.

GUIDED CONVERSATION LESSONS

Introducing Model Conversations

Given the importance of the model conversation, it is essential that students practice it several times in a variety of ways before going on to the exercises. This Teacher's Guide offers the following comprehensive 8-step approach for introducing the model:

1. Have students look at the model illustration. This helps establish the context of the conversation.

2. Set the scene.

3. *Present the model.* With books closed, have students listen as you present the model or play the audio one or more times. To make the presentation of the model as realistic as possible, you might draw two stick figures on the board to represent the speakers in the dialog. You can also show that two people are speaking by changing your position or by shifting your weight from one foot to the other as you say each speaker's lines.

4. *Full-Class Repetition.* Model each line and have the whole class repeat in unison.

5. Have students open their books and look at the dialog. Ask if there are any questions, and check understanding of new vocabulary.

6. *Group Choral Repetition.* Divide the class in half. Model line A and have Group 1 repeat. Model line B and have Group 2 repeat. Continue with all the lines of the model.

7. *Choral Conversation.* Have both groups practice the dialog twice, without a teacher model. First Group 1 is Speaker A and Group 2 is Speaker B; then reverse.

8. Call on one or two pairs of students to present the dialog.

In steps 6, 7, and 8, encourage students to look up from their books and *say* the lines rather than read them. (Students can of course refer to their books when necessary.)

The goal is not memorization or complete mastery of the model. Rather, students should become familiar with the model and feel comfortable saying it.

At this point, if you feel that additional practice is necessary before going on to the exercises, you can do Choral Conversation in small groups or by rows.

Alternative Approaches to Introducing Model Conversations

Depending upon the abilities of your students and the particular lesson you're teaching, you might wish to try the following approaches to vary the way in which you introduce model conversations.

- **Pair Introduction**

  Have a pair of students present the model. Then practice it with the class.

- **Trio Introduction**

  Call on *three* students to introduce the model. Have two of them present it while the third acts as the *director,* offering suggestions for how to say the lines better. Then practice the dialog with the class.

- **Cloze Introduction**

  Write a cloze version of the model conversation on the board for student reference as you introduce the model. For lessons that provide a skeletal framework of the model (Book 3 pp. 28–29, 48, 62–63, 86–87, 88–89, 90–91, 104–105, 106–107, 122–123), you can use that as the cloze version. For other lessons, you can decide which words to delete from the dialog.

- **Scrambled Dialog Introduction**

  Write each line of the dialog on a separate card. Distribute the cards to students and have them practice saying their lines and then talk with each other to figure out what the correct order of the lines should be. Have them present the dialog to the class, each student in turn reading his or her line. Have the class decide if the dialog is in the correct order. Then practice the dialog with the class.

Warning: Do a scrambled dialog introduction *only* for conversations in which there is only one possible sentence order!

- **Disappearing Dialog Introduction**

  Write the dialog on the board and have students practice saying it. Erase a few of the words and practice again. Continue practicing the dialog several times, each time erasing more of the words, until the dialog has completely *disappeared* and students can say the lines without looking at them.

- **Eliciting the Model**

  Have students cover up the lines of the model and look only at the illustration. Ask questions based on the illustration and the situation. For example: *Who are these people? Where are they? What are they saying to each other?* As a class, in groups, or in pairs, have students suggest a possible dialog. Have students present their ideas and then compare them with the model conversation in the book. Then practice the dialog with the class.

Side by Side Exercises

The numbered exercises that follow the model form the core learning activity in each conversation lesson. Here students use the illustrations and word cues to create conversations based on the structure of the model. Since all language practice in these lessons is conversational, you will always call on a pair of students to do each exercise. Your primary role is to serve as a resource to the class—to help students with new structures, new vocabulary, intonation, and pronunciation.

The Teacher's Guide recommends the following three steps for practicing the exercises. (Students should be given thorough practice with the first two exercises before going on.)

1. **Exercise 1:** Introduce any new vocabulary in the exercise. Call on two students to present the dialog. Then do Choral Repetition and Choral Conversation practice.

2. **Exercise 2:** Same as for Exercise 1.

3. For the remaining exercises, there are two options: either Full-Class Practice or Pair Practice.

   Full-Class Practice: Call on a pair of students to do each exercise. Introduce new vocabulary one exercise at a time. (For more practice, you can call on other pairs of students or do Choral Repetition or Choral Conversation.)

   Pair Practice: Introduce new vocabulary for all the exercises. Next have students practice all the exercises in pairs. Then have pairs present the exercises to the class. (For more practice, you can do Choral Conversation or Choral Repetition.)

The choice of Full-Class Practice or Pair Practice should be determined by the content of the particular lesson, the size and composition of the class, and your own teaching style. You might also wish to vary your approach from lesson to lesson.

- **Suggestions for Pairing Students**

  Whether you use Full-Class Practice or Pair Practice, you can select students for pairing in various ways.

  - You might want to pair students by ability, since students of similar ability might work together more efficiently than students of dissimilar ability.

  - On the other hand, you might wish to pair a weaker student with a stronger one. The slower student benefits from this pairing, while the more advanced student strengthens his or her abilities by helping a partner.

  You should also encourage students to look at each other when speaking. This makes the conversational nature of the language practice more realistic. One way of ensuring this is *not* to call on two students who are sitting next to each other. Rather, call on students in different parts of the room and encourage them to look at each other when saying their lines.

- **Presenting New Vocabulary**

  Many new words are introduced in each conversation lesson. The illustration usually helps to convey the meaning, and the new words are written for students to see and use in these conversations. In addition, you might:

  - write the new word on the board or on a word card.

  - say the new word several times and ask students to repeat chorally and individually.

  - help clarify the meaning with visuals.

Students might also find it useful to keep a notebook in which they write each new word, its meaning, and a sentence using that word.

- **Open-Ended Exercises**

  In many lessons, the final exercise is open-ended. This is indicated in the text by a *blank box*. Here students are expected to create conversations based on the structure of the model, but with vocabulary that they select themselves. This provides students with an opportunity for creativity, while still focusing on the particular structure being practiced. These open-ended exercises can be done orally in class and/or assigned as homework for presentation in class the following day. Encourage students to use dictionaries to find new words they want to use.

General Guiding Principles for Working with Guided Conversations

- *Speak*, Don't *Read*, the Conversations

  When doing the exercises, students should practice *speaking* to each other, rather than *reading* to each other. Even though students will need to refer to the text to be able to practice the conversations, they should not read the lines word by word. Rather, they should scan a full line and then look up from the book and *speak* the line to the other person.

- **Intonation and Gesture**

  Throughout, you should use the book to teach proper intonation and gesture. (Capitalized words are used to indicate spoken emphasis.) Encourage students to truly *act out* the dialogs in a strong and confident voice.

- **Student-Centered Practice**

  Use of the texts should be as student-centered as possible. Modeling by the teacher should be efficient and economical, but students should have every opportunity to model for each other when they are capable of doing so.

- **Vocabulary in Context**

  Vocabulary can and should be effectively taught in the context of the conversation being practiced. Very often it will be possible to grasp the meaning from the conversation or its accompanying illustration. You should

spend time drilling vocabulary in isolation only if you feel it is absolutely essential.

- **No "Grammar Talk"**

  Students need not study the grammar formally or be expected to produce grammatical rules. The purpose of the texts is to engage students in active communication that gets them to *use* the language according to these rules.

Relating Lesson Content to Students' Lives and Experiences

- **Personalize the Exercises**

  While doing the guided conversation exercises, whenever you think it is appropriate, ask students questions that relate the situations in the exercises to their own lives and personal experiences. This will help make the leap from practicing language in the textbook to using language for actual communication.

- **Interview the Characters**

  When appropriate, as students present the exercises to the class, encourage them to feel as though they really *are* the characters in those conversations. Ask questions and have students respond "in character" using their imaginations.

SHORT STRUCTURED STORIES

If you wish, preview the story by having students talk about the story title and/or the illustrations. You may choose to introduce new vocabulary beforehand or have students encounter the new vocabulary in context while reading.

Have students read silently or follow along silently as the story is read aloud by you, by one or more students, or on the audio program. Ask students if they have any questions and check understanding of new vocabulary. Then do the Reading Check-Up exercises.

HOW TO SAY IT!

How to Say It! activities help students develop important communication strategies. Present the conversations the same way you introduce model guided conversations: set the scene, present the model, do full-class and choral repetition, and have pairs of students present the dialog. Then divide the class into pairs and have students practice other conversations based on the *How to Say It!* model and then present them to the class.

HOW ABOUT YOU?

How About You? activities offer students additional opportunities to tell about themselves. Have students do these activities in pairs or as a class.

ON YOUR OWN

On Your Own activities invite students to contribute content of their own within the grammatical framework of the lesson. You should introduce these activities in class and assign them as homework for presentation in class the next day. In this way, students will automatically review the previous day's grammar while contributing new and inventive content of their own.

These activities are meant for simultaneous grammar reinforcement and vocabulary building. Encourage students to use a dictionary when completing the *On Your Own* activities. In this way, they will use not only the words they know but also the words they would *like* to know in order to really bring their interests, backgrounds, and imaginations into the classroom. As a result, students will teach each other new vocabulary as they share a bit of their lives with others in the class.

IN YOUR OWN WORDS

Have students do the activity as written homework, using a dictionary for any new words they wish to use. Then have students present and discuss what they have written, in pairs or as a class.

ROLE PLAY

Have pairs of students practice role-playing the activity and then present their role plays to the class.

INTERACTIONS

Divide the class into pairs and have students practice conversations based on the skeletal models. Then call on students to present their conversations to the class.

INTERVIEW

Have students circulate around the room to conduct their interviews and then report back to the class.

TALK ABOUT IT!

Call on a few different pairs of students to present the model dialogs. Then divide the class into pairs and have students take turns using the models to ask and answer questions about the characters and situations depicted on the page. Then call on pairs to present conversations to the class.

THINK ABOUT IT!

Divide the class into pairs or small groups. Have students discuss the questions and then share their thoughts with the class.

PRONUNCIATION

Pronunciation exercises provide students with models of natural English pronunciation. The goal of these exercises is to enable learners to improve their own pronunciation and to understand the pronunciation of native speakers using English in natural conversational contexts.

Have students first focus on listening to the sentences. Say each sentence in the left column or play the audio one or more times and have students listen carefully and repeat. Next, focus on pronunciation. Have students say each sentence in the right column and then listen carefully as you say it or play the audio. If you wish, you can have students continue practicing the sentences to improve their pronunciation.

JOURNAL

The purpose of the *Side by Side* Journal activity is to show students how writing can become a vehicle for communicating thoughts and feelings. Have students begin a journal in a composition notebook. In these journals, students have the opportunity to write about things that are meaningful to them.

Have students write their journal entries at home or in class. Encourage students to use a dictionary to look up words they would like to use. They can share their written work with other students if appropriate. Then as a class, in pairs, or in small groups, have students discuss what they have written.

If time permits, you may want to write a response in each student's journal, sharing your own opinions and experiences as well as reacting to what the student has written. If you are keeping portfolios of students' work, these compositions serve as excellent examples of students' progress in learning English.

GRAMMAR FOCUS

Review the grammar charts in class. Have students do the grammar exercises either in class or at home. Then go over the answers in class and determine if any grammar points need further review or reinforcement.

LIFE SKILLS LESSONS (THE "YELLOW PAGES")

Teaching strategies for each unit's life skills lessons are customized for the specific content and competency objectives of each activity. See each Teacher's Guide unit for detailed step-by-step instructions for the conversation, teamwork, critical thinking, problem solving, community task, life skills reading, narrative reading, and life skills writing activities. These Teacher's Guide sections also offer multilevel variations for many activities, instructions for real-life reading and writing practice using the Life Skills Worksheets, and an array of multilevel expansion activities.

ASSESSMENT

Check-Up Tests

(Note: Have students use pencils for the Check-Up Tests.) Read item number 1 aloud. After students have identified the correct answer, show them how to fill in the bubble on the Answer Sheet. Have students do the Check-Up Test and then review the answers as a class.

Skills Check: Words

Explain to students that this is a list of words they have learned in the unit. Have students take turns reading each item aloud to the class. Have students put a check next to the item if they feel they have learned it. Encourage students to get a small notebook where they

can write down words that are difficult for them.

Skills Check: I can . . .

Explain to students that this is a list of skills they have learned in the unit. Read each item aloud to the class. Ask a student to demonstrate the skill. Have students put a check next to the item if they feel they have learned it. Use this information to determine which lessons you may want to review or reinforce for the entire class or for particular students.

SIDE BY SIDE GAZETTE

The magazine-style Gazette sections are ideal for use both at home and in class. Students can listen to the Gazette Audio CD included with their student books as they read the Gazette sections and complete the reproducible worksheets provided for some of the activities. Many teachers find that the most effective and time-efficient way to use the Gazettes is to have students complete the worksheets at home, go over them briefly in class, and devote more class time to the discussions and role-playing that are stimulated by many of the Gazette lessons. Here are some suggestions for using the various Gazette activities in class:

FEATURE ARTICLE

Have students read silently or follow along silently as the article is read aloud by you, by one or more students, or on the audio program. You may choose to introduce new vocabulary beforehand or have students encounter it within the context of the article. Ask students if they have any questions, and check understanding of vocabulary. (A Gazette Worksheet for each feature article provides valuable reading comprehension practice.)

FACT FILE

Present the information and have the class discuss it. (A Gazette Worksheet for each Fact File offers students important practice interpreting data in charts, graphs, and lists.)

INTERVIEW

Have students read silently or follow along silently as the interview is read aloud by you, by one or more students, or on the audio program. (A Gazette Worksheet for each interview provides reading comprehension practice and a follow-up activity in which students interview each other.)

FUN WITH IDIOMS

Have students look at the illustrations. Say each expression or play the audio and have the class repeat it chorally and individually. Check students' understanding and pronunciation of the expressions. Then have students match the expressions with their meanings. (A Gazette Worksheet provides a variety of activities for supplemental practice with the idioms in the lesson.)

AROUND THE WORLD

Divide the class into pairs or small groups and have students react to the photographs and answer the questions. Then have students report back to the class.

WE'VE GOT MAIL!

Have students read silently or follow along silently as the letters are read aloud by you, by one or more students, or on the audio program. Check students' understanding of the grammar explanations contained in the letters. (A Gazette Worksheet offers focused practice with the grammatical structures in a variety of multiple-choice formats found on standardized tests.)

GLOBAL EXCHANGE

Have students read silently or follow along silently as the message is read aloud by you, by one or more students, or on the audio program. For additional practice, you can have students write back to the person and then share their writing with the class. You may also wish to have students correspond with a keypal on the Internet and then share their experience with the class.

WHAT ARE THEY SAYING?

Have students talk about the people and the situation in the cartoon and then create role plays based on the scene. Students may refer back to previous lessons as a resource, but they should not simply reuse specific conversations. You may want to assign this exercise as written homework, having students prepare their role plays, practice them the next day with other students, and then present them to the class.

Multilevel Expansion Activities

This Teacher's Guide offers a rich variety of Multilevel Expansion Activities for review and reinforcement. Feel free to pick and choose or vary the activities to fit the particular ability-levels, needs, and learning styles of your students. Activity levels are indicated through a three-star system:

★ **One-star activities** are designed for *below-level* students who need extra support and some re-teaching of skills and content to master basic objectives;

★★ **Two-star activities** are for *at-level* students who are performing well in class and can benefit from reinforcement;

★★★ **Three-star activities** are for *above-level* students who want and deserve opportunities for enrichment and greater challenge.

See pages vi–vii for a complete description of these ability-levels.

While offering you these approaches and strategies for using *Side by Side Plus,* we hope that we have also conveyed the spirit: that the language-learning experience we create for our students is most effective when it is dynamic and interactive . . . responsive to our students' differing levels and learning styles . . . and fun!

Steven J. Molinsky
Bill Bliss

Scope and Sequence

Unit	Topics & Vocabulary	Grammar	Functional Communication	Listening & Pronunciation	Writing
1	• Describing habitual & ongoing activities • Telling about likes & dislikes • Describing frequency of actions • Telling about personal background & interests • Emergency room check-in • Preventing identity theft • Civics: U.S. government • Reading a social studies textbook lesson	REVIEW: • Simple present tense • Present continuous tense • Subject & object pronouns • Possessive adjectives • Time expressions	• Engaging in small talk about self, family, interests, & leisure activities • Asking for & reacting to information • Giving personal information	• Listening for correct tense & person in information questions • Pronouncing reduced *are*	• Writing about studying English • Writing about yourself, your family, & your interests • Filling out a patient information form • Writing the names of current federal, state, & local government officials
2	• Reporting past activities • Mishaps • Difficult experiences • Describing a trip • Apologizing for lateness at work • Giving an excuse • Traffic accident report • Civics: U.S. history	REVIEW: • Simple past tense (Regular & irregular verbs) • Past continuous tense	• Asking for & reporting information • Reacting to bad news • Apologizing • Giving excuses	• Listening for correct tense & meaning in information questions • Pronouncing *Did you*	• Writing about a trip you took • Filling out a traffic accident report • Creating a timeline
3	• Describing future plans & intentions • Telling about the future • Expressing time & duration • Talking on the telephone • Plans for the future • Asking a favor • Calling in sick at work • Calling school to report a child's absence • Writing a note to the teacher • Parent-school communication • Reading a campus map	REVIEW: • Future: Going to • Future: Will • Future continuous tense • Time expressions • Possessive pronouns	• Asking & telling about future plans • Engaging in small talk about weekend plans • Making a telephone call to someone you know • Asking a favor • Asking to borrow an item	• Listening to conversations & making deductions about people's plans • Pronouncing *going to*	• Writing about something you're looking forward to • Writing a note to the teacher to explain a child's absence
Gazette	• Immigration around the world • Ellis Island • Interpreting a chart with population statistics • Culture concept: Immigrant neighborhoods around the world • Interview with an immigrant • Idioms	• Simple present tense • Simple past tense • Using present tense to express future • Future: Going to • Future: Will	• Describing neighborhoods • Describing personal history • Using idiomatic expressions	• Listening to messages on a telephone answering machine	• Writing an e-mail or instant message to tell about what you did last weekend & what you plan to do next weekend

CORRELATION and PLACEMENT KEY

Side by Side Plus 3 correlates with the following standards-based curriculum levels and assessment system score ranges:

NRS (National Reporting System) Educational Functioning Level	Low Intermediate
SPL (Student Performance Level)	4
CASAS (Comprehensive Adult Student Assessment System)	201–210
BEST Plus (Basic English Skills Test)	439–472
BEST Oral Interview	42–50
BEST Literacy	47–53

For correlation keys to other major state and local curriculum frameworks, please visit:
www.pearsonlongman.com/sidebysideplus

LIFE SKILLS, CIVICS, TEST PREPARATION, CURRICULUM STANDARDS AND FRAMEWORKS

Life Skills, Civics, & Test Preparation	EFF	SCANS/Employment Competencies	CASAS	LAUSD	Florida*
• Asking & answering personal information questions: name, address, telephone number, social security number, date of birth, place of birth, height, weight, marital status • Providing information about family members • Checking in at an emergency room • Interpreting a narrative reading about identity theft • Civics: Describing three branches of government, their functions, & their elected officials • Identifying current federal, state, & local government officials	• Interact in a way that is friendly • Identify family relationships • Develop & express sense of self • Work together • Keep pace with change • Provide for family members' safety	• Sociability • Self-esteem • Participate as a member of a team	0.2.1, 0.2.2, 0.2.4, 5.5.2, 5.5.3, 5.5.4, 5.5.8	1, 2, 3, 32	4.05.01, 4.05.02, 4.05.04, 4.12.03
• Apologizing & giving a reason for being late for work • Critical thinking: Good & bad excuses for being late for work • Interpreting & filling out traffic accident reports • Civics: U.S. history—major events, historical documents, key leaders • Study skill: Creating a history timeline	• Work together • Reflect & evaluate • Understand, interpret, & work with symbolic information	• Self-management: Assess self accurately • Responsibility • Participate as a member of a team • See things in the mind's eye (Interpret a diagram)	0.1.4, 1.9.7, 5.2.1, 5.2.2	4b, 23	4.02.02, 4.02.05, 4.12.04, 4.15.03
• Calling in sick at work • Calling school to report a child's absence • Parent-school communication • Interpreting a letter to parents from a school principal • Identifying U.S. school structure & grading system • Describing school expectations for students & parents • Interpreting a campus map to locate classrooms, offices, & other facilities	• Interact in a way that is friendly • Plan: Set a goal • Provide for family members' safety & physical needs • Understand, interpret, & work with symbolic information	• Sociability • Allocate time • Responsibility • Understand an organizational system (high school) • See things in the mind's eye (Interpret a chart & a map)	0.1.2, 0.1.3, 0.1.4, 0.2.4, 2.5.4, 2.5.5	3, 5a, 5b, 10, 11, 12b, 57	4.14.01, 4.14.02, 4.15.12
• Interpreting narrative readings about immigration & Ellis Island • Civics: U.S. immigration • Interpreting statistical facts in a table • Interpreting telephone messages on an answering machine	• Respect others & value diversity • Understand, interpret, & work with numerical information • Identify family relationships • Use technology	• Acquire & evaluate information • Work with cultural diversity • Identify goal-relevant activities • Work with technology	0.2.1, 0.2.3, 2.1.7, 2.7.2, 4.8.7, 7.2.4	1, 9, 18, 50	4.05.01, 4.06.02, 4.15.09, 4.15.12

EFF: Equipped for the Future (Content standards, Common activities, & Key activities for Citizen/Community Member, Worker, & Parent/Family role maps; EFF Communication and Reflection/Evaluation skills are covered in every unit)

SCANS: Secretary's Commission on Achieving Necessary Skills (U.S. Department of Labor)

CASAS: Comprehensive Adult Student Assessment System

LAUSD: Los Angeles Unified School District (ESL Intermediate Low content standards)

Florida: Adult ESOL High Beginning Standardized Syllabi

(*Florida benchmarks 4.15.0, 4.16.0, and 4.17.0 are covered in every unit.)

Scope and Sequence

Unit	Topics & Vocabulary	Grammar	Functional Communication	Listening & Pronunciation	Writing
4	• Describing skills • Describing actions that have occurred • Describing actions that haven't occurred yet • Making recommendations • Things to do where you live • Making lists • Employment application procedures • Job application forms • Employment history • Job search strategies	• Present perfect tense	• Expressing ability • Expressing jealousy • Engaging in small talk about experiences, movies, books, videos, and restaurants • Inquiring about & indicating completion of tasks • Expressing satisfaction	• Listening to narratives about tasks accomplished & indicating these tasks on a checklist • Pronouncing contractions with *is* & *has*	• Making a checklist of tasks done at school, at work, or at home • Writing about things you have done & haven't done in the place where you live • Filling out a job application form
5	• Discussing duration of activity • Medical symptoms & problems • Career advancement • Telling about family members • Job interview • Giving employment history • Cover letters & resumes • Employee manual: Workplace policies & expectations	• Present perfect vs. present tense • Present perfect vs. past tense • Since/For • Time expressions	• Asking for & reporting information • Engaging in small talk about interests & experiences • Reacting to information • Asking for clarification	• Listening for information about time & duration in conversations • Pronouncing reduced *have* & *has*	• Writing a story about your English teacher • Writing about your activities & interests • Writing a cover letter & a simple resume
Gazette	• "24/7" work schedules • Culture concept: Unique jobs around the world • Interview with a working couple about their work schedule • Interpreting a bar graph with information about vacation time in different countries • Idioms	• Present perfect tense • Simple present tense • Since/For	• Describing people's work schedules • Giving your opinion • Describing vacation time in different countries • Using idiomatic expressions	• Listening to voice-mail messages at work	• Writing an e-mail or instant message to tell about things you have done
6	• Discussing duration of activity • Reporting household repair problems • Describing tasks accomplished • Describing experiences • Job interviews • Renting an apartment • Lease information • Apartment rules • Utility bills • Housing maintenance & repairs • Yellow pages	• Present perfect continuous tense • Since/For • Time expressions	• Asking for & reporting information • Expressing surprise • Expressing nervousness • Reassuring someone • Asking about & telling about previous experiences	• Listening for particular forms of verbs in sentences • Listening & making deductions about who is speaking • Pronouncing reduced *for*	• Writing about places where you have lived, worked, & gone to school • Making a list of apartment building rules
7	• Discussing recreation preferences • Discussing things you dislike doing • Habits • Describing talents & skills • Telling about important decisions • Requests at work • Thanking someone • Borrow & lending • Workplace notes & messages • "Small talk" at work	• Gerunds • Infinitives • Review: Present perfect & present perfect continuous tenses	• Engaging in small talk about leisure activities • Introducing yourself • Attracting someone's attention • Offering & responding to advice • Expressing envy • Expressing appreciation • Sharing news about future plans • Congratulating	• Listening & making deductions about the context of conversations • Pronouncing reduced *to*	• Writing about an important decision • Making a list of topics for small talk

Life Skills, Civics, & Test Preparation	EFF	SCANS/Employment Competencies	CASAS	LAUSD	Florida*
• Job responsibilities • Following a sequence of employment application procedures • Describing employment history including employer, dates of employment, position, salary, supervisor, & reason for leaving • Identifying sources of job opportunities • Identifying job search strategies	• Interact in a way that is friendly • Create & pursue vision & goals • Work together • Plan: Develop an organized approach of activities & objectives	• Sociability • Self-management: Monitor progress • Decision-making • Allocate time • Understand an organizational system (workplace operations) • Identify goal-relevant activities • Self-management: Set personal goals • Participate as a member of a team • Identify human resources (occupations & work skills)	0.2.2, 0.2.4, 4.1.2, 4.1.3, 4.1.5, 4.6.1, 4.6.4	2, 3, 42, 43, 44, 45, 47b	4.01.01, 4.01.02, 4.01.04, 4.01.05, 4.01.06
• Describing medical symptoms & problems during an examination • Describing family members • Career advancement • Job interview • Describing work experience • Cover letters & resumes • Interpreting a new employee manual • Identifying workplace policies & expectations	• Identify problems • Identify a strong sense of family • Identify family relationships • Work together • Create & pursue vision & goals • Exercise rights & responsibilities	• Understand an organizational system (workplace) • Participate as a member of a team • Identify human resources (occupations & work skills)	0.1.6, 0.2.1, 0.2.3, 0.2.4, 4.1.2, 4.1.5, 4.2.1, 4.2.4	1, 3, 7, 9, 43, 44, 46	4.01.01, 4.01.02, 4.01.03, 4.01.05, 4.01.06, 4.01.07
• Interpreting a narrative reading about work schedules • Describing working parents' activities & responsibilities • Interpreting statistical information in a bar graph • Interpreting voice-mail messages at the workplace	• Keep pace with change • Respect others & value diversity • Identify a strong sense of family • Identify supportive family relationships • Provide for family members' safety & physical needs • Analyze & use information • Understand, interpret, & work with numbers • Use technology	• Work with cultural diversity • Acquire & evaluate information • See things in the mind's eye (Interpret a bar graph) • Work with technology	0.2.3, 2.1.7, 4.8.7, 6.7.2	9, 18, 50	4.01.01, 4.01.02, 4.02.01, 4.02.02, 4.06.02, 4.15.09, 4.15.12
• Reporting apartment maintenance & repair problems • Job interview • Job responsibilities • Inquiring about lease information when renting an apartment • Apartment building rules & regulations • Interpreting utility bills • Credit ratings • Interpreting an apartment building notice to tenants • Interpreting yellow pages listings	• Provide for family members' safety & physical needs • Develop & express sense of self • Work together • Manage resources • Analyze & use information	• Allocate time • Identify goal-relevant activities • Self-esteem • Understand a social system (apartment building rules & regulations) • Participate as a member of a team • Acquire & evaluate information	1.4.2, 1.5.3, 1.8.1, 1.8.2, 4.1.5	25, 26, 27, 43	4.01.06, 4.05.03, 4.06.04, 4.06.05, 4.08.03, 4.11.07, 4.11.08
• Making & responding to requests at work • Workplace tasks • Borrowing & lending items • Thanking someone • Workplace notes • Workplace e-mail messages • Making small talk at work • Understanding the importance of small talk • Interpreting paycheck & pay stub information	• Interact in a way that is friendly • Advocate & influence • Develop & express sense of self • Interact in a way that is courteous • Create & pursue vision & goals • Work together • Interact in a way that is tactful	• Sociability • Self-esteem • Identify goal-relevant activities • Self-management: Set personal goals • Participate as a member of a team • Understand an organizational system (workplace operations)	0.1.3, 0.1.4, 0.2.4, 4.6.4	3, 4a, 5a, 5b, 5e, 47d	4.01.02, 4.02.05, 4.02.06

Scope and Sequence

Unit	Topics & Vocabulary	Grammar	Functional Communication	Listening & Pronunciation	Writing
8	• Discussing things people had done • Discussing preparations for events • Describing consequences of being late • Describing accomplishments • Scheduling medical appointments • Medical appointment cards • Medical history forms • Preventive care recommendations • Public health information • Nutrition: The food pyramid • Reading a health textbook lesson	• Past perfect tense • Past perfect continuous tense	• Asking for & reporting information • Engaging in small talk about leisure activities • Sharing news about someone • Discussing feelings • Sharing experiences	• Listening to questions & choosing the correct response • Pronouncing reduced *had*	• Writing about plans that fell through • Writing about something you accomplished
Gazette	• The Jamaican bobsled team • Culture concept: Children & sports training around the world • Interview with an athlete • Interpreting a line graph with number facts • Idioms	• Gerunds • Infinitives	• Describing popular sports & children's sports training • Using idiomatic expressions	• Listening to sports broadcasts on the radio	• Writing an e-mail or instant message to tell about a favorite hobby
9	• Discussing when things are going to happen • Remembering & forgetting • Discussing obligations • Asking for & giving advice • School assignments • Making plans by telephone • Talking about important people in your life • Shopping for clothing • Identifying bargains • Returning & exchanging defective items • Advertisements • Store coupons	• Two-word verbs: Separable, Inseparable	• Asking for & reporting information about future events • Reminding someone • Remembering & forgetting • Making & responding to invitations • Expressing obligation • Asking for & offering advice	• Listening to determine subject matter of conversations • Pronouncing linked "t" between vowels	• Writing letters to offer advice • Writing about someone you admire
10	• Coincidences • Asking for & giving reasons • Describing people's backgrounds, interests, & personalities • Looking for a job • Referring people to someone else • Discussing opinions • Describing people's similarities & differences • Requesting help at work • Giving & following a sequence of instructions • Operating equipment • Career advancement • Continuing education • Developing a personal education plan	• Connectors: And . . . too And . . . either So, But, Neither	• Engaging in small talk • Giving excuses • Asking for & reporting information • Offering a suggestion • Describing family members	• Listening to determine subject matter of conversations • Pronouncing contrastive stress	• Writing about how you & another person are the same & different
Gazette	• Traditions, customs, modern life, & the ways people meet • Interpreting a bar graph with number facts about social behavior in different countries • Culture concept: Wedding customs & traditions around the world • Interviews with couples about how they met • Idioms	• Two-word verbs: Separable, Inseparable • Simple present tense • Simple past tense	• Describing customs & traditions • Describing how people met • Using idiomatic expressions	• Listening to answering machine messages to make deductions about people's likes & plans	• Writing an e-mail or instant message to tell about a best friend

Life Skills, Civics, & Test Preparation	EFF	SCANS/Employment Competencies	CASAS	LAUSD	Florida*
• Making, confirming, rescheduling, & canceling medical appointments • Interpreting medical appointment cards • Identifying public health clinics & other medical offices offering free or inexpensive medical care • Medical history forms • Preventive care recommendations • Immunizations • Medical screening tests available in the community • Public health information • Nutrition: The food pyramid	• Create & pursue vision & goals • Manage resources • Develop & express sense of self • Provide for family members' safety & physical needs • Identify community needs & resources • Analyze & use information	• Identify goal-relevant activities • Self-management: Set personal goals • Allocate resources • Acquire & evaluate information • See things in the mind's eye (Interpret a chart & a diagram)	0.2.4, 1.1.1, 1.1.7, 3.1.1, 3.2.1, 3.2.2	3, 31, 36, 37, 38, 39, 40, 41	4.05.03, 4.07.01, 4.07.03, 4.07.05, 4.07.06, 4.07.07, 4.07.08, 4.07.09
• Interpreting a narrative reading about international sports • Interpreting statistical facts in a line graph • Interpreting sports broadcasts on the radio	• Respect others & value diversity • Analyze & use information • Understand, interpret, & work with numbers	• Work with cultural diversity • Self-management: Set personal goals • Acquire & evaluate information • See things in the mind's eye (Interpret a line graph)	0.2.1, 0.2.3, 4.8.7, 6.7.1	1, 9, 50	4.05.01, 4.15.09, 4.15.12
• Family chores & responsibilities • Feedback on performance • Child-rearing • Offering assistance to a customer • Asking for clothing in a store • Describing clothing • Identifying sale prices & bargains • Returning & exchanging defective products • Interpreting store advertisements • Calculating sale prices • Comparing products & prices at different stores • Interpreting food product coupons	• Manage resources • Identify supportive family relationships • Meet family needs & responsibilities • Guide & support others • Work together • Gather, analyze, & use information	• Identify goal-relevant activities • Self-management: Assess self accurately • Responsibility • Participate as a member of a team • Allocate money • Acquire & evaluate information	1.2.1, 1.2.2, 1.2.3, 1.3.3, 1.3.5, 1.3.9	28, 29, 30	4.08.02, 4.11.01, 4.11.02, 4.11.04, 4.11.06, 4.11.10, 4.15.12
• Job interview • Requesting & offering help at work • Giving & following a sequence of instructions for operating equipment at work • Identifying skills, education, & positive job evaluations necessary for job retention & promotion • Identifying appropriate behavior, attire, attitudes, & social interactions for job retention & promotion • Identifying programs & classes available in adult & career education	• Interact in a way that is friendly • Develop & express sense of self • Guide & support others • Identify a strong sense of family • Seek & receive assistance • Give direction • Work together • Create & pursue vision & goals • Analyze & use information • Keep pace with change • Plan: Set a goal; Develop an organized approach of activities & objectives	• Sociability • Teach others new skills • Participate as a member of a team • Acquire & evaluate information • Identify goal-relevant activities • Self-management: Set personal goals	0.1.4, 0.2.1, 0.2.4, 2.5.5, 4.8.2, 7.1.1	1, 3, 4b, 13, 47b, 48, 53	4.03.01, 4.03.02, 4.03.03, 4.03.04, 4.05.01, 4.05.02, 4.05.04
• Interpreting statistical facts in a bar graph • Interpreting answering machine messages	• Respect others & value diversity • Identify the family system • Analyze & use information • Understand, interpret, & work with numbers • Use technology	• Work with cultural diversity • See things in the mind's eye (Interpret a bar graph) • Work with technology	0.2.1, 0.2.3, 4.8.7, 6.7.2	1, 9, 50	4.06.02, 4.15.09, 4.15.12

GRAMMAR

PRESENT CONTINUOUS TENSE

(I am)	I'm	
(He is)	He's	
(She is)	She's	eating.
(It is)	It's	
(We are)	We're	
(You are)	You're	
(They are)	They're	

Am	I	
Is	he	
	she	
	it	eating?
Are	we	
	you	
	they	

TO BE: SHORT ANSWERS

	I	am.
Yes,	he	
	she	is.
	it	
	we	
	you	are.
	they	

	I'm	not.
No,	he	
	she	isn't.
	it	
	we	
	you	aren't.
	they	

SIMPLE PRESENT TENSE

I	
We	eat.
You	
They	
He	
She	eats.
It	

Do	I	
	we	
	you	eat?
	they	
Does	he	
	she	
	it	

	I	
Yes,	we	do.
	you	
	they	
	he	
	she	does.
	it	

	I	
No,	we	don't.
	you	
	they	
	he	
	she	doesn't.
	it	

Subject Pronouns	Possessive Adjectives	Object Pronouns
I	my	me
he	his	him
she	her	her
it	its	it
we	our	us
you	your	you
they	their	them

FUNCTIONS

ASKING FOR AND REPORTING INFORMATION

Are you busy?
   Yes, I am. I'm *studying.*
What are you *studying*?
   I'm *studying* English.

Who are you calling?

What are you doing?
   I'm *practicing the piano.*

What *are George and Herman* talking about?

What *are you* complaining about?

What's *your teacher's* name?
What are their names?

What do you do?

When do you *go to class*?

Where are you from?
Where do you live now?
Where do you *work*?

How often do you *watch TV*?

Do you *practice* very often?
   Yes, I do.

Is *she* a good *tennis player*?
   Yes, *she* is.

Are you married?
Are you single?

Her tennis coach says *she's* *excellent.*
Her friends tell *her she plays tennis better than anyone else.*

INQUIRING ABOUT LIKES/DISLIKES

Do you like to *ski*?

What do you like to do *in your free time*?

EXPRESSING INABILITY

I'm not a very good *skier.*

NEW VOCABULARY

Occupations and Agent Nouns

ballet dancer
ballet instructor
coach
cook
instructor
music teacher
skater
soccer coach
swimmer
tennis coach
typist
violinist

Verbs

appoint
approve
belong
carry
compose
declare
die
elect
enforce
explain
hold
interpret
judge
prevent
report
serve
shred
sign
stay after
withdraw

Personal Information

divorced
form of identification
marital status
patient information form
personal information
signature
widowed

Finances

account statement
bank account number
bill
cash machine
credit card account
credit card number
credit information
pay
pay stub

U.S. Government

armed forces
bill
branch of government
cabinet
chief executive
citizen
Commander-in-Chief
Congress
executive branch
federal court
government
House of Representatives
judicial branch
legislative branch
Senate
senator
Supreme Court
Supreme Court justice
term
Vice President
voter

Miscellaneous

army
away
Beethoven
bribe
business
crime
decision
final
household
identify theft

immediately
interests (n)
land
Little Red Riding Hood
Madagascar
member
million
natural-born
Orlando
population
professional
Scrabble
shredder
talk show
telephone bill
war
whenever

for several *days*
once *a day*
twice *a day*
three times *a day*

Text Page 1: Unit Opening Page

VOCABULARY PREVIEW

You may want to introduce these words before beginning the unit, or you may choose to wait until they first occur in a specific lesson. If you choose to introduce them at this point, here are some suggestions:

1. Have students look at the illustrations on text page 1 and identify the words they already know.

2. Present the vocabulary. Say each word and have the class repeat it chorally and individually. Check students' understanding and pronunciation of the words.

3. Practice the vocabulary as a class, in pairs, or in small groups. Have students cover the word list and look at the pictures. Practice the words in the following ways:

   • Say a word and have students tell the number of the illustration.

   • Give the number of an illustration and have students say the word.

Text Page 2: They're Busy

FOCUS

- Review: Present Continuous Tense

CLOSE UP

RULE: The present continuous tense is used to express events that are happening right now.

EXAMPLES: What's she doing?
　　　　　She's reading.
　　　　　What's she reading?
　　　　　She's reading the newspaper.

GETTING READY

1. Review Yes/No questions and affirmative short answers. Form sentences with the words in the left and center boxes at the top of text page 2. Have students repeat chorally. For example:

   Am I eating?　　Is he eating?
   Yes, I am.　　　Yes, he is.

2. Use *Side by Side* Picture Cards or your own visuals to practice short answers.

   a. Point to each visual and ask:

   Is ___ _____ing?

   Have students respond with the affirmative short answer. For example:

   A. Is she eating?
   B. Yes, she is.

   A. Are they studying?
   B. Yes, they are.

   b. Point to each visual and call on pairs of students to ask and answer as above.

3. Review the present continuous tense.

   a. Form sentences with the words in the right-hand box at the top of the page. Have students repeat chorally. For example:

   I'm eating.

He's eating.

Check students' pronunciation of the final *s* sound in *He's, She's, It's.*

b. Use your own visuals or *Side by Side* Picture Cards for verbs.

Ask students: "What ___ doing?" and have students answer individually, then chorally. For example:

A. What's he doing?
B. He's cooking.

A. What's she doing?
B. She's reading.

A. What are they doing?
B. They're studying.

c. Have students role-play people in the visuals. Ask students: "What are you doing?" For example:

A. What are you doing?
B. I'm cooking.

A. What are you and (*Jim*) doing?
B. We're cooking.

INTRODUCING THE MODEL

1. Have students look at the model illustration.

2. Set the scene: "A daughter is talking to her father."

3. With books closed, have students listen as you present the model or play the audio one or more times.

4. **Full-Class Repetition:** Model each line and have students repeat.

Pronunciation Note

The pronunciation focus of Unit 1 is **Reduced *are*** (text page 10). You may wish to model this pronunciation at this point (*What are you studying?*) and encourage students to incorporate it into their language practice.

5. Have students open their books and look at the dialog. Ask students if they have any questions. Check understanding of vocabulary.

6. **Group Choral Repetition:** Divide the class in half. Model line A and have Group 1 repeat. Model line B and have Group 2 repeat, and so on.

7. **Choral Conversation:** Groups 1 and 2 practice the dialog twice, without teacher model. First, Group 1 is Speaker A and Group 2 is Speaker B. Then reverse.

8. Call on one or two pairs of students to present the dialog.

(For additional practice, do Choral Conversation in small groups or by rows.)

SIDE BY SIDE EXERCISES

Examples

1. A. Is Alan busy?
   B. Yes, he is. He's baking.
   A. What's he baking?
   B. He's baking cookies.

2. A. Is Doris busy?
   B. Yes, she is. She's reading.
   A. What's she reading?
   B. She's reading the newspaper.

1. **Exercise 1:** Call on two students to present the dialog. Then do Choral Repetition and Choral Conversation practice.

2. **Exercise 2:** Same as above.

3. **Exercises 3–9:**

New Vocabulary

9. compose

Culture Note

Exercise 9: Ludwig van Beethoven (1770–1827) was a German composer of classical music.

Either

Full-Class Practice: Introduce the new vocabulary before doing Exercise 9. Call on a pair of students to do each exercise.

(For more practice, call on other pairs of students, or do Choral Repetition or Choral Conversation.)

or

Pair Practice: Introduce all the new vocabulary. Next have students practice all the exercises in pairs. Then have pairs present the exercises to the class.

(For more practice, do Choral Repetition or Choral Conversation.)

WORKBOOK

Pages 2–3

EXPANSION ACTIVITIES

1. What Are They Doing? ★

Use *Side by Side* Picture Cards for verbs and community locations or your own visuals to review the present continuous tense.

Hold up each visual and call on students to ask and answer as many questions as possible about what the person or people in the visual are doing. For example:

A. What's she doing?
B. She's cleaning her apartment.

A. What's he doing?
B. He's playing the piano.
A. What are the other people doing?
B. They're listening to the concert/music.

2. Dictation ★

Dictate the following sentences to your students. Read each sentence twice.

1. She's painting the kitchen.
2. What's he doing?
3. He's baking cookies.
4. They're studying.
5. We're cooking dinner.
6. He's knitting.
7. What are you doing?
8. I'm composing a song.

3. Can You Hear the Difference? ★

a. Write on the board:

①	②
I am studying.	I'm studying.
You are ironing.	You're ironing.
He is cooking dinner.	He's cooking dinner.
They are watching TV.	They're watching TV.
She is composing music.	She's composing music.
We are painting the house.	We're painting the house.

b. Choose a sentence randomly from one of the two columns and say it to the class. Have the class listen and respond "One" if the sentence is not contracted, and "Two" if the sentence is contracted.

c. Have students continue the activity in pairs. One student says a sentence, and the other identifies its form. Then have students reverse roles.

d. Write other similar sentences on the board and continue the practice.

4. Telephone ★

a. Divide the class into large groups. Have each group sit in a circle.

b. Whisper the following message to one student:

   "Billy is sitting, Willy is knitting, Eve is reading, and Steve is eating."

c. The first student whispers the message to the second student, and so forth around the circle. The student listening may ask for clarification by saying, "I'm sorry. Could you repeat that?"

d. When the message gets to the last student, that person says it aloud. Is it the same message you started with? The group with the most accurate message wins.

5. Miming ★

a. Write on cards the following activities:

bake a cake	paint a wall	read a newspaper
knit a sweater	iron a shirt	eat ice cream
study mathematics	make a pizza	ride a motorcycle
listen to rock music	put on mittens	feed the dog

b. Have students take turns picking a card from the pile and pantomiming the action on the card.

(continued)

c. The class must guess exactly what the person is doing—both the verb and the object.

Variation: This can be done as a game with competing teams.

6. Role Play: I'm Sorry, But I Can't ★★

a. Write the following conversation model on the board:

> A. Hi, _____. This is _____. Do you want to come over and visit?
> B. I'm sorry, but I can't. I'm _____ right now.
> A. Oh, well. Maybe some other time.
> B. Sure. Thanks for calling.

b. Call on pairs of students to role-play the telephone conversation, using any vocabulary they wish. For example:

> A. Hi, Tom. This is Paul. Do you want to come over and visit?
> B. I'm sorry, but I can't. I'm studying right now.
> A. Oh, well. Maybe some other time.
> B. Sure. Thanks for calling.

7. Describe the Pictures ★★★

a. Bring in several pictures or ask students to bring in pictures of interesting scenes or events.

b. In pairs, have students select a picture and write a description of what's happening in the picture.

c. Have students read their descriptions aloud as the class listens and tries to identify the correct picture.

8. Information Gap: Alan's Family ★★★

a. Tell students that Alan's family is home today. Make up a map of his house with his family members placed in each room and a

description of what they are doing, but divide the information between two different maps. For example:

House Map A:

Living room	Kitchen	Basement
_____ _____	Alan's mother baking a cake	_____ _____
Yard Alan's grandparents planting flowers		Dining room Alan's younger brother doing his homework
Attic _____ _____	Bedroom Alan's sister listening to the radio and cleaning her room	Bathroom _____ _____

Questions:
Who's in the *living room*?
What's he doing?
What's she doing?
What are they doing?

House Map B:

Living room	Kitchen	Basement
Alan's aunt and uncle watching videos	_____ _____	Alan's older brother playing the guitar
Yard _____ _____		Dining room _____ _____
Attic Alan's father looking for old photographs	Bedroom _____ _____ and _____	Bathroom Alan's cousin brushing her hair

Questions:

Who's in the *kitchen*?
What's he doing?
What's she doing?
What are they doing?

b. Divide the class into pairs. Give each member of the pair a different map. Have students ask each other questions and fill in their house maps. For example:

Student A: Who's in the living room?
Student B: Alan's aunt and uncle.
Student A: What are they doing?
Student B: They're watching videos.
Student A [writes the information in House Map A]

c. The pairs continue until each has a filled map.

d. Have students look at their partner's map to make sure that they have written the information correctly.

Text Page 3: What Are They Doing?

FOCUS

- Contrast: Simple Present and Present Continuous Tenses
- Review of Question Formation

CLOSE UP

RULE: The simple present tense expresses habitual activity.

EXAMPLES: **Do** you **practice** the piano often?
          Yes, I **do**. I **practice** the piano whenever I can.

GETTING READY

1. Review the simple present tense by talking about habitual activities.

   a. Write the following adverbs on the board: *always, often, sometimes, rarely, never.* Review the pronunciation. Say each word and have students repeat chorally.

   b. Make a statement about yourself, such as:

        I always see a movie on the weekend.
        I never worry about things.
        I sometimes drive too fast.
        I usually sing in the shower.
        I never dance at parties.

      After each statement, ask students: "How about you?" Have students respond with statements about themselves. For example:

            Teacher: I always see a movie on the
                      weekend. How about you?
            Student A: I rarely see a movie on the
                      weekend.
            Student B: I usually see a movie on the
                      weekend.

2. Review *he, she*, and *they* forms in the simple present tense.

   a. Put the following cues on the board:

	Bob	Betty
work:	bank	museum
study:	math	business
eat:	Italian	Mexican
do exercises:	morning	night

   b. Set the scene: "Bob and Betty are happily married. They like each other very much, but they're very different." Then tell the story:

        Bob and Betty both work.
        He works in a bank.
        She works in a museum.

        They both study in the evening.
        He studies math.
        She studies business.

        They both like to eat in restaurants.
        He likes to eat in Italian restaurants.
        She likes to eat in Mexican restaurants.

        They both do exercises every day.
        He does exercises in the morning.
        She does exercises at night.

   c. Put the following guide on the board and call on pairs of students to create conversations about Bob and Betty.

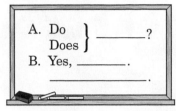

A. Do⎫
Does⎭ ⎯⎯⎯ ?
B. Yes, ⎯⎯⎯ .
⎯⎯⎯ .

For example:

    A. Do Bob and Betty work?
    B. Yes, they do.
       Bob works in a bank, and Betty
       works in a museum.

    A. Does Betty study in the evening?
    B. Yes, she does.
       She studies business.

INTRODUCING THE MODEL

1. Have students look at the model illustration.

2. Set the scene: "Two people are talking."

3. Present the model.

4. Full-Class Repetition.

5. Ask students if they have any questions. Check understanding of the word *whenever*.

6. Group Choral Repetition.

7. Choral Conversation.

8. Call on one or two pairs of students to present the dialog.

   (For additional practice, do Choral Conversation in small groups or by rows.)

SIDE BY SIDE EXERCISES

Examples

1. A. What's Carol doing?
   B. She's watching the news.
   A. Does she watch the news very often?
   B. Yes, she does. She watches the news whenever she can.

2. A. What's Edward doing?
   B. He's swimming.
   A. Does he swim very often?
   B. Yes, he does. He swims whenever he can.

1. **Exercise 1:** Call on two students to present the dialog. Then do Choral Repetition and Choral Conversation practice.

2. **Exercise 2:** Same as above.

3. **Exercises 3–8:** Either Full-Class Practice or Pair Practice.

New Vocabulary

5. Scrabble

Culture Note

Scrabble is a popular game in which players have to create words using letter blocks.

4. **Exercise 9:** Have students use the model as a guide to create their own conversations, using vocabulary of their choice. (They can use any names and activities they wish.) Encourage students to use dictionaries to find new words they want to use. This exercise can be done orally in class or for written homework. If you assign it for homework, do one example in class to make sure students understand what's expected. Have students present their conversations in class the next day.

WORKBOOK

Pages 4–5

EXPANSION ACTIVITIES

1. He or They? ★

a. Put on the board:

He   They

b. Have students listen as you read each of the following sentences with blanks:

——— goes to school every day.
——— play baseball every weekend.
——— practice the piano often.
——— reads at night.
——— always studies English.
——— always go to the movies after work.
——— never drive carefully.
——— usually speaks very slowly.
——— usually take the bus to school.
——— always cleans the apartment.

c. Have students choose the correct pronoun on the board, say it, and then repeat the entire sentence chorally and individually. For example:

Teacher: ——— goes to school every day.
Student: He. He goes to school every day.

2. Pronunciation Practice ★

Write pairs of verbs on the board with and without the final -s. Have students practice saying these words chorally and individually. For example:

cook – cooks
read – reads
fix – fixes
study – studies
write – writes
go – goes
take – takes
watch – watches
swim – swims
exercise – exercises

3. That's Strange! ★★

a. Put the following conversation model on the board:

A. What _____ doing?
B. _____ing.
A. That's strange! _____ never
   _____ !
B. Well, _____ing today!

Use *Side by Side* Picture Cards for verbs, your own visuals, or word cues on the board. If you use word cues, include a name and a verb. For example:

Mrs. Murphy dance	Howard roller-blade

b. Point to a visual or word cue and call on a pair of students to create a conversation based on the model. For example:

(Side by Side Picture Card 44: play cards)

A. What are they doing?
B. They're playing cards.
A. That's strange! They never play cards!
B. Well, they're playing cards today!

4. How Many Sentences? ★★★

a. Write the following on the board:

bake	-s
cook	-ing
chicken	the
kitchen	is
clean	in
chef	are

b. Divide the class into pairs or small groups.

c. Tell students that the object of the game is to see how many sentences they can think of based on these words. Explain that *-ing* can be added to verbs (for example: *cooking, baking*), and *-s* can be added to verbs (*cooks,*

12   UNIT 1

bakes) and to nouns (*chickens, chefs*). Students can say their sentences or they can write them.

Some possible sentences:

The chicken is cooking in the kitchen.
The chefs are cleaning chickens in the kitchen.
The chickens are clean.
Clean the kitchen!
The chef's kitchen is clean.
The chicken is baking in the kitchen.
The chef bakes chickens in the clean kitchen.

Variation: You can do this activity as a game in which the pair or group of students who comes up with the most sentences wins.

5. Class Story: The Brown Family ★★

a. Begin the following story:

The Brown family is always busy on the weekend. For example, today is Saturday. Mr. Brown is washing his car. He washes his car every Saturday morning.

b. Have each student continue the story by telling about another member of the Brown family. For example:

Mrs. Brown is vacuuming the living room rug. She vacuums the living room rug every Saturday morning.

c. The story continues until each student has added similar sentences about other family members to the story.

Note: If your class is large, you might want to divide the class into groups of 6 to 8 students and have each group create its own story. Have the groups compare their stories after they have completed them.

6. Dictate and Discuss ★★★

a. Divide the class into pairs or small groups.

b. Dictate sentences such as the following:

He never listens to the radio in the basement, but he's listening to the radio in the basement today.

They never walk to work, but they're walking to work today.

She never washes her clothes in the sink, but she's washing her clothes in the sink today.

We never eat spaghetti for breakfast, but we're eating spaghetti for breakfast today.

c. Have students discuss possible reasons for the strange behavior. For example:

He's listening to the radio in the basement because he wants to the listen to the baseball game, and his teenage children are listening to music on the radio in the living room.

d. Call on students to share their ideas with the rest of the class.

7. What Do You Think They're Doing Now? ★★★

a. Write the names of some famous people on the board. For example:

the president
the queen
the prime minister
(popular entertainment star)

b. Ask about these famous people. For example:

Teacher: It's midnight in Washington, D.C. What's the president doing?

Student 1: He's sleeping.
Student 2: He's probably talking on the hot line.
Student 3: I think he's meeting with the secretary of state.

Teacher: It's 4 P.M. in London. What's the queen doing?

Student 1: She's probably having tea.
Student 2: She's working in her office.
Student 3: Maybe she's playing with her dogs.

Encourage students to be imaginative when thinking about possible answers to your questions.

FOCUS

- Review:
  Don't and *Doesn't*
  Like to
  Agent Nouns
  Negative forms of *To Be*

CLOSE UP

RULE: The simple present tense is used to express a fact.

EXAMPLE: I **don't like** to skate.

RULE: In the simple present tense, the verb *to be* can contract with *not* or with the subject. In this lesson, the following negative forms are presented:

he isn't	we aren't
she isn't	you aren't
it isn't	they aren't

Equally correct alternatives are:

he's not	we're not
she's not	you're not
it's not	they're not

GETTING READY

1. Review short answers with *don't* and *doesn't*.

   a. Have students look at the left-hand box at the top of the page as you ask questions about people in the class, using each pronoun and the simple present tense. Have students respond with negative short answers. For example:

Teacher	Student
Do you speak (*German*)?	No, I don't.
Do you and (*Mary*) wear glasses?	No, we don't.
Do I live in (*Tokyo*)?	No, you don't.
Do (*Bill*) and (*Bob*) drive too fast?	No, they don't.
Does (*Barbara*) live in (*London*)?	No, she doesn't.
Does (*Tom*) like to cook?	No, he doesn't.

   b. Call on students to make up other questions such as those above, and have other students answer.

2. Review short answers with the verb *to be*.

   a. Have students look at the right-hand box at the top of the page. Ask questions about people in the class, using each pronoun and the verb *to be*. Have students answer with negative short answers. For example:

Teacher	Student
Are you married?	No, I'm not.
Are you and (*Carol*) sisters?	No, we aren't.
Am I a student?	No, you aren't.
Are (*Tom*) and (*Jim*) teachers?	No, they aren't.

Is (*Ted*) a truck driver?   No, he isn't.
Is (*Betty*) a doctor?   No, she isn't.

b. Call on students to make up other questions such as those above, and have other students answer.

INTRODUCING THE MODEL

1. Have students look at the model illustration.

2. Set the scene: "Two people are riding on a ski lift. They just met each other."

3. Present the model.

4. Full-Class Repetition.

5. Ask students if they have any questions. Check understanding of vocabulary.

6. Group Choral Repetition.

7. Choral Conversation.

8. Call on one or two pairs of students to present the dialog.

   (For additional practice, do Choral Conversation in small groups or by rows.)

SIDE BY SIDE EXERCISES

Examples

1. A. Does Richard like to sing?
   B. No, he doesn't. He isn't a very good singer.

2. A. Does Brenda like to swim?
   B. No, she doesn't. She isn't a very good swimmer.

3. A. Do Mr. and Mrs. Adams like to skate?
   B. No, they don't. They aren't very good skaters.

1. **Exercise 1:** Call on two students to present the dialog. Then do Choral Repetition and Choral Conversation practice.

2. **Exercise 2:** Introduce the word *swimmer*. Same as above.

3. **Exercise 3:** Introduce the word *skater*. Same as above.

4. **Exercises 4–9:** Either Full-Class Practice or Pair Practice.

New Vocabulary

5. typist
9. cook

WORKBOOK

Pages 6–8

EXPANSION ACTIVITIES

1. Chain Game ★

a. Start the chain game by asking Student A: "Do you like to swim?"

b. Student A answers and asks Student B, who then continues the chain. For example:

Student A: No, I don't.
(to Student B):   Do you like to ski?

Student B: Yes, I do.
(to Student C):   Do you like to . . . ?

2. Is That True? ★★

a. Write on cards statements such as those below, using names of students in your class if you wish:

(Rita) dances beautifully.

(Richard) doesn't ski very well.

(Michael) and (Maria) type very quickly.

You're a very good skier.

(Peter) doesn't act very well.

(Carol) skates very badly.

I sing beautifully.

You and (Jane) cook very well.

(Sam) writes very interesting stories.

(Thomas) drives very carelessly.

(Shirley) swims very badly.

b. Put this conversation model on the board:

A. Everybody says _____. Is that true?

B. { Yes, it is. / No, it isn't. } ___ a/an { great / fantastic / wonderful / terrible / awful / very bad } _____!

c. Give the cards to pairs of students. Have students create conversations, using the model on the board, and then present them to the class. Students may choose to agree or disagree with the first speaker. For example:

A. Everybody says (Rita) dances beautifully. Is that true?
B. Yes, it is. She's a wonderful dancer!
   or
No, it isn't. She's an awful dancer!

3. What's the Occupation? ★★

a. Put the following on the board:

He's a/an _____.
She's a/an _____.
They're _____s.

b. Have students listen as you read the following job descriptions. After each description, have students tell the occupation, using the sentence models on the board. If you wish, you can do the activity as a game with competing teams.

Walter plays the violin in concerts.
   (He's a violinist.)

Carla types for a company downtown.
   (She's a typist.)

Michael and his brother fix broken sinks.
   (They're plumbers.)

Alice drives a truck between Chicago and Denver.
   (She's a truck driver.)

Tom plays tennis all around the world.
(*He's a tennis player.*)

Barbara paints houses for a living.
(*She's a painter/house painter.*)

David acts in plays and movies and on TV.
(*He's an actor.*)

His girlfriend also acts.
(*She's a actress.*)

Brian repairs televisions.
(*He's a TV repairperson.*)

Tony and Greta repair cars and trucks.
(*They're mechanics.*)

Boris plays chess in countries all around the world.
(*He's a chess player.*)

Diane cleans people's chimneys.
(*She's a chimneysweep.*)

Bob takes pictures at weddings and other special occasions.
(*He's a photographer.*)

Olga translates from English into Russian.
(*She's a translator.*)

Frank and his brother cook in a very good restaurant downtown.
(*They're cooks/chefs.*)

Barbara designs beautiful clothes.
(*She's a designer.*)

Joe bakes bread, cakes, and special desserts.
(*He's a baker.*)

George and Paul plant flowers in people's yards.
(*They're gardeners.*)

Betty helps doctors and takes care of people in the hospital.
(*She's a nurse.*)

Peter takes care of sick dogs and cats.
(*He's a veterinarian.*)

c. Find out what other occupations your students are interested in. Have students use their dictionaries to find out the names of these occupations and tell what the people do.

4. Tell About Yourself! ★★

a. Set the scene by telling about yourself or about a person on the board. For example:

"This is Mary. Mary likes to swim, and she's a good swimmer. She likes to type, but she isn't a very good typist. She doesn't like to cook because she isn't a very good cook. She likes to play the piano, and she plays whenever she can."

b. Divide students into pairs.

c. Have students interview each other to find out about their likes and dislikes and related abilities.

d. Then have each student tell the class about the person he or she interviewed.

Variation: You can do this as a writing activity. For homework, have students write about themselves: their likes, dislikes, and related abilities.

5. Common Interests ★★★

a. Put the following on the board:

I like to _____.
He/She likes to _____.
He's/She's a good _____.
We both like to _____.
We're both good _____.

b. Divide the class into pairs.

c. Have students interview each other about what they like to do. The object is for students to find things they have in common and then report back to the class. For example:

(continued)

I interviewed Maria. I like to ski. She likes to skate. She's a good skater. We both like to dance. We're both good dancers. Also, we both like to sing. We're both good singers.

6. Classroom Interviews ★★★

a. On an index card, have each student write three things that he or she likes to do. For example:

> I like to swim.
> I like to watch TV.
> I like to play tennis.

b. Collect the cards and distribute them randomly to all the students in the class.

c. Have students interview others in the class to match the correct person with each card, that is, to find out which student likes to do the three activities written on each card.

d. When the interviews are completed, call on students to tell about the others in the class, based on their interviews. For example:

> Alexander likes to swim.
> He likes to watch TV.
> And he likes to play tennis.

📖 READING *Practicing*

FOCUS

- Review:
  Simple Present Tense
  Present Continuous Tense
  Subject Pronouns
  Possessive Adjectives

NEW VOCABULARY

ballet dancer
ballet instructor
coach (n)
instructor
music teacher
professional
soccer coach
stay after
tennis coach
violinist

READING THE STORY

Optional: Preview the story by having students talk about the story title and/or illustrations. You may choose to introduce new vocabulary beforehand, or have students encounter the new vocabulary within the context of the reading.

1. Have students read silently or follow along silently as the story is read aloud by you, by one or more students, or on the audio program.

2. Ask students if they have any questions. Check understanding of vocabulary.

3. Check students' comprehension, using some or all of the following questions:

   What am I doing?
   How often do I practice?

What does my soccer coach tell me?
What do my friends tell me?
What do I want to be when I grow up?

What's Anita doing?
How often does she practice?
What does her tennis coach tell her?
What do her friends tell her?
What does she want to be when she grows up?

What's Hector doing?
How often does he practice?
What does his music teacher tell him?
What do his friends tell him?
What does he want to be when he grows up?

What are Jenny and Vanessa doing?
How often do they practice?
What does their ballet instructor tell them?
What do they want to be when they grow up?

✔ READING *CHECK-UP*

Q & A

1. Call on a pair of students to present the model.

2. Have students work in pairs to create new dialogs.

3. Call on pairs to present their new dialogs to the class.

READING EXTENSION

1. Question the Answers!

a. Choose one of the four paragraphs. Dictate answers such as these to the class:

   Every day after school.
   Her tennis coach.
   Her friends.
   A professional tennis player.
   Because she wants to be a professional tennis player.

b. Have students write questions for which these answers would be correct. For example:

Answer: Every day after school.
Question: How often does Anita practice?

Answer: Her tennis coach.
Question: Who tells her she's an excellent tennis player?

Answer: Her friends.
Question: Who tells her she's better than anyone else in school?

Answer: A professional tennis player.
Question: What does she want to be when she grows up?

Answer: Because she wants to be a professional tennis player.
Question: Why does she practice every day?

c. Have students compare their questions with each other.

Variation: Write the answers on cards. Divide the class into groups and give each group a set of cards as cues for the activity.

2. Pair Discussion

Have pairs of students discuss the following questions and then report back to the class:

Do you have a hobby? Do you play sports or a musical instrument?
What do you play?
How often do you practice?
Do you want to be a professional player?
Did you practice when you were a child?
When you were a child, what did you want to be when you grew up?

 LISTENING

Listen and choose the correct answer.

1. What are you doing?

2. Do you watch the news very often?

3. Are you a good swimmer?

4. What's Cathy reading?

5. Who cooks in your family?

6. Do they like to skate?

7. Does your sister want to be a ballet dancer?

8. Do you and your friends play basketball very often?

9. Are your parents good dancers?

10. What does Peter want to be when he grows up?

Answers

1. b
2. b
3. a
4. b
5. a
6. b
7. b
8. a
9. a
10. b

 IN YOUR OWN WORDS

1. Make sure students understand the instructions.

2. Have students do the activity as written homework, using a dictionary for any new words they wish to use.

3. Have students present and discuss what they have written, in pairs or as a class.

Text Pages 7–8: How Often?

FOCUS

- Pronoun Review
- Contrast: Simple Present and Present Continuous Tenses

CLOSE UP

RULE: In spoken English, **who** is used to refer to both a subject and an object.

EXAMPLES: **Who** are you calling? (I'm calling *my brother*.)
           Who is calling your brother? (*I* am calling my brother.)
           Who are you arguing with? (I am arguing with *my neighbor*.)

RULE: In formal and written English, **whom** is used to refer to an object.

EXAMPLES: **Whom** are you calling?
           With **whom** are you arguing?

GETTING READY

1. Review pronouns.

   a. Write on the board:

   My { friend / friends } ———— { likes / likes } to visit me here in ————.

   When ———— { comes / come } to visit, I always take ———— to ———— favorite { museum / restaurant / theater }.

   b. Set the scene: "My friend Bob likes to visit me here in (*name of your city*). When he comes to visit, I always take him to his favorite restaurant."

   c. Have students use this model to review other pronouns. Ask students: "What about your friend(s) ————?" Students can refer to the box at the top of text page 7 for the pronoun. For example:

   A. What about your friend Maria?
   B. My friend Maria likes to visit me here in ————. When she comes to visit, I always take her to her favorite museum.

   A. What about your friends Dave and Donna?
   B. My friends Dave and Donna like to visit me here in ————. When they come to visit, I always take them to their favorite theater.

d. Change *my* to *our* in the model on the board. Have students make all the necessary changes as they tell about *our friend(s)* _____ and _____.

2. Review time expressions.

a. Write on the board:

study English	play soccer
clean your house	watch the news
call your grandparents	read poetry
read the newspaper	iron clothes
ask questions in class	exercise
do your homework	chat online

b. Ask students a few questions based on the cues on the board, and have students respond, using the expressions with *every* in the chart on text page 7. For example:

Teacher: How often do you study English?
Student: I study English every day.

c. Introduce the new expressions with *once, twice.* Ask students: "How often do you *play soccer?*" Have students respond, using the time expressions with *once, twice,* and *(three) times,* which are presented in the chart on text page 7. For example:

Teacher: How often do you play soccer?
Student: I play soccer twice a week.

d. In pairs, have students ask and answer *How often* questions, using the cues on the board.

INTRODUCING THE MODELS

There are two model conversations. Introduce and practice each separately. For each model:

1. Have students look at the model illustration.

2. Set the scene:

1st model: "Two friends are talking. One of them is making a phone call."
2nd model: "Two friends are sitting and talking in the park."

3. Present the model.

4. Full-Class Repetition.

5. Ask students if they have any questions. Check understanding of vocabulary.

6. Group Choral Repetition.

7. Choral Conversation.

8. Call on one or two pairs of students to present the dialog.

9. After the 1st model:

a. Go over the alternative vocabulary at the top of the page.

b. Have several pairs of students present the dialog again, using alternative vocabulary in place of *every Sunday evening.*

10. After the 2nd model, have several pairs of students present the dialog again, using alternative vocabulary in place of *all the time.*

SIDE BY SIDE EXERCISES

Students can use any time expression they wish to complete these conversations.

Examples

1. A. Who is Mr. Tanaka calling?
   B. He's calling his son in New York.
   A. How often does he call him?
   B. He calls him *(every week).*

2. A. Who is Mrs. Kramer writing to?
   B. She's writing to her daughter in the army.
   A. How often does she write to her?
   B. She writes to her *(once a month).*

1. **Exercise 1:** Call on two students to present the dialog. Then do Choral Repetition and Choral Conversation practice.

2. **Exercise 2:** Introduce the word *army.* Same as above.

3. **Exercises 3–9:** Either Full-Class Practice or Pair Practice.

New Vocabulary

7. telephone bill
8. talk show

Whenever possible, after each exercise ask students to compare their own experiences with that of the people in the exercise. For example, after Exercise 4 ask: "How about you? Do you argue with your landlord?" After Exercise 5 ask: "How about you? How often do you send e-mail messages to friends and family members?" After Exercise 6 ask: "Do you know someone who shouts a lot?" After Exercise 7 ask: "Do you get large telephone bills? Do you make many long-distance phone calls?" After Exercise 8 ask: "How often do you watch TV talk shows? Which is your favorite?" After Exercise 9 ask: "How often do you visit your grandparents?"

Culture Note

Exercise 9: *Little Red Riding Hood* is a well-known folk tale about a little girl wearing a red hood who goes to visit her grandmother in her house in the woods. In the story, a clever wolf pretends to be the grandmother and nearly succeeds in eating Little Red Riding Hood.

4. **Exercise 10:** Have students use the model as a guide to create their own conversations, using vocabulary of their choice. Encourage students to use dictionaries to find new words they want to use. This exercise can be done orally in class or for written homework. If you assign it for homework, do one example in class to make sure students understand what's expected. Have students present their conversations in class the next day.

WORKBOOK

Pages 9–11

EXPANSION ACTIVITIES

1. Pronoun Review: A Story About Peggy and John ★

   a. Put the following on the board:

   b. Set the scene: "I want to tell you about my friends Peggy and John."

   c. Read each sentence below while pointing to the faces on the board. Have students listen and repeat each sentence, changing all the nouns to pronouns.

   Example: Peggy and John are married.
   (They're married.)

   Peggy likes John.
   (She likes him.)

John likes Peggy.
(He likes her.)

Peggy and John live in Canada.
(They live in Canada.)

Peggy and John's last name is Jones.
(Their last name is Jones.)

Peggy met John at a party.
(She met him at a party.)

John liked Peggy right away.
(He liked her right away.)

John and Peggy got married at Peggy's parents' house.
(They got married at her parents' house.)

On Peggy's last birthday, John gave Peggy a watch.
(On her last birthday, he gave her a watch.)

On John's last birthday, Peggy gave John a new coat.
(On his last birthday, she gave him a new coat.)

(continued)

2. Mystery Word ★★

a. Divide the class into pairs.

b. Give each pair a card with a *mystery word* on it. Possibilities include:

granddaughter	complain	shout
army	bill	argue
landlord	employees	practice

c. Have each pair create a sentence in which that word is in final position. For example:

> My son's daughter is my _____.
> *(granddaughter)*
> Before you leave the hotel, don't forget to pay the _____. *(bill)*

d. One student from the pair then reads aloud the sentence with the final word missing. The other pairs of students try to guess the missing word.

Variation: This can be done as a game in which each pair scores a point for identifying the correct *mystery word*. The pair with the most points wins the game.

3. Expand the Sentence! ★★

Tell students that the object of the activity is to build a long sentence on the board, one word at a time.

a. Call on a student to write a pronoun or someone's name on the far left side of the board. For example:

George

b. Have another student come to the board and add a word. For example:

George likes

c. Have a third student add a third word. For example:

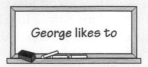

George likes to

d. Continue until each student in the class has had one or more turns to add a word to expand the sentence into the longest one they can think of. For example:

> George likes to talk to his brother on the telephone every Sunday night because his brother lives in Russia, and George doesn't see his brother very often.

4. Grammar Chain: How Often? ★★

a. Write the following activities on the board:

see a movie	argue with someone
write a letter	visit your grandparents
bake cookies	paint your house
iron your shirts	pay bills
play baseball	play the piano
knit a sweater	watch the news
read poetry	play tennis
cook dinner	read the newspaper
chat online	watch a talk show
compose music	send e-mail messages

b. Start the chain game by saying:

> Teacher (*to Student A*): How often do you see a movie?

c. Student A answers truthfully and then makes a new question, using another verb phrase on the board. Student A asks the new question to Student B, who then continues the chain. For example:

Student A: I see a movie every weekend.
(to Student B): How often do you write a letter?

Student B: I write a letter once a week.
(to Student C): How often do you read poetry?

5. Find the Right Person! ★★

a. Collect some information about students' habits.

b. Put the information on a handout in the following form:

> Find someone who . . .
> 1. watches talk shows every night. _____
> 2. bakes bread once a week.   _____
> 3. knits sweaters.   _____
> 4. chats online every evening.   _____
> 5. reads a novel once a month.   _____

c. Have students circulate around the room, asking each other questions to identify the above people. For example:

How often do you watch talk shows?
Do you bake bread? How often?

d. The first student to find all the people, raise his or her hand, and tell the class who they are is the winner of the game.

6. Role Play: At the Doctor's Office ★★

a. Put the following conversation model on the board:

> A. How often do you _____?
> B. I _____ { all the time.
>   every _____.
>   once a _____.
>   twice a _____.
>   _____ times a _____.
> A. I see. And how often do you _____?
> B. I _____.
> A. Well, you don't have any serious medical problems. I'll see you next year.

b. Also put these word cues on the board:

> exercise
> take vitamins
> eat rich desserts
> go to bed late
> listen to loud music
> go to the dentist
> eat fatty foods
> eat healthy foods

c. Set the scene: "You're at the doctor's office for your annual physical examination."

d. Call on pairs of students to role-play the conversation. Speaker A is the *doctor*. Speaker B is the *patient*. For example:

A. How often do you exercise?
B. I exercise once a week.
A. I see. And how often do you take vitamins?
B. I take vitamins every morning.
A. Well, you don't have any serious medical problems. I'll see you next year.

Encourage students to expand the conversation in any way they wish.

7. Interview the Characters ★★★

Have students pretend to be the different characters from this lesson. *Interview* them to find out more about their situations. For example:

Model 1:   Tell us, what do you and your sister usually talk about?

Model 2:   George and Herman, tell us about your grandchildren.

Exercise 1: Mr. Tanaka, what do you usually talk to your son about?

Exercise 2: Mrs. Kramer, what do you write to your daughter about?

Exercise 3: What are you saying about your teachers?

Exercise 4: Lenny, what's the problem? What are you arguing about with your landlord?

(continued)

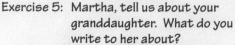

Exercise 5: Martha, tell us about your granddaughter. What do you write to her about?

Exercise 6: Mr. Crabapple, why are you shouting at your employees? (Also interview some employees: Why is Mr. Crabapple shouting at you? How often does that happen? What kind of a boss is he?)

Exercise 7: What's the problem with your telephone bill?

Exercise 8: George, what's your favorite talk show? Why is it your favorite? Tell us about it.

Exercise 9: Little Red Riding Hood, does your grandmother look a little different today?

8. Role Plays ★★★

a. Divide the class into pairs.

b. Have each pair choose one of the situations in the lesson—either of the models or any of the exercises—and create a role play based on that situation.

c. Have the pairs present their role plays to the class and compare their interpretations of the situation.

9. Little Red Riding Hood ★★★

Little Red Riding Hood appears in Exercise 9 in the student text. If you think your students would be interested, go to the library or look on the Internet, find the story of Little Red Riding Hood, and read it to the class. Possible follow-up activities:

a. Call on students to retell the story.

b. Read the story and have students write it as best they can remember it.

c. Have students tell the class famous folk tales from their countries.

How to Say It!

> **Asking for and Reacting to**
> **Information:** *Tell me* is a common way to
> preface a question. There are many ways
> to react to new information. "Oh," "Really?"
> "Oh, really?" and "That's interesting" are
> four common phrases. The intonation rises
> to indicate interest in what the other
> person has just said.

1. Set the scene: "Two diplomats at the United
   Nations are talking."

2. Present the conversation.

3. Full-Class Repetition.

4. Ask students if they have any questions.
   Bring a world map to class and point out the
   location of Madagascar.

5. Group Choral Repetition.

6. Choral Conversation.

 INTERACTIONS

There are three topics of conversation, with
suggested questions under each. For each topic:

1. Go over the questions and introduce the new
   vocabulary: *What do you do?, interests.*

   ### Culture Note

   The question *What do you do?* is
   commonly asked to find out what
   someone's profession is. The importance of
   this question in U.S. culture reflects the
   value of work as a means of establishing
   one's identity.

2. Divide the class into pairs. Have students
   interview each other, using the questions on
   student text page 9. Remind students to use
   the phrases in ***How to Say It!*** to express
   interest in what the other person is saying.
   Have students take notes during their
   interviews in order to remember each other's
   answers.

3. Call on several students to report back to the
   class about the people they interviewed.

   Option: As the class changes topics, have
   students change partners so they may get to
   know many different people in the class.

4. For homework, have students write several
   sentences about each person they
   interviewed.

EXPANSION ACTIVITIES

1. Silent Letters ★

Write the words below on the board. Have
students try to find the silent letter or letters
in each word:

knit	neighbor
plumber	ballet
daughter	right
knife	wrong

2. Who Is Your Favorite? ★★

Have students talk about their favorite writers,
singers, painters, actors, actresses, and
composers.

a. Put on the board:

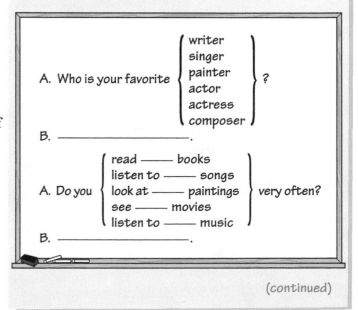

A. Who is your favorite { writer / singer / painter / actor / actress / composer } ?

B. _____.

A. Do you { read ___ books / listen to ___ songs / look at ___ paintings / see ___ movies / listen to ___ music } very often?

B. _____.

(continued)

EXPANSION ACTIVITIES (Continued)

b. Have pairs of students create conversations based on the model. This can be done as Full-Class Practice or Pair Practice. Examples:

A. Who is your favorite singer?
B. *(Timmy Martin.)*
A. Do you listen to his songs very often?
B. Yes, I do. I listen to them every day.

A. Who is your favorite actress?
B. *(Julie Richards.)*
A. Do you see her movies very often?
B. Yes. I see them whenever I can.

JOURNAL

Have students write their journal entries at home or in class. Encourage students to use a dictionary to look up words they would like to use. Students can share their written work with other students if appropriate. Have students discuss what they have written as a class, in pairs, or in small groups.

GRAMMAR FOCUS

Answers

1. He's ironing
2. chats
3. We, our
4. are, doing, They're, their
5. are, arguing
6. Does, practice
7. I call
8. Is, isn't, doesn't

MULTILEVEL VARIATION ★★★

Challenge *above-level* students to cover the grammar boxes as they complete the grammar exercises.

1 CONVERSATION
Giving Personal Information

1. Have students look at the patient information form. Ask questions about the patient so students understand the form—for example: "What's the patient's first name?" (Rita) "What's her last name?" (Sanchez) "What's her address?" (84 Central Avenue, Apartment 14G, Los Angeles, California) Introduce the new vocabulary: *divorced, household, marital status, patient information form*, and *widowed*.

2. Model the first two questions with a student volunteer. For example:

   A. What's your name?
   B. My name is Rita Sanchez.
   A. What's your address?
   B. My address is 84 Central Avenue, Apartment 14G, Los Angeles, California.

3. In pairs, have students practice the conversation as you circulate around the classroom, helping students find the information in the form. (Students don't need to write the answers for B in the Student Book. This is a conversation practice exercise.)

4. Have students switch roles and repeat the conversation.

5. Call on a pair of students to present their conversation to the class.

2 TEAMWORK *Checking in at an Emergency Room*

1. Model the activity with a student. Copy several lines of the form onto the board and write in your own information (or any information you wish). Have a student ask you questions from student text page 10a. Answer the questions with the information on the board.

2. Divide the class into pairs. First have students complete the form using any information they wish and then ask and answer one another's questions.

MULTILEVEL VARIATION ★★★

Have *above-level* students ask their partners the questions and then complete the form with their partners' information. For example:

   A. What's your last name?
   B. Fernandez.
   [Student A writes *Fernandez* in the form on student book page 10a.]

LIFE SKILLS ENRICHMENT

Personal Information Form

Life Skills Worksheet 1

Make copies of Life Skills Worksheet 1 and give one to each student. Have students complete the worksheet as homework. In the next class, have students compare their answers in pairs.

EXPANSION ACTIVITIES

1. Find the Words! ★

a. Write the following words or abbreviations on the board and have students circle the corresponding word on student book page 10a. For example:

social security number	(SSN)
DOB	(date of birth)
ft.	(feet)
in.	(inches)
lbs.	(pounds)
apt.	(apartment)
Ave.	(Avenue)

b. Have students share their answers with the class. Write their answers on the board.

2. Question the Answers! ★★

a. Dictate answers such as the following to the class:

William Jones.
October 21, 1986.
829–77–2731.

b. Have students write questions for which these answers would be correct. For example:

Answer: William Jones.
Question: What's your name?

c. Have students compare their questions with each other.

3. The 50 States ★★

Activity Master 1

Make multiple copies of Activity Master 1 and give one to each student. Have students look at the map on student text page 162 and complete the Activity Master. Then have students compare their answers in pairs.

4. Interview ★★★

Activity Master 2

a. Make multiple copies of Activity Master 2 and give one to each student.

b. Have students complete the form with their own information or any information they wish.

c. Divide the class into pairs. Have students ask their partners questions and write their information into the form. For example:

Student A. What's your last name?
Student B. Valdivia.
Student A. How do you spell that?
Student B. V-A-L-D-I-V-I-A.

d. When the pairs have finished completing the form, have them show their partner the form to make sure they have written the information correctly.

MULTILEVEL VARIATION ★★★

Challenge *above-level* students by having them cover the question box and form the questions on their own.

NEWS ARTICLE *Identity Theft*

1. Have students look at the title. Ask: "What do you think *identity theft* means?" Write students' ideas on the board. Have students read the first paragraph. Ask: "Was your definition of identity theft correct?"

2. Have students look at the photograph. Ask: "What's that?" (It's paper from a paper shredder.) Introduce the new vocabulary: *account statement, bank account number, bribe (v), business, carry, cash machine, credit card account, credit card number, credit*

information, crime, for several days, form of identification, hold, identity theft, immediately, million, pay (v), pay stub, personal information, prevent, report (v), shred, shredder, signature, and *withdraw.*

3. Have students do all the comprehension exercises individually and then compare their answers in pairs.

Answers

1.	B	**4.**	C
2.	C	**5.**	A
3.	D	**6.**	D

EXPANSION ACTIVITIES

1. Identity Theft Prevention Checklist ★

Activity Master 3

Make multiple copies of Activity Master 3 and give one to each student. Have students read the article again on student text page 10b and complete the checklist. Then have students compare answers in small groups.

Variation: ★/★★ Have pairs of students take turns reading the lines of Activity Master 3 aloud and checking each other's comprehension of the article.

Variation: ★★★ Have students draw two columns on a separate piece of paper and write <u>Yes</u> above one column and <u>No</u> above the other. Dictate lines from Activity Master 3 and have students write the lines in the correct column. For example:

<u>Yes</u>	<u>No</u>
Leave your social security card at home.	Leave your mail in your mailbox.

2. True or False? ★★

Make statements using new vocabulary from the reading and have students decide whether the statements are true or false. If a statement is false, have students correct it. For example:

A thief can buy a car with your credit information. [True.]
You should always carry all of your credit cards with you. [False.]
You should shred important documents before you throw them out. [True.]
To *withdraw* money means to take money out of an account. [True.]

You are a victim of identity theft if someone steals your money. [False. You are a victim of identity theft when someone steals your personal information and uses it.]

Variation: Do the activity as a game with competing teams.

3. Identity Theft Prevention Poster Contest ★★

a. Bring poster board, markers, old magazines, and glue sticks to class.

b. Divide the class into pairs. Have each pair make a poster with the most important information about preventing identity theft from the article.

c. Have a poster contest. Award each poster with a prize. For example:

the most colorful poster
the most informative poster
the most artistic poster

d. Have students hang their posters up on classroom walls and school hallways so other students may learn about identity theft.

4. Dictate and Discuss ★★★

Divide the class into pairs or small groups. Dictate sentences such as the following and have students discuss whether they agree or disagree with the statements.

It's dangerous to shop on the Internet.
It's safer to carry cash than to carry credit cards.
It's possible to buy things on the phone with somebody else's credit card information.
Anyone can be a victim of identity theft.

THE THREE BRANCHES OF GOVERNMENT

1. Have students look at the photos and answer the questions in the caption. (The first picture is of the White House. The President lives and works there. The second picture is of the Supreme Court. Supreme Court justices work there. The third picture is of the Capitol building. The Congress works there.) Explain that these three buildings represent the three branches of government—the executive branch, the judicial branch, and the legislative branch.

2. Introduce the new vocabulary: *appoint, approve, armed forces, belong, bill, branch of government, Cabinet, chief executive, citizen, Commander-in-Chief, Congress, decision, declare, die, elect, enforce, executive branch, explain, federal court, final, government, House of Representatives, interpret, judge, judicial branch, land, legislative branch, member, natural-born, population, Senate, senator, serve, sign, Supreme Court, Supreme Court justice, term, Vice President, voter,* and *war.*

3. Have students work individually to complete the comprehension exercise and then compare answers in pairs, small groups, or as a class.

Answers

1.	C	**4.**	B
2.	D	**5.**	D
3.	C	**6.**	A

Civics Today

Have students work individually to read the questions and write their responses. Then have students share their responses with the class.

LIFE SKILLS ENRICHMENT

The Three Branches of Government

Life Skills Worksheet 2

Make copies of Life Skills Worksheet 2 and give one to each student. Have students complete the worksheet as homework. In the next class, have students compare their answers in pairs.

EXPANSION ACTIVITIES

1. Association Game ★

a. Write on the board the three branches of the U.S. government:

> legislative branch
> executive branch
> judicial branch

b. Divide the class into several teams. Have the students in each team work together to see how many words they can associate with each branch. For example:

legislative branch:	[Congress/Capitol building/Senate]
executive branch:	[President/Cabinet/White House/Vice President]
judicial branch:	[Supreme Court/justices/judges/court]

c. Set a time limit for the game. When the time limit is up, call on the teams to read their list of associations to the class. The team with the most correct items wins.

2. Category Dictation ★

a. Have students make three columns on a piece of paper and write the following at the top of each column:

> Legislative Branch
> Executive Branch
> Judicial Branch

b. Dictate words from the reading and have students write them in the appropriate column.

c. As a class, in pairs, or in small groups, have students check their work.

3. U.S. Government Match Game ★★

Activity Master 4

a. Make a copy of Activity Master 4 and cut it into cards. Distribute the cards randomly, one to each student.

   Note: The large cards are questions and the small cards are answers.

b. Have students memorize the question or response on their cards. Then have students circulate around the room saying their lines until they find their match. Make sure students don't show their cards to their classmates since this is a listening and speaking exercise.

c. When students have found their match, have them compare their cards and then come show you.

d. Continue until students have found all the matches.

MULTILEVEL VARIATION ★

Below-level students can look at the cards as they do the activity.

4. True or False? ★★★

Make statements about the U.S. government and have students decide whether the statements are true or false. If a statement is false, have students correct it. For example:

The President can serve up to two four-year terms. [True.]
The three branches of the U.S. government are legislative, judicial, and military. [False. The three branches are legislative, judicial, and executive.]
There are eight Supreme Court justices. [False. There are nine.]
The number of representatives from a state depends on the number of people in the state. [True.]

Variation: Do the activity as a game with competing teams.

(continued)

5. Who Am I? ★★★

Tell about people described in the reading and have students guess who it is. For example:

   A. I am a judge on the highest court in the country. Who am I?

   B. A Supreme Court justice.

   A. I become President if the President dies. Who am I?

   B. The Vice President.

   A. I represent my state in the U.S. Senate. Who am I?

   B. A senator.

   A. I can appoint Cabinet members. Who am I?

   B. The President.

   A. We can declare war. Who are we?

   B. Congress.

   A. I represent my district in the U.S. House of Representatives. Who am I?

   B. A representative.

   A. I can serve two four-year terms. Who am I?

   B. The President.

   A. We give the President advice. Who are we?

   B. The Cabinet.

Variation: Do the activity in pairs, in small groups, or as a game with competing teams.

6. Concentration: The Branches of Government ★★★

Activity Master 4

a. Divide the class into pairs. Make multiple copies of Activity Master 4, cut them into cards, and distribute one set to each pair.

   Note: The large cards are questions and the small cards are answers.

b. Have students shuffle the cards and place the large cards in two rows and the small cards in two rows face down.

c. The object of the game is for students to find the matching questions and answers. Both students should be able to see the cards,

since *concentrating* on their location is an important part of playing the game.

d. Student A turns over a large card and a small card, and if they match the student keeps the cards. If the cards don't match, the student turns them face down and Student B takes a turn.

The game continues until all the questions and answers have been matched. The student with the most correct *matches* wins the game.

MULTILEVEL VARIATION ★

Below-level students can read through the questions and answers all at once and then match the cards face up.

7. U.S. Government Quiz ★★★

Activity Master 5

a. Make a copy of Activity Master 5, cut it into cards, and put the cards in a pile on a table or desk in the front of the room.

b. Divide the class into two teams. Have students take turns coming up to the front of the class, picking up a card, and reading it to the team. The team must answer the question in one minute. For each correct answer, the team gets one point. The team with the most points wins.

MULTILEVEL VARIATIONS

★ *Below-level* students can refer to the reading on student text page 10c to answer the questions.

★★/★★★ Challenge *at-level* and *above-level* students to close their textbooks and try to recall the information from memory.

CHECK-UP TEST Ⓐ Ⓑ Ⓒ Ⓓ

Have students do the check-up test and then
review the answers as a class.

Answers

1.	C	**6.**	D
2.	B	**7.**	A
3.	D	**8.**	B
4.	A	**9.**	D
5.	C	**10.**	C

SKILLS CHECK

Words:

Explain to students that this is a list of words
they have learned in the unit. Have students
take turns reading each item aloud to the class.
Have students put a check next to the item if
they feel they have learned it. Encourage
students to get a small notebook where they can
write down words that are difficult for them.

I can:

Explain to students that this is a list of skills
they have learned in the unit. Read each item
aloud to the class. Ask individual students or
pairs of students to demonstrate the skill. For
example:

> Teacher: Are you busy?
> Student: No, I'm not.

> Teacher: I can name state officials.
> Student: Mr. Richardson is governor.
> Ms. Belmont and Mr. Wong are
> senators.

Have students put a check next to the item if
they feel they have learned it. Use this
information to determine which lessons you may
want to review or reinforce for the entire class
or for particular students.

EXPANSION ACTIVITIES

1. **Do You Remember the Words?** ★

   Check students' retention of the vocabulary
   depicted on the opening page of Unit 1 by doing
   the following activity:

   a. Have students open their books to page 1 and
      cover the list of vocabulary words.

   b. Either call out a number and have students
      tell you the noun, or say a noun and have
      students tell you the number.

   Variation: You can also do this activity as a game
   with competing teams.

2. **Agent Noun Concentration** ★

   Activity Master 6

   a. Divide the class into pairs. Make multiple
      copies of Activity Master 6, cut them into
      cards, and distribute one set to each pair.

   b. Have students shuffle the cards and place
      them face down in 2 rows of eleven each.

   c. The object of the game is for students to find
      the matching cards. Both students should
      be able to see the cards, since *concentrating*
      on their location is an important part of
      playing the game.

   d. Student A turns over two cards, and if they
      match, the student keeps the cards. If the
      cards don't match, the student turns them
      face down and Student B takes a turn.

   The game continues until all the cards have been
   matched. The student with the most correct
   matches wins the game.

   MULTILEVEL VARIATION ★★/★★★

   Tell *at-level* and *above-level* students to use the
   word in a sentence that's true about themselves
   after they make a match. For example:

   > I'm a good singer.
   > I'm not a very good skier.

   (continued)

3. Miming Game ★★

Activity Master 7

a. Make a copy of Activity Master 7, cut it into cards, and put the cards in a pile face down on a table or desk in the front of the room.

b. Have students take turns picking a card from the pile and pantomiming the action on the card. Ask: "What's _____ doing?" and have students answer in a complete sentence. For example:

> Teacher: What's Sascha doing?
> Student: He's ironing clothes.

Variation: Do the activity as a game with competing teams.

4. Who Is It? ★★

Divide the class into teams and quiz them with the following clues:

your mother's mother	[grandmother]
your mother's brother	[uncle]
your father's sister	[aunt]
your father's father	[grandfather]
your daughter's son	[grandson]
your son's children	[grandchildren]
your mother and father	[parents]
the man you married	[husband]
the woman you married	[wife]
your parents' son	[brother]
your parents' daughter	[sister]

5. Board Game ★★

Activity Master 8

For this activity, you will need a die, markers, and a piece of paper. (If students use a coin as a die, the class should decide which side of the coin will indicate a move of one space and which will indicate a move of two spaces.)

a. Make multiple copies of Activity Master 8. Divide the class into small groups and give each group a copy of Activity Master 8 along with a die, markers, and a piece of paper.

b. Have students place their markers on *Start*. The group should decide who goes first. That student begins the game by rolling the die or flipping the coin and moving his or her marker. If the student responds to the question or task correctly, he or she may take one more turn. If the student doesn't respond correctly, the next student takes a turn. No one may take more than two turns at a time.

Option 1: The first person to reach *Finish* is the winner.

Option 2: The game continues until each student reaches *Finish*. This way everybody is a winner.

6. Question the Answers! ★★

a. Dictate answers such as the following to the class:

> Yes, she is.
> No, they aren't.
> Yes, I do.
> No, we don't.
> I'm an actor.
> Her name is Alex.
> I read the papers every morning.
> I'm from Brazil.
> She lives in Atlanta.

b. Divide the class into groups of four. Have them write questions for which these answers are correct. For example:

> Answer: Yes, she is.
> Question: Is Anita married?

> Answer: No, they aren't.
> Question: Are they good skiers?

c. Have students share some of their questions and answers with the class.

7. Dialog Builder! ★★★

a. Divide the class into pairs. Write a line on the board from a conversation such as the following:

Yes, I am.

Other possible lines are:

> Do you like to _____?
> How often do you _____?
> Really?
> That's interesting.

b. Have each pair create a conversation incorporating that line. Students can begin and end their conversations any way they wish, but they must include that line in their dialogs.

c. Call on students to present their conversations to the class.

8. What's Wrong? ★★★

a. Write several sentences such as the following on the board or on a handout that you give to students. Some of the sentences should be correct and others incorrect. For example:

> Are you busy?
> Yes, she's.
> Does they eat cookies?
> Who does she sending an e-mail to?
> What do you doing?
> I'm swimming whenever I can.
> How often do you practice the piano?
> I'm calling my brother. I call her every Friday.
> Do you like to skier?
> What is your date of birth?
> What is your birth of place?
> Why is he shouting at the landlord?
> Who they calling?
> What's your marital status?
> I'm not very good cook.
> What is she knitting?
> Who family members live in you household?

b. Divide the class into pairs. The object of the activity is for students to identify which sentences are incorrect and then correct them. Have students compare their answers in small groups.

Variation: Do the activity as a game with competing teams. For each team's turn, write one sentence on the board and have the team decide whether the sentence is correct or not. If it isn't correct, the team must correct it. Every time a team is right, that team receives one point. The team with the greatest number of points wins.

MULTILEVEL VARIATION ★

For *below-level* students, underline the errors and have the below-level pairs focus only on correcting them.

GRAMMAR

SIMPLE PAST TENSE

What did	I he she it we you they	do?

I He She It We You They	worked.

Did	I he she it we you they	fall asleep?

Yes,	I he she it we you they	did.

No,	I he she it we you they	didn't.

I He She It	was	tired.
We You They	were	

I He She It	wasn't	tired.
We You They	weren't	

PAST CONTINUOUS TENSE

I He She It	was	working.
We You They	were	

FUNCTIONS

ASKING FOR AND REPORTING INFORMATION

Who *did you meet*?

What did you *buy*?

What did *she* do *yesterday*?

What were you doing?

What happened?

What language *did you speak*?

What kind of *hotel did you stay in*?

Where were you?

Where did you *go*?

Why?

How did *John break his arm*?
How did you feel?
How did you get there?
How many *pictures did you take*?
How long were you there?

Did *Robert shout at his dog*?
    Yes, *he* did.
    No, *he* didn't.
Did you have a good time?

ADMITTING POOR PERFORMANCE

I didn't *teach* very well *this morning*.
I *taught* very badly.

INITIATING A TOPIC

You know . . .

Tell me about . . .

MAKING A DEDUCTION

I bet *that was a difficult experience for you*.

REACTING TO BAD NEWS

What a shame!
What a pity!
That's a shame.

NEW VOCABULARY

Verbs

bet	occur
break down	prepare
declare	realize
fight	rip
form	sign
free	snowboard
grow	sprain
hike	wave
kill	

U.S. History

Abraham Lincoln
Blacks
central government
civil rights movement
Civil War
Colonial Army
colony
Confederacy
Constitution
Declaration of Independence
demonstration
discrimination
Emancipation Proclamation
freedom
George Washington
immigrant
Immigration Act

Independence Day
Independence Hall
independent
John Hancock
March on Washington
Martin Luther King, Jr.
nation
national government
national holiday
North
Northern states
plantation
Presidents' Day
protest (n)
representative
Revolutionary War
slave
slavery
soldier
South
Southern states
state government
Thomas Jefferson
Union

Travel and Tourism

boat	take pictures
Colosseum	tourist
Mediterranean	Vatican
souvenir	

Miscellaneous

ankle	light conditions
audience	lines
black eye	magic trick
chart	magician
cotton	meeting
daily	prepared
daily exercises	red light
dawn	right (n)
daylight	road surface
demonstrator	signature
driver	slippery
dusk	speaker
experience	timeline
farm	vehicle
fog	weather
icy	conditions
kid	west
leader	

EXPRESSIONS

at the back of
get around by taxi/by bus
I bet
look over *his* shoulder
sleep well

PAST TENSE VERB FORMS

Irregular

am/is – was	keep – kept
are – were	lose – lost
break – broke	meet – met
buy – bought	ride – rode
come – came	see – saw
cut – cut	shake – shook
do – did	sing – sang
drink – drank	sit – sat
eat – ate	sleep – slept
fall – fell	speak – spoke
feel – felt	stand – stood
fight – fought	swim – swam
forget – forgot	take – took
get – got	teach – taught
go – went	tell – told
have – had	write – wrote
hurt – hurt	

Regular

burn	realize
chop	rip
cover	shave
cry	shout
deliver	snowboard
finish	sprain
growl	stay
hike	study
jump	talk
look	trip
paint	type
play	wash
poke	watch
practice	wave
prepare	work

Text Page 11: Unit Opening Page

VOCABULARY PREVIEW

You may want to introduce these words before beginning the unit, or you may choose to wait until they first occur in a specific lesson. If you choose to introduce them at this point, here are some suggestions:

1. Have students look at the illustrations on text page 11 and identify the verbs they already know.

2. Present the vocabulary. Say each word and have the class repeat it chorally and individually. Check students' understanding and pronunciation of the verbs.

3. Practice the vocabulary as a class, in pairs, or in small groups. Have students cover the word list and look at the pictures. Practice the words in the following ways:

   • Say a verb in its present or past form and have students tell the number of the illustration.

   • Give the number of an illustration and have students say the verb in its present and past forms.

FOCUS

- Past Tense Review:
    Regular and Irregular Verbs
    To Be
    Was / Were
    Questions with *Did*
    Affirmative Short Answers

CLOSE UP

The simple past tense is used to express events that happened in the past.

RULE:	The simple past tense describes events that occurred at a particular point in time.
EXAMPLE:	**Did** you **sleep** well last night? Yes, I **did**.
RULE:	The simple past tense also describes events that took place over a period of time.
EXAMPLES:	I **studied** English all day. She **taught** all day.
RULE:	When a verb ending with *t* or *d* takes the regular past tense *-ed* ending, an additional syllable is formed at the end of the word.
EXAMPLE:	He **painted** his apartment all day.

GETTING READY

Review the past tense.

1. Practice listening for the *-ed* ending.

    a. Write on the board:

    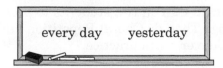

    every day   yesterday

    b. Read statements such as the following one or more times:

    > She works.
    > He worked.
    > They worked.

    They work.
    We study.
    I bake a cake.
    He studied.
    She plays the piano.
    We played cards.
    They need some books.
    I study.
    She needed some bread.

    c. Have students respond by saying "every day" when they hear a verb in the present tense and "yesterday" when they hear a verb in the past tense. For example:

Teacher	Students
I work.	every day
I worked.	yesterday

2. Practice forming sentences that contrast verb endings in the simple present and simple past tenses.

   a. Write on the board:

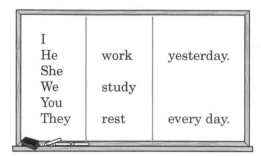

I He She We You They	work study rest	yesterday. every day.

   b. Call on students to form sentences with these words. For each student, point to one word in each column. The student then makes a sentence using these words. For example:

     (She) (work) (every day) → She works every day.

     (He) (study) (yesterday) → He studied yesterday.

     (They) (rest) (yesterday) → They rested yesterday.

3. Review a few irregular verbs in the past tense.

   a. Using the same columns on the board from 2 above, change the verbs to *teach, write,* and *meet people.*

   b. Review the past tense forms *taught, wrote,* and *met.*

   c. Again, have students form sentences, using one word from each column.

4. Review the past tense of the verb *to be.*

   a. Write on the board:

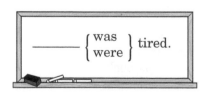

_____ { was / were } tired.

   b. Say each pronoun and have students form sentences using the correct verb. Have students respond chorally and individually. For example:

     (He):   He was tired.
     (They):   They were tired.

INTRODUCING THE MODEL

1. Have students look at the model illustration.

2. Set the scene: "Two people are talking about Emma."

3. Present the model.

4. Full-Class Repetition.

   Pronunciation Note

   The pronunciation focus of Unit 2 is ***Did you*** (text page 20). You may wish to model this pronunciation at this point *(What did you do yesterday?)* and encourage students to incorporate it into their language practice.

5. Ask students if they have any questions. Check understanding of the expression *sleep well.*

6. Group Choral Repetition.

7. Choral Conversation.

8. Call on one or two pairs of students to present the dialog.

   (For additional practice, do Choral Conversation in small groups or by rows.)

SIDE BY SIDE EXERCISES

Examples

1. A. Did you sleep well last night?
   B. Yes, I did. I was VERY tired.
   A. Why? What did you do yesterday?
   B. I studied English all day.

2. A. Did Rick sleep well last night?
   B. Yes, he did. He was VERY tired.
   A. Why? What did he do yesterday?
   B. He painted his apartment all day.

1. **Exercise 1:** Call on two students to present the dialog. Then do Choral Repetition and Choral Conversation practice.

2. **Exercise 2:** Same as above.

3. **Exercises 3–8:** Either Full-Class Practice or Pair Practice.

4. **Exercise 9:** Have students use the model as a guide to create their own conversations, using vocabulary of their choice. (They can use any names and activities they wish.) Encourage students to use dictionaries to find new words they want to use. This exercise can be done orally in class or for written homework. If you assign it for homework, do one example in class to make sure students understand what's expected. Have students present their conversations in class the next day.

WORKBOOK

Pages 12–13

EXPANSION ACTIVITIES

1. Can You Hear the Difference? ★

a. Write on the board:

I study English.	I studied English.
You work all day.	You worked all day.
They wash windows.	They washed windows.
They deliver pizzas.	They delivered pizzas.
We paint the apartment.	We painted the apartment

b. Choose a sentence randomly from one of the two columns and say it to the class. Have the class listen and identify whether the sentence is *present or past*.

c. Have students continue the activity in pairs. One student says a sentence and the other identifies its time frame. Then have students reverse roles.

d. Write other similar sentences on the board and continue the practice.

2. Tell More About Situation 8 ★★

Have students look at the illustration for Situation 8. Ask students the questions below. These questions allow students to use their imaginations to *tell you more* about the people in the situation.

Did the president sleep well last night?
What did he do yesterday?
Who did the president meet?
What did they talk about?

3. Interview ★★

a. Write the following on the board:

What did you do yesterday?

b. Have pairs of students interview each other about what they did yesterday and then report back to the class.

Option: Have the class decide who had *the most interesting day* yesterday.

4. Find the Right Person! ★★

a. From the prior activity, write down information about what students did yesterday.

b. Put the information on a handout in the following form:

Find someone who . . .

1. cleaned the house. _____
2. wrote a letter. _____
3. worked late. _____
4. rode her bicycle. _____
5. studied math. _____

c. Have students circulate around the room, asking each other information questions to identify the above people. For example:

What did you do yesterday?
Where did you go? (continued)

UNIT 2   45

d. The first student to find all the people, raise his or her hand, and identify the students is the winner of the game.

5. Sense or Nonsense? ★★

a. Divide the class into four groups.

b. Make four sets of split-sentence cards with beginnings and endings of sentences. For example:

She worked	in the office all day.
He washed	windows all day.
I met	a professional soccer player yesterday.
We rode	our bicycles all day.
They taught	English all day.
I studied	for the English test.
She painted	the living room.
We delivered	mail all morning.
He wrote	letters all afternoon.

c. Mix up the cards and distribute sets of cards to each group, keeping the beginning and ending cards in different piles.

d. Have students take turns picking up one card from each pile and reading the sentence to the group. For example:

I washed	mail all morning.

e. The group decides if the sentence makes sense or is nonsense.

f. After all the cards have been picked, have the groups lay out all the cards and put together all the sentence combinations that make sense.

6. Miming: Why Am I So Tired? ★★

a. On cards write activities such as the following:

paint my apartment	cook	wash clothes
ride my bicycle	write letters	vacuum my rugs
plant flowers	play soccer	bake a cake
clean my apartment	rearrange furniture	do exercises
pay bills	rake leaves	fix my car
work	study	type letters

b. Have students take turns picking three cards from the pile and pantomiming the actions on the cards in succession.

c. The class must guess what the person did yesterday. For example:

You studied, you painted your apartment, and you washed clothes.

Variation: This can be done as a game with competing teams.

7. Sequencing ★★

a. Dictate the following sentences to students:

He was late for an important meeting.
Then he quickly ate breakfast and left the house.
He took a shower and got dressed.
He arrived at work at ten o'clock.

He took the bus to the office.
Henry got up late this morning.

b. Have students then sequence these sentences from *one* to *six*, with *one* being the first thing that happened to Henry:

1. Henry got up late this morning.
2. He took a shower and got dressed.
3. Then he quickly ate breakfast and left the house.
4. He took the bus to the office.
5. He arrived at work at ten o'clock.
6. He was late for an important meeting.

c. As a class, in pairs, or in small groups, have students compare their sequences.

8. What's New in the News? ★★★

Have students look in the newspaper for an article that tells about a recent local, national, or international event. Have them take notes on the article and come to the next class prepared to tell the class about it. Encourage the rest of the class to ask questions.

Text Page 13: Did Robert Shout at His Dog?

FOCUS

- Past Tense Review:
    Regular and Irregular Verbs
    Yes/No Questions and Short Answers
    with *Did*
    Negative Statements with *To Be*

GETTING READY

Contrast *did* and *was/were*.

1. Write on the board:

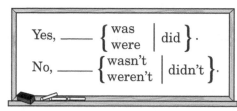

2. Make up questions, such as those below, that will pertain to your students' experience. Pick questions that will allow students to practice all the forms on the board. Read each question and have students respond chorally and/or individually.

Was it (*sunny*) yesterday?
Did it (*rain*) yesterday?
Were (*Bob*) and (*Jane*) late for class today?
Did (*Mary*) miss class last week?
Were (*you*) on time this morning?
Did (*Alice*) and (*George*) ride their bicycles
    to class today?
Were we at school last (*Wednesday*)?
Was (*Gloria*) at the beach yesterday?
Did you sleep for (*15*) hours last night?
Was (*John*) tired this morning?
Did we study (*French*) in class last week?

INTRODUCING THE MODELS

There are two model conversations. Introduce and practice each separately. For each model:

1. Have students look at the model illustration in the book.

2. Set the scene:

  1st model: "Two people are talking about Robert."
  2nd model: "Two people are talking about Helen."

3. Present the model.

4. Full-Class Repetition.

5. Ask students if they have any questions.

6. Group Choral Repetition.

7. Choral Conversation.

8. Call on one or two pairs of students to present the dialog.

    (For additional practice, do Choral Conversation in small groups or by rows.)

SIDE BY SIDE EXERCISES

Examples

1. A. Did Howard fall asleep in class?
    B. Yes, he did. He was bored.

2. A. Did Amy take the plane to Rio?
    B. No, she didn't. She wasn't on time.

1. **Exercise 1:** Call on two students to present the dialog. Then do Choral Repetition and Choral Conversation practice.

2. **Exercise 2:** Same as above.

3. **Exercises 3–8:** Either Full-Class Practice or Pair Practice.

> **New Vocabulary**
>
> 4. prepared
> 5. lines

WORKBOOK

Pages 14–17

EXPANSION ACTIVITIES

1. What Did They Do? ★

Use your own visuals or *Side by Side* Picture Cards 36–67, 141–148, and 158–162 to review verbs in the past tense.

a. Hold up a visual and ask a student:

What did _____ do (yesterday/last night . . .)?

You can use any appropriate time expression or name in your questions. For example:

What did (*Bill*) do last weekend?
What did (*your friends*) do yesterday?
What did (*Sally*) do this morning?
What did (*you*) do today?
What did (*we*) do last week?

b. Give the visuals to students and have them ask and answer questions in the past tense.

2. Finish the Sentence! ★

a. Write the following words on the board:

angry	hungry	on time	scared	tired
bored	nervous	prepared	thirsty	upset

b. Say the sentences below. Have students complete each sentence with the appropriate word on the board.

He drank two bottles of soda because he was very . . .
I didn't know the answers on the test because I wasn't . . .
Kathy didn't want to go into that dark room herself because she was . . .
It rained all day yesterday. I stayed home and didn't do anything. I was . . .
I didn't have any lunch today, and now I'm . . .
Class began at nine. I arrived at nine thirty. I wasn't . . .
My little brother cried because he was . . .
Bob fell asleep in class because he was . . .
Your big exam is tomorrow. Are you feeling . . .?
Paul had an accident with his father's car. His father was very . . .

3. Tic Tac Adjective! ★★

a. Have students draw a tic tac grid on their papers and fill in the grid with any nine of the ten adjectives in the previous activity.

b. Read the sentences from Activity 2, and tell students to cross out any word on their grids that finishes the sentence.

c. The first person to cross out three words in a straight line—either vertically, horizontally, or diagonally—wins the game.

d. Have the winner call out the words to check the accuracy.

4. Question the Answers! ★★

a. Dictate answers such as the following to the class:

Yes, she did. She was prepared.
No, he didn't. He wasn't on time.
Yes, they did. They were very angry.
No, he didn't. He wasn't hungry.
Yes, we did. We were tired.
No, she didn't. She wasn't nervous.

b. Have students write questions for which these answers would be correct. For example:

Answer: Yes, she did. She was prepared.
Question: Did Betty do well on her English exam?

Answer: No, he didn't. He wasn't on time.
Question: Did your husband take the bus to Denver this morning?

c. Have students compare their questions with each other.

Variation: Write the answers on cards. Divide the class into groups and give each group a set of cards.

5. Match the Conversations ★★

a. Make a set of matching cards. For example:

Did you enjoy yourself?	No, I didn't. I was bored.

(continued)

Did you drink that whole glass of water?	Yes, I did. I was thirsty.
Did you do well on the test?	No, I didn't. I wasn't prepared.
Did you miss the bus?	No, I didn't. I was on time.
Did you finish the apple pie?	Yes, I did. I was hungry.
Did you shout at those people?	Yes, I did. I was angry.
Did you cry at the play?	No, I didn't. It wasn't sad.
Did you laugh during the movie?	No, I didn't. It wasn't funny.
Did you bite your nails?	Yes, I did. I was nervous.

b. Distribute a card to each student.

c. Have students memorize the sentences on their cards, and then have students walk around the room saying their sentences until they find their match.

d. Then have pairs of students say their matched sentences aloud to the class.

6. Extend the Conversations ★★★

a. Review the following verb forms from student text page 13:

> *Model Conversations*
> shout–shouted
> sleep–slept
>
> *Exercises*
> 1. fall–fell
> 2. take–took
> 3. cry–cried
> 4. do–did
> 5. forget–forgot
> 6. cover–covered

b. Divide the class into pairs and have each pair prepare a short role play to present to the class. Use both model conversations and Exercises 1–6. Have students pretend to be the people in the situations and create a possible 4- to 6-line dialog based on the situation. Encourage students to use their imaginations to embellish the dialogs. Suggest that students begin their dialogs like this: "Hi, _____ What's new?" For example:

(Model 1)

A. Hi, Robert. What's new?
B. Well, I'm very upset.
A. What happened?
B. My dog ate today's newspaper. I was so angry that I shouted at him.
A. Hmm. Maybe you should feed your dog more often.

7. Pronunciation Story: The Boys at Dover Academy ★★

Use the story below to have students practice past tense verbs in *-ted* and *-ded*.

a. Put on the board:

Peter painted	Sam started	Nick went needed	Paul planted

Walter went wanted	Richard didn't feel well rested	Frank went fainted

b. Set the scene: "The boys at Dover Academy are always very busy."

c. Point to the appropriate cue as you tell each part of the story below.

"Last Saturday afternoon, . . .
   Peter painted his room.
   Sam started to study for a history exam.
   Nick went to the store because he needed a new notebook.
   Paul planted flowers in front of the school.
   Walter went to the library because he wanted to be by himself.
   Richard didn't feel very well, so he rested in bed.
   Frank went jogging in the hot sun and fainted."

d. Ask questions about the story. You can pause as you tell it and ask questions, or you can wait until the end. Then call on one or two students to retell the whole story.

e. As an optional writing assignment, have students write the story, using only the cues on the board.

8. Guess How They're Feeling! ★★★

a. Write the following words on the board:

| angry | bored | hungry | nervous |
| scared | thirsty | tired | |

b. Divide the class into pairs.

c. Give each pair a situation card. Possibilities include:

> You're at the movies, and you're talking about the movie you're watching.

> You and a friend are at a restaurant, and the service is very slow tonight.

> You and a friend are at a lecture.

> You and a friend are sitting in the waiting room at the doctor's office.

> You and a friend are talking before English class.

d. Give each pair a card with one of the *feeling* words from the board written on it.

e. Have each pair prepare a short role play based on their situation and then act it out for the class, according to the *feeling* on their card.

f. The rest of the class has to guess what was on the card:

   They're angry.
   They're nervous.
      Etc.

9. Tell About a Time . . . ★★★

a. Write the following words on the board:

angry
bored
nervous
sad
scared

In the lesson on student text page 13, some people were *angry, bored, sad, nervous,* and *scared.*

b. Divide the class into pairs and have students talk with each other about a time *they* were angry, bored, sad, nervous, or scared.

c. Call on students to share their experiences with the class.

FOCUS

• Review: Past Continuous Tense

CLOSE UP

RULE: The past continuous tense is commonly used to show a past activity that was in progress when another event happened.

EXAMPLES: He **broke** his leg while he **was snowboarding**.
She **sprained** her ankle while she **was playing** volleyball.

GETTING READY

1. Use your own visuals or *Side by Side* Picture Cards for verbs to review the past continuous tense.

   a. Hold up visuals and ask students questions in the past continuous tense. For example:

      (*Side by Side* Picture Card 44)
      A. What were they doing last night?
      B. They were playing cards.

      (*Side by Side* Picture Card 36)
      A. What was she doing last night?
      B. She was reading.

   b. Hold up visuals and have pairs of students ask and answer, using the past continuous tense.

2. Review the irregular past forms of the following verbs: *lose–lost, cut–cut, fall–fell, get–got, hurt–hurt*.

   a. Write the following verbs on the board:

   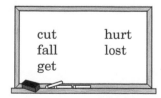

cut	hurt
fall	lost
get	

   b. Call on students to pantomime actions with those verbs and have the class tell what the person just *did*.

INTRODUCING THE MODEL

1. Have students look at the model illustration.
2. Set the scene: "Two people are talking about Marty's accident."
3. Present the model.
4. Full-Class Repetition.
5. Ask students if they have any questions. Check understanding of the word *snowboard*.
6. Group Choral Repetition.
7. Choral Conversation.
8. Call on one or two pairs of students to present the dialog.

   (For additional practice, do Choral Conversation in small groups or by rows.)

SIDE BY SIDE EXERCISES

Examples

1. A. How did Greta sprain her ankle?
   B. She sprained it while she was playing volleyball.
   A. That's too bad!

2. A. How did Larry lose his wallet?
   B. He lost it while he was hiking in the woods.
   A. That's too bad!

1. **Exercise 1:** Introduce the words *sprain, ankle*. Call on two students to present the dialog. Then do Choral Repetition and Choral Conversation practice.

2. **Exercise 2:** Introduce the words *hike, woods*. Same as above.

3. **Exercises 3–10:** Either Full-Class Practice or Pair Practice.

New Vocabulary

4. prepare
5. rip
   daily exercises
9. black eye
   fight
   kid
10. magician
    magic trick

WORKBOOK

Pages 18–19

EXPANSION ACTIVITIES

1. Do You Remember? ★

a. Divide the class into pairs.

b. Show the class a picture for two or three minutes of a scene with many people engaged in many activities.

c. Put the picture away and have students write down what the characters in the picture *were doing*.

d. Have the partners compare their sentences and then look at the picture again to see how much they remembered.

2. Find the Right Person! ★★

a. Find out what students were doing last night at 8:00.

b. Put the information on a handout in the following form:

Find someone who . . .

1. was cleaning the house.   _____
2. was watching TV.   _____
3. was listening to music.   _____
4. was studying for a math exam.   _____
5. was preparing dinner.   _____

---

c. To identify the above people, have students circulate around the room, asking each other information questions about their activities yesterday. For example: "What were you doing last night at 8:00?"

d. The first student to find all the people, raise his or her hand, and identify the people is the winner of the game.

3. What Were They Doing? ★★★

a. Divide the class into pairs or small groups.

b. Dictate sentences such as the following:

> He fell off the train while he was . . .
> She sprained her ankle while she was . . .
> They burned their hands while they were . . .
> I lost my glasses while I was . . .
> He hurt his finger while he was . . .
> We met the president while we were . . .
> She ripped her jacket while she was . . .

c. Have students write possible endings for the sentences.

d. Call on students to share their ideas with the rest of the class.

(continued)

4. I Saw You! ★★

Have pairs of students role play the conversation below. Use your own visuals or *Side by Side* Picture Cards as cues for community locations. Students can use any vocabulary they wish to finish the dialog as long as the verb is in the past continuous tense.

a. Briefly review some or all of the locations in the community below, using visuals if possible. Say each word and then have students tell what people usually do in that location. For example:

library: read/study/borrow books

airport	hospital
bakery	laundromat
bank	library
bus station	movie theater
butcher shop	museum
cafeteria	park
candy store	pet shop
clinic	playground
concert hall	police station
courthouse	post office
department store	school
doctor's office	shopping mall
drug store	supermarket
gas station	train station
hardware store	zoo

b. Write on the board:

> A. Were you at the _____ yesterday?
> B. Yes, I was. How did you know?
> A. I was there, too. I was _____. I saw you, but I guess you didn't see me.
> B. I'm sorry I didn't see you. I was _____, and I was in a hurry.

c. Call on pairs of students to role play the dialog. For each pair, signal a location in the community with a visual or word card. For example:

Cue: *department store*

> A. Were you at the department store yesterday?
> B. Yes, I was. How did you know?
> A. I was there, too. I was (*looking for a new coat*). I saw you, but I guess you didn't see me.
> B. I'm sorry I didn't see you. I was (*buying a birthday present for my brother*), and I was in a hurry.

5. Chain Story ★★

a. Begin by saying: "Henry had a bad day today. He fell while he was getting out of bed."

b. Student 1 repeats what you said and continues the story. For example:

Henry had a bad day today. He fell while he was getting out of bed. Then he cut himself while he was shaving.

c. Continue around the room in this fashion, with each student repeating what the previous one said and adding another sentence.

d. You can do the activity again, beginning and ending with different students.

If the class is large, you may want to divide students into groups to give students more practice.

6. A Bad Day ★★

a. Write the following conversation model on the board:

> A. I had a bad day today.
> B. Why? What happened?
> A. I _____ while _____.
> B. That's too bad!

b. Write the following cues on the board or on word cards:

burn	forget
cut	lose
fall asleep	rip
fall down	spill

c. Have pairs of students create conversations based on the word cues and the model on the board. For example:

A. I had a bad day today.
B. Why? What happened?
A. I cut myself while I was cooking dinner.
B. That's too bad!

A. I had a bad day today.
B. Why? What happened?
A. I lost my homework while I was walking to school.
B. That's too bad!

7. Student Discussion: Accidents ★★★

a. Write on the board:

> Were you ever in an accident?
> What happened?
> What were you doing when the accident happened?

b. In pairs or small groups, have students share their stories and then share them with the class.

8. How Did You Meet? ★★★

a. Put the following on the board:

> How did you meet your boyfriend/ girlfriend/ best friend/husband/wife?
> Where were you?
> What were you doing?
> What was he/she doing?

b. Divide the class into pairs and have students discuss the questions on the board. Have them tell how they met their boyfriend, girlfriend, best friend, husband, or wife. Where were they? What were they doing? What was the other person doing?

c. Have students share their stories with the class.

How to Say It!

> **Reacting to Bad News:** There are many ways to respond with sympathy to bad news. "That's too bad!" "That's a shame!" "What a shame!" "What a pity!" and "I'm sorry to hear that" are five common sympathetic responses.

1. Set the scene: "Someone just heard some bad news."

2. Present the expressions.

3. Full-Class Repetition.

4. Ask students if they have any questions.

5. Group Choral Repetition.

6. Have students practice the conversations in the lesson again, reacting to the bad news with any of these five expressions.

7. Call on students to present their conversations to the class.

READING *Difficult Experiences*

FOCUS

- Review:
  Simple Past Tense
  Past Continuous Tense

NEW VOCABULARY

at the back of	look over *his* shoulder
audience	principal
demonstrator	realize
experience	wave

READING THE STORY

Optional: Preview the story by having students talk about the story title and/or illustrations. You may choose to introduce new vocabulary beforehand, or have students encounter the new vocabulary within the context of the reading.

1. Have students read silently or follow along silently as the story is read aloud by you, by one or more students, or on the audio program.

2. Ask students if they have any questions. Check understanding of vocabulary.

   ### Culture Note

   Demonstrators often go to listen to a politician's speech. During the speech, they shout and disrupt the politician because they disagree and are angry with what the person has to say.

3. Check students' comprehension, using some or all of the following questions:

   Did Ms. Henderson teach well this morning?
   How did she teach?

Why?
Why was it a difficult experience for Ms. Henderson?
Why couldn't she do anything about it?

Did Stuart type well today?
How did he type?
Why?
Why was it a difficult experience for Stuart?
Why couldn't he do anything about it?

Did the Baxter Boys sing well last night?
How did they sing?
Why?
Why was it a difficult experience for the Baxter Boys?
Why couldn't they do anything about it?

Did the president speak well this afternoon?
How did he speak?
Why?
Why was it a difficult experience for the president?
Why couldn't he do anything about it?

✓ READING *CHECK-UP*

Q & A

1. Call on a pair of students to present the model. Check understanding of the expression *I bet*.

2. Have students work in pairs to create new dialogs.

3. Call on pairs to present their new dialogs to the class.

MATCH

1. f
2. c
3. h
4. a
5. g
6. d
7. e
8. b

READING EXTENSION

1. Class Discussion

   a. Have students discuss the following:

      In each situation, the character was too upset to do a good job. What advice can you give each of these people? What are some simple ways to relax?

   b. Call on students to share their thoughts with the class.

2. Stories Alive!

   a. Divide some of the students into pairs, and have them choose either the story about Ms. Henderson or the story about Stuart, and then create a dramatization of the situation.

   b. Divide the rest of the class into groups. Have them choose either the story about the Baxter Boys or the story about the president, and then create a dramatization of the situation.

   c. Call on students to present their *dramas* to the class.

How About You?

Have students answer the questions, in pairs or as a class. If you do it as pair practice, call on students to report to the class about their conversation partner.

 **LISTENING**

Listen and choose the correct answer.

1. Did you do well at your job interview yesterday?

2. Were your children tired last night?

3. What was he doing when he broke his leg?

4. Did you finish your dinner last night?

5. How did your husband lose his wallet?

6. What was your supervisor doing?

7. Did you do well on the exam?

8. What happened while you were preparing lunch?

Answers

1. a

2. b

3. b

4. a

5. b

6. b

7. a

8. a

FOCUS

> - Past Tense Review:
>   Regular and Irregular Verbs
>   Information Questions

GETTING READY

Review the irregular past forms of the following verbs: *get–got, eat–ate, speak–spoke, take–took, buy–bought, swim–swam, see–saw, meet–met, come–came.*

1. Write the following cues on the board:

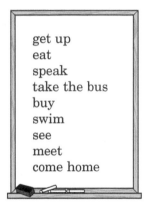

get up
eat
speak
take the bus
buy
swim
see
meet
come home

2. Call on students to pantomime actions with those verbs, and have the class tell what the person just *did.*

INTRODUCING THE MODEL (EXERCISE 1)

1. Have students look at the illustration at the top of the page and then the illustration for Exercise 1.

2. Set the scene: "One neighbor is telling the other about her vacation."

3. Present the introductory conversation and Exercise 1.

4. Full-Class Repetition.

5. Ask students if they have any questions. Check understanding of vocabulary.

6. Group Choral Repetition.

7. Choral Conversation.

8. Call on one or two pairs of students to present the dialog.

   (For additional practice, do Choral Conversation in small groups or by rows.)

SIDE BY SIDE EXERCISES

Examples

> 1. A. Did you go to Paris?
>   B. No, we didn't.
>   A. Where did you go?
>   B. We went to Rome.
>
> 2. A. Did you get there by boat?
>   B. No, we didn't.
>   A. How did you get there?
>   B. We got there by plane.

1. **Exercise 2:** Introduce the expressions *get there, by boat.* Call on two students to present the dialog. Then do Choral Repetition and Choral Conversation practice.

2. **Exercise 3:** Same as above.

3. **Exercises 4–12:** Either Full-Class Practice or Pair Practice.

> **New Vocabulary**
>
> 6. take pictures
> 7. souvenir
> 8. Mediterranean
> 9. Colisseum
>   Vatican
> 10. get around by taxi/by bus
> 11. tourist

Culture Note

Exercise 9: Each year many people in Rome visit the Vatican, the seat of the Roman Catholic church and home of the pope. The Roman Colosseum, an ancient amphitheater, is a major tourist attraction in the city.

WORKBOOK

Pages 20–23

1. Correct the Statement! ★★

Make statements about the characters' vacation in Italy described in the exercises on text pages 18 and 19. Some statements should be true, and others false. Have students respond to your statements. If a statement is false, a student should correct it. For example:

Teacher: They went to Italy.
Student: That's right.

Teacher: They went to Venice.
Student: No, they didn't. They went to Rome.

Variation 1: ★★★ Have students make statements for others to react to.

Variation 2: ★★ Do the activity as a game with competing teams.

2. Tell a Story! ★★

a. Tell the following short story to the class:

"Mr. and Mrs. Lane took a vacation last month. They went to Paris. They took the plane, but it was a terrible experience. The plane left three hours late, and they had very bad weather during the flight. When they arrived in Paris, it was raining. In fact, it rained for three days. They stayed in a small hotel and tried to eat in restaurants that weren't too expensive. They visited the Eiffel Tower and other famous places in Paris, they bought a few souvenirs, and they took a lot of photographs. They sent postcards to all their friends and told them about their trip. Mr. and Mrs. Lane didn't meet a lot of people because they didn't speak any French. But they didn't care. They had a very good time."

b. After you finish telling the story, make several statements about it. Some should be true, and others should be false.

c. Students listen to the statements and decide if they're true or false. If a statement is false, have students correct it. For example:

Teacher: Mr. and Mrs. Lane went to Madrid.

Student: False. They didn't go to Madrid. They went to Paris.

Variation: This activity can be done as a game with competing teams. The teams take turns deciding whether the statements are true or false.

3. Question Game ★★★

a. Write the following sentence on the board:

Mrs. Watson went to Paris last week.

b. Underline different elements of the sentence, and have students create a question based on that portion of the sentence. For example:

<u>Mrs. Watson</u> went to Paris last week.

Who went to Paris last week?

Mrs. Watson went to Paris <u>last week</u>.

When did Mrs. Watson go to Paris?

Mrs. Watson went <u>to Paris</u> last week.

Where did Mrs. Watson go last week?

Mrs. Watson <u>went to Paris</u> last week.

What did Mrs. Watson do last week?

c. Continue with other sentences.

(continued)

4. I'm Sorry I Can't Hear You! ★★★

In real-life conversations, people often miss some of what was said because of noise and distractions or a bad telephone connection. In this exercise, students practice asking for clarification about the part of the conversation they missed.

a. Give students cards with statements on them such as the following:

> I went to (Hawaii) last week.

> My (father) just got back from Spain.

> When my family went to Korea, our plane was (three) hours late.

> While we were visiting Rome, we ate in a lot of (expensive) restaurants.

> My friend and I went to Africa by (boat) last summer.

> I remember when I went to Chicago. The weather was (terrible).

> When I went to Germany, I spoke only (English).

> My family and I bought a lot of (clothing) when we went to France last year.

> I really enjoyed my trip to Greece. We (swam) every day.

> The best thing about my trip to New York was that I saw (the Statue of Liberty).

> I'll never forget my trip to Argentina because I lost my (suitcase).

> When I was in England, I traveled everywhere by (bicycle).

> I flew to (Tokyo) last summer, and I loved it.

> We wanted to go to (Portugal) two years ago, but we just weren't able to go.

b. Set the scene: "We're all at a party. We're talking about vacations and trips, but it's noisy and we can't always hear very well."

c. Have students who are holding cards choose another student to begin a conversation with. Have each student begin by reading the statement, but substituting the nonsense syllable *Bzzz* for the word in parentheses. For example:

  A. I went to (*Bzzz*) last week.

Student B must answer "I'm sorry" and ask a question about the part of the communication he or she didn't understand. For example:

  B. I'm sorry. WHERE did you go last week?

Student A repeats the statement, but this time he or she says the word in parentheses. The two students must then continue the dialog for two more lines, using any vocabulary they wish.

Example:

  A. My (*Bzzz*) just got back from Spain.
  B. I'm sorry. WHO just got back from Spain?

A. My *father* just got back from Spain.
B. Oh. How long was he there?
A. He was there for a few weeks.

5. Grammar Chain: The Bakers' Bad Vacation ★★

a. Start the chain game by saying:

> Teacher: The Bakers went to Los Angeles last week. They had a terrible time!
>
> (to Student A): Did they *eat in good restaurants?*

b. Student A must answer the question negatively, then ask Student B another past tense question. For example:

> Student A: No, they didn't. They ate in very bad restaurants.
>
> (to Student B): Did they *meet any famous people?*

c. The chain continues. For example:

> Student B: No, they didn't. They didn't meet anyone.
>
> (to Student C): Did they *take many pictures?*

6. Group Story ★★★

a. Begin the following story: "The Jacksons went to Los Angeles last week. They had a wonderful time!"

b. Divide the class into small groups of 3 to 5 students.

c. Have each group continue the story with at least ten sentences about the Jacksons' vacation. Encourage students to use any vocabulary they wish and to draw from their own knowledge in describing the vacation.

d. Have one person from each group present that group's story to the class.

e. Have the class decide which group's story describes the best vacation of all.

7. Find the Right Person! ★★★

a. Collect information about the students' last vacation. Ask them:

> Where did you go on your last vacation?
> How did you get there?
> What interesting sights did you see?
> What did you do?

b. Put the information on a handout in the following form:

> Find someone who . . .
>
> 1. went to New York. _____
> 2. took a plane. _____
> 3. went to museums. _____
> 4. met famous people. _____
> 5. saw the Statue of Liberty. _____
> 6. ate in very good restaurants. _____

c. Have students circulate around the room, asking each other information questions to identify the above people.

d. The first student to find all the people, raise his or her hand, and identify the students is the winner of the game.

8. Telling About Our Travels ★★★

a. Have students tell the class about a tourist sight they visited. If possible, have students show the class photographs, postcards, and souvenirs.

b. As students listen, have them ask questions such as those in the lesson.

 JOURNAL

Have students write their journal entries at home or in class. Encourage students to use a dictionary to look up words they would like to use. Students can share their written work with other students if appropriate. Have students discuss what they have written as a class, in pairs, or in small groups.

PRONUNCIATION

> ***Did you:*** The final /d/ sound of *did* combines with the initial /y/ sound of *you* to form a /j/ sound. This is very common in everyday conversational English.

Focus on Listening

Practice the sentences in the left column. Say each sentence or play the audio one or more times. Have students listen carefully and repeat.

Focus on Pronunciation

Practice the sentences in the right column. Have students say each sentence and then listen carefully as you say it or play the audio.

If you wish, have students continue practicing the sentences to improve their pronunciation.

 GRAMMAR FOCUS

Answers
1. did you do, went
2. eat, didn't, weren't
3. did they burn, were baking
4. sleep, did, was
5. Did he take, didn't, took
6. How did, fall, fell, she was

MULTILEVEL VARIATION ★★★

Challenge *above-level* students to cover the grammar boxes as they complete the grammar exercises.

1 CONVERSATION
Apologizing for Being Late

1. Have students look at the photograph. Ask: "Where are they?" (At work.) "Who are they?" (They're both employees. He's the supervisor.)

2. Divide the class in half. Model the A lines and have Group 1 repeat. Model the B lines and have Group 2 repeat. Point out that it's customary in the U.S. to give a reason for being late. It isn't enough simply to apologize without explaining why.

3. In pairs, have students practice the conversations as you circulate around the classroom, helping students as necessary. Introduce the expression: *break down.*

2 TEAMWORK *Critical Thinking*

1. Tell the class that missing a bus is a good reason for arriving late to work. Ask: "What are other good reasons for arriving late to work? What are bad reasons?" Write a few student ideas on the board.

2. Have students continue brainstorming in pairs and taking notes on student text page 20a. Have the pairs practice conversations with good excuses. Circulate around the classroom, helping students as necessary.

3. Call on students to share their ideas with the class. Write a common list on the board of good and bad reasons for being late for work.

LIFE SKILLS ENRICHMENT

Apologizing for Being Late for Work

Life Skills Worksheet 3

Make copies of Life Skills Worksheet 3 and give one to each student. Have students complete the worksheet as homework. In the next class, have students compare their answers in pairs.

1. Disappearing Dialog ★

Write a conversation from student text page 20a on the board and ask for two student volunteers to read the conversation. Erase a few of the words from the dialog and have two different students read the conversation. Erase more words and call on two more students to read the conversation. Continue erasing words and calling on pairs of students until everyone has had a turn and the dialog has *disappeared*.

2. Telephone Story ★

a. Divide the class into large groups. Have each group sit in a circle. Whisper a short story to one student in each group. For example:

Alex had a terrible morning. He woke up late. The traffic was terrible. And then his car broke down. He had to call a mechanic. He was three hours late for work.

b. The first student whispers the story to the second student, who whispers it to the third student, and so forth around the circle. When the story gets to the last person, that student says it aloud. Is it the same story you started with? The group with the most accurate story wins.

3. Category Dictation ★★

a. Have students make two columns on a piece of paper and write the following at the top of each column:

Good Reasons
Bad Reasons

b. Dictate reasons for requesting a schedule change and have students write them in the appropriate column. For example:

Good Reasons	Bad Reasons
I had to take my son to the doctor.	There was a long line at the coffee shop.
I had a parent-teacher conference.	I met an old friend on my way to work.
The bus broke down.	I forgot to turn on my alarm clock.
The train was late.	I got a phone call.
I had an accident.	

c. As a class, in pairs, or in small groups, have students check their work.

4. Dictate and Discuss ★★★

Divide the class into pairs or small groups. Dictate sentences such as the following and have students discuss whether they agree or disagree with the statements.

It's okay to be five minutes late for work.
There is never a good excuse for being late.
If you are often late to work, you don't really care about your job.

5. Problem Solving ★★★

Activity Master 9

a. Make multiple copies of Activity Master 9 and give one to each student.

b. Have students work individually to read the story and complete the comprehension exercise.

c. In pairs, have students compare answers, discuss the question, and complete the sentence.

d. Have students share their sentences with the class.

REPORT OF TRAFFIC ACCIDENT

1. Have students look at the traffic accident report. Ask questions to orient students to the diagram—for example: "Where's Clark Street? Where's 23rd Street? Which way is north? South? East? West?" Introduce the new vocabulary: *dawn, daylight, driver, dusk, fog, icy, light conditions, red light, road surface, slippery, vehicle, weather conditions,* and *west*.

2. Give students a few minutes to read the report silently. Ask questions about the report to check students' comprehension. For example: "Where was the accident?" (At the intersection of 23rd Street and Clark Street.) "What was the weather?" (It was raining.)

3. Have students work individually to read the text again and complete the comprehension exercise. Have them compare answers in pairs, small groups, or as a class.

MULTILEVEL VARIATION ★

Have *below-level* students work in pairs to provide each other with more support while doing the comprehension exercise.

Answers

1. C	**4.** C
2. D	**5.** A
3. B	**6.** D

LIFE SKILLS ENRICHMENT

A Traffic Accident Report

Life Skills Worksheet 4

Make copies of Life Skills Worksheet 4 and give one to each student. Have students complete the worksheet as homework. In the next class, have students compare their answers in pairs.

1. Listen for the Verbs ★

a. Read the accident report description on student text page 20b to the class and have students write down all the verbs they hear. For example:

> was driving
> stopped
> turned
> entered
> was going
> was making
> didn't stop
> hit
> was talking

b. Have pairs of students check each others' answers.

MULTILEVEL VARIATION ★★/★★★

At-level and *above-level* students can sort the verbs into verb tense categories as they do the activity. For example:

Past Continuous Tense	Simple Past Tense
was driving	stopped

2. True or False? ★★

Make statements about the accident report on student text page 20b and have students decide whether the statements are true or false. If a statement is false, have students correct it. For example:

> Vehicle 1 was driving on 23rd Street. [True.]
> Vehicle 2 was turning right on Clark Street. [False. Vehicle 2 was turning left on Clark Street.]

Variation: Do the activity as a game with competing teams.

3. Retell What Happened ★★

Divide the class into pairs. Have students close their books and retell what they remember about the accident report on student text page 20b. Then have them open their books and check to see how much they remembered.

4. Role Play: What Happened? ★★★

a. Brainstorm with the class questions a police officer might ask the drivers about the accident. Write their questions on the board. For example:

> What happened?
> Where were you when your cars hit?
> What were you doing when the accident happened?
> What direction were you driving?

b. Divide the class into pairs. Have students write a conversation between the police officer and the driver of Vehicle 1 or the driver of Vehicle 2.

c. Circulate to help students as necessary.

d. Have students perform their role plays for the class.

5. Writing from a Different Point of View ★★★

The description of the accident on student text page 20b is from the perspective of the driver of Vehicle 1. Have students write a paragraph description of the accident from the point of view of the driver of Vehicle 2. Call on students to read their paragraphs to the class.

HISTORY OF THE UNITED STATES 1

1. Have students look at each photograph and ask: "What's happening?" (Photo 1: General Washington is fighting in the Revolutionary War. Photo 2: Representatives from the American colonies are signing the Declaration of Independence.) Have students look at the documents and ask: "What's this? Why is it important?" (Document 1: It's the Declaration of Independence. It's important because it talks about people's rights. Document 2: It's the U.S. Constitution. It's important because it is the highest law in the United States.)

2. Introduce the new vocabulary: *central government, colony, Constitution, Declaration of Independence, Independence Day, Independence Hall, independent, John Hancock, meeting, national government, national holiday, representative, Revolutionary War, right* (n), *signature, soldier, state government,* and *Thomas Jefferson.*

3. Have students work individually to complete the cloze exercise and then compare answers in pairs, small groups, or as a class.

Answers

1. began
2. ended
3. fought
4. lost
5. met

6. wrote
7. signed
8. needed
9. sent
10. described

LIFE SKILLS ENRICHMENT

U.S. History 1

Life Skills Worksheet 5

Make copies of Life Skills Worksheet 5 and give one to each student. Have students complete the worksheet as homework. In the next class, have students compare their answers in pairs.

EXPANSION ACTIVITIES

1. Verb Review ★

Have students circle all the irregular verbs on student text page 20c. On a separate piece of paper, have them write each irregular verb in its base form. For example:

Past Form	Base Form
began	begin
fought	fight
had	have
lost	lose
met	meet
sent	send
wrote	write

2. U.S. History Match Game I ★★

Activity Master 10

a. Make a copy of Activity Master 10 and cut it into cards. Distribute the cards randomly, one to each student.

   Note: The large cards are questions and the small cards are answers.

b. Have students memorize the question or response on their cards. Then have students circulate around the room saying their lines until they find their match. Make sure students don't show their cards to their classmates since this is a listening and speaking exercise.

c. When students have found their match, have them compare their cards and then come show you.

d. Continue until students have found all the matches.

MULTILEVEL VARIATION ★

Give *below-level* students the small cards, which are easier to memorize.

3. True or False? ★★

Make statements about U.S. history from Civics Reading 1 on student text page 20c and have students decide whether the statements are true or false. If a statement is false, have students correct it. For example:

John Hancock wrote the Declaration of Independence. [False. Thomas Jefferson wrote it.]

The American colonies wanted to be independent from England. [True.]

The American colonies declared independence from England in 1976. [False. They declared independence in 1776.]

There were twelve American colonies. [False. There were thirteen colonies.]

Variation: Do the activity as a game with competing teams.

4. Concentration: Early U.S. History ★★★

Activity Master 10

a. Divide the class into pairs. Make multiple copies of Activity Master 10, cut them into cards, and distribute one set to each pair.

   Note: The large cards are questions and the small cards are answers.

b. Have students shuffle the cards and place the large cards in two rows and the small cards in two rows face down.

c. The object of the game is for students to find the matching questions and answers. Both students should be able to see the cards, since *concentrating* on their location is an important part of playing the game.

d. Student A turns over a large card and a small card, and if they match, the student keeps the cards. If the cards don't match, the student turns them face down and Student B takes a turn.

The game continues until all the questions and answers have been matched. The student with the most correct *matches* wins the game.

Below-level students can read through the questions and answers all at once and then match the cards face up.

5. U.S. History Quiz ★★★

Activity Master 11

a. Make a copy of Activity Master 11, cut it into cards, and put the cards in a pile on a table or desk in the front of the room.

b. Divide the class into two teams. Have students take turns coming up to the front of the class, picking up a card, and reading it to the team. The team must answer the question in one minute. For each correct answer, the team gets one point. The team with the most points wins.

MULTILEVEL VARIATIONS

★ *Below-level students can refer to the reading on student text page 20c to answer the questions.*

★★/★★★ Challenge *at-level* and *above-level* students to close their student texts and try to recall the information from memory.

HISTORY OF THE UNITED STATES 2

1. Have students look at each photograph and ask questions to get them oriented—for example: "Who's that?" (Photo 1: President George Washington. Photo 3: President Abraham Lincoln.) "What's happening?" (Photo 2: Soldiers are going to war.)

2. Introduce the new vocabulary: *Abraham Lincoln, Civil War, Colonial Army, Confederacy, cotton, Emancipation Proclamation, farm, form* (v), *free* (v), *freedom, George Washington, grow, kill, leader, nation, national holiday, North, Northern states, plantation, Presidents' Day, slave, slavery, South, Southern States,* and *Union.*

3. Have students work individually to complete the cloze exercise and then compare answers in pairs, small groups, or as a class.

Answers

1.	met	7.	thought
2.	became	8.	fought
3.	served	9.	lost
4.	began	10.	was
5.	grew	11.	led
6.	bought	12.	signed

LIFE SKILLS ENRICHMENT

U.S. History 2

Life Skills Worksheet 6

Make copies of Life Skills Worksheet 6 and give one to each student. Have students complete the worksheet as homework. In the next class, have students compare their answers in pairs.

1. Verb Review ★

Have students circle all the irregular verbs on student text page 20d. On a separate piece of paper, have them write each irregular verb in its base form. For example:

Past Form	Base Form
became	become
began	begin
bought	buy
fought	fight
grew	grow
had	have
kept	keep
led	lead
lost	lose
met	meet
thought	think
wrote	write

2. U.S. History Match Game II ★★

Activity Master 12

a. Make a copy of Activity Master 12 and cut it into cards. Distribute the cards randomly, one to each student.

   Note: The large cards are questions and the small cards are answers.

b. Have students memorize the question or response on their cards. Then have students circulate around the room saying their lines until they find their match. Make sure students don't show their cards to their classmates since this is a listening and speaking exercise.

c. When students have found their match, have them compare their cards and then come show you.

d. Continue until students have found all the matches.

MULTILEVEL VARIATION ★

Give below-level students the small cards, which are easier to memorize.

3. True or False? ★★

Make statements about U.S. history from Civics Reading 2 on student text page 20d and have students decide whether the statements are true or false. If a statement is false, have students correct it. For example:

> George Washington signed the Emancipation Proclamation. [False. Abraham Lincoln signed it.]
> The Civil War began in 1861. [True.]
> President Lincoln led the Southern states in the war against the North. [False. He represented the Northern states.]
> People in the North thought slavery was wrong. [True.]

Variation: Do the activity as a game with competing teams.

4. Concentration: U.S. History II ★★★

Activity Master 12

a. Divide the class into pairs. Make multiple copies of Activity Master 12, cut them into cards, and distribute one set to each pair.

   Note: The large cards are questions and the small cards are answers.

b. Have students shuffle the cards and place the large cards in two rows and the small cards in two rows face down.

c. The object of the game is for students to find the matching questions and answers. Both students should be able to see the cards, since *concentrating* on their location is an important part of playing the game.

d. Student A turns over a large card and a small card, and if they match the student keeps the cards. If the cards don't match, the student turns them face down and Student B takes a turn.

The game continues until all the questions and answers have been matched. The student with the most correct *matches* wins the game.

(continued)

MULTILEVEL VARIATION ★

Below-level students can read through the questions and answers all at once and then match the cards face up.

5. Category Dictation ★★

a. Have students make two columns on a piece of paper and write the following at the top of each column:

   Revolutionary War
   Civil War

b. Dictate key words and phrases from Civics Readings 1 and 2 (student text pages 20c and 20d) and have students write them in the appropriate column. For example:

Revolutionary War	Civil War
George Washington	Abraham Lincoln
The American colonies and England	The North and the South
1775 to 1783	1861 to 1865

c. As a class, in pairs, or in small groups, have students check their work.

6. Tic Tac Question ★★★

a. Draw a tic tac grid on the board and write the following answers in random order on the grid:

Abraham Lincoln.	1865.	George Washington.
1861.	The Emancipation Proclamation.	The Civil War.
The Confederacy.	The Union.	1787.

b. Divide the class into two teams. Give each team a mark: X or O.

c. Give the teams five minutes to write the questions for each of the answers on the grid. Then have the teams take turns calling out an answer and the corresponding question. If the question is correct, the team gets to put its mark in that space. For example:

   X Team: The Emancipation Proclamation.
   What document freed the slaves?

d. The first team to mark out three boxes in a straight line—vertically, horizontally, or diagonally—wins.

HISTORY OF THE UNITED STATES 3

1. Have students look at each photograph and ask questions to get them oriented—for example: "Who is in the picture? What are the people doing?" (Photo 1: These people are workers. They're working in a clothing factory. Photo 2: That's Martin Luther King, Jr. People are protesting in Washington.)

2. Introduce the new vocabulary: *Blacks, civil rights movement, demonstration, discrimination, immigrant, Immigration Act, March on Washington, Martin Luther King, Jr., occur, protest* (n), and *speaker.*

3. Have students work individually to complete the cloze exercise and then compare answers in pairs, small groups, or as a class.

Answers

1. opened	5. gave
2. came	6. led
3. worked	7. was
4. made	8. spoke

HISTORY QUIZ

Have students ask and answer the history quiz questions in pairs, small groups, or as a class.

Answers

1. 1775.
2. Thomas Jefferson.
3. July 4th.
4. The Constitution.
5. George Washington.
6. The South (the Confederacy) and the North (the Union).
7. The Emancipation Proclamation.
8. Abraham Lincoln.
9. The Immigration Act of 1965.
10. Martin Luther King, Jr.

MULTILEVEL VARIATIONS

★ *Below-level* students can refer to the text as they answer the questions.

★★/★★★ Challenge *at-level* and *above-level* students to close their texts and try to answer the questions.

TEAMWORK

1. Explain to the class what a timeline is. Have students read the directions silently. Then divide the class into pairs.

2. Have students read text pages 20c, 20d, and 20e again. Have them underline eight important events in U.S. history and then create a timeline with these events and their dates in chronological order.

3. When the pairs have completed their timelines, have them compare the timeline they created with a timeline created by another pair of students.

MULTILEVEL VARIATION ★★/★★★

As *at-level* and *above-level* students finish this activity, give them a copy of Life Skills Worksheet 7 to work on individually.

LIFE SKILLS ENRICHMENT

U.S. History 3: Timeline

Life Skills Worksheet 7

Make copies of Life Skills Worksheet 7 and give one to each student. Have students complete the worksheet as homework. In the next class, have students compare their answers in pairs.

1. Scrambled Words ★

a. Choose key words or phrases from the Civics readings on student text pages 20c, 20d, and 20e and write them on the board or on a card with the letters scrambled out of order. For example:

liciv ihtgsr

b. Have students take turns guessing what the word or phrase is. [civil rights]

Variation 1: Do the activity in pairs or small groups, with students taking turns scrambling words and phrases for others to guess.

Variation 2: Do the activity as a class game with competing teams.

2. Association Game ★

a. Write on the board the following historical events from the Civics readings on student text pages 20c, 20d, and 20e:

> The Civil War
> The Revolutionary War
> The Civil Rights Movement

b. Divide the class into several teams. Have the students in each team work together to see how many words and phrases they can associate with each historical event. For example:

> The Civil Rights Movement: [Martin Luther King, Jr./the March on Washington/Blacks/Whites/protests/demonstrations]
> The Civil War: [Abraham Lincoln/the North/the South/the Confederacy/the Union/plantations/slavery/slaves]

c. Set a time limit for the game. When the time limit is up, call on the teams to read their list of associations to the class. The team with the most correct items wins.

3. Stand in Order: Events in U.S. History ★

Activity Master 13

Make two copies of Activity Master 13 and cut them into cards. Divide the class into two groups. Give each group member a card. Have students in each group read their historical event aloud and arrange themselves in a line from the earliest event to the most recent event.

Variation: Do the activity as a game with competing teams. The team that correctly puts the events in order in the shortest time is the winner.

4. True or False? ★★

Make statements about U.S. history from Civics Reading 3 on student text page 20e and have students decide whether the statements are true or false. If a statement is false, have students correct it. For example:

> George Washington led the civil rights movement. [False. Martin Luther King, Jr. led it.]
> In the 1800s many immigrants came to the U.S. [True.]
> The March on Washington was in 1965. [False. It was in 1963.]
> The Immigration Act of 1965 gave people from any country in the world the right to apply to come to the United States. [True.]

Variation: Do the activity as a game with competing teams.

5. Can You Guess? ★★

a. Write the following historical events and people on the board:

> The Civil Rights Movement
> Immigration in the U.S.
> The Civil War
> Abraham Lincoln
> George Washington
> Thomas Jefferson
> The Declaration of Independence
> The Revolutionary War
> The Constitution

b. Divide the class into pairs. Have each pair choose one of these people or events and write three sentences without naming the person or event. For example:

> He was the first President of the United States.
> He helped write the Constitution.
> He led the Revolutionary Army.

c. Have the pairs read their sentences to the class and see if students can identify the historical figure or event. [George Washington]

6. Tic Tac Question ★★★

a. Draw a tic tac grid on the board and write the following answers in random order on the grid:

Martin Luther King, Jr.	The 1950s and 1960s.	The 1800s.
In 1963.	In factories.	The third Monday in January.
To end discrimination against Blacks.	The Immigration Act of 1965.	Washington D.C.

b. Divide the class into two teams. Give each team a mark: X or O.

c. Give the teams five minutes to write the questions for each of the answers on the grid. Then have the teams take turns calling out an answer and the corresponding question. If the question is correct, the team gets to put its mark in that space. For example:

> X Team: The Immigration Act of 1965.
> What law made immigration easier?

d. The first team to mark out three boxes in a straight line—vertically, horizontally, or diagonally—wins.

CHECK-UP TEST (A) (B) (C) (D)

Have students do the check-up test and then review the answers as a class.

Answers

1. B	**6.** D
2. A	**7.** B
3. D	**8.** C
4. C	**9.** A
5. B	**10.** A

SKILLS CHECK ✔

Words:

Explain to students that this is a list of verbs they have learned or reviewed in the unit. Have students take turns reading each item aloud to the class. Have students put a check next to the item if they feel they have learned it. Encourage students to get a small notebook where they can write down words that are difficult for them.

I can:

Explain to students that this is a list of skills they have learned in the unit. Read each item aloud to the class. Ask individual students or pairs of students to demonstrate the skill. For example:

> Teacher: I can react to bad news.
> Student A: I lost my cell phone.
> Student B: What a shame!

> Teacher: I can apologize for being late.
> Student: I'm sorry I'm late. I missed the bus.

Have students put a check next to the item if they feel they have learned it. Use this information to determine which lessons you may want to review or reinforce for the entire class or for particular students.

EXPANSION ACTIVITIES

1. **Do You Remember the Verbs? ★**

Check students' retention of the vocabulary depicted on the opening page of Unit 2 by doing the following activity:

a. Have students open their books to page 11 and cover the list of verbs.

b. Either call out a number and have students tell you the verb, or say a verb and have students tell you the number.

Variation: You can also do this activity as a game with competing teams.

2. **Miming Game ★★**

Activity Master 14

a. Make a copy of Activity Master 14, cut it into cards, and put the cards face down in a pile on a table or desk in the front of the room.

b. Have students take turns picking a card from the pile and pantomiming the action on the card. Then ask: "What did ____ do?" or "What was ____ doing?" and have students answer in a complete sentence. For example:

> Teacher: What was Pedro doing?
> Student: He was riding a bike.

> Teacher: What did Wanda do?
> Student: She cut herself.

Variation: Do the activity as a game with competing teams.

3. **Expand the Sentence ★★**

Tell students that the object of the game is to build a long sentence on the board, one word at a time.

a. Call on a student to write a pronoun or someone's name on the far left side of the board. For example:

> Jose

b. Have another student come to the board and add a word. For example:

Jose was

c. Have a third student add a third word. For example:

Jose was walking

d. Continue until each student in the class has had one or more turns to add a word to the sentence into the longest one they can think of. For example:

Jose was walking down the street yesterday afternoon when he saw a very bad accident at the corner of Main Street and Central Boulevard.

e. Begin a new sentence and continue the story.

4. Board Game ★★

Activity Master 15

For this activity, you will need a die, markers, and a piece of paper. (If students use a coin as a die, the class should decide which side of the coin will indicate a move of one space and which will indicate a move of two spaces.)

a. Make multiple copies of Activity Master 15. Divide the class into small groups and give each group a copy of Activity Master 15 along with a die, markers, and a piece of paper.

b. Have students place their markers on *Start.* The group should decide who goes first. That student begins the game by rolling the die or flipping the coin and moving his or her marker. If the student responds to the question or task correctly, he or she may take one more turn. If the student doesn't respond correctly, the next student takes a turn. No one may take more than two turns at a time.

Option 1: The first person to reach *Finish* is the winner.

Option 2: The game continues until each student reaches *Finish.* This way everybody is a winner.

5. Question the Answers! ★★

a. Dictate answers such as the following to the class:

Yes, I did.
Yes, I was.
No, I didn't.
No, I wasn't.
I sprained my ankle while I was skiing.
She cut herself while she was chopping vegetables.
He lost it while he was going to work.
They went by bus.
She went to Rome.
He stayed in a small hotel.
I met a lot of tourists.
We saw the Vatican.

b. Divide the class into groups of four. Have them write questions for which these answers are correct. For example:

Answer: Yes, I did.
Question: Did you work last night?

Answer: They went by bus.
Question: How did they go?

c. Have students share some of their questions and answers with the class.

6. Question Game ★★★

a. Write the following sentence on the board:

Martin sprained his ankle while he was walking in the woods.

b. Underline different elements of the sentence and have students create a question based on that portion of the sentence. For example:

<u>Martin</u> sprained his ankle while he was walking in the woods.

(continued)

Who sprained his ankle while he was walking in the woods?

> Martin sprained <u>his ankle</u> while he was walking in the woods.

What did Martin sprain while he was walking in the woods?

> Martin sprained his ankle while <u>he was walking in the woods</u>.

What was Martin doing when he sprained his ankle?

c. Continue with other sentences.

7. What's Wrong? ★★★

a. Write several sentences such as the following on the board or on a handout that you give to students. Some of the sentences should be correct and others incorrect. For example:

> Did they study for the exam?
> What did you delivered?
> Why was he waving?
> I waked up with a high fever.
> He cutted himself with a knife.
> She didn't sang well.
> They didn't embarrassed.
> I sprained my ankle while I was hiking in the woods.
> He ripped his pants while he got on the bus.
> How did they got there?
> What did they see at the museum?
> Were you watch a movie last night?
> I poked myself in the eye at work.
> The father teached his son how to ride a bicycle.
> The South fighted against the North in the Civil War.

b. Divide the class into pairs. The object of the activity is for students to identify which sentences are incorrect and then correct them. Have students compare their answers in small groups.

Variation: Do the activity as a game with competing teams. For each team's turn, write one sentence on the board and have the team decide whether the sentence is correct or not. If it isn't correct, the team must correct it. Every time a team is right, that team receives one point. The team with the greatest number of points wins.

MULTILEVEL VARIATION ★

For *below-level* students, underline the errors and have the below-level pairs focus only on correcting them.

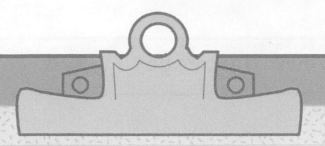

Teacher's Notes

GRAMMAR

FUTURE: GOING TO

What	am	I		
	is	he she it	going to do?	
	are	we you they		

(I am)	I'm	
(He is)	He's	
(She is)	She's	going to read.
(It is)	It's	
(We are)	We're	
(You are)	You're	
(They are)	They're	

POSSESSIVE PRONOUNS

| mine |
| his |
| hers |
| — |
| ours |
| yours |
| theirs |

FUTURE: WILL

(I will)	I'll	
(He will)	He'll	
(She will)	She'll	
(It will)	It'll	work.
(We will)	We'll	
(You will)	You'll	
(They will)	They'll	

I	
He	
She	
It	won't work.
We	
You	
They	

FUTURE CONTINUOUS TENSE

(I will)	I'll	
(He will)	He'll	
(She will)	She'll	
(It will)	It'll	be working.
(We will)	We'll	
(You will)	You'll	
(They will)	They'll	

FUNCTIONS

ASKING FOR AND REPORTING INFORMATION

Will *Ms. Martinez return soon*?
　Yes, *she* will.
　No, *she* won't.

Will you *be home this evening*?
　Yes, I will. I'll be *watching videos*.
　No, I won't. I'll be *working overtime*.

Will *the play* begin soon?
Will *the train* arrive soon?

How much longer will you be *doing homework*?
　I'll probably be *doing homework* for another
　　30 minutes.

What are you looking forward to?

What's the weather forecast?

Do you know anybody who does?

Tell me, *Milton*, _____.

INQUIRING ABOUT INTENTION

What are you going to do?
What are you going to do *this weekend*?
What are you going to *buy*?

Are you going to *buy a donut this morning*?

EXPRESSING INTENTION

I'm going to *buy a muffin*.

I'll *call you in 30 minutes*.
I'll *call him* right away.

EXPRESSING PROBABILITY

I'll probably be *doing homework for another 30 minutes*.

REQUESTING

Could you do me a favor?
Could you possibly do me a favor?
Could you do a favor for me?
Could I ask you a favor?

Could I possibly *borrow yours*?

RESPONDING TO REQUESTS

Sure. What is it?

GREETING PEOPLE

Hi, ———. This is ———.

Can you talk for a minute?
   I'm sorry. I can't talk right now. I'm *doing homework*. Can you call back a little later?

LEAVE-TAKING

Well, have a nice weekend.
   You, too.

Speak to you soon.
   Good-bye.

APOLOGIZING

I'm sorry.

EXPRESSING INABILITY

I'm sorry. I can't *talk right now*.

EXPRESSING OBLIGATION

I have to *fix a flat tire*.

ADMITTING

I'm afraid *I don't have one*.

OFFERING ADVICE

You should *call Joe*.

EXPRESSING CERTAINTY

I'm sure *he'll be happy to lend you his*.

EXPRESSING GRATITUDE

Thanks.

NEW VOCABULARY

Time Expressions
a little later
for a long time
four times a year
last *January*
last *spring*
last *Sunday*
next *January*
next *spring*
next *Sunday*
this *Friday night*
this *January*
this *spring*
this *Sunday*

Verbs
adjust
browse the web
call back
come back
contain
do research
give *the kids* a bath
go water-skiing
ice skate
include
manage
participate
relax
say good-bye
stay with
supervise
volunteer (v)
work out
work overtime

Adjectives
absent
compulsory
emotional
excited
lonely
satisfactory
unsatisfactory

Adverbs
independently
perhaps
permanently
possibly

School/College
administration building
after-school program
art
astronomy
attendance line
biology
campus
freshman
honor roll
junior
latch-key children
learning
music building
open house
parent-teacher
   association
photography
report card
school attendance line

school event
school year
science center
security
semester
senior
sophomore
vocational center

Medical
dental appointment
illness
medical appointment
rash

Music
Broadway show tunes
folk songs

Free Time
day off
retirement
summer vacation

Foods
onion soup
pea soup

Superheroes
Batman
Superman

Places in the Community
art museum
child-care center

Miscellaneous
absence
activity
channel
composition
Europe
favor
flight
Halloween
income tax form
jack
jail
meeting
opportunity
part
plan (n)
safety
screwdriver
tone
tree house

EXPRESSIONS

as you can imagine
Dear ———,
Fine.
have a good life
Have a nice weekend
have a party for
look forward to
Sincerely, ———
Speak to you soon.

VOCABULARY PREVIEW

You may want to introduce these time expressions before beginning the unit, or you may choose to wait until they first occur in a specific lesson. If you choose to introduce them at this point, here are some suggestions:

1. Have students look at the illustrations on text page 21 and identify the time expressions they already know.

2. Present the vocabulary. Say each time expression and have the class repeat it chorally and individually. Check students' understanding and pronunciation.

3. Practice the vocabulary as a class, in pairs, or in small groups. Have students cover the word list and look at the pictures. Practice the time expressions in the following ways:

   To practice time expressions for *yesterday*, ask about 1, 4, 7, 10.
   To practice time expressions for *today*, ask about 2, 5, 8, 11.
   To practice time expressions for *tomorrow*, ask about 3, 6, 9, 12.

   To practice *morning* time expressions, ask about 1, 2, 3.
   To practice *afternoon* time expressions, ask about 4, 5, 6.
   To practice *evening* time expressions, ask about 7, 8, 9.
   To practice *night* time expressions, ask about 10, 11, 12.

   • Say a time expression and have students tell the number of the illustration.

   • Give the number of an illustration and have students say the time expression.

4. For further practice, ask about the situations that are depicted:

   Situations 1–3—morning:

   What did they do yesterday morning?
   Where are they this morning?
   Where are they going to be tomorrow morning?

   Situations 4–6—afternoon:

   What did he do yesterday afternoon?
   What's he doing this afternoon?
   What's going to happen tomorrow afternoon?

   Situations 7–9—evening:

   What did they do yesterday evening?
   What's happening this evening?
   What are they going to do tomorrow evening?

   Situations 10–12—night:

   What happened last night?
   What's happening tonight?
   Where are they going to be tomorrow night?

FOCUS

- Review: Future: Going to
- Contrast: Future and Past Tenses
- Contrast: Future and Past Time Expressions

CLOSE UP

RULE: *Going to* + verb is used to express future plans or intentions.

EXAMPLES: **I'm going to buy** a muffin.
She**'s going to sing** Broadway show tunes.
We**'re going to go** to Hawaii.
They**'re going to watch** the news program.

GETTING READY

Review time expressions and contracted forms with *going to*.

1. Have students look at the list of time expressions on text page 22 as you read the examples below.

> George couldn't go shopping yesterday.
> He's going to go shopping TODAY.
>
> Jane didn't study last night.
> She's going to study TONIGHT.
>
> It isn't going to rain this week.
> It's going to rain NEXT week.

2. Read the statements below and call on students to respond following the pattern above, using *going to* and a corresponding future time expression.

> Mr. and Mrs. Mason didn't come home from their vacation yesterday.
> Marylou didn't clean her apartment last week.
> David can't write to his girlfriend this week.
> Shirley couldn't take a trip last year.
> We didn't study very hard last month.
> Mr. Davis didn't visit his son last spring.
> Jim and Bob aren't going to study today.
> Bill didn't come to work last Monday.
> Gloria couldn't go skiing last January.
> Our neighbors didn't have a party yesterday.

INTRODUCING THE MODEL

1. Have students look at the model illustration.
2. Set the scene: "Two friends are talking."
3. Present the model.
4. Full-Class Repetition.

   ### Pronunciation Note

   The pronunciation focus of Unit 3 is **Going to** (text page 32). Tell students that this is very common in informal speech. You may wish to model this pronunciation at this point and encourage students to incorporate it into their language practice.

   > Are you "gonna" buy a donut this morning?
   > I'm "gonna" buy a muffin.

5. Ask students if they have any questions. Check understanding of vocabulary.
6. Group Choral Repetition.
7. Choral Conversation.
8. Call on one or two pairs of students to present the dialog.

   (For additional practice, do Choral Conversation in small groups or by rows.)

SIDE BY SIDE EXERCISES

Examples

1. A. Is Mr. Hopper going to have cake for dessert tonight?
   B. No, he isn't. He had cake for dessert LAST night.
   A. What's he going to have?
   B. He's going to have ice cream.

2. A. Is Valerie going to sing folk songs this evening?
   B. No, she isn't. She sang folk songs YESTERDAY evening.
   A. What's she going to sing?
   B. She's going to sing Broadway show tunes.

1. **Exercise 1:** Call on two students to present the dialog. Then do Choral Repetition and Choral Conversation practice.

2. **Exercise 2:** Introduce the expressions *folk songs, Broadway show tunes*. Same as above.

   ### Culture Notes

   Folk songs are traditional songs of ordinary country people. They are usually accompanied by instruments such as a guitar, banjo, or harmonica.

   Broadway show tunes are songs from musical productions that have been performed in theaters in the Broadway area of New York City.

3. **Exercises 3–10:** Either Full-Class Practice or Pair Practice.

New Vocabulary

3. Europe
4. Channel
   this Friday night
7. onion soup
   pea soup
8. biology
   semester
   astronomy
10. Superman
    Halloween
    Batman

Culture Notes

Exercise 10: *Superman* is a superhero who saves people in trouble. He can fly, see through objects, and hear sound from very far away. He wears a large *S* on his red, yellow, and blue costume.

Batman is a futuristic superhero who saves the world from bad people. A cave under his house is equipped with special technology. Batman has a special vehicle that can move very fast. His black and gray costume resembles a bat.

Halloween is a popular holiday in the United States. It takes place on October 31st. Children dress up as their favorite characters and go door to door asking for candy. If children don't receive candy, they play tricks on people.

WORKBOOK

Pages 24–26

1. Memory Chain ★★

a. Divide the class into groups of 5 or 6 students each.

b. Have students answer the question *What are you going to do tomorrow?*

c. One group at a time, have Student 1 begin. For example:

> I'm going to have dinner at my favorite restaurant.

d. Student 2 repeats what Student 1 said and adds a statement about himself or herself. For example:

> Maria is going to have dinner at her favorite restaurant, and I'm going to go bowling.

e. Student 3 continues in the same way. For example:

> Maria is going to have dinner at her favorite restaurant, Edward is going to go bowling, and I'm going to visit my grandparents.

f. Continue until everyone has had a chance to play the *memory chain*.

2. Sense or Nonsense? ★★

a. Divide the class into four groups.

b. Make four sets of split sentence cards with beginnings and endings of sentences. For example:

I'm not going to have cake for dessert, . . .	I'm going to have pie.
I'm not going to sing folk songs, . . .	I'm going to sing show tunes.
I'm not going to take biology this semester, . . .	I'm going to take astronomy.
I'm not going to play chess this afternoon, . . .	I'm going to play cards.

I'm not going to make soup today, . . .	I'm going to make stew.
I'm not going to wear a suit today, . . .	I'm going to wear jeans.
I'm not going to plant vegetables this year, . . .	I'm going to plant flowers.
I'm not going to go out with my friends, . . .	I'm going to go out with my cousins.
I'm not going to go to Europe this summer, . . .	I'm going to go to Canada.

c. Mix up the cards and distribute sets of cards to each group, keeping the beginning and ending cards in different piles.

d. Have students take turns picking up one card from each pile and reading the sentence to the group. For example:

I'm not going to take biology this semester, . . .	I'm going to sing show tunes.

e. That group decides if the sentence makes *sense* or is *nonsense*.

f. After all the cards have been picked, have the groups lay out all the cards and put together all the sentence combinations that make sense.

3. Concentration ★★

a. Use the cards from the above activity. Place them face down in three rows of 6 each.

b. Divide the class into two teams. The object of the game is for students to find the

(continued)

matching cards. Both teams should be able to see all the cards since *concentrating* on their location is an important part of playing the game.

c. A student from Team 1 turns over two cards. If they match, the student picks up the cards, that team gets a point, and the student takes another turn. If the cards don't match, the student turns them face down, and a member of Team 2 takes a turn.

d. The game continues until all the cards have been matched. The team with the most correct matches wins the game.

Variation: This game can also be played in groups or pairs.

4. Expand the Sentence ★★

Tell students that the object of the activity is to build a long sentence on the board, one word at a time.

a. Call on a student to write a pronoun or someone's name on the far left side of the board. For example:

Jennifer

b. Have another student come to the board and add a word. For example:

Jennifer isn't

c. Have a third student add a third word. For example:

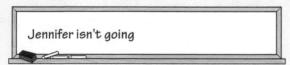

Jennifer isn't going

d. Continue until each student in the class has had one or more turns to add a word to expand the sentence into the longest one they can think of. For example:

Jennifer isn't going to go to work today because she has a terrible sore throat, and she thinks she should go to the clinic to see her doctor instead.

5. You Just Did That! ★★

a. Put the following on the board:

A. I'm going to _____ tomorrow.
B. But you _____ last week!
A. I know. But I'm going to _____ again.
B. Why are you going to do that?
A. _____.

b. Put the following cues on the board or on word cards that you can distribute to students:

paint my _____
fly to _____
go to _____
visit _____
drive to _____
go _____ing
take a _____ to _____
have _____ for dessert
ride my bicycle to _____
write a letter to _____
complain about _____

c. Divide the class into pairs and have students create conversations based on the model on the board and the cues. Encourage students to expand their conversations any way they wish. For example:

A. I'm going to paint my kitchen tomorrow.
B. But you painted your kitchen last week!
A. I know. But I'm going to paint my kitchen again.
B. Why are you going to do that?
A. Because I don't like the color.

A. I'm going to fly to Rio tomorrow.
B. But you flew to Rio last week!
A. I know. But I'm going to fly to Rio again.
B. Why are you going to do that?
A. I'm going to meet a friend and travel around Brazil.

6. Find the Right Person! ★★★

a. Write the following times on the board:

after class
tonight
this weekend

b. On a separate piece of paper, have students write three sentences about plans they have, using the time expressions on the board. For example:

I'm going to have lunch after class.
I'm going to watch TV tonight.
I'm going to see a movie this weekend.

c. Collect the papers and distribute them randomly to different students in the class.

d. Have each student interview others (for example: "What are you going to do tonight?" "Are you going to see a movie this weekend?") in order to find out whose plans match those on his or her particular card.

e. Once everybody has identified the correct person, call on students to tell about the people on their cards. For example:

Thomas is going to go home after class.
He's going to study tonight.
He's going to visit his cousins this weekend.

7. Class Story ★★★

a. Begin by saying "The Jones family is going to take a very exciting trip next summer. They're going to travel around the world."

b. Student 1 begins the story. For example: "First, they're going to go to Europe."

c. Student 2 continues. For example: "They're going to spend a week in London."

d. Continue around the room in this fashion, with each student telling more about the Jones family trip.

READING *Plans for the Weekend*

FOCUS

- Future: Going to

NEW VOCABULARY

go water-skiing
plan (n)
tree house

READING THE STORY

Optional: *Preview the story by having students talk about the story title and/or illustration. You may choose to introduce new vocabulary beforehand, or have students encounter the new vocabulary within the context of the reading.*

1. Have students read silently or follow along silently as the story is read aloud by you, by one or more students, or on the audio program.

2. Ask students if they have any questions. Check understanding of vocabulary.

   ### Language Note

   To rain cats and dogs means to rain very hard.

3. Check students' comprehension, using some or all of the following questions:

   What's Milton going to do this weekend?
   What's Diane going to do?
   What are Carmen and Tom going to do?
   What's Jack going to do?
   What's Kate going to do?
   What are Ray and his family going to do?
   Why are they all going to be disappointed?

✓READING *CHECK-UP*

Q & A

1. Call on a pair of students to present the model.

2. Ask students if they have any questions. Check understanding of the expression *Have a nice weekend.*

3. Have students work in pairs to create new dialogs.

4. Call on pairs to present their new dialogs to the class.

READING EXTENSION

Have students answer the following questions in groups and then share their ideas with the class:

What are all the activities the employees at the Liberty Insurance Company want to do?
What season of the year is it in the story?
What are some popular outdoor activities for summer?
What are some popular outdoor activities for fall?
What are some popular outdoor activities for winter?
What are some popular outdoor activities for spring?

How About You?

Have students answer the questions in pairs or as a class. If you do it as pair practice, call on students to report to the class about their conversation partner.

 **LISTENING**

Answers

1. a

2. a

3. b

4. a

5. b

6. b

Listen to the conversation and choose the answer that is true.

1. A. Are you going to wear your brown suit today?
   B. No, I don't think so. I wore my brown suit yesterday. I'm going to wear my gray suit.

2. A. Let's make beef stew for dinner!
   B. But we had that last week. Let's make spaghetti and meatballs instead.
   A. Okay.

3. A. Do you want to watch the game show on Channel 5 or the news program on Channel 9?
   B. Let's watch the news program.

4. A. What's the matter with it?
   B. The brakes don't work, and it doesn't start very well in the morning.

5. A. What are you going to do tomorrow?
   B. I'm going to plant carrots, tomatoes, and lettuce.

6. A. This computer is very powerful, but it's too expensive.
   B. You're right.

FOCUS

- Review: Future Tense: Will

CLOSE UP

RULE:	The future tense with *will* expresses a predictable or expected future event.

EXAMPLES:	Will the play begin soon?
	    Yes, **it will**.
	    It'll begin at 7:30.
	
	Will Flight 216 arrive soon?
	    No, **it won't**.
	    It won't arrive for several hours.

RULE:	*Will* does not contract with subject pronouns in short answers.

EXAMPLES:	Will Ms. Martinez return soon?
	    Yes, **she will**.
	    (**She'll** return in a little while.)
	
	Will Ken and Kim see each other again soon?
	    Yes, **they will**.
	    (**They'll** see each other again this Saturday night.)

GETTING READY

Review *will* and *won't*.

1. Write the following on the board:

Yes, _____ will.

No, _____ won't. (____'ll _____.)

2. Ask Yes/No questions about some predictable future event in your students' lives. Have students respond, using any of the forms on the board. For example:

Will we finish class at *(12 o'clock)*?
Yes, we will.

Will class start at *(9 o'clock)* tomorrow?
No, it won't. It'll start at *(10 o'clock)*.

Will you come to school *(next Sunday)*?
No, I won't. I'll come to school *(next Monday)*.

INTRODUCING THE MODELS

There are two model conversations. Introduce and practice each separately. For each model:

1. Have students look at the model illustration.

2. Set the scene:

1st model: "Someone is asking about Ms. Martinez."
2nd model: "Two friends are talking."

3. Present the model.

4. Full-Class Repetition.

5. Ask students if they have any questions. Check understanding of new vocabulary:

2nd model: *for a long time*

6. Group Choral Repetition.

7. Choral Conversation.

8. Call on one or two pairs of students to present the dialog.

(For additional practice, do Choral Conversation in small groups or by rows.)

SIDE BY SIDE EXERCISES

Examples

1. A. Will the play begin soon?
   B. Yes, it will. It'll begin at 7:30.

2. A. Will the concert begin soon?
   B. No, it won't. It won't begin until 8:00.

1. Exercise 1: Call on two students to present the dialog. Then do Choral Repetition and Choral Conversation practice.

2. Exercise 2: Same as above.

3. Exercises 3–8: Either Full-Class Practice or Pair Practice.

New Vocabulary

6. flight
8. jail

WORKBOOK

Page 27

EXPANSION ACTIVITIES

1. Can You Hear the Difference? ★

a. Write on the board:

Present	Future
They return at 7:00.	They'll return at 7:00.
I get out soon.	I'll get out soon.
You see each other every day.	You'll see each other every day.
We call each other.	We'll call each other.

b. Choose a sentence randomly from one of the two columns and say it to the class. Have the class listen and identify whether the sentence is in the *present* or in the *future*.

c. Have students continue the activity in pairs. One student says a sentence, and the other identifies the tense. Then have them reverse roles.

d. Write other similar sentences on the board and continue the practice.

2. Information Gap Handouts ★★

a. Tell students: "Ken and Kim plan to see each other this Saturday night." Write out their

plans, but divide the information between two different charts. For example:

Chart A:

6:00	
6:30	eat in a fancy restaurant
7:30	walk to the theater
8:00	
11:00	go out for dessert
12:00	

Chart B:

6:00	take a taxi downtown
6:30	
7:30	
8:00	see a Broadway play
11:00	
12:00	make plans for their next date

(continued)

b. Divide the class into pairs. Give each member of the pair a different chart. Have students share their information and fill in their charts. For example:

Student A: What will they do at 6:00?
Student B: They'll take a taxi downtown.
Student A: [writes the information in Chart A]

c. The pairs continue until each has a complete chart.

d. Have students look at their partner's chart to make sure that they have written the information correctly.

3. At the Office ★★

a. Write the following on the board:

> A. Hello, _____. May I help you?
> B. Yes. Is _____ in?
> A. I'm sorry. ____ isn't in the office right now.
> B. When do you think ____'ll be back?
> A. ____'ll probably be back in _____.
> B. Thank you very much. I'll call back later.
> A. You're welcome. Good-bye.

b. Divide the class into pairs and have students role play the telephone conversation. Students can use any names and time expressions they wish.

c. Give Speaker A in each pair a card showing the name of a business, such as those below. Encourage students to make up other names of businesses if they wish.

Carlson Computers
Smith Tire Company
Gold Star Travel
Sure Technology Company
Wilson Trucking
Presto Furniture
Rock Village Apartments
Real Engineering Corporation
True Insurance Company
Big Boy Paper Company
Goodman's Department Store
Dr. Peterson's Office

d. Call on pairs to present their conversations to the class without referring to the model on the board. For example:

A. Hello, Carlson Computers. May I help you?
B. Yes. Is Ms. Blake in?
A. I'm sorry. She isn't in the office right now.
B. When do you think she'll be back?
A. She'll probably be back in a few hours.
B. Thank you very much. I'll call back later.
A. You're welcome. Good-bye.

4. Question the Answers! ★★

a. Dictate answers such as the following to the class:

Yes, he will. He'll get out in a week.
Yes, she will. She'll return in an hour.
No, it won't. It won't arrive for several hours.
Don't worry. They'll be back soon.
No, they won't. They won't see each other for several weeks.

b. Have students write questions for which these answers would be correct. For example:

Answer: Yes, he will. He'll get out in a week.
Question: Will your brother get out of the hospital soon?

Answer: Yes, she will. She'll return in an hour.
Question: Will Ms. Parker return to her office soon?

c. Have students compare their questions with each other.

Variation: Write the answers on cards. Divide the class into groups and give each group a set of cards.

5. Jigsaw Contest: When Will They Get Home? ★★★

a. Divide the class into groups of four. Give each member of the group one of these cards:

> • Larry won't get home for four hours
>
> • John won't get home until 4:00.

- It's now 1:00.
- Ralph will get home an hour before John.

- Lisa will get home in an hour.
- Julie will get home at the same time as John.

- Valerie will arrive an hour after Larry gets home.
- David will get home at the same time as Lisa.

---

b. Have students share their information to create the correct schedule. Answer Key:

> It's now 1:00.
> Lisa and David will get home at 2:00.
> Ralph will get home at 3:00.
> John and Julie will get home at 4:00.
> Larry will get home at 5:00.
> Valerie will arrive at 6:00.

c. The first group to finish wins.

6. Mystery Conversations ★★★

a. Divide the class into pairs.

b. Write the following conversation framework on the board:

> A. Will _____ soon?
> B. No, ____ won't. ____ won't _____ until _____ .

c. Write roles such as the following on word cards and give one to each pair of students:

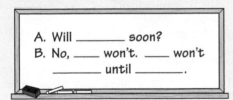

| a parent and a child | a boss and an employee |

---

a teacher and a student	a mechanic and a car owner
a soccer coach and a player	a doctor and a patient
a wife and a husband	a ballet teacher and a dancer

d. Have each pair create a short dialog that begins "Will _____ soon?" The dialogs should be appropriate for the roles the students have on their cards.

e. Have each pair present their dialog to the class. Then have the other students guess who the people are: Are they married? Is a teacher talking to a student? For example:

> [soccer coach–player]
> A. Will I play in the game soon?
> B. No, you won't. You won't play until the second half of the game.

7. Predictions for the Future ★★★

a. Divide the class into pairs or small groups.

b. Have students write predictions for the future and then discuss them with the class. For example:

> We'll have a very hot summer this year.
> (Maria) will be the president of her own company some day.
> (George) will become a famous Hollywood movie star.
> People will soon be able to fly in the air by themselves.
> The world will be a safer place in the future.

Text Page 26: Will You Be Home This Evening?

FOCUS

- Review: Future Continuous Tense

CLOSE UP

RULE: The future continuous tense emphasizes the ongoing nature or duration of an activity in the future.

EXAMPLES: Will you be home this evening?
Yes, I will. **I'll be watching** videos *(this evening)*.

Will Frank be home this evening?
Yes, he will. **He'll be paying** bills *(this evening)*.

GETTING READY

Review the future continuous tense.

1. Write on the board:

Mr. Davis	Spanish
Mrs. Davis	Arabic
Betty and Fred Davis	Russian
Martha Davis	Chinese
Bob Davis	German

2. Set the scene: "Everyone in the Davis family loves languages. This year they'll all be studying new languages. For example, Mr. Davis will be studying Spanish."

3. Have students ask and answer about the others, using the future continuous tense. For example:

   A. What will Mrs. Davis be studying?
   B. She'll be studying Arabic.

   A. What will Bob Davis be studying?
   B. He'll be studying German.

   A. Martha, what will you be studying?
   B. I'll be studying Chinese.

INTRODUCING THE MODELS

There are two model conversations. Introduce and practice each separately. For each model:

1. Have students look at the model illustration in the book.

2. Set the scene:

   1st model: "Two friends are talking."
   2nd model: "Two people are talking about Nancy."

3. Present the model.

4. Full-Class Repetition.

5. Ask students if they have any questions. Check understanding of vocabulary.

Culture Note

Work overtime. Employees often have to work after their scheduled hours in order to finish a project or meet a deadline. This extra work time is called *overtime*. When employees are paid by the hour, they receive a higher rate for their overtime work.

6. Group Choral Repetition.

7. Choral Conversation.

8. Call on one or two pairs of students to present the dialog.

(For additional practice, do Choral Conversation in small groups or by rows.)

SIDE BY SIDE EXERCISES

Examples

> 1. A. Will you be home this evening?
>   B. Yes, I will. I'll be paying bills.
>
> 2. A. Will Angela be home this evening?
>   B. No, she won't. She'll be shopping at the mall.

1. Exercise 1: Call on two students to present the dialog. Then do Choral Repetition and Choral Conversation practice.

2. Exercise 2: Same as above.

3. Exercises 3–9: Either Full–Class Practice or Pair Practice.

New Vocabulary

4. meeting
5. ice skate
6. browse the web
7. do research
8. income tax form
9. work out

Culture Note

Exercise 8: Federal income taxes in the United States are due on April 15th of every year. Many people fill out the forms themselves, while others hire an accountant to fill out these forms for them.

WORKBOOK

Pages 28–29

EXPANSION ACTIVITIES

1. What Will They Be Doing? ★★

a. Have the class listen as you tell about people who are getting new jobs or changing jobs.

b. Then call on several students to tell what the person will be doing in his or her new job. Whenever possible, hold up a visual for the occupation as you talk about it. (You can use *Side by Side* Picture Cards 131–140.) For example:

> Jane will start her new job as an English teacher next week.

Possible responses:

> She'll be going to school every day.
> She'll be teaching English.
> She'll be speaking English to students.

Other possible introductions:

> *(Larry)* just got a new job as a *(truck driver)*. He'll start his new job next month.
> A company just hired *(Marie)* as a *(secretary)*. She'll start work next Monday.
> *(John)* studied *(cooking)* for several years. A very good *(restaurant)* just hired him to be the *(chef)*.
> *(Susan)* is a *(plumber)*. She'll start her first job soon.

2. Writing Predictions: Five Years from Now ★★

a. Write on the board:

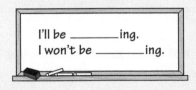

I'll be _____ing.
I won't be _____ing.

(continued)

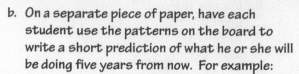

b. On a separate piece of paper, have each student use the patterns on the board to write a short prediction of what he or she will be doing five years from now. For example:

> Five years from now, I'll be living in Mexico City. I won't be studying English anymore. I'll be working for a large import-export company.

c. Collect the papers and read them aloud. Have the class guess which student wrote each prediction.

3. Find the Right Person ★★

a. Collect information about students' plans for a specific time later in the day (for example: *What will you be doing today at six o'clock?*).

b. Put this information in the following form:

> Find someone who . . .
>
> 1. will be doing research. _____
> 2. will be working out. _____
> 3. will be studying English. _____
> 4. will be driving home. _____
> 5. will be eating dinner. _____

c. Have students circulate around the room, asking each other information questions to identify the above people. For example:

> Student A: What will you be doing today at six o'clock?
> Student B: I'll be working out. How about you?

d. The first student to identify all the people wins.

4. Change the Sentence! ★★

a. Write a sentence on the board, underlining and numbering different portions of the sentence. For example:

> | 1 | 2 | 3 | 4 |
> |-------|---------|--------|---------------|
> | I'll be | watching | videos | this evening. |

b. Have students sit in a circle.

c. Tell them that when you say a number, the first student in the circle makes a change in that part of the sentence. For example:

> Teacher: Two.
> Student 1: I'll be <u>buying</u> videos this evening.

d. The second student keeps the first student's sentence, but changes it based on the next number you say. For example:

> Teacher: Three.
> Student 2: I'll be buying <u>ice cream</u> this evening.

e. Continue this way with the rest of the students in the circle. For example:

> Teacher: Four.
> Student 3: I'll be buying ice cream <u>this afternoon</u>.

5. Memory Chain ★★

a. Divide the class into groups of 5 or 6 students each.

b. Tell each student to say what he or she will be doing tonight.

c. One group at a time, have Student 1 begin. For example:

> I'll be watching TV.

d. Student 2 repeats what Student 1 said and adds a statement about himself or herself. For example:

> Jane will be watching TV, and I'll be visiting my aunt in the hospital.

e. Student 3 continues in the same way. For example:

> Jane will be watching TV, Albert will be visiting his aunt in the hospital, and I'll be studying in the library.

f. Continue until everyone has had a chance to play the *memory chain*.

6. Likely or Unlikely? ★★★

a. Write the following on the board:

likely?
unlikely?

b. Make statements such as the following and have students tell you whether the statements are *likely* or *unlikely*:

Fred will be watching TV at home tonight.
Sally will be swimming in her office tomorrow morning.
We'll be browsing the web at the bakery this afternoon.
Mr. and Mrs. Chang will be planting flowers in their yard tomorrow.
I'll be ice skating in my living room tonight.
The president will be meeting several important people tomorrow.
The electrician will be fixing our bathtub tomorrow morning.
I'll be doing research at the library today.
We'll be working at the office all day.
Bob will be working out at the meeting this afternoon.

Variation: Divide the class into pairs or small groups and have students make up statements for others to react to.

Text Page 27: Can You Call Back a Little Later?

FOCUS

- Review: Future Continuous Tense

INTRODUCING THE MODEL

1. Have students look at the model illustration.

2. Set the scene: "Two friends are talking on the telephone."

3. Present the model, using any names, activity, and time expression you wish.

4. Full-Class Repetition.

5. Ask students if they have any questions. Check understanding of new vocabulary: *a little later, call back, Fine., Speak to you soon.*

6. Group Choral Repetition.

7. Choral Conversation.

8. Call on one or two pairs of students to present the dialog.

    (For additional practice, do Choral Conversation in small groups or by rows.)

SIDE BY SIDE EXERCISES

Examples

1. A. Hi, *(Karen)*. This is *(Bill)*. Can you talk for a minute?
   B. I'm sorry. I can't talk right now. I'm doing homework. Can you call back a little later?
   A. Sure. How much longer will you be doing homework?
   B. I'll probably be doing homework for another *(twenty)* minutes.
   A. Fine. I'll call you in *(twenty)* minutes.
   B. Speak to you soon.
   A. Good-bye.

2. A. Hi, *(Tim)*. This is *(Frank)*. Can you talk for a minute?
   B. I'm sorry. I can't talk right now. I'm ironing. Can you call back a little later?
   A. Sure. How much longer will you be ironing?
   B. I'll probably be ironing for another *(thirty)* minutes.
   A. Fine. I'll call you in *(thirty)* minutes.
   B. Speak to you soon.
   A. Good-bye.

1. **Exercise 1:** Call on two students to present the dialog. Then do Choral Repetition and Choral Conversation practice.

2. **Exercise 2:** Same as above.

3. **Exercises 3–5:** Either Full-Class Practice or Pair Practice.

New Vocabulary

5. give the kids a bath

---

4. **Exercise 6:** Have students use the model as a guide to create their own conversations, using vocabulary of their choice. Encourage students to use dictionaries to find new words they want to use. This exercise can be done orally in class or for written homework. If you assign it for homework, do one example in class to make sure students understand what's expected. Have students present their conversations in class the next day.

WORKBOOK

Page 30

EXPANSION ACTIVITIES

1. Disappearing Dialog ★

a. Write the model conversation on the board, using any names, time expression, and activity you wish.

b. Ask for two student volunteers to read the conversation.

c. Erase a few of the words from each line of the dialog. Have two different students read the conversation.

d. Erase more words and call on two more students to read the conversation.

e. Continue erasing words and calling on pairs of students to say the model until all the words have been erased and the dialog has *disappeared*.

2. Students' Plans ★★

a. Write the following on the board:

> What will you be doing next summer?
> What will you be studying next semester?

b. Divide the class into pairs or small groups.

c. Have students answer the questions on the board and then report to the class about each other's plans.

3. Information Gap Role Plays ★★★

a. Divide the class into pairs.

b. Write the following situations on index cards and give one of the situations to each pair. Give Role A to one member of the pair and Role B to the other.

c. Have students practice their role plays and then present them to the class. Compare different students' versions of the same situations.

Role A:

Your car is at the repair shop. Call the mechanic. You want to find out when your car will be ready. You need to have your car right away.

Role B:

You're a mechanic at a repair shop. Someone is going to call you about his or her car. You're still working on it. You found a lot of problems with the car.

Role A:

Call your friend. You really need to talk to her. It's very important. Someone else is going to answer the phone.

Role B:

Someone is calling your daughter, but she's busy now. She's fixing her bicycle. Then she has to study for a test.

Role A:

You're going to be late for work this morning. You have a flat tire, and you're fixing it right now. Call your boss from your cell phone.

Role B:

One of your employees is going to call you. This person is late for work, and you're very upset. This person needs to be at an important meeting.

Role A:

It's late. You made dinner for your wife and children, but your wife isn't home yet. Call her at the office.

Role B:

Your husband is going to call you. It's late, but you're very busy at your office. You still have to do a lot of things.

(continued)

4. Celebrity Travel Plans: Who Am I? ★★★

   a. Divide the class into small groups.

   b. Give each person a card with the name of a famous person. For example:

the president	the prime minister	(famous athlete)

(famous singer)	(famous movie star)

   c. Write the following cues on the board:

   I'll be _____ing.

   leave _____ for _____
   meet with _____
   go to _____
   visit _____
   talk to _____
   have lunch/dinner with _____
   return to _____

   d. Have each group work together, choosing expressions from the board, to write imaginary travel plans for the person on their card.

   e. When the groups have finished, call on one person to read each group's itinerary and have the other students in the class try to guess who the famous person is. For example:

   Tonight I'll be leaving Washington for Miami. Tomorrow morning I'll be meeting with local politicians. In the afternoon, I'll be talking to the mayor about problems of the city. Then I'll be returning to Washington. Who am I?

FOCUS

- Review: Possessive Pronouns
- Review: Should
- Review: Requests with *Could*

GETTING READY

Review possessive pronouns.

1. Write on the board:

Doris   Steve   Susan and Michael

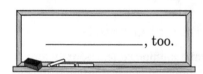

_____, too.

2. Read statements such as those below and point to one of the three illustrations on the board. Have students make a similar statement about the person or people you are pointing to, using the possessive pronoun. For example:

Teacher:	I lost my wallet *(point to Doris)*
Students:	Doris lost hers, too.
Teacher:	I lost my book. *(point to Steve)*
Students:	Steve lost his, too.

Possible statements:

I found my book.
I lost my cat.
I did well on the test.
I like my job.
I like my friends.
I sold my bicycle.
I called my boss.
I want to sell my car.

INTRODUCING THE MODEL

1. Have students look at the model illustration.

2. Set the scene: "Two neighbors are talking. One of them is asking a favor."

3. Present the model.

4. Full-Class Repetition.

5. Ask students if they have any questions. Check understanding of new vocabulary and expressions: *Could you do me a favor? jack, possibly.*

6. Group Choral Repetition.

7. Choral Conversation.

8. Call on one or two pairs of students to present the dialog.

(For additional practice, do Choral Conversation in small groups or by rows.)

SIDE BY SIDE EXERCISES

Examples

1. A. Could you do me a favor?
    B. Sure. What is it?
    A. I have to fix my front steps, and I don't have a hammer. Could I possibly borrow yours?
    B. I'm sorry. I'm afraid I don't have one.
    A. Oh. Do you know anyone who does?
    B. Yes. You should call Janet. I'm sure she'll be happy to lend you hers.
    A. Thanks. I'll call her right away.

2. A. Could you do me a favor?
    B. Sure. What is it?
    A. I have to assemble my new bookshelf, and I don't have a screwdriver. Could I possibly borrow yours?
    B. I'm sorry. I'm afraid I don't have one.
    A. Oh. Do you know anyone who does?
    B. Yes. You should call Bruce. I'm sure he'll be happy to lend you his.
    A. Thanks. I'll call him right away.

1. **Exercise 1:** Call on two students to present the dialog. Then do Choral Repetition and Choral Conversation practice.

2. **Exercise 2:** Introduce the word *screwdriver*. Same as above.

3. **Exercises 3–5:** Either Full-Class Practice or Pair Practice.

> **New Vocabulary**
>
> 3. composition
> 4. adjust

4. **Exercise 6:** Have students use the model as a guide to create their own conversations, using vocabulary of their choice. Encourage students to use dictionaries to find new words they want to use. This exercise can be done orally in class or for written homework. If you assign it for homework, do one example in class to make sure students understand what's expected. Have students present their conversations in class the next day.

WORKBOOK

Pages 31–33

EXPANSION ACTIVITIES

1. Different Emotions ★★

Have students practice reading the model conversation, using any combination of these different emotions:

Speaker A is very worried.
Speaker A isn't worried.
Speaker B wants to help Speaker A.
Speaker B isn't very friendly and doesn't want to help.

2. Match the Conversations ★★

a. Make a set of matching cards. For example:

I have to assemble a desk.	I'll be happy to lend you my hammer and screwdriver.
I have to write a composition.	I'll be happy to lend you my dictionary.
I have to to a fancy party.	I'll be happy to lend you my tuxedo.
I have to adjust my TV antenna.	I'll be happy to lend you my ladder.
I have to change a flat tire.	I'll be happy to lend you my jack.

I have to move to my new apartment.	I'll be happy to lend you my truck.
I have to bake a cake for my friend's party.	I'll be happy to give you my recipe.

b. Distribute a card to each student.

c. Have students memorize the sentences on their cards, and then have students walk around the room saying their sentences until they find their match.

d. Then have pairs of students say their matched sentences aloud to the class.

3. Tic Tac Vocabulary ★★

a. Have students draw a tic tac grid and fill it in with any 9 of the following words:

camcorder	headphones
camera	jack
cell phone	ladder
cookbook	screwdriver
dictionary	tuxedo
fan	

b. Say the beginnings of the following sentences, and tell students to cross out the word that finishes each sentence:

It's very hot in my apartment. Could I possibly borrow your . . . ?

I have to fix my satellite dish. Could I possibly
   borrow your . . . ?
I want to take photographs at our family
   reunion. Could I possibly borrow your . . . ?
My brother is going to a very fancy party.
   Could he possibly borrow your . . . ?
I've got to fix a flat tire on my car. Could I
   possibly borrow your . . . ?
I've got to write a composition for my English
   class. Could I possibly borrow your . . . ?
I'm looking for a good recipe for apple pie.
   Could I possibly borrow your . . . ?
I need to call my mother right away. Could I
   possibly borrow your . . . ?
I want to take videos at my daughter's
   wedding. Could I possibly borrow your . . . ?
I'm trying to assemble a new bookshelf. I have
   a hammer. Could I possibly borrow your . . . ?
I want to listen to some music on my CD
   player. Could I possibly borrow your . . . ?

c. The first student to cross out three words in
   a straight line—either horizontally, vertically,
   or diagonally—wins the game.

d. Have the winner call out the words to check
   for accuracy.

4. Information Gap Role Play: Could I Ask You a Favor? ★★★

a. Divide the class into pairs.

b. Write the following situations on index cards
   and give one situation to each pair. Give Role
   A to one member of the pair and Role B to the
   other.

c. Have students practice their role plays and
   then present them to the class. Compare
   different students' versions of the same
   situations.

Role A:

Your car is broken, and you need a ride to
work today. Ask your friend.

Role B:

You aren't going to work today because you
have a bad cold.

Role A:

Your car has a flat tire, and you can't find
your jack. Ask your friend.

Role B:

Your sister borrowed your jack last week, and
she forgot to return it.

Role A:

You're baking a cake, and you just realized you
don't have any more flour! Your next-door
neighbor is walking out of the building. Maybe
your neighbor is going to the supermarket.

Role B:

You're walking out of your apartment
building. First, you're going to the bank. Then
you're going to the post office. After that,
you're going to the drug store. And finally,
you're going to the supermarket.

---

5. Category Dictation: Lending Practices ★★★

a. Have students draw two columns on a piece
   of paper. At the top of one column, have
   students write I'll be happy to lend you my . . .
   At the top of the other column, have them
   write I don't really like to lend my . . . .

b. Dictate items to the class. Tell the class to
   imagine lending each item to a close friend,
   and have students choose the appropriate
   column. For example:

I'll be happy to lend you my . . .	I don't really like to lend my . . .
bicycle	car
pen	cell phone
calculator	laptop computer

(continued)

c. Have students compare their lists in small groups. Ask the class:

> What items are easy to lend?
> What items are difficult to lend?
> Why don't you like to lend these items to a friend?
> What do you do when a friend forgets to return an item?

6. Class Discussion ★★★

a. Write the following questions on the board or on a handout for students:

> Do your friends or neighbors ever ask you to do a favor for them?
> How do you feel when someone asks you to do a favor?
> What was the biggest favor someone asked you to do? Tell about it.

b. Divide the class into small groups and have students discuss doing favors. Then call on students to tell about their discussions.

How to Say It!

Asking for a Favor: There are many ways to request a favor. "Could you do me a favor?" "Could you possibly do me a favor?" "Could you do a favor for me?" "Could I ask you a favor?" are four common ways. The word *possibly* makes the request less direct and therefore more polite.

1. Set the scene: "The neighbors from text page 28 are talking."

2. Present the expressions.

3. Full-Class Repetition.

4. Ask students if they have any questions.

5. Group Choral Repetition.

6. Have student practice the conversations in this lesson again, asking for favors with any of these four expressions.

7. Call on pairs to present their conversations to the class.

READING *Saying Good-bye*

FOCUS

- Future Tense: Will
- Future Continuous Tense

NEW VOCABULARY

as you can imagine	lonely
Canada	perhaps
come back	permanently
emotional	say good-bye
excited	stay with
have a good life	Toronto

READING THE STORY

Optional: Preview the story by having students talk about the story title and/or illustrations. You may choose to introduce new vocabulary beforehand, or have students encounter the new vocabulary within the context of the reading.

1. Have students read silently or follow along silently as the story is read aloud by you, by one or more students, or on the audio program.

2. Ask students if they have any questions. Check understanding of vocabulary.

3. Check students' comprehension, using some or all of the following questions:

> Where are Mr. and Mrs. Karpov?
> What are they doing?
> What will Sasha and his family do in a few minutes?
> Why won't Mr. and Mrs. Karpov be seeing them for a long time?
> Where are Sasha and his family going to live?

> Who are they going to stay with?
> What will Sasha do?
> What will his wife, Marina, do?
> What will their children do?
> Why are Mr. and Mrs. Karpov happy?
> Why are Mr. and Mrs. Karpov sad?
> Why are they going to be lonely?
> What will Mr. and Mrs. Karpov do some day?

✓ READING *CHECK-UP*

TRUE OR FALSE?

1. False
2. True
3. False
4. True
5. False

READING EXTENSION

Class Discussion

1. Have students work in pairs to write several sentences in which they give advice to Sasha and Marina as they begin their new life in Canada. For example:

> They should try to learn English as quickly as possible.
> They should try to learn about their children's school.
> They should find a good doctor right away.

2. Have students share their sentences with the class and explain the rationale for their answers.

How About You?

Have students answer the questions in pairs or as a class. If you do it as pair practice, call on students to report to the class about their conversation partner.

ON YOUR OWN *Looking Forward*

FOCUS

> • Review: Going to

For each situation:

1. Have students look at the illustrations and cover the text as you read or play the audio.

2. Then have students look at the text and follow along as you read or play the audio again.

3. Ask students if they have any questions. Check understanding of new vocabulary: *have a party for, look forward to, relax, retirement, summer vacation.*

4. Ask questions about the situations and/or have students ask each other questions. For example:

> What's Jerry looking forward to?
> Is he going to think about work this
>   weekend?
> What's he going to do?

> What's Amanda looking forward to?
> Why?
> Who's going to be at the party?

> What are Mr. and Mrs. Cook looking forward
>   to?
> Where are they going to go?
> What are they going to do there?

> What are Mr. and Mrs. Lee looking forward
>   to?
> Why?

5. Have students talk about what *they* are looking forward to.

   a. Check understanding of the expression *day off*.

   b. Divide the class into pairs. Have each student find out something the other is looking forward to and then report back to the class. For example:

   > Barbara is looking forward to this weekend because she's going to go to her sister's wedding. She's looking forward to it because everybody in her family is going to be there.

   > Richard is looking forward to his winter vacation because he's going to go skiing during the day and sit in front of a warm fireplace every evening.

 JOURNAL

Have students write their journal entries at home or in class. Encourage students to use a dictionary to look up words they would like to use. Students can share their written work with other students if appropriate. Have students discuss what they have written as a class, in pairs, or in small groups.

PRONUNCIATION

> ***Going to:*** In daily English usage, the pronunciation of the verb phrase *going to* is reduced to *gonna*.

Focus on Listening

Practice the sentences in the left column. Say each sentence or play the audio one or more times. Have students listen carefully and repeat.

Focus on Pronunciation

Practice the sentences in the right column. Have students say each sentence and then listen carefully as you say it or play the audio.

If you wish, have students continue practicing the sentences to improve their pronunciation.

WORKBOOK

Check-Up Test: Pages 34–35

 GRAMMAR FOCUS

Answers

1. are, going to, I'm going to
2. Will, she will, She'll be
3. mine, he'll, his
4. going to, we'll, go
5. Will, it won't, It won't arrive
6. Will, they will, They'll be

MULTILEVEL VARIATION ★★★

Challenge *above-level* students to cover the grammar boxes as they complete the grammar exercises.

Text Page 32a
LIFE SKILLS

• Calling in sick at work
• Writing a note to the teacher
• Calling school to report a child's absence

① CONVERSATION
Calling in Sick at Work

1. Have students look at the photos. Ask: "What's the matter with these people?" (1— He has a stomachache. 2—He hurt his back. 3—She has a fever.) For Conversation 4, brainstorm other health problems that may keep an employee away from work and write students' ideas on the board.

2. Model the conversation with a student volunteer. For example:

   A. Hello. This is Lisa Carter.
      I won't be able to come to work today.
      I have a sore throat.
   B. I'm sorry to hear that.
   A. If I feel better tomorrow, I'll come to work.
   B. Okay. Thank you for calling.

3. In pairs, have students practice the conversations as you circulate around the classroom.

4. Call on pairs of students to present their version of Conversation 4 to the class.

② CONVERSATION *Calling School to Report a Child's Absence*

1. Have students look at the photos. Ask: "What's the matter with these people?" (1—He has a cold. 2—She has a toothache. 3—She has a rash.) For Conversation 4, brainstorm other health problems that may keep a child away from school and write students' ideas on the board. Introduce the new vocabulary: *absence, rash, school attendance line,* and *tone.*

2. Model the conversation with a student volunteer, using your own information and the information from Exercise 1. For example:

   A. This is the school attendance line. After the tone, please give your name, your child's name, and the reason for our child's absence. Thank you.

   B. Hello. This is Wilma Gomes. My son Victor won't be in school today. He has a bad cold. Thank you.

3. In pairs, have students practice the conversations as you circulate around the classroom, helping students as necessary.

4. Call on students to present their conversations to the class.

③ CLOZE READING & WRITING
A Note to the Teacher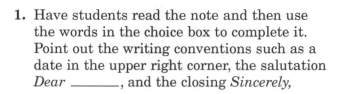

1. Have students read the note and then use the words in the choice box to complete it. Point out the writing conventions such as a date in the upper right corner, the salutation *Dear* _____, and the closing *Sincerely,* _____.

2. Have students compare answers in pairs.

3. For homework, have students write a note to the teacher and submit it to you for your review.

Answers

1. will
2. She'll
3. won't
4. She's
5. going to

EXPANSION ACTIVITIES

1. Scrambled Sentences ★

Activity Master 16

Divide the class into pairs. Make enough copies of Activity Master 16 for half the class. Cut them into cards and distribute one set to each pair of students. Have students take turns picking up a scrambled sentence prompt and then saying the sentence in the correct order.

Variation: Students can write their sentences and then compare their answers with other pairs.

2. Role Play ★★

Activity Master 17

a. Make multiple copies of Activity Master 17. Cut the role-play cards into A cards and B cards and clip each role play (1, 2, or 3) together.

b. Divide the class into pairs. Give each partner one set of role-play cards—A or B. Tell students they have five minutes to act out the role play.

c. As students are acting out the role play, circulate to help as necessary.

d. After five minutes, call on a few pairs to perform their role plays for the class.

MULTILEVEL VARIATIONS ★/★★/★★★

Allow *below-level* students to look at each other's cards. If *at-level* or *above-level* students finish their role plays quickly, give them another set of role-play cards.

3. Survey ★★★

Activity Master 18

a. Make copies of Activity Master 18 and give one to each student.

b. Have students interview others in the class by asking: "Why do you miss class? What's the usual reason for your absence?"

c. The interviewer should write the person's name next to the appropriate response.

d. When students have completed their surveys, have them add up the number of people for each response. Talk as a class about the results. Follow-up with the question: What can you do to come to class more often?

Option: Have students create a bar graph illustrating their survey findings.

4. Dictate and Discuss ★★★

Divide the class into pairs or small groups. Dictate sentences such as the following and have students discuss whether they agree or disagree with the statements.

A child with a sore throat shouldn't go to school.
A person with a fever shouldn't go to work.
Too many people call in sick when they aren't sick.
All people should be paid for sick days.
There should be a limit to how many times a person can call in sick.

1. Have students look at the letterhead and signature. Ask: "Who wrote this letter?" (The Principal of Jefferson High School.) Introduce the new vocabulary: *absent, activity, after-school* (adj), *art, compulsory, contain, dental appointment, four times a year, freshman, get into trouble, honor roll, illness, include, independently, junior, latch-key children, learning, manage, medical appointment, meeting, open house, opportunity, parent-teacher association, part, participate, photography, report card, satisfactory, school event, school year, senior, sophomore, unsatisfactory,* and *volunteer* (v).

2. Have students do all the comprehension exercises individually and then compare their answers in pairs.

Answers

1.	B	4.	D
2.	D	5.	A
3.	C	6.	B

EXPANSION ACTIVITIES

1. **Guess the Word!** ★

   a. Divide the class into two teams. Choose a vocabulary word or phrase from the reading, and on the board, write a blank for each letter in the word. For example: [*report card*]

   b. Give students a clue about the word. For example: "a list of a students' grades."

   c. The team that guesses the word gets a point. The team with the most points wins the guessing game.

2. **Schools in the United States** ★

   Activity Master 19

   Make multiple copies of Activity Master 19 and give one to each student. Have students read the letter again on student text page 32b and complete the activity master. Then have students compare answers in small groups.

   Variation: ★/★★ Have pairs of students take turns reading the lines of Activity Master 19 aloud and checking each other's comprehension of the letter.

   Variation: ★★★ Have students draw two columns on a separate piece of paper and write <u>True</u> above one column and <u>False</u> above the other. Dictate lines from Activity Master 19 and have students write the lines in the correct column. For example:

<u>True</u>	<u>False</u>
There are four years in high school.	C and D are excellent grades.

3. **Match Game** ★★

   Activity Master 20

   a. Make a copy of Activity Master 20 and cut it into cards. Distribute the cards randomly, one to each student.

Note: The large cards are sentence beginnings and the small cards are sentence endings.

b. Have students memorize the phrase on their cards. Then have students circulate around the room saying their lines until they find their match to make a logical and complete sentence. Make sure students don't show their cards to their classmates since this is a listening and speaking exercise.

c. When students have found their match, have them compare their cards and then come show you.

d. Continue until students have found all the matches.

MULTILEVEL VARIATION ★

Below-level students can look at each other's cards as they do the activity.

4. True or False? ★★

Make statements using new vocabulary from the reading and have students decide whether the statements are true or false. If a statement is false, have students correct it. For example:

High school is four years long. [True.]
The final year of high school is called the junior year. [False. It's called the senior year.]
An A is a very good grade. [True.]
All children must attend school from ages 5 to 15. [False. From ages 6 to 16.]

Variation: Do the activity as a game with competing teams.

5. Concentration: Sentence Completion ★★★

Activity Master 20

a. Divide the class into pairs. Make multiple copies of Activity Master 20, cut them into cards, and distribute one set to each pair.

   Note: The large cards are sentence beginnings and the small cards are sentence endings.

b. Have students shuffle the cards and place the large cards in two rows and the small cards in two rows face down.

c. The object of the game is for students to match sentence beginnings and endings. Both students should be able to see the cards, since *concentrating* on their location is an important part of playing the game.

d. Student A turns over a large card and a small card, and if they match the student keeps the cards. If the cards don't match, the student turns them face down and Student B takes a turn.

The game continues until all the sentences have been completed. The student with the most correct matches wins the game.

MULTILEVEL VARIATION ★

Below-level students can read through the sentence beginnings and endings all at once and then match the cards face up.

6. How Much Do You Remember? ★★★

Write the following topics on the board:

> Absences
> Report Cards
> Parent-Teacher Communication
> After-School Programs
> Homework

Divide the class into pairs. Have students close their books and retell to each other what they remember about the topics from the letter on student text page 32b. Then have them open their books and check to see how much they remembered.

7. Dictate and Discuss ★★★

Divide the class into pairs or small groups. Dictate sentences such as the following and have students discuss whether they agree or disagree with the statements.

Too many students get A's.
School should be compulsory until age eighteen.
Students today get too much homework.
After-school programs are good for kids.
Parents should meet their children's teachers.

CLARKSDALE COMMUNITY COLLEGE

1. Have students look at the campus map. Introduce the new vocabulary word *campus*. Ask questions such as the following to get students oriented to the map: What street names do you see? How many buildings are there on the map? What is Building 3? What is Building 7? What number is the Epinosa Theater? What number is Rossi Hall?

2. Introduce the new vocabulary: *administration building, art museum, child-care center, music building, safety, science center, security, student center,* and *vocational center.* Have students brainstorm what is in each building. For example:

   Security/Safety: campus police office, parking permits
   Administration Building: offices, report cards
   Music Building: music rooms, classrooms
   Student Center: student clubs, cafeteria, bookstore

3. Have students work individually to complete the comprehension exercise and then compare answers in pairs, small groups, or as a class.

Answers

1.	B	**5.**	D
2.	C	**6.**	C
3.	D	**7.**	A
4.	B	**8.**	C

LIFE SKILLS ENRICHMENT

Reading a Campus Map

Life Skills Worksheet 10

Make copies of Life Skills Worksheet 10 and give one to each student. Have students complete the worksheet as homework. In the next class, have students compare their answers in pairs.

EXPANSION ACTIVITIES

1. Do You Remember? ★

   a. Tell students to spend two minutes looking carefully at the campus map of Clarksdale Community College on student text page 32c.

   b. Have students close their books and write down all the places they can remember from the campus map. For example:

      Vocational Center
      Library
      Administration Building
      Music Building

   c. Have students compare their lists with a partner and then look at the map again to see how well they remembered the school buildings.

   MULTILEVEL VARIATION ★★★

   Have *above-level* students work together to see if they can remember the names of specific places. For example: Burton Library, Danson Art Center, Tamworth Vocational Center.

2. Association Game ★

   a. Write common campus buildings on the board. For example:

      Student Center
      Library
      Science Center
      Administration Building
      Gym
      Theater

   b. Divide the class into pairs or small groups. Have students work together to see how many activities they can associate with each campus building. For example:

      Student Center: [eat lunch/go to a student club/meet a friend/go to the bookstore]

Library: [study/borrow a book/read a magazine]

Science Center: [go to science class/meet a professor/work in the science lab]

c. Set a time limit for the game. When the time limit is up, call on the teams to read their list of associations to the class. The team with the most correct items wins.

3. True or False? ★★

Make statements about the map on student text page 32c and have students decide whether the statements are true or false. If a statement is false, have students correct it. For example:

The Science Center and the Library are on the same block. [False. They're on different blocks.]

The Theater and the Art Museum are both on Pine Street. [True.]

The Student Center and the Science Center are on different blocks. [True.]

The Student Center is next to the parking lot. [False. They're on different streets.]

Variation: Do the activity as a game with competing teams.

4. The "Write" Location ★★

a. Divide the class into pairs. Have each pair choose one building from the campus map on student text page 32c and write two sentences describing the location of the building. For example:

It's on Warren Street.
It's between the Child-Care Center and the Student Center.

b. Have the pairs read their sentences to the class and see if students can guess which building is being described. [Building 9, Carter Hall]

5. Location! Location! ★★

a. Divide the class into two teams.

b. Describe the location of a building on the campus map on student text page 32c and

have individual students in each team take turns identifying the building. For example:

Teacher: It's on Russell Avenue. It's next to the Student Center.
Team A Student: Rossi Hall.

c. A team gets one point for every correct answer. The team with the most points wins.

6. Make a Neighborhood Map ★★★

a. Have students work in pairs to draw a map of your school's street or neighborhood. Have them number and then label the buildings and businesses. (Encourage students to leave the classroom and explore the immediate neighborhood for fifteen minutes so they can draw an accurate map.)

b. Have students share their maps in groups.

Text Page 32d
ASSESSMENT
• **Check-up test**
• **Self-evaluation checklists**

CHECK-UP TEST

Have students do the check-up test and then review the answers as a class.

Answers

1.	A	**6.**	D
2.	C	**7.**	B
3.	D	**8.**	A
4.	B	**9.**	D
5.	C	**10.**	C

SKILLS CHECK

Words:

Explain to students that this is a list of verbs they have learned in the unit. Have students take turns reading each item aloud to the class. Have students put a check next to the item if they feel they have learned it. Encourage students to get a small notebook where they can write down verbs that are difficult for them.

I can:

Explain to students that this is a list of skills they have learned in the unit. Read each item aloud to the class. Ask individual students or pairs of students to demonstrate the skill. For example:

Teacher: I can ask and answer: What are you going to do?
Student A: What are you going to do tonight?
Student B: I'm going to pay bills.

Teacher: I can call in sick at work.
Student A: Hello. This is Lisa Carter. I won't be able to come to work today. I have a bad toothache.
Student B: I'm sorry to hear that.
Student A: If I feel better tomorrow, I'll come to work.
Student B: Okay. Thank you for calling.

Have students put a check next to the item if they feel they have learned it. Use this information to determine which lessons you may want to review or reinforce for the entire class or for particular students.

EXPANSION ACTIVITIES

1. Category Dictation ★

a. Have students make four columns on a piece of paper and write the following at the top of each column:

This
Yesterday
Last
Tomorrow

b. Dictate time words from the unit and have students write them in the appropriate columns. For example:

This	Yesterday	Last	Tomorrow
morning	morning	night	morning
afternoon	afternoon	March	afternoon
evening	evening	year	evening
March		Sunday	night
year			
Sunday			

c. As a class, in pairs, or in small groups, have students check their work.

2. Board Game ★★

Activity Master 21

For this activity, you will need a die, markers, and a piece of paper. (If students use a coin as a die, the class should decide which side of the coin will indicate a move of one space and which will indicate a move of two spaces.)

a. Make multiple copies of Activity Master 21. Divide the class into small groups and give each group a copy of Activity Master 21 along with a die, markers, and a piece of paper.

b. Have students place their markers on *Start*. The group should decide who goes first. That student begins the game by rolling the die or flipping the coin and moving his or her marker. If the student responds to the question or task correctly, he or she may take one more turn. If the student doesn't respond correctly, the next student takes a turn. No one may take more than two turns at a time.

Option 1: The first person to reach *Finish* is the winner.

Option 2: The game continues until each student reaches *Finish.* This way everybody is a winner.

3. Question the Answers! ★★

a. Dictate answers such as the following to the class:

No I'm not. I played basketball last night.
No, she isn't. She had ice cream for dessert yesterday.
No, we aren't. We went to Florida for vacation last year.
Yes, he will. He'll return in a little while.
No, they won't. They won't see each other for months.
I'm sorry. I can't right now.
I'm sorry. I'm afraid I don't have one.
No, I won't. I'll be working overtime.
No, we won't. We'll be watching TV at home.

b. Divide the class into groups of four. Have them write questions for which these answers are correct. For example:

Answer: No, I'm not. I played basketball last night.
Question: Are you going to play basketball tonight?

Answer: No, she isn't. She had ice cream for dessert yesterday.
Question: Is she going to have ice cream for dessert today?

c. Have students share some of their questions and answers with the class.

4. Dialog Builder! ★★★

a. Divide the class into pairs. Write a line on the board from a conversation such as the following:

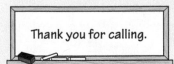

Thank you for calling.

Other possible lines are:

Could you do me a favor?
Could I possibly borrow your _____?
I'm afraid I don't have one.
I can't talk right now.

Speak to you soon.
I'm sorry to hear that.

b. Have each pair create a conversation incorporating that line. Students can begin and end their conversations any way they wish, but they must include that line in their dialogs.

c. Call on students to present their conversations to the class.

5. Scrambled Phrase Game ★★★

Activity Master 22 (two pages)

a. Divide the class into groups of four. Make a copy of Activity Master 22 for each group. Cut the Activity Masters into two sets of cards, shuffle the cards, and place them face down in two piles—one for verbs and the other for object phrases.

Note: The small cards are verbs and the large cards are object phrases.

b. Have students take turns picking up one card from each pile and reading the phrase to the group. For example:

| stay with | the kitchen |

The group decides if the phrase *makes sense* or *doesn't make sense.*

c. After all the cards have been chosen, have the group lay out all the cards and put together all the phrase combinations that make sense.

Multilevel Variation ★

Below-level students can read through the verbs and object phrases all at once and then match the cards face up.

6. Time Capsule! ★★★

Activity Master 23

a. Make multiple copies of Activity Master 23 and give one to each student.

b. Have students write their predictions as homework.

(continued)

c. After you have reviewed their writing, have students seal their predictions in an envelope and write on the front "Time Capsule: Open five years from (today's date)."

7. What's Wrong? ★★★

a. Write several sentences such as the following on the board or on a handout that you give to students. Some of the sentences should be correct and others incorrect. For example:

> What will he going to do?
> What will they doing tonight?
> She's going to read a magazine.
> That book is their.
> Those tools are his.
> They're be working tomorrow night.
> Were going to go hiking.
> That's our car. That's ours.
> I'll be home. I'll be fix the TV.
> Could you give me a favor?
> I'm sure he'll be happy to borrow you his.
> They're be seeing each other soon.
> What's he will wear?
> This is my ladder. this is my.
> Theirs going to be a retirement party
>   for Mrs. Lee.

b. Divide the class into pairs. The object of the activity is for students to identify which sentences are incorrect and then correct them. Have students compare their answers in small groups.

Variation: Do the activity as a game with competing teams. For each team's turn, write one sentence on the board and have the team decide whether the sentence is correct or not. If it isn't correct, the team must correct it. Every time a team is right, that team receives one point. The team with the greatest number of points wins.

MULTILEVEL VARIATION ★

For *below-level* students, underline the errors and have the below-level pairs focus only on correcting them.

Text Pages 33–36: *Side by Side* Gazette

 FEATURE ARTICLE
Immigration Around the World

PREVIEWING THE ARTICLE

1. Have students talk about the title of the article and the accompanying photograph.

2. You may choose to introduce the following new vocabulary beforehand, or have students encounter it within the context of the article:

> earthquake
> economic
> flood
> flow (n)
> for example
> foreign
> foreign born
> historic
> immigrant
> immigration
> living conditions
> marry
> native
> natural disaster
> political
> public school
> reason
> republic
> total
> war

> *Places Around the World*
>
> Africa
> Albania
> Asia
> Bulgaria
> Eastern Europe
> former Soviet republics
> Latin America
> Middle East
> Moldova
> North Africa
> Saudi Arabia
> Ukraine
> Western Europe

READING THE ARTICLE

1. Have students read silently, or follow along silently as the article is read aloud by you, by one or more students, or on the audio program.

2. Ask students if they have any questions and check understanding of new vocabulary. Show the class a world map and have students identify the locations of all the place names mentioned in the article.

3. Check students' comprehension by asking the following questions:

> Why do people move to other countries?
> What are examples of natural disasters?
> Name three different flows of immigrants.
> Where do immigrants often live in their new countries?
> What changes do immigrants bring to their new neighborhoods?
> In the Los Angeles public schools, how many different languages do children speak?
> How many people in New York are foreign born?

EXPANSION ACTIVITIES

1. World Map ★★

Cut out seven large arrows that can be taped to a large world map. Have students tape the arrows on the world map to indicate the flows of immigrants according to the feature article.

2. Class Discussion ★★★

a. In small groups, have students discuss the following questions:

> Are there immigrants in your city, your town, or your neighborhood?
> Where do these immigrants come from?
> Why did they come to your country?
> What changes have they brought to your community?

b. Have the groups report back to the class.

2nd ARTICLE
Ellis Island

PREVIEWING THE ARTICLE

1. Have students talk about the title of the article and the accompanying photograph.

2. You may choose to introduce the following new vocabulary beforehand, or have students encounter it within the context of the article:

> check
> come through
> document
> former
> harbor
> immigration official
> island
> medical examination
> official
> pass through
> reception hall

> *Places Around the World*
>
> Austria
> Austria-Hungary
> England
> Germany
> Hungary
> Ireland
> Italy
> Russia

READING THE ARTICLE

1. Have students read silently, or follow along silently as the article is read aloud by you, by one or more students, or on the audio program.

2. Ask students if they have any questions and check understanding of new vocabulary. Show the class a world map and have students identify the locations of all the place names.

3. Check students' comprehension by having them decide if the following statements are true or false:

Ellis Island was an immigration center in the United States. *(True)*
Ellis Island was an immigration center for 75 years. *(False)*
At Ellis Island, officials checked immigrants' health and their documents. *(True)*
Some immigrants couldn't stay in the United States. *(True)*
Most immigrants who came through Ellis Island were from the Soviet Republics. *(False)*
Forty percent of the present U.S. population came through Ellis Island. *(False)*

EXPANSION ACTIVITY

Class Discussion ★★★

1. In small groups, have students discuss the following questions:

   How do you think immigrants traveled to Ellis Island?
   What do you think they brought with them?
   How do you think they felt when immigration officials checked their documents and gave them medical exams?
   Which immigrants probably had to return to their countries?

2. Have the groups report back to the class.

FACT FILE *Countries with Large Number of Immigrants*

1. Before reading the Fact File, show the class a world map. Have students identify the locations of the following place names:

> Australia
> Canada
> France
> Germany
> Saudi Arabia
> the United States

2. Have students rank the countries according to which they believe would have the largest immigrant populations. Write students' ideas on the board. Then have students read the table on text page 33 to check their predictions.

3. Read the table aloud as the class follows along. Ask students: "Is this list different from your list? How is your list different?"

4. For a comprehension activity, have students read the Feature Article again and identify where the immigrants in the listed countries probably came from. For example:

> United States: *Latin America and Asia*
> Germany: *Eastern Europe, the former Soviet republics, and North Africa*
> France: *Eastern Europe, the former Soviet republics, and North Africa*
> Saudi Arabia: *Africa and Asia*

AROUND THE WORLD
Immigrant Neighborhoods

1. Have students read silently or follow along silently as the text is read aloud by you, by one or more students, or on the audio program.

2. Bring a world map to class and point out the locations of the places depicted in the photographs. Introduce the words *Chinatown, Cuban, Sydney, Turkish*.

3. Have students first work in pairs or small groups, responding to the question. Then have students tell the class what they talked about. Write any new vocabulary on the board.

EXPANSION ACTIVITY

Investigating Interesting Immigrant Neighborhoods ★★★

1. Brainstorm with the class interesting immigrant neighborhoods in your area.

2. Have students think of information they would like to learn about each neighborhood. For example:

> What are the directions to the neighborhood?
> What are some interesting things to do there?
> Is there a special festival that is interesting to visit?
> What are the best restaurants?

3. Have each student chose a neighborhood to investigate. Have students begin their investigations by circulating around the room to see if other classmates know the answers to the questions. Students may also want to interview people outside the classroom. Students can also visit the neighborhood to get the information firsthand.

4. For homework, have students write up the information they learned and present it in class.

Option: The class can publish their information as a *Neighborhood Guide to Our City.*

INTERVIEW

1. Have students read silently, or follow along silently as the interview is read aloud by you, by one or more students, or on the audio program.

2. Ask students if they have any questions. Check understanding of the words *immigrate, Melbourne, opportunity, recently,* and the expression *seven days a week.*

3. Check students' comprehension by having them decide if the following statements are true or false:

> Mr. Nguyen came from Vietnam with his brother. *(False)*
> Mr. Nguyen never takes a day off from work. *(True)*
> Mr. Nguyen wants his children to work in the restaurant when they grow up. *(False)*
> Mr. Nguyen likes to teach mathematics. *(True)*
> Mr. Nguyen works in the restaurant so he can send his children to college. *(True)*
> Mr. Nguyen likes the way Australians spend their time. *(False)*
> Mr. Nguyen likes the opportunities in Australia. *(True)*

EXPANSION ACTIVITIES

1. Before and After Immigrating ★★

a. Write the following on the board:

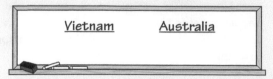

Vietnam   Australia

b. Have students read the article again and compare Mr. Nguyen's life in Vietnam to his life in Australia by completing the chart. For example:

Vietnam
He lived with his wife and children.
He was a mathematics teacher.
People took care of each other.
There wasn't a very good future.

Australia
He lives with his wife and children.
He works in a restaurant.
People don't have much time to be with
    friends.
There are many opportunities.

c. Have students share their ideas.

d. Discuss with the class:

How did Tran Nguyen's life change when he
    moved to Australia?
Is he happy he moved?
What is the most important opportunity for
    Tran Nguyen and his family in Australia?

2. Student Interviews ★★★

a. If possible, have students ask the same interview questions of an immigrant they know.

b. Have students report their findings to the class.

 WE'VE GOT MAIL!

THE LETTER TO *SIDE BY SIDE*

1. Have students read silently, or follow along silently as the letter is read aloud by you, by one or more students, or on the audio program.

2. Ask students if they have any questions. Check understanding of the words *future tense, present tense, sincerely, tense (adj), tense (n), TV program.*

3. Check students' comprehension by having them decide whether these statements are true or false:

The writer is confused about why English
    speakers use the present tense to talk
    about the past. (*False*)
"I'm flying to London" is in the present
    continuous tense. (*True*)
"My plane leaves at 9:30" is in the simple
    future tense. (*False*)
The writer thinks it isn't correct to say "I'm
    flying to London tomorrow" because it's in
    the present tense, and tomorrow is in the
    future. (*True*)

4. Ask students:

Did you ever have this question?
Can you think of another example in
    English where someone uses the present
    tense to talk about the future?

THE RESPONSE FROM *SIDE BY SIDE*

1. Have students read silently, or follow along silently as the letter is read aloud by you, by one or more students, or on the audio program.

2. Ask students if they have any questions. Check understanding of the words *definite, event, regular, schedule.*

3. Check students' comprehension by having them decide whether these statements are true or false:

The man made a mistake when he said "I'm
    flying to London tomorrow." (*False*)
People use the present continuous tense to

talk about definite plans in the future. *(True)*

People use the simple present tense to talk about special schedules and unusual events. *(False)*

"My planes leaves at 9:30" means the same as "My plane will leave at 9:30." *(True)*

4. Ask students:

Can you use the present tense for the future in your language?

GLOBAL EXCHANGE

1. Set the scene: "Two keypals are writing to each other."

2. Have students read silently or follow along silently as the messages are read aloud by you, by one or more students, or on the audio program.

3. Ask students if they have any questions. Check understanding of the following new words and expressions: *after midnight, campfire, computer lab, family reunion, final exam, lake, turn off.*

4. Options for additional practice:

• Have students write about their activities last weekend and their plans for next weekend and share their writing in pairs.

• Have students correspond with a keypal on the Internet and then share their experience with the class.

LISTENING *You Have Five Messages!*

Set the scene: "Dave invited his friends to a party. These are phone messages that his friends left for him."

LISTENING SCRIPT

Listen to the messages on Dave's machine. Match the messages

You have five messages.

Message Number One: "Hi, Dave. It's Sarah.

Thanks for the invitation, but I can't come to your party tomorrow. I'll be taking my uncle to the hospital. Maybe next time." *[beep]*

Message Number Two: "Hello, Dave. It's Bob. I'm sorry that my wife and I won't be able to come to your party tomorrow. We'll be attending a wedding out of town. I hope it's a great party. Have fun!" *[beep]*

Message Number Three: "Dave? It's Paula. How's it going? I got your message about the party tomorrow. Unfortunately, I won't be able to go. I'll be studying all weekend. Talk to you soon." *[beep]*

Message Number Four: "Hi, Dave. It's Joe. Thanks for the invitation to your party. I'll be visiting my parents in New York City, so I'm afraid I won't be around. I'll call you when I get back." *[beep]*

Message Number Five: "Hello, Dave? It's Carla. Thanks for the invitation to your party. I don't have anything to do tomorrow night, so I'll definitely be there. I'm really looking forward to it. See you tomorrow. " *[beep]*

Answers

1. e

2. c

3. b

4. a

5. d

FUN WITH IDIOMS

a piece of cake
give someone a ring
no picnic
raining cats and dogs
tied up
What's cooking?

INTRODUCTION AND PRACTICE

For each idiom, do the following:

1. Have students look at the illustration.

2. Present the idiom. Say the expression and have the class repeat it chorally and individually. Check students' pronunciation of the words.

DO YOU KNOW THESE EXPRESSIONS?

Have students match the expressions with their meanings.

Answers

1. e

2. d

3. f

4. a

5. c

6. b

EXPANSION ACTIVITIES

1. Line Prompts ★★

Call out one of the following line prompts and have students respond appropriately with one of the idioms:

You look terrible. How was your English test?
(It was no picnic!)

You look very happy. How was your English test?
(It was a piece of cake!)

Do you have a minute to talk?
(I'm tied up right now.)

Let's talk soon.
(I'll give you a ring tomorrow.)

How's the weather?
(It's raining cats and dogs!)

Hi!
(What's cooking?)

2. Idiom Challenge! ★★★

a. Divide the class into pairs.

b. Have each pair create a conversation in which they use as many of the idioms from text page 36 as they can.

c. Have the pairs present their conversations to the class. Which pair used the most idioms?

 WHAT ARE THEY SAYING?

FOCUS

- Saying Good-bye, Giving Personal Information

Have students talk about the characters and the situations, and then create role plays based on the scenes. Students may refer back to previous lessons as a resource, but they should not simply reuse specific conversations.

Note: You may want to assign this exercise as written homework, having students prepare their role plays, practice them the next day with other students, and then present them to the class.

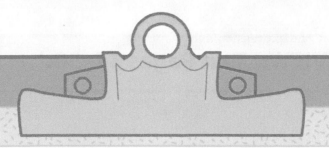

Teacher's Notes

GRAMMAR

PRESENT PERFECT TENSE

(I have) (We have) (You have) (They have)	I've We've You've They've	
(He has) (She has) (It has)	He's She's It's	eaten.

	I We You They	haven't	
	He She It	hasn't	eaten.

Have	I we you they	
Has	he she it	eaten?

Yes,	I we you they	have.
	he she it	has.

No,	I we you they	haven't.
	he she it	hasn't.

FUNCTIONS

ASKING FOR AND REPORTING INFORMATION

Why isn't *Charlie going to go bowling tonight*?
  He's already *gone bowling this week.*
Really? When?
  He went bowling yesterday.

I've *driven trucks* for many years.

I've never *eaten lunch with the boss.*

I haven't *swum* in a long time.
  Why not?
I haven't had the time.

Have you ever *seen a rainbow*?
  Yes, I have. *I saw a rainbow last year.*

Have you *written the report* yet?
  Yes, I have. *I wrote it a little while ago.*
Has *David gone to the bank* yet?
  Yes, *he* has. *He went to the bank a little while ago.*

Has *Timmy gone to bed* yet?
  No, *he* hasn't.

I still haven't *typed two important letters.*

Have you *seen any good movies* recently?
  Yes, I have. *I saw a very good movie last week.*
What *movie* did you *see*?
  I *saw The Wedding Dancer.*

INTENTION

I'm going to *eat lunch with the boss tomorrow.*

INQUIRING ABOUT ABILITY

Do you know how to *drive trucks*?

INQUIRING ABOUT LIKES/DISLIKES

Do you like to *swim*?

EXPRESSING OBLIGATION

I have to *take it now.*
He has to *go to bed now.*

EXPRESSING AN OPINION

It's one of the best *movies* I've ever *seen*.

EXPRESSING SATISFACTION

How was it?
  It was excellent/very good/wonderful/great/
  fantastic/terrific/phenomenal/
  awesome.

INITIATING A CONVERSATION

I see *you haven't gone home yet.*

EXPRESSING AGREEMENT

That's right.

LEAVE-TAKING

Have a good weekend.
  You, too.

NEW VOCABULARY

Job Search

application
classified ad
cold call
dates of
  employment
education
  history
employer
employment
  history
employment
  website

help-wanted
  sign
job application
  form
job bank
job fair
job opening
job opportunity
job posting
job search
reference
  website

At Work

bookkeeper
client
inventory
mail room
manager

office assistant
office clerk
paycheck
presentation
report

Free Time

Bingo
Broadway show
cruise
hot-air balloon
Monopoly

Tourist Attractions

Alcatraz Prison
Chinatown
Empire State Building
Fisherman's Wharf
Golden Gate Park
Statue of Liberty
Times Square
United Nations

Time Expressions

already
at the beginning
at this point
ever
for many years
in a long time
recently
yet

Transportation

cable car
helicopter
limousine

Medical Words

aspirin
blood
change dressings
do lab tests
first-aid course
injection
medical assistant
medical records
medicine

Verbs

apply for
create
draw
explain
fill in
get a raise
get rid of
get stuck
give blood
go kayaking

go scuba
  diving
go to bed
greet
have the time
leave for *school*
list
look through
network
schedule

state
take a cruise
take a ride

take a tour
take *your*
  medicine

Adjectives

complete
former
jealous
local

present
recent
surprised

Miscellaneous

beginning (n)
best friend
cash register
chopsticks
cotton candy
dance lesson
electric bill
extremely
horse
Internet
  service
kimono
middle name
online
present
  perfect tense

public building
public library
rainbow
speech
Swahili
talent
term paper
thousands
tip
tool
top
vocational
  school

EXPRESSIONS

as for me
Have a good weekend.
Look!
on the spot

VOCABULARY PREVIEW

These are the irregular past participles that are introduced in Unit 4. You may want to introduce these forms before beginning the unit, or you may choose to wait until they first occur in a specific lesson. If you choose to introduce them at this point, here are some suggestions:

1. Write the phrases with their base forms on the board:

1. go to the bank
2. do the laundry
3. get a haircut
4. write to Grandma
5. take the dog for a walk
6. give the dog a bath
7. speak to the landlord
8. drive the kids to their dance lesson
9. eat lunch
10. ride my exercise bike
11. swim
12. see a movie

2. Have students look at the illustrations on text page 37. Tell the class that these are all the things this person has to do today. Say each phrase and have the class repeat after you. Check students' understanding and pronunciation of the words.

3. One phrase at a time, erase the base form of the verb and replace it with the past participle form. Tell students that this person *has done* all these things. Say each phrase in the present perfect (for example: "I've gone to the bank, I've done the laundry") and have students repeat it chorally and individually. Check students' understanding and pronunciation of the verb forms.

4. After students have practiced saying the present perfect forms, erase the phrases on the board and have students look again at the illustrations on text page 37.

5. Practice the vocabulary as a class, in pairs, or in small groups. Have students cover the word list and look at the pictures. Practice the words in the following way:

   • Give the number of an illustration and have students say the phrase in the present perfect.

FOCUS

- Introduction of the Present Perfect Tense:
  1st Person Positive Statements

CLOSE UP

RULE: The present perfect tense is formed with the auxiliary verb *have* + the past participle. The auxiliary verb can contract with the subject pronoun unlike the verb *have*, which cannot contract with the subject pronoun.

EXAMPLES:

I **have driven**.	I**'ve driven**.
You **have driven**.	You**'ve driven**.
He **has driven**.	He**'s driven**.
We **have driven**.	We**'ve driven**.
They **have driven**.	They**'ve driven**.

RULE: The past participle of all regular verbs and some irregular verbs is the same as the past tense form.

EXAMPLES: Yesterday I **washed** the dishes.
I**'ve washed** dishes for many years.

Yesterday I **played** the piano.
I**'ve played** the piano for many years.

Yesterday I **bought** oranges from Florida.
I**'ve bought** oranges from Florida for many years.

RULE: Most irregular verbs have a different past participle form.

EXAMPLES:

Present	Past	Past Participle
be	was/were	been
do	did	done
draw	drew	drawn
drive	drove	driven
eat	ate	eaten
fall	fell	fallen
fly	flew	flown
get	got	gotten
go	went	gone
give	gave	given
ride	rode	ridden
see	saw	seen
sing	sang	sung
speak	spoke	spoken
swim	swam	swum

(continued)

Present	Past	Past Participle
take	took	taken
wear	wore	worn
write	wrote	written

RULE: When the present perfect tense is used with *for*, it describes a situation that began in the past and continues until the present. *For* is followed by a length of time.

EXAMPLES: **I've driven** trucks **for** many years.
(I continue to drive trucks.)

I've written reports **for** many years.
(I continue to write reports.)

GETTING READY

Review the language of ability.

1. Write on the board:

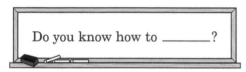

Do you know how to _____?

2. Ask students the above question with the following:

ride a motorcycle
drive a car
eat with chopsticks
speak Spanish
do karate
write in Chinese

For example:

Teacher: Do you know how to ride a
motorcycle?
Student: Yes, I do.

Teacher: Do you know how to write in
Chinese?
Student: No, I don't.

INTRODUCING THE MODEL

1. Have students look at the model illustration.

2. Set the scene: "Someone is at a job interview."

3. Present the model.

4. Full-Class Repetition.

5. Ask students if they have any questions. Check understanding of vocabulary.

6. Group Choral Repetition.

7. Choral Conversation.

8. Call on one or two pairs of students to present the dialog.

(For additional practice, do Choral Conversation in small groups or by rows.)

SIDE BY SIDE EXERCISES

Examples

1. A. Do you know how to write reports?
B. Yes. I've written reports for many years.

2. A. Do you know how to fly airplanes?
B. Yes. I've flown airplanes for many years.

1. **Exercise 1:** Introduce the word *report*. Call on two students to present the dialog. Then do Choral Repetition and Choral Conversation practice.

2. **Exercise 2:** Same as above.

3. Exercises 3–9: Either Full-Class Practice or Pair Practice.

> **New Vocabulary**
>
> 4. Swahili
> 5. chopsticks
> 6. injection
> 7. draw
> 9. horse

WORKBOOK

Page 36

EXPANSION ACTIVITIES

1. Tic Tac Grammar ★

   a. Have students draw a tic tac grid on a piece of paper and fill it in with any nine of the following verbs:

drive	write
fly	take
speak	eat
give	draw
do	ride

   b. Call out the past participle of any of these verbs. Tell students to cross out any present tense verb on their grid for which you have given a past participle form.

   c. The first person to cross out three verbs in a straight line—either vertically, horizontally, or diagonally—wins the game.

   d. Have the winner call out the words to check the accuracy.

2. Concentration ★

   a. Write the following verbs on separate cards:

drive	drove
ride	rode
write	wrote
give	given

fly	flown
take	taken
speak	spoken
eat	eaten
draw	drawn
do	done

   b. Shuffle the cards and place them face down in five rows of 4 each.

   c. Divide the class into two teams. The object of the game is for students to find the matching cards. Both teams should be able to see all the cards, since *concentrating* on their location is an important part of playing the game.

   d. A student from Team 1 turns over two cards. If they match, the student picks up the cards, that team gets a point, and the student takes another turn. If the cards don't match, the student turns them face down, and a member of Team 2 takes a turn.

   e. The game continues until all the cards have been matched. The team with the most correct matches wins the game.

(continued)

Variation: This game can also be played in groups and pairs.

3. Grammar Chain ★★

a. Write the following conversation model and verbs on the board:

> A. Do you know how to _____?
> B. Yes. I've _____ for many years.
>   Do you know how to _____?

do	give
drive	ride
draw	speak
eat	take
fly	write

b. Start the chain game by saying:

> Teacher *(to Student A):* Do you know how to speak Spanish?

c. Student A answers "Yes." and makes a statement using the present perfect: "I've spoken Spanish for many years." Then Student A asks Student B another ability question, using another verb on the board, and the chain continues. For example:

> Student A: Yes. I've spoken Spanish for many years.
> *(to Student B):* Do you know how *to ride a bicycle?*
>
> Student B: Yes. I've ridden a bicycle for many years.
> *(to Student C):* Do you know how *to fly an airplane?*

d. Continue until everyone has had a chance to answer and ask a question.

4. Match the Conversations ★★

a. Make a set of matching cards based on the model and exercises on text page 38.

Do you know how to drive trucks?	Yes. I've driven trucks for many years.
Do you know how to write reports?	Yes. I've written reports for many years.
Do you know how to fly airplanes?	Yes. I've flown airplanes for many years.
Do you know how to take X-rays?	Yes. I've taken X-rays for many years.
Do you know how to speak Swahili?	Yes. I've spoken Swahili for many years.
Do you know how to eat with chopsticks?	Yes. I've eaten with chopsticks for many years.
Do you know how to draw cartoons?	Yes. I've drawn cartoons for many years.
Do you know how to do yoga?	Yes. I've done yoga for many years.
Do you know how to ride horses?	Yes. I've ridden horses for many years.

b. Distribute a card to each student.

c. Have students memorize the sentences on their cards, and then have students walk around the room saying their sentences until they find their match.

d. Then have pairs of students say their matched sentences aloud to the class.

5. Which One Isn't True? ★★★

a. Put the following verb list on the board:

do   give
draw   ride
drive   speak
eat   take
fly   write

b. Tell students to write two true statements and one false statement about themselves using any of the verbs on the board and the phrase "for many years." For example:

I've driven a car for many years.
I've done yoga for many years.
I've ridden a motorcycle for many years.

c. Have students take turns reading their statements to the class. Have the class determine which statement isn't true.

FOCUS

- Present Perfect Tense: 1st Person Negative Statements with *never*

CLOSE UP

RULE: When the present perfect tense is used with *never*, it describes a situation that began in the past and continues until the present.

EXAMPLES: I've **never eaten** lunch with the boss.
I've **never flown** in a helicopter.

INTRODUCING THE MODEL

1. Have students look at the model illustration.

2. Set the scene: "Two co-workers are talking."

3. Present the model.

4. Full-Class Repetition.

5. Ask students if they have any questions. Check understanding of the word *jealous*.

6. Group Choral Repetition.

7. Choral Conversation.

8. Call on one or two pairs of students to present the dialog.

   (For additional practice, do Choral Conversation in small groups or by rows.)

SIDE BY SIDE EXERCISES

Examples

1. A. I'm going to fly in a helicopter tomorrow.
   B. I'm jealous. I've never flown in a helicopter.

2. A. I'm going to see a Broadway show tomorrow.
   B. I'm jealous. I've never seen a Broadway show.

1. **Exercise 1:** Introduce the word *helicopter*. Call on two students to present the dialog. Then do Choral Repetition and Choral Conversation practice.

2. **Exercise 2:** Introduce the expression *Broadway show*. Same as above.

3. **Exercises 3–9:** Either Full-Class Practice or Pair Practice.

New Vocabulary

3. cruise
6. get a raise
8. take a ride
   hot-air balloon
9. limousine

WORKBOOK

Page 37

1. Tic Tac Grammar ★

a. Have students draw a tic tac grid on a piece of paper and fill it in with any nine of the following verbs:

see	go
sing	swim
get	be
drive	write
fly	take
speak	eat
give	draw
do	ride

b. Call out the past participle of any of these verbs. Tell students to cross out any present tense verb on their grid for which you have given a past participle form.

c. The first person to cross out three verbs in a straight line—either vertically, horizontally, or diagonally—wins the game.

d. Have the winner call out the words to check the accuracy.

2. Grammar Chain: Tall Tales ★★

a. Write on the board:

> A. Tomorrow I'm going to _____.
> B. I've never _____, but tomorrow I'M going to _____.

b. Start the chain game by saying:

Teacher (to Student A): Tomorrow I'm going to fly in a hot-air balloon.

c. Student A responds to Student B according to the model on the board. For example:

Student A: (to Student B) I've never flown in a hot-air balloon, but tomorrow I'M going to swim in the Mediterranean.

Student B continues the chain. For example:

Student B: (to Student C) I've never swum in the Mediterranean, but tomorrow I'M going to be on TV.

3. Which One Isn't True? ★★★

a. Tell students to write two true statements and one false statement about themselves in the present perfect with never. For example:

I've never ridden a motorcycle.
I've never eaten with chopsticks.
I've never gone to the White House.

b. Have students take turns reading their statements to the class, and have the class guess which statement isn't true.

4. Category Dictation ★★

a. Have students draw two columns on a piece of paper. At the top of one column, have students write I've never. At the top of the other column, have them write I've.

b. Dictate phrases such as the following to the class:

go out all night
speak Greek
take guitar lessons
get a raise
be in a boat
swim in a lake
draw a picture of our teacher
meet a famous person
give a ring to someone
be on the radio
see a Broadway show
be on TV
go on a cruise
take a ride on the back of a bicycle
write a love letter
sing with an orchestra

c. Have students choose the appropriate column according to their own experience and write the verb with its past participle. For example:

I've never	I've
met a famous person	gone out all night
been on the radio	seen a Broadway show

d. In pairs, have students compare their lists.

(continued)

5. Class Discussion: Our Greatest Wishes ★★★

a. Divide the class into groups of three. Have students answer the following question:

What is something you have always wanted to do but have never done?

b. Have the groups share their greatest wishes with the class.

FOCUS

- Present Perfect Tense:
    Yes/No Questions with *You*
    Affirmative Short Answers
- Contrast: Present Perfect and Simple Past

CLOSE UP

RULE:	The present perfect describes an activity that occurred at an unspecified time in the past.
EXAMPLE:	**Have** you ever **seen** a rainbow? *(In your general past, have you seen a rainbow?)*
RULE:	The simple past describes an activity that occurred at a specific time in the past.
EXAMPLE:	I **saw** a rainbow last year. *(I saw a rainbow at a specific time in the past.)*
RULE:	*Ever* is placed between the subject and the past participle.
EXAMPLES:	Have you **ever** given a speech? Have you **ever** been in the hospital?
RULE:	The short answer response in the present perfect is formed with the auxiliary verb *have*.

EXAMPLES:	**Have** you ever **eaten** cotton candy?
	   Yes, I **have**.
	Have you ever **fallen** asleep in class?
	   Yes, I **have**.

INTRODUCING THE MODEL

1. Have students look at the model illustration.

2. Set the scene: "Two people on a date are talking."

3. Present the model.

4. Full-Class Repetition.

5. Ask students if they have any questions. Check understanding of the word *rainbow*.

6. Group Choral Repetition.

7. Choral Conversation.

8. Call on one or two pairs of students to present the dialog.

   (For additional practice, do Choral Conversation in small groups or by rows.)

SIDE BY SIDE EXERCISES

Examples

> 1. A. Have you ever gone scuba diving?
>   B. Yes, I have. I went scuba diving last year.
>
> 2. A. Have you ever given a speech?
>   B. Yes, I have. I gave a speech last year.

1. **Exercise 1:** Introduce the expression *go scuba diving*. Call on two students to present the dialog. Then do Choral Repetition and Choral Conversation practice.

2. **Exercise 2:** Introduce the word *speech*. Same as above.

3. **Exercises 3–9:** Either Full-Class Practice or Pair Practice.

> **New Vocabulary**
>
> 3. kimono
> 4. cotton candy
> 5. first-aid course
> 8. get stuck

Culture Notes

Exercise 3: A *kimono* is a long Japanese dress for women. In modern times it is used for very formal occasions such as weddings.

Exercise 4: *Cotton candy* is a sweet treat of spun sugar wrapped around a stick. It is usually served at carnivals and amusements parks.

Exercise 5: A *first-aid course* teaches people how to treat minor medical emergencies.

WORKBOOK

Page 38

EXPANSION ACTIVITIES

1. Match the Conversations ★

a. Make the following set of matching cards:

Have you ever seen one?	Yes, I have. I saw one last year.
Have you ever gotten one?	Yes, I have. I got one last year.
Have you ever written one?	Yes, I have. I wrote one last year.
Have you ever worn one?	Yes, I have. I wore one last year.

Have you ever taken one?	Yes, I have. I took one last year.
Have you ever given one?	Yes, I have. I gave one last year.
Have you ever driven one?	Yes, I have. I drove one last year.
Have you ever ridden one?	Yes, I have. I rode one last year.
Have you ever drawn one?	Yes, I have. I drew one last year.

Have you ever eaten one?	Yes, I have. I ate one last year.
Have you ever flown there?	Yes, I have. I flew there last year.
Have you ever gone there?	Yes, I have. I went there last year.
Have you ever swum there?	Yes, I have. I swam there last year.
Have you ever sung there?	Yes, I have. I sang there last year.
Have you ever been there?	Yes, I have. I was there last year.

b. Distribute a card to each student.

c. Have students memorize the sentences on their cards, and then have students walk around the room saying their sentences until they find their match.

d. Then have pairs of students say their matched sentences aloud to the class.

2. Clap in Rhythm ★★

a. Write the following verbs on the board:

be	fly	sing
do	get	speak
draw	give	swim
drive	go	take
eat	ride	wear
fall	see	write

b. Have students sit in a circle.

c. Establish a steady, even beat—one-two-three-four, one-two-three-four—by having students clap their hands to their laps twice and then clap their hands together twice. Repeat throughout the game, maintaining the same rhythm.

d. In this activity, Student 1 says a verb (for example: *see*). Student 2 gives the past of that verb (for example: *saw*), and Student 3 gives the past participle of that verb (for example: *seen*). Student 4 says a new verb (for example: *go*), and the activity continues until all the verbs on the board have been practiced.

The object is for each student in turn to give a verb form each time the hands are clapped together twice. Nothing is said when students clap their hands on their laps.

Note: The beat never stops! If a student misses a beat, he or she can either wait for the next beat or pass to the next student.

3. Grammar Chain ★★

a. Write the following verb phrases on the board:

go to a ballgame
swim in the ocean
eat a pizza
give advice to a friend
wear a tuxedo
take the subway
fall asleep on your couch
get stuck in traffic
go on a merry-go-round
be late for class
draw a picture of a friend
write a letter to a famous person
fly to Rio
see the president

b. Start the chain game by saying:

Teacher (*to Student A*): Have you ever *gone to a ballgame?*

c. Student A answers: "Yes, I have. I went to a ballgame last week." Then Student A asks Student B another question using another phrase on the board, and the chain continues. For example:

(continued)

Student A: Yes, I have. I went to a ballgame last week.

(to Student B):   Have you ever *eaten* a pizza?

Student B: Yes, I have. I ate a pizza last week.

(to Student C):   Have you ever *gotten* stuck in traffic?

d. Continue until everyone has had a chance to answer and ask a question.

4. Question the Answers! ★★

a. Dictate answers such as the following to the class:

> Yes, I have. I went to Japan last summer.
> Yes, I have. I took a French course last semester.
> Yes, I have. I saw a famous person last week.

b. Have students write questions for which these answers would be correct.

For example:

Answer: Yes, I have. I went to Japan last summer.

Question: Have you ever gone to Japan?

Answer: Yes, I have. I took a French course last summer.

Question: Have you ever taken a French course?

c. Have students compare their questions with each other.

Variation: Write the answers on cards. Divide the class into groups and give each group a set of cards.

5. Question Game: How Many Questions? ★★

a. Divide the class into pairs.

b. Dictate the following answers to the class:

> Yes, I have.
> Yes, I did.

c. Tell students that in five minutes, they should write as many questions as they can think of for which these answers would be correct. For example:

Yes, I have.   Have you ever driven a truck?
Have you ever gone fishing?
Have you ever worn jeans to work?

Yes, I did.   Did you write your report last night?
Did you see a movie last weekend?
Did you go to a ballgame yesterday?

d. Have students read their questions to the class. The pair with the most correct questions wins the *question game*.

6. Class Survey: Have You Ever? ★★

a. Make up the following handout based on the lesson on student text page 40, and give each student a copy:

Have you ever . . .	Yes	No
seen a rainbow?	____	____
gone scuba diving?	____	____
given a speech?	____	____
worn a kimono?	____	____
eaten cotton candy?	____	____
taken a first-aid course?	____	____
fallen asleep in class?	____	____
been in the hospital?	____	____
gotten stuck in an elevator?	____	____

b. Have students go around the room interviewing each other.

c. Have students report their findings to the class.

Variation: Have students do the same activity with questions based on the situations on text pages 38 and 39.

7. Find the Right Person! ★★

a. Write the following on the board:

I've _____.

b. Have each student write one special thing that he or she has done.

c. Collect the information and put it on a handout in the following form:

Find someone who . . .
1. has gone scuba diving. _____
2. has given a speech in front _____
   of a hundred people.
3. has eaten octopus. _____
4. has ridden in a limousine. _____
5. has flown in a helicopter. _____

d. Have students circulate around the room, asking each other questions to identify the above people. For example:

Student A: Have you ever gone scuba diving?
Student B: Yes, I have. I went scuba diving last summer.

e. The first student to find all the people, raise his or her hand, and identify the students is the winner of the game.

FOCUS

- Present Perfect Tense:
    Yes/No Questions
    Affirmative Short Answers
- Questions with *Yet*

CLOSE UP

RULE:	Yes/No questions with *yet* express the expectation that something has happened before now. The word *yet* is always at the end of the question.
EXAMPLES:	Have you driven the new van **yet**? Has Nancy given her presentation **yet**?

INTRODUCING THE MODELS

There are two model conversations. Introduce and practice each separately. For each model:

1. Have students look at the model illustration.

2. Set the scene.

    1st model: "A supervisor is talking to an employee."
    2nd model: "Two co-workers are talking about David."

3. Present the model.

4. Full-Class Repetition.

5. Ask students if they have any questions.

6. Group Choral Repetition.

7. Choral Conversation.

8. Call on one or two pairs of students to present the dialog.

    (For additional practice, do Choral Conversation in small groups or by rows.)

SIDE BY SIDE EXERCISES

Examples

1. A. Have you driven the new van yet?
    B. Yes, I have. I drove the new van a little while ago.

2. A. Has Nancy given her presentation yet?
    B. Yes, she has. She gave her presentation a little while ago.

1. **Exercise 1:** Call on two students to present the dialog. Then do Choral Repetition and Choral Conversation practice.

2. **Exercise 2:** Introduce the word *presentation*. Same as above.

3. **Exercises 3–6:** Either Full-Class Practice or Pair Practice.

New Vocabulary

3. paycheck
4. take inventory
6. explain
   present perfect tense

EXPANSION ACTIVITIES

1. Tic Tac Grammar ★

a. Have students draw a tic tac grid on a piece of paper and fill it in with any nine of the following verbs:

be	fly	sing
do	get	speak
draw	give	swim
drive	go	take
eat	ride	wear
fall	see	write

b. Call out the past participle of any of these verbs. Tell students to cross out any present tense verb on their grid for which you have given a past participle form.

c. The first person to cross out three verbs in a straight line—either vertically, horizontally, or diagonally—wins the game.

d. Have the winner call out the words to check the accuracy.

2. Match the Conversations ★

a. Make the following set of matching cards:

Has he seen them?	Yes, he has. He saw them a little while ago.
Has she seen them?	Yes, she has. She saw them a little while ago.
Have you seen them?	Yes, I have. I saw them a little while ago.

Have they seen you?	Yes, they have. They saw me a little while ago.
Have you seen him?	Yes, we have. We saw him a little while ago.
Have I seen them?	Yes, you have. You saw them a little while ago.

b. Distribute a card to each student.

c. Have students memorize the sentences on their cards, and then have students walk around the room saying their sentences until they find their match.

d. Then have pairs of students say their matched sentences aloud to the class.

3. Concentration ★

a. Write the following sentences on separate cards:

Have you gone there?	Yes, I have.
Have they gone there?	Yes, they have.
Have I gone there?	Yes, you have.
Has she gone there?	Yes, she has.

(continued)

Has he gone there?	Yes, he has.
Has it gone there?	Yes, it has.

b. Shuffle the cards and place them face down in three rows of four each.

c. Divide the class into two teams. The object of the game is for students to find the matching cards. Both teams should be able to see all the cards, since *concentrating* on their location is an important part of playing the game.

d. A student from Team 1 turns over two cards. If they match, the student picks up the cards, that team gets a point, and the student takes another turn. If the cards don't match, the student turns them face down, and a member of Team 2 takes a turn.

e. The game continues until all the cards have been matched. The team with the most correct matches wins the game.

Variation: This game can also be played in groups and pairs.

4. Question the Answers! ★★

a. Dictate answers such as the following to the class:

Yes, he has. He wore his new suit yesterday.
Yes, she has. She went to the post office a few minutes ago.
Yes, they have. They ate there yesterday.

b. Have students write questions for which these answers would be correct. For example:

Answer: Yes, he has. He wore his new suit yesterday.
Question: Has Tom worn his new suit yet?

Answer: Yes, she has. She went to the post office a few minutes ago.
Question: Has Nancy gone to the post office yet?

Answer: Yes, they have. They ate there yesterday.
Question: Have your friends eaten there yet?

c. Have students compare their questions with each other.

Variation: Write the answers on cards. Divide the class into groups and give each group a set of cards.

FOCUS

- Present Perfect Tense
- Contrast: Present Perfect, Simple Past, Future: Going to

CLOSE UP

RULE: *Already* is placed between the auxiliary and the past participle.

EXAMPLES: He's **already** gone bowling this week.
She's **already** seen a movie this week.
They've **already** eaten at a restaurant this week.

INTRODUCING THE MODEL

1. Have students look at the model illustration.

2. Set the scene: "Charlie's wife and a friend are talking about Charlie."

3. Present the model.

4. Full-Class Repetition.

5. Ask students if they have any questions. Check understanding of the word *already*.

6. Group Choral Repetition.

7. Choral Conversation.

8. Call on one or two pairs of students to present the dialog.

   (For additional practice, do Choral Conversation in small groups or by rows.)

9. Use the sentence *He's already gone bowling this week* to practice the other forms of the present perfect tense.

   a. Point to yourself and say: "I've already gone bowling this week." Have students repeat chorally and individually.

   b. Continue in the same way with the other pronouns. For example:

      We've already gone bowling this week.
      She's already gone bowling this week.
      They've already gone bowling this week.

Have students refer to the grammar box at the top of text page 42. Check pronunciation of contractions with *have* and provide additional practice if necessary.

SIDE BY SIDE EXERCISES

Examples

1. A. Why isn't Vicky going to see a movie this evening?
   B. She's already seen a movie this week.
   A. Really? When?
   B. She saw a movie yesterday.

2. A. Why aren't Mr. and Mrs. Kendall going to eat at a restaurant tonight?
   B. They've already eaten at a restaurant this week.
   A. Really? When?
   B. They ate at a restaurant yesterday.

1. **Exercise 1:** Call on two students to present the dialog. Then do Choral Repetition and Choral Conversation practice.

2. **Exercise 2:** Call on two students to present the dialog.

3. Exercises 3–14: Either Full-Class Practice or Pair Practice.

> **New Vocabulary**
>
> 4. give blood
> 8. best friend
> 14. Bingo

Culture Note

Exercise 14: *Bingo* is a popular game. Numbers are called out, and players listen to match the numbers they hear with those on their game cards.

WORKBOOK

Pages 40–43

EXPANSION ACTIVITIES

1. Practice Makes It Perfect! ★

a. Write the following on the board:

> No. ____'ve already _____.
> No. ____'s already _____.

b. Ask students each of the following questions. Have students respond, using the present perfect model on the board. For example:

> Teacher: Are you going to write your English composition tonight?
> Student: No. I've already written it.
>
> Teacher: Is Maria going to go to the dentist today?
> Student: No. She's already gone to the dentist.

Questions:

Are you going to write your English composition tonight?

Is (Maria) going to go to the dentist today?

Are your friends going to do their homework this afternoon?

It's late. Is your brother going to get dressed for the party?

Tomorrow is your sister's birthday. Are you going to give her a birthday gift?

Are you and your (husband) going to do your laundry this morning?

Sally's dog is sick. Is she going to take him to the vet today?

Are you going to write to your uncle in (Chicago) this weekend?

Are you going to go jogging after class today?

Are you going to see the new movie at the (Regency) Theater?

Are your friends (Barbara) and (Bill) going to get married this weekend?

Are you going to do your exercises tonight before you go to bed?

Is (Peter) going to eat lunch with us today?

Are you going to ride your new exercise bike today?

Are you going to take your daughter to her piano lessons this afternoon?

(Tom) isn't feeling very well. Is he going to see the doctor this afternoon?

Is Professor (Jones) going to give his famous lecture on American birds tonight?

2. Grammar Chain ★★

a. Write on the board:

> A. Why aren't you going to _____?
> B. Because I've already _____ this week. I _____ yesterday. Why aren't you _____?

b. Start the chain game by saying:

> Teacher (to Student A): Why aren't you going to see a movie tonight?

c. Student A answers according to the model on the board and then asks Student B another present perfect question. For example:

> Student A: Because I've already seen a movie this week. I saw a movie yesterday.
>
> (to Student B): Why aren't you going to go skating tomorrow?

Student B: Because I've already gone skating this week. I went skating yesterday.

(to Student C):   Why aren't you going to write your report today?

d. Continue until everyone has had a chance to answer and ask a question.

3. Can You Hear the Difference? ★

a. Write the following sentences on the board:

A	B
He's eating here.	He's eaten here.
We drive there.	We've driven there.
She had time.	She's had time.
I wore it.	I've worn it.
We bought them.	We've bought them.
He sees her.	He's seen her.
I go there.	I've gone there.

b. Choose a sentence randomly from one of the two columns and say it to the class. Have the class listen and identify whether the sentence is from Column A or Column B.

c. Have students continue the activity in pairs. One student pronounces a sentence, and the other identifies whether it's from Column A or Column B. Then have them reverse roles.

d. Write other similar sentences on the board and continue the practice.

4. Sentence Cues ★★

a. On separate cards, write key words that can be put together to form sentences or questions. Clip together the cards for each sentence. For example:

you	speak	to	grandparents	yet	?
she	speak	boyfriend		last night	.
they	ever	go bowling		with you	?

she	wear	kimono	last year	.
he	ever	fall asleep	in the library	?
they	already	get	their paychecks	?

b. Divide the class into small groups and give a clipped set of cards to each group.

c. Have each group write a sentence based on their set of cards.

d. Have one member of each group write that group's sentence on the board. Then compare everybody's sentences. Did they choose the correct tense? What words helped them choose the correct tense?

5. What's Wrong? ★★★

a. Divide the class into pairs or small groups.

b. Write several sentences such as the following on the board or on a handout. Some of the sentences should be correct, and others incorrect. For example:

I flew there last month.
I've never went there.
She's already written the letter.
I've never saw them.
We've already done that.
I drive trucks for many years.
I've never saw her.
They've never swum there.
Have you ever be to Chicago?
I've gotten a very short haircut last week.

c. The object of the activity is for students to identify which sentences are incorrect and then correct them.

d. Have students compare their answers.

Variation: Do the activity as a game with competing teams. The team that successfully completes the task in the shortest time is the winner.

(continued)

6. Don't You Remember? ★★★

a. Write the following on the board:

> A. You know, _____.
> B. But { ___'s / ___'ve } already _____.
> A. Really? When?
> B. Don't you remember? _____ a few days ago.
> A. Oh. That's right. I forgot.

b. Call on pairs of students to create conversations based on the model on the board. Give one member of the pair one of these cards as a cue for the conversation.

You know, we should see the new science fiction movie at the Regency Theater.	You know, Timmy should get a haircut.
You know, we really should do the laundry.	You know, we should write to Uncle Charlie.
You know, you should wear the wool sweater your grandmother gave you for your birthday.	You know, you should take the car to the mechanic.
You know, your sister should really invite us for dinner.	You know, our friends should visit us in our new apartment.

READING *We Can't Decide*

FOCUS

- Present Perfect Tense

READING THE STORY

Optional: Preview the story by having students talk about the story title and/or illustration. You may choose to introduce new vocabulary beforehand, or have students encounter the new vocabulary within the context of the reading.

1. Have students read silently or follow along silently as the story is read aloud by you, by one or more students, or on the audio program.

2. Ask students if they have any questions. Check understanding of vocabulary.

3. Check students' comprehension, using some or all of the following questions:

> What don't I want to do tonight?
> Why not?
> What doesn't Maggie want to do tonight?
> Why not?
> What doesn't Mark want to do tonight?
> Why not?
> What don't Betty and Mike want to do tonight?
> Why not?
> Who wants to go dancing?
> Why not?

ROLE PLAY

1. Make sure students understand the instructions. Check understanding of the expression *Look!*

2. Have students work in groups to create a role play based on the model. Encourage them to continue the conversation any way they wish.

3. Call on groups to present their role plays to the class.

READING EXTENSION

Have students answer these questions in groups and then share their ideas with the class.

> What have you done in your free time this week?

> What are you going to do in your free time next weekend?

COMPLETE THE STORY

Before doing the activity, introduce the following new vocabulary:

> aspirin
> at the beginning
> at this point
> extremely
> get rid of

Answers

1. gone
2. seen
3. stayed
4. taken
5. drunk
6. eaten
7. rested
8. done

FOCUS

• Present Perfect Tense: Negative Statements

CLOSE UP

RULE: In spoken and informal written English, the auxiliary verb *have/has* contracts with *not*.

EXAMPLES: I **haven't** (have not) had the time.
She **hasn't** (has not) drawn in a long time.

INTRODUCING THE MODELS

There are two model conversations. Introduce and practice each separately. For each model:

1. Have students look at the model illustration.

2. Set the scene.

   1st model: "Two co-workers are talking after work."
   2nd model: "A friend is asking Rita's mother a question."

3. Present the model.

4. Full-Class Repetition.

5. Ask students if they have any questions. Check understanding of the expressions *in a long time, have the time.*

6. Group Choral Repetition.

7. Choral Conversation.

8. Call on one or two pairs of students to present the dialog.

   (For additional practice, do Choral Conversation in small groups or by rows.)

SIDE BY SIDE EXERCISES

Examples

1. A. Do you like to ride your bicycle?
   B. Yes, but I haven't ridden my bicycle in a long time.
   A. Why not?
   B. I haven't had the time.

2. A. Does Arthur like to write poetry?
   B. Yes, but he hasn't written poetry in a long time.
   A. Why not?
   B. He hasn't had the time.

1. **Exercise 1:** Call on two students to present the dialog. Then do Choral Repetition and Choral Conversation practice.

2. **Exercise 2:** Same as above.

3. **Exercises 3–8:** Either Full-Class Practice or Pair Practice.

Culture Note:

Exercise 4: *Monopoly* is a popular board game.

4. **Exercise 9:** Have students use the model as a guide to create their own conversations, using vocabulary of their choice. Encourage students to use dictionaries to find new words they want to use. This exercise can be done orally in class or for written homework. If you assign it for homework, do one example in class to make sure students understand what's expected. Have students present their conversations in class the next day.

WORKBOOK

Pages 44–45

EXPANSION ACTIVITIES

1. Can You Hear the Difference? ★

a. Write on the board:

Positive	Negative
I have seen that play.	I haven't seen that play.
You have met them before.	You haven't met them before.
She has written many letters.	She hasn't written many letters.
It has been a long time.	It hasn't been a long time.
We have eaten all the pie.	We haven't eaten all the pie.
They have bought the milk.	They haven't bought the milk.

b. Choose a sentence randomly from one of the two columns and say it to the class. Have the class listen and identify whether the sentence is *positive* or *negative*.

c. Have students continue the activity in pairs. One student says a sentence, and the other tells whether it's positive or negative. Then have them reverse roles.

d. Write other similar sentences on the board and continue the practice.

2. Telephone ★

a. Divide the class into large groups. Have each group sit in a circle.

b. Whisper the following sentence to a student:

"He's gotten up, he's taken a shower, he's done his exercises, and he's eaten breakfast, but he hasn't gone to work yet."

c. The first student whispers the message to the second student, and so forth around the circle. The student listening may ask for clarification by saying "I'm sorry. Could you repeat that?"

d. When the message gets to the last student, that person says it aloud. Is it the same message you started with? The group with the most accurate message wins.

3. Match the Sentences ★★

a. Make the following set of split sentence cards:

I like to swim, . . .	but I haven't swum in a long time.
I like to sing, . . .	but I haven't sung in a long time.
I like to draw, . . .	but I haven't drawn in a long time.
I like to write music, . . .	but I haven't written music in a long time.

(continued)

I like to ride my bicycle, . . .	but I haven't ridden my bicycle in a long time.
I like to see movies, . . .	but I haven't seen a movie in a long time.
I like to eat pizza, . . .	but I haven't eaten pizza in a long time.
I like to go dancing, . . .	but I haven't gone dancing in a long time.
I like to speak French, . .	but I haven't spoken French in a long time.

b. Distribute a card to each student.

c. Have students memorize the phrases on their cards, and then have students walk around the room saying their phrases until they find their match.

d. Then have pairs of students say their matched sentences aloud to the class.

4. Change the Sentence! ★★

a. Write a sentence on the board, underlining and numbering different portions of the sentence. For example:

> 1   2   3   4
> I haven't   seen   my friends   in a long time.

b. Have students sit in a circle.

c. Tell them that when you say a number, the first student in the circle makes a change in that part of the sentence. For example:

> Teacher: Two.
> Student 1:   I haven't <u>spoken to</u> my friends in a long time.

d. The second student keeps the first student's sentence, but changes it based on the next number you say. For example:

> Teacher: Three.
> Student 2:   I haven't spoken to <u>my neighbors</u> in a long time.

e. Continue this way with the rest of the students in the circle. For example:

> Teacher: Four.
> Student 3:   I haven't spoken to my neighbors <u>this week</u>.

5. Not This Week! ★★

a. Write the following on the board:

> I know. But this week _____ { hasn't / haven't }
> _____ at all.

b. Read each of the following sentences, and have students complete the follow-up sentence on the board. For example:

> Teacher: Rita usually draws cartoons.
> Student: I know. But this week she hasn't drawn cartoons at all.

Possible sentences:

Rita usually draws cartoons.
David usually does yoga in the morning.
We usually see our friends after class.
Bob usually rides his bicycle to work.
Susan usually takes the bus to work.
Arthur usually writes in his journal every day.
My father usually drives his car to work.
My friends and I usually meet at a cafe.
Vicky usually eats lunch in a restaurant.
Nancy usually goes to the health club every evening.

6. Plans for the Weekend ★★

a. Write the following on the board:

> A. What are you going to do this weekend?
> B. I'm not sure. I think I'll _____.
>   I haven't _____ in a long time.

b. Have pairs of students create conversations about their weekend plans, using the model on the board.

c. Call on pairs to present their conversations to the class.

Example:

> A. What are you going to do this weekend?
> B. I'm not sure. I think I'll drive to the beach.
>   I haven't driven to the beach in a long time.

7. Category Dictation ★★

a. Have students draw two columns on a piece of paper. At the top of one column, have students write <u>Things I've Done This Week</u>. At the top of the other column, have them write <u>Things I Haven't Done This Week</u>.

b. Dictate activities such as the following:

do my laundry	ride my bicycle
write to a friend	swim
go to the bank	see a movie
get a haircut	fly in an airplane
take the bus	draw a picture
drive my car	

c. Have students write sentences about these activities in the appropriate column. For example:

<u>Things I've Done This Week</u>	<u>Things I Haven't Done This Week</u>
I've gone to the bank.	I haven't done my laundry.
I've gotten a haircut.	I haven't written to a friend.
I've taken the bus.	I haven't ridden my bicycle.

8. Which One Isn't True? ★★

a. Tell students to write three true present perfect statements and one false statement about themselves. For example:

> I've never gone kayaking.
> I've done yoga for many years.
> I've seen ten Broadway shows.
> I've had a bad headache all day.

b. Have students take turns reading their statements to the class, and have the class guess which statement isn't true.

9. New in Town! ★★★

a. Put the following on the board:

> The Henderson Family
>
> Joan   Mark   Bob   Sally
>
> A. { Has / Have } _____ yet?
> B. Yes, _____.
>   or
>   No. They haven't had the time.

b. Set the scene: "Mr. and Mrs. Henderson and their children are new in town. They've just moved here, and they've been very busy. I think they're going to like *(name of your city)* very much."

c. Have students create conversations in which they ask about all the experiences the Hendersons have had in their new city. For example, students can ask about getting an apartment, finding work, starting school, and going to local tourist sights and landmarks.

Examples:

> A. Have the Hendersons found an apartment yet?
> B. Yes, they have. They found an apartment on Maple Street.

> A. Have the children started school yet?
> B. Yes, they have. They started school last month, and they like it very much.

> A. Have they visited the museum yet?
> B. No. They haven't had the time.

Text Page 46: Has Timmy Gone to Bed Yet?

FOCUS

- Present Perfect Tense:
  Negative Short Answers
  Questions with *Yet*

INTRODUCING THE MODEL

1. Have students look at the model illustration.

2. Set the scene: "Timmy's parents are talking about Timmy."

3. Present the model.

4. Full-Class Choral Repetition.

5. Ask students if they have any questions. Check understanding of the expression *go to bed*.

6. Group Choral Repetition.

7. Choral Conversation.

8. Call on one or two pairs of students to present the dialog.

   (For additional practice, do Choral Conversation in small groups or by rows.)

SIDE BY SIDE EXERCISES

Examples

1. A. Has Amanda done her homework yet?
   B. No, she hasn't. She has to do her homework now.

2. A. Have you taken your medicine yet?
   B. No, I haven't. I have to take my medicine now.

1. **Exercise 1:** Call on two students to present the dialog. Then do Choral Repetition and Choral Conversation practice.

2. **Exercise 2:** Introduce the word *medicine*. Same as above.

3. **Exercises 3–9:** Either Full-Class Practice or Pair Practice.

New Vocabulary

4. leave for school
6. term paper
9. electric bill

WORKBOOK

Pages 46–47

EXPANSION ACTIVITIES

1. Grammar Chain ★★

a. Write on the board:

> A. Have you _____ yet?
> B. No, I haven't. I have to _____ now.
>   Have you _____ yet?

b. Start the chain game by saying:

> Teacher (to Student A): Have you *done your homework* yet?

c. Student A answers according to the model, then asks Student B another present perfect question, and the chain continues. For example:

> Student A: No, I haven't. I have to do my homework now.
> (to Student B): Have you *written your paper* yet?
> Student B: No, I haven't. I have to write my paper now.
> (to Student C): Have you *eaten lunch* yet?

d. Continue until everyone gets a chance to answer and ask a question.

2. Tic Tac Question the Answer ★★

a. Draw a tic tac grid on the board and fill it in with the following short answers to questions:

Yes, we have.	No, she hasn't.	Yes, he did.
No, I didn't.	Yes, I have.	No, it hasn't.
No, they haven't.	Yes, he has.	No, we didn't.

b. Divide the class into teams. Give each team a mark: *X* or *O.*

c. Have each team ask a question for an answer in the grid. For example:

> X Team: Have you done your homework yet?
>   Yes, I have.

d. If the question is appropriate and is stated correctly, that team may replace the answer with its team mark. For example:

Yes, we have.	No, she hasn't.	Yes, he did.
No, I didn't.	X	No, it hasn't.
No, they haven't.	Yes, he has.	No, we didn't.

e. The first team to mark out three boxes in a straight line—either vertically, horizontally, or diagonally—wins.

3. Mystery Conversations ★★★

a. Divide the class into pairs.

b. Write the following conversation framework on the board:

> Have you _____ yet?

c. Write roles such as the following on word cards and give one to each pair of students:

a parent and a child	a boss and an employee
a teacher and a student	two friends
two neighbors	a nurse and a patient
a wife and a husband	a brother and a sister

(continued)

d. Have each pair create a short dialog that begins "Have you _____ yet?" The dialogs should be appropriate for the roles the students have on their cards.

e. Have each pair present their dialog to the class. Then have the other students guess who the people are: Are they friends? Is a teacher talking to a student? For example:

[parent-child]
A. Have you cleaned your room yet?
B. No, I haven't. But I'm going to clean it tonight.
A. Well, please don't forget. I've already asked you two times.
B. Don't worry. I won't forget.

[boss-employee]
A. Have you typed those letters yet?
B. Yes, I have. I just finished them a few minutes ago.
A. Can I see them, please?
B. Certainly. Here they are.

4. Asking Questions ★★★

a. Write the following on the board:

Have/Has _____?	
take his medicine	finish her homework
get up	say good-bye
feed him	call her boss
go to bed	speak to your
pay his electric bill	landlord

b. Read the situations below and call on students to respond, using the present perfect and an appropriate phrase from the list on the board. For example:

Teacher: I don't have any heat in my apartment!
Student: Have you spoken to your landlord?

Situations:

I don't have any heat in my apartment!
(Have you spoken to your landlord?)

The lights in Henry's house won't go on.
(Has he paid his electric bill?)

Walter is feeling very sick.
(Has he taken his medicine?)

The dog is very hungry, and he's barking loudly.
(Have you fed him?)

My daughter wants to watch TV.
(Has she finished her homework?)

Mary's alarm clock is ringing.
(Has she gotten up?)

Alice has decided to stay home from work today.
(Has she called her boss?)

My son is very tired.
(Has he gone to bed?)

Margaret and Michael are leaving for the airport.
(Have they said good-bye?)

5. Going Abroad ★★★

a. Write the following on the board:

Have you _____ yet?
get your passport
apply for your visa
buy _____ for the trip
make hotel reservations
pack
buy your plane ticket
_____

b. Divide the class into pairs and set the scene: "One of you is going on a trip and you have a lot of things to do before you go. Your friend is trying to help you remember everything you have to do."

c. Using cues on the board, have pairs create conversations about the trip one of them is going to take.

d. After the students have rehearsed their conversations, call on several pairs to present their conversations to the class. For example:

A. Where are you going?
B. To China.
A. When are you leaving?
B. Next month.
A. Have you gotten your passport yet?
B. Yes, I have. I got it yesterday.
A. Have you bought clothes for the trip yet?
B. Yes. I've already bought everything I need.
A. Have you packed yet?
B. No, I haven't. I'll pack the night before I leave.
A. Have you learned any Chinese phrases yet?
B. Yes. I've learned how to say "Hello" and "Good-bye."

READING *Working Overtime*

FOCUS

- Present Perfect Tense
- Expressions with *Still*

NEW VOCABULARY

as for me	office clerk
bookkeeper	surprised

READING THE STORY

Optional: Preview the story by having students talk about the story title and/or illustration. You may choose to introduce new vocabulary beforehand, or have students encounter the new vocabulary within the context of the reading.

1. Have students read silently or follow along silently as the story is read aloud by you, by one or more students, or on the audio program.

2. Ask students if they have any questions. Check understanding of vocabulary.

   #### Culture Note

   Overtime is any work done over the 40-hour work week. Workers are usually paid more per hour than their normal salary, usually one and a half times their hourly wage.

3. Check students' comprehension, using some or all of the following questions:

   Have the employees of the Goodwell
       Computer Company gone home yet?
   Why not?
   Why hasn't the secretary gone home yet?

Why hasn't the bookkeeper gone home yet?
Why haven't the office clerks gone home yet?
Why hasn't the boss gone home yet?
Why hasn't the custodian gone home yet?
Why hasn't he cleaned all the offices?
Why isn't he surprised?

✔ READING *CHECK-UP*

Q & A

1. Call on a pair of students to present the model. Check understanding of the expression *Have a good weekend.*

2. Have students work in pairs to create new dialogs.

3. Call on pairs to present their new dialogs to the class.

READING EXTENSION

Tic Tac Question Formation

1. Draw a tic tac grid on the board and fill it with question words. For example:

Have?	Who?	What?
Has?	How many?	What day?
Is?	Are?	Where?

2. Divide the class into two teams. Give each team a mark: *X* or *O.*

3. Have each team ask a question that begins with one of the question words and then provide the answer to the question. If the question and answer are correct, the team gets to put its mark in that space. For example:

   X Team: Have the office clerks delivered all
       the mail?
           No, they haven't.

X	Who?	What?
Has?	How many?	What day?
Is?	Are?	Where?

4. The first team to mark out three boxes in a straight line—vertically, horizontally, or diagonally—wins.

What's the Word?

Before doing the exercise, check understanding of the expression *mail room* in Exercise 7.

1. seen
   saw

2. eaten
   ate

3. gone
   has, went

4. spoken
   have, spoke

5. made
   made

6. read
   read

7. taken
   hasn't, took
   he hasn't taken

8. finished
   has, gone

FOCUS

- Present Perfect Tense
- Expressions with *Recently* and *Ever*

INTRODUCING THE MODEL

1. Have students look at the model illustration.

2. Set the scene: "Two co-workers are talking during a break on the job."

3. Present the model.

4. Full-Class Repetition.

5. Ask students if they have any questions. Check understanding of the word *recently*.

6. Group Choral Repetition.

7. Choral Conversation.

8. Call on one or two pairs of students to present the dialog.

   (For additional practice, do Choral Conversation in small groups or by rows.)

SIDE BY SIDE EXERCISES

Example

1. A. Have you read any good books recently?
   B. Yes, I have. I read a very good book last week.
   A. Really? What book did you read?
   B. I read *(War and Peace)*.
   A. Oh. How was it?
   B. It was excellent. It's one of the best books I've ever read.

1. **Exercise 1:** Call on two students to present the dialog. Then do Choral Repetition and Choral Conversation practice.

2. **Exercises 2–3:** Either Full-Class Practice or Pair Practice.

How to Say It!

Expressing Satisfaction: In informal and spoken English, there are many ways to express satisfaction, such as the ones listed on text page 48. "Awesome" and "phenomenal" are popular expressions among younger speakers.

1. Set the scene: "The co-workers from the conversation above are talking."

2. Present the expressions.

3. Full-Class Repetition.

4. Ask students if they have any questions.

5. Group Choral Repetition.

6. Have students practice the conversations in this lesson again, using any of these new expressions.

7. Call on pairs to present their conversations to the class.

WORKBOOK

Pages 48–50

1. Disappearing Dialog ★

a. Write the model conversation on the board.

b. Ask for two student volunteers to read the conversation.

c. Erase a few of the words from each line of the dialog. Have two different students read the conversation.

d. Erase more words and call on two more students to read the conversation.

e. Continue erasing words and calling on pairs of students to say the model until all the words have been erased and the dialog has disappeared.

2. Role Play: Meeting a Famous Person ★★

a. Ask students to name a few of their favorite writers, actors/actresses, dancers, singers, or other artists.

b. Write on the board:

> A. Excuse me. Aren't you _____?
> B. Yes, I am.
> A. (Mr./Mrs./Miss/Ms.) _____, I've always wanted to meet you! I've _____ all your _____s, and I think they're the _____ _____s I've ever _____.
> B. Thank you very much.
>
> (Have students expand the dialog.)

c. Set the scene: "Imagine that you're walking down the street and you see a famous person you have always wanted to meet."

d. Call on pairs of students to role play this *chance encounter*. Student A can pretend to meet the writer/actor/etc, he or she really admires. For example:

> A. Excuse me. Aren't you Sophia Loren?
> B. Yes, I am.
> A. Ms. Loren, I've always wanted to meet you! I've seen all your movies, and I think they're the best movies I've ever seen.
> B. Thank you very much.

(Possible expansion)

> A. Ms. Loren. Could you possibly do me a favor?
> B. Of course. What is it?
> A. Could you please give me your autograph?
> B. I'll be happy to.

3. Our Recommendations ★★

a. Write the following conversation model on the board:

> A. Can you recommend a good { book / movie / restaurant / hotel / TV program / _____ }?
> B. Yes. _____ is a good _____. As a matter of fact, I think it's one of the best _____s I've ever _____.
> A. _____.
> B. _____.
> A. That's great! Thanks for the recommendation.

b. Call on pairs of students to create conversations based on the model, using names of real books, movies, restaurants, hotels, etc. For example:

> A. Can you recommend a good restaurant?
> B. Yes. Luigi's is a good restaurant. As a matter of fact, I think it's one of the best restaurants I've ever eaten at.
> A. Is it very expensive?
> B. No, not at all.
> A. That's great! Thanks for the recommendation.

> A. Can you recommend a good hotel?
> B. Yes. The Windsor is a good hotel. As a matter of fact, I think it's one of the best hotels I've ever stayed at.
> A. Where is it located?
> B. It's on Jackson Boulevard, near the park.
> A. That's great! Thanks for the recommendation.

(continued)

4. Write a Review ★★★

a. Have students pretend they work for a newspaper and write a review of one of the following:

  a movie they've seen
  a play they've seen
  a book they've read
  a restaurant where they've eaten

b. Have students read their reviews to the class, and have others react to the reviews by agreeing or disagreeing, or perhaps by asking for more information about the movie, play, book, or restaurant.

5. The Best! ★★

a. Divide the class into small groups. Have students develop a listing of their recommendations for the following:

  the best restaurant
  the best fast-food restaurant
  the best newspaper
  the best magazine
  the best new movie
  the best TV program
  the best CD

b. Have the groups share their ideas with the class and compile the top three picks for each category, if necessary through voting.

Option: ★★★ Have students "publish" their listing and distribute it to other classes in your school.

READING *Linda Likes New York*

FOCUS

• Present Perfect Tense

NEW VOCABULARY

Empire State Building
Statue of Liberty
take a tour
Times Square
top
United Nations

READING THE STORY

Optional: Preview the story by having students talk about the story title and/or illustration. You may choose to introduce new vocabulary beforehand, or have students encounter the new vocabulary within the context of the reading.

1. Have students read silently or follow along silently as the story is read aloud by you, by one or more students, or on the audio program.

2. Ask students if they have any questions. Check understanding of vocabulary.

3. Check students' comprehension, using the following questions:

   What has Linda done in New York?
   What hasn't she done yet?

   #### Culture Note

   Times Square on New Year's Eve:
   Thousands of people gather in Times Square in New York City to count down the last minute of the old year as a giant ball descends. Everyone cheers when the ball touches down and marks the new year.

READING EXTENSION

Have students answer these questions in pairs or small groups and then share their ideas.

1. *Places We Have Visited*

   Have students tell about interesting places they have visited.

   > Where did they go?
   > What interesting things did they see?
   > What did they do there?

2. *Places We Want to Visit*

   Have students tell about interesting places they *want to* visit.

   > What places around the world do you want to visit?
   > What do you want to do and see in those places?
   > What are some places you want to visit in your own city or region?

 LISTENING

Before doing the listening, introduce the new words *cable car, Golden Gate Bridge, Golden Gate Park, Alcatraz Prison, Chinatown, Fisherman's Wharf.*

1. **Linda is on vacation in San Francisco. This is her list of things to do. Check the things on the list Linda has already done.**

   Linda has already seen the Golden Gate Bridge. She hasn't visited Golden Gate Park yet. She took a tour of Alcatraz Prison yesterday. She's going to go to Chinatown tomorrow. She hasn't ridden a cable car yet. She's eaten at Fisherman's Wharf, but she hasn't had time to buy souvenirs.

2. **Alan is a secretary in a very busy office. This is his list of things to do before 5 P.M. on Friday. Check the things on the list Alan has already done.**

Alan has already called Mrs. Porter. He has to type the letter to the Mervis Company. He hasn't taken the mail to the post office yet. He's gone to the bank. He hasn't sent an e-mail to the company's office in Denver, and he's going to speak to the boss about his salary next week.

3. **It's Saturday, and Judy and Paul Johnson are doing lots of things around the house. This is the list of things they have to do today. Check the things on the list they've already done.**

Judy and Paul haven't done the laundry. They have to wash the kitchen windows. They've paid the bills. They haven't given the dog a bath. They'll clean the garage later. They couldn't fix the bathroom sink or repair the fence, but they vacuumed the living room rug.

Answers

✓	see the Golden Gate Bridge
____	visit Golden Gate Park
✓	take a tour of Alcatraz Prison
____	go to Chinatown
____	ride a cable car
✓	eat at Fisherman's Wharf
____	buy souvenirs

✓	call Mrs. Porter
____	type the letter to the Mervis Company
____	take the mail to the post office
✓	go to the bank
____	send an e-mail to the company's office in Denver
____	speak to the boss about my salary

____	do the laundry
____	wash the kitchen windows
✓	pay the bills
____	give the dog a bath
____	clean the garage
____	the bathroom sink
____	repair the fence
✓	vacuum the living room rug

Make a List!

Have students share their lists of *things they have and haven't done this week* with each other in pairs or small groups.

PRONUNCIATION
Contractions with *is* & *has*

Contractions with *is* & *has*: When the auxiliary verbs *is* and *has* are contracted, they are indistinguishable. *He's (he is)* is pronounced and written the same way as *he's (he has)*.

Focus on Listening

Practice the sentences in the left column. Say each sentence or play the audio one or more times. Have students listen carefully and repeat.

Focus on Pronunciation

Practice the sentences in the right column. Have students say each sentence and then listen carefully as you say it or play the audio.

If you wish, have students continue practicing the sentences to improve their pronunciation.

WORKBOOK

Page 51

EXPANSION ACTIVITY

Category Dictation ★★

1. Have students draw two columns on a piece of paper. At the top of one column, have students write <u>is</u>. At the top of the other column, have them write <u>has</u>.

2. Dictate various sentences with *is* and *has* (as an auxiliary), and have students write them in the appropriate columns. For example:

<u>is</u>	<u>has</u>
He's going to see a movie.	He's seen a movie.
She's very tired.	She's been very tired.
It's working well.	It's worked well.

JOURNAL

Have students write their journal entries at home or in class. Encourage students to use a dictionary to look up words they would like to use. Students can share their written work with other students if appropriate. Have students discuss what they have written as a class, in pairs, or in small groups.

GRAMMAR FOCUS

Answers

1. I've drawn
2. Have, seen
3. have, taken
4. We've, sung, sang
5. hasn't ridden
6. Have, been, have
7. has, worn, wore
8. Has, gone, she has, went

MULTILEVEL VARIATIONS

★ Tell *below-level* students the verb for each exercise, so they can focus only on putting it in the correct form.

★★★ Challenge *above-level* students to cover the grammar boxes as they complete the grammar exercises.

1 READING How to Fill Out an Employment Application

1. Have students read the brief introduction and look at the photograph. Ask: "What's she doing?" (She's filling out a job application form.) Then ask: "What information do you give on a job application form?" Write students' ideas on the board. (For example: name, address, social security number, previous jobs, contact numbers.)

2. Introduce the new vocabulary: *application, apply for, complete* (adj), *dates of employment, education history, employer, fill in, former, job application form, list* (v), *reference, state* (v), and *vocational school.*

3. Have students read the list silently. Then read the list aloud to the class. Then call on students to take turns reading the list aloud.

2 CONVERSATION Applying for a Job

1. Have students look at the photograph. Ask: "What's she doing?" (She's giving the employer a completed job application form.)

2. Model the completed A lines and have the class repeat. Then make sure students can say all the verbs in the reading in Exercise 1 in the present perfect. Have students look at the opening verbs in each sentence and say them in the present perfect tense (*have filled in, have stated, have completed, have listed, have written, have given, have described,* and *have checked*).

3. In pairs, have students practice the conversations as you circulate around the classroom, helping students as necessary.

3 TEAMWORK Application Forms

1. Brainstorm places where you can get application forms and write students' ideas on the board (restaurants, small businesses, supermarkets, retail businesses, etc.).

2. Have students visit different places in the community and obtain job application forms. Tell students to bring the forms to class.

3. In class, have students complete one of the job application forms and then go over the checklist with a partner. (If you wish, you can have students submit their applications to you for your review and comments.)

MULTILEVEL VARIATION ★★/★★★

As *at-level* and *above-level* students finish this activity, give them a copy of Life Skills Worksheet 11 to work on individually.

LIFE SKILLS ENRICHMENT

Job Application Vocabulary

Life Skills Worksheet 11

Make copies of Life Skills Worksheet 11 and give one to each student. Have students complete the worksheet as homework. In the next class, have students compare their answers in pairs.

EXPANSION ACTIVITIES

1. Guess the Word! ★

a. Divide the class into two teams. Choose a vocabulary word from the lesson, and on the board, write a blank for each letter in the word. For example: [reference]

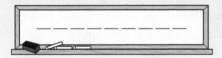

b. Give students a clue about the word. For example: "A person who knows you and can say you are a good employee and good person."

c. The team that guesses the word gets a point. The team with the most points wins the guessing game.

2. How Much Do You Remember? ★★

Divide the class into pairs. Have students close their books and retell to each other what they remember about the steps for completing a job application form on student text page 50a. Then have them open their books and check to see how much they remembered.

3. Associations ★★

a. Write the following six categories of job application information on the board.

> Personal Information
> Education History
> Current and Past Employment
> Skills
> References
> Position Applying For

b. Divide the class into pairs or small groups. Have students work together to write a list of the information required for each category in an application form. For example:

Personal Information: [name/address/phone number/social security number]
Education History: [high school/adult education program/college/community college/degrees/dates attended/date of graduation]
Current and Past Employment: [employment dates/reason for leaving job/employer name and address]

c. Have students share their lists with the class.

4. Dictate and Discuss ★★★

Divide the class into pairs or small groups. Dictate sentences such as the following and have students discuss whether they agree or disagree with the statements.

Employers never check references.
A family member is a good reference.
A former teacher is a good reference.
You should complete a job application with a blue or black pen.
You must tell the truth on a job application.

5. Problem Solving ★★★

Activity Master 24

a. Make multiple copies of Activity Master 24 and give one to each student.

b. Have students work individually to read the story and complete the comprehension exercise.

c. In pairs, have students compare answers, discuss the question, and complete the sentence.

d. Have students share their sentences with the class.

1. Have students look at the job application. Ask questions to orient students to the form—for example: "Who is the person applying for a job? Where does Daniel Lessard work now? Where did Daniel work from January 2005 to February 2008?" Introduce the new vocabulary: *cash register, change dressings, client, do lab tests, employment history, greet, medical assistant, medical records, middle name, office assistant, present, recent, schedule* (v), and *tool*.

2. Have students work individually to read the text and complete the comprehension exercise. Have them compare answers in pairs, small groups, or as a class.

MULTILEVEL VARIATIONS

★ Have *below-level* students work in pairs to provide each other with more support while doing the comprehension exercise.

★★/★★★ As *at-level* and *above-level* students finish this activity, give them copies of Life Skills Worksheet 12 to work on individually.

Answers

1. A	**4.** C
2. B	**5.** B
3. A	**6.** D

LIFE SKILLS ENRICHMENT

Job Application Form

Life Skills Worksheet 12 (two pages)

Make copies of Life Skills Worksheet 12 and give one to each student. Have students complete the application form as homework. In the next class, have students compare their answers in pairs.

EXPANSION ACTIVITIES

1. Put in Order ★

Activity Master 25

Make multiple copies of Activity Master 25, cut them up, and distribute one set to every pair of students. Have pairs of students work together to put the job cards in chronological order starting with the most recent. Call on a pair to read their list and have the class decide whether or not the order is correct.

2. True or False? ★★

Make statements about the application form on student text page 50b and have students decide whether the statements are true or false. If a statement is false, have students correct it. For example:

> Daniel now works as a medical assistant. [True.]
> Daniel was a receptionist in Tampa. [False. He was a receptionist in Miami.]
> Daniel worked as a cashier for two years. [False. He worked as a cashier for eight months.]

Variation: Do the activity as a game with competing teams.

3. How Much Do You Remember? ★★★

Divide the class into pairs. Have students close their books and retell to each other what they remember about Daniel Lessard's employment history on student text page 50b. Then have them open their books and check to see how much they remembered.

4. Information Gap ★★★

Activity Master 26

a. Make multiple copies of Activity Master 26 and cut them in half (Julie's Employment History A and Julie's Employment History B).

b. Divide the class into pairs. Give each partner a different employment history—A or B. Have students share their information and fill in their forms. For example:

A. How much does Julie make at her current job?

B. $11 an hour.

c. When the pairs have finished completing their forms, have them look at their partner's form to make sure they have written the information correctly.

MULTILEVEL VARIATIONS

★/★★ Have *below-level* and *at-level* students look at the questions at the end of each form as they do the activity.

★★★ Challenge *above-level* students to fold the questions under the activity master and form their own questions to ask their partner.

5. Guess Who! ★★★

a. Write the following on the board:

> I've worked as a _____.
> I worked as a _____ for
> _____ years.
> In my home country I was a _____.

b. Have students take out a piece of paper and use these as guidelines to write true sentences about themselves.

c. Collect the papers and mix them up. Read each paper aloud to the class and have students guess who the person is.

MAGAZINE ARTICLE *Find the Right Job!*

1. Have students look at the title and ask: "What is this article about?" Introduce the new vocabulary: *classified ad, cold call, create, employment website, help-wanted sign, Internet service, job bank, job fair, job listing, job opening, job opportunity, job posting, job search, local, look through, manager, network (v), on the spot, online, public building, public library, talent, thousands, tip,* and *website.*

2. Read the article aloud to the class as students follow along silently.

3. Have students work individually to complete the comprehension exercises and then compare answers in pairs, small groups, or as a class.

Answers

1. D	**4.** C
2. A	**5.** B
3. C	**6.** D

EXPANSION ACTIVITIES

1. Job Search Strategies ★

Activity Master 27

Make multiple copies of Activity Master 27 and give one to each student. Have students read the article again on student text page 50c and complete the activity master. Then have students compare answers in small groups.

Variation: ★/★★ Have pairs of *below-level* and *at-level* students take turns reading the lines of Activity Master 27 aloud and checking each other's comprehension of the article.

Variation: ★★★ Have pairs of *above-level* students work together. Tell them to draw two columns on a separate piece of paper and write True above one column and False above the other. Have the pairs take turns dictating lines from Activity Master 27 and have their partners write the lines in the correct column. For example:

True	False
There are many ways to find out about job openings.	To network means to look for a job online.

2. Job Search Match Game ★★

Activity Master 28

a. Make a copy of Activity Master 28 and cut it into cards. Distribute the cards randomly, one to each student.

   Note: The large cards are sentence beginnings and the small cards are sentence endings.

b. Have students memorize the sentence segment on their cards. Then have students circulate around the room saying their lines until they find their match. Make sure students don't show their cards to their classmates since this is a listening and speaking exercise.

c. When students have found their match, have them compare their cards and then come show you.

d. Continue until students have found all the matches.

MULTILEVEL VARIATION ★

Give below-level students the small cards, which are easier to memorize.

3. True or False? ★★

Make statements about the information on job search strategies on student text page 50c and have students decide whether the statements are true or false. If a statement is false, have students correct it. For example:

> Some people call businesses and ask if there are any openings. [True.]
> You can find a help-wanted sign on the Internet. [False. Help-wanted signs are usually in store windows.]
> It's possible to create a job for yourself. [True.]
> You can complete an application on the phone. [False. You can complete applications online.]

Variation: Do the activity as a game with competing teams.

4. Survey ★★★

Activity Master 29

a. Make copies of Activity Master 29 and give one to each student.

b. Have students interview others in the class by asking: "How did you find your current job?"

   Note: For students who are not currently employed, they can talk about a strategy they used to find a job in the past.

c. The interviewer should write the person's name next to the appropriate response.

d. When students have completed their surveys, have them add up the number of people for each response. Talk as a class about the results. Follow-up with the question: "What are the most common ways for students in our class to find jobs?"

Option: Have students create a bar graph illustrating their survey findings.

5. Advantages and Disadvantages ★★★

Activity Master 30

a. Divide the class into groups of three. Make multiple copies of Activity Master 30 and distribute one to each group.

b. Have students talk about the advantages and disadvantages of each job search strategy. Have one student in each group take notes on the activity master. For example:

Job Fairs	
Advantages (+)	Disadvantages (-)
There are many jobs in one place.	The jobs may not be local.
You can meet the people in the company.	There may be only certain kinds of jobs.

c. Have students tell the class their ideas.

6. Your Dream Job ★★★

Have students write a paragraph description of their dream job. Have students share their paragraphs in pairs.

CHECK-UP TEST

Have students do the check-up test and then review the answers as a class.

Answers

1. D	**6.** B
2. C	**7.** A
3. A	**8.** D
4. B	**9.** B
5. C	**10.** C

SKILLS CHECK

Words:

Explain to students that this is a list of words and phrases they have learned or reviewed in the unit. Have students take turns reading each item aloud to the class. Have students put a check next to the item if they feel they have learned it. Encourage students to get a small notebook where they can write down words that are difficult for them.

I can:

Explain to students that this is a list of skills they have learned in the unit. Read each item aloud to the class. Ask individual students or pairs of students to demonstrate the skill. For example:

Teacher: Have you ever seen the movie *Titanic*?
Student: Yes, I have. I saw it two years ago.

Teacher: I can identify employment application procedures.
Student 1: You get a job application.
Student 2: You fill out your personal information.
Student 3: You give the names and numbers of references.
Student 4: You write the dates of your employment.
Student 5: You complete your education history.
Student 6: You sign and date the application.

Have students put a check next to the item if they feel they have learned it. Use this information to determine which lessons you may want to review or reinforce for the entire class or for particular students.

EXPANSION ACTIVITIES

1. Concentration: Past Participles ★

Activity Master 31

a. Divide the class into pairs. Make multiple copies of Activity Master 31, cut them into cards, and distribute one set to each pair.

b. Have students shuffle the cards and place them face down in 8 rows of three each.

c. The object of the game is for students to find the matching verbs. Both students should be able to see the cards, since *concentrating* on their location is an important part of playing the game.

d. Student A turns over two cards, and if they match the student keeps the cards. If the verbs don't match, the student turns them face down and Student B takes a turn.

The game continues until all the cards have been matched. The student with the most correct matches wins the game.

2. Job Search Bingo ★★★

Activity Master 32

a. Make multiple copies of Activity Master 32 and give one to each student.

b. Have students write any nine words from the word box onto their grid.

c. Randomly define the words in the word box using the following definitions. Tell students to identify that word and look for it on their grids. If they have that word on their grids, they should cross it out.

education history—the names of the schools you have attended
employment history—your current and past jobs
job bank—a list of job openings on an employment website
job fair—an event where company representatives hire new employees
employer—the person who hires you

online—on the Internet
position—job
skills—things you know how to do
reference—a person who knows you well and can say good things about you
fill out—complete
hire—give someone a job
network—talk to people you know about your job search

d. The first student to mark out three boxes in a straight line—vertically, horizontally, or diagonally—wins.

3. Board Game ★★

Activity Master 33

For this activity, you will need a die, markers, and a piece of paper. (If students use a coin as a die, the class should decide which side of the coin will indicate a move of one space and which will indicate a move of two spaces.)

a. Make multiple copies of Activity Master 33. Divide the class into small groups and give each group a copy of Activity Master 33 along with a die, markers, and a piece of paper.

b. Have students place their markers on *Start*. The group should decide who goes first. That student begins the game by rolling the die or flipping the coin and moving his or her marker. If the student responds to the question or task correctly, he or she may take one more turn. If the student doesn't respond correctly, the next student takes a turn. No one may take more than two turns at a time.

Option 1: The first person to reach *Finish* is the winner.

Option 2: The game continues until each student reaches *Finish*. This way everybody is a winner.

4. Question Game ★★★

a. Write the following sentence on the board:

Laura likes to go to the museum, but she hasn't gone in a long time because she hasn't had the time.

b. Underline different elements of the sentence and have students create a question based on that portion of the sentence. For example:

Laura likes to go <u>to the museum</u>, but she hasn't gone in a long time because she hasn't had the time.

Where does Laura like to go?

Laura likes to go to the museum, but she hasn't gone in a long time <u>because she hasn't had the time</u>.

Why hasn't Laura gone to the museum in a long time?

c. Continue with other sentences.

5. Dialog Builder! ★★★

a. Divide the class into pairs. Write a line on the board from a lesson in the unit, such as the following:

I'm jealous.

Other possible lines are:

Yes, I have.
No, not yet.
A little while ago.
Really? When?
It was awesome!
Have you given the names and numbers of three references?

b. Have each pair create a conversation incorporating that line. Students can begin and end their conversations any way they wish, but they must include that line in their dialogs.

c. Call on students to present their conversations to the class.

(continued)

6. What's Wrong? ★★★

a. Write several sentences such as the following on the board or on a handout that you give to students. Some of the sentences should be correct and others incorrect. For example:

> I have flew airplanes for many years.
> Do you know how speak Spanish?
> I've sung on Broadway.
> Have you gone to the zoo ever?
> Never I've eaten lunch with my boss.
> Have you ever fallen asleep in class?
> Is the teacher explained it yet?
> She's given a speech last year.
> They've yet gone to the mall.
> We've done all our homework yesterday.
> He hasn't gotten a haircut yet.
> I've already went to the bank.
> We have to pay the bills now.
> You've to finish your homework.
> That was one of the best book I've ever ridden.
> Have you gave the reason for leaving each position?
> Have you completed your education history on your application?

b. Divide the class into pairs. The object of the activity is for students to identify which sentences are incorrect and then correct them. Have students compare their answers in small groups.

Variation: Do the activity as a game with competing teams. For each team's turn, write one sentence on the board and have the team decide whether the sentence is correct or not. If it isn't correct, the team must correct it. Every time a team is right, that team receives one point. The team with the greatest number of points wins.

MULTILEVEL VARIATION ★

For *below-level* students, underline the errors and have the below-level pairs focus only on correcting them.

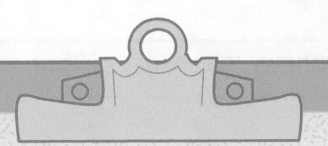

Teacher's Notes

GRAMMAR

SINCE/FOR

We've known each other	since	three o'clock. yesterday afternoon. last week. 2000. we were in high school.
	for	three hours. two days. a week. a long time.

PRESENT PERFECT VS. PRESENT TENSE

I **know** how to ski.

I**'ve known** how to ski since I was a little girl.

PRESENT PERFECT VS. PAST TENSE

Victor **was** an engineer.

He**'s been** a taxi driver since he immigrated.

FUNCTIONS

ASKING FOR AND REPORTING INFORMATION

How long *has your neck been stiff*?
For *more than a week*.

Do you know *how to ski*?
Yes, I do. I've known *how to ski* since *I was a little girl*.

How long have you *known each other*?
We've known each other for *three years*.
We've known each other since *1998*.

Has *Victor* always been *a taxi driver*?
No. *He's been a taxi driver* since *he immigrated*.
Before that, *he was an engineer*.

Have you always *taught history*?

No. I've *taught history* for *the past three years*.
Before that, I *taught geography*.

Do you still *live on Main Street*?
No. I haven't *lived on Main Street for several years*.

Are you still *a barber*?
No. I haven't been *a barber for several years*.

So how are you feeling today, *George*?
Not very well, *Dr. Fernando*.
What seems to be the problem?
My neck is stiff.

What is your present address?
How long have you lived there?
What was your last address?
How long did you live there?

Tell me, _____.
Tell me, *Tony*, _____.
And how about YOU?

REACTING TO INFORMATION

Oh. I didn't know that.
Oh. I didn't realize that.
Oh. I wasn't aware of that.

INDICATING UNDERSTANDING

I see.

GREETING PEOPLE

George!
  Tony!

How have you been?
  Fine. And how about YOU?
Everything's fine with me, too.

EXPRESSING SURPRISE-DISBELIEF

I can't believe it's you!

EXPRESSING AGREEMENT

That's right, *George*.

LEAVE-TAKING

Well, *George*, I'm afraid I have to go now. We should get together soon.
Good idea, *Tony*.

NEW VOCABULARY

Employment

cover letter
hours of work
lunch break
management
medical reason
paycheck
payment schedule
payroll office
sick day
sick leave
sick time
staff
supplies
team
time clock
time sheet
vacation day
work shift

Occupations

assistant manager
astronaut
barber
clerk
computer programmer
engineer
guidance counselor
guitarist
manager
musician
physician
store manager
taxi driver
vice president

Medical Care

black and blue
body
dizzy
feel dizzy
have *the measles*
high fever
neck
pain
patient
stiff
swollen
waiting room

The Arts

art
modern art
photography
Picasso

Time Expressions

early this morning
more than *a week*
the past *three years*

Verbs

arrange
count
get paid
graduate
handle
immigrate
infect
own
package
peel
punch in
punch out
record
save up
sign up
take time
weigh

Adjectives

dedicated
engaged
fortunate
incarcerated
interested (in)
necessary
present
successful
terminated
unused

Food

deli counter
family restaurant
salad plate
seafood
takeout food
vegetable dish

School

medical school
music school

Musical Instruments

cello
saxophone

Places Around the World

Dallas
Georgia
Singapore
Texas

Miscellaneous

accent
  New York accent
  southern accent
bachelor
bottom
complaint
department
direct deposit
form (n)
inn
leader
lottery
personal computer
satellite
space
tardiness
termites
whole milk

EXPRESSIONS

Good idea.
happily married
in love
It's been a long time.
start at the bottom
"the birds and the bees"
the facts of life
work *his* way up to the top

VOCABULARY PREVIEW

You may want to introduce these words before beginning the unit, or you may choose to wait until they first occur in a specific lesson. If you choose to introduce them at this point, here are some suggestions:

1. Have students look at the illustrations on text page 51 and identify the words they already know.

2. Present the vocabulary. Say each word and have the class repeat it chorally and individually. Check students' understanding and pronunciation of the words.

3. Practice the vocabulary as a class, in pairs, or in small groups. Have students cover the word list and look at the pictures. Practice the words in the following ways:

   • Say a word and have students tell the number of the illustration.

   • Give the number of an illustration and have students say the word.

FOCUS

- Present Perfect Tense:
  Questions with *How Long*
  Expressions with *For* and *Since*

CLOSE UP

Time expressions with *for* and *since* are commonly used with the present perfect tense to describe something that began in the past and continues in the present.

RULE: *For* is used with expressions describing a period of time.

EXAMPLES: We've known each other **for three years**.
She's had the measles **for five days**.

RULE: *Since* is used with expressions referring to a definite point in time.

EXAMPLES: I've been sick **since last Friday**.
They've been married **since 1985**.

INTRODUCING THE MODELS

There are two model conversations. Introduce and practice each separately. For each model:

1. Have students look at the model illustration.

2. Set the scene:

> 1st model: "A salesperson in a jewelry store is talking to a couple who are looking for a wedding ring."
> 2nd model: "One friend is visiting another friend who is sick."

3. Present the model.

4. Full-Class Repetition.

Pronunciation Note

The pronunciation focus of Unit 5 is **Reduced *have* & *has*** (text page 64). You may wish to model this pronunciation at this point (*How long have you been sick? How long have you known each other?*) and encourage students to incorporate it into their language practice.

5. Ask students if they have any questions. Check understanding of the word *known* in the 1st model.

6. Group Choral Repetition.

7. Choral Conversation.

8. Call on one or two pairs of students to present the dialog.

   (For additional practice, do Choral Conversation in small groups or by rows.)

9. Further practice with *for* and *since*:

   a. After the 1st model, call on pairs of students to present the model again, using some of the other expressions under *for* in the box at the top of text page 52. For example:

   > *a long time*
   >
   > A. How long have you known each other?
   > B. We've known each other for a long time.

   b. After the 2nd model, same as above, using some of the expressions under *since* in the box at the top of text page 52. For example:

last week

   A. How long have you been sick?
   B. I've been sick since last week.

SIDE BY SIDE EXERCISES

Examples

> 1. A. How long have Tom and Janet known
>   each other?
>   B. They've known each other for two
>   years.
> 2. A. How long have Mr. and Mrs. Garcia
>   been married?
>   B. They've been married since 1995.

1. **Exercise 1:** Call on two students to present the dialog. Then do Choral Repetition and Choral Conversation practice.

2. **Exercise 2:** Same as above.

3. **Exercises 3–12:** Either Full-Class Practice or Pair Practice.

New Vocabulary

  5. guidance
    counselor
  6. satellite
    space
  7. own (v)
  9. interested in
 10. photography

Culture Note

Exercise 5: A *guidance counselor* is a person who helps high school students select classes according to their interests and career plans.

WORKBOOK

Pages 52–54

EXPANSION ACTIVITIES

1. *For or Since?* ★

a. Write on the board:

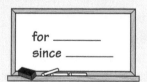

    for _____
    since _____

b. Say time expressions such as those below and have students rephrase them with *for* or *since*. For example:

  Teacher: a long time
  Student: for a long time

  Teacher: last week
  Student: since last week

Time expressions:

  yesterday   (since)
  two hours   (for)

a few minutes	(for)
this morning	(since)
2000	(since)
several weeks	(for)
a long time	(for)
a quarter to three	(since)
ten years	(for)
Wednesday	(since)
last month	(since)
three days	(for)
1999	(since)
three and a half weeks	(for)
eleven o'clock last night	(since)

Variation: Do the activity as a game with competing teams.

2. Rephrase the Sentences! ★★

a. Have students open their books to text pages 52 and 53.

b. Write the current year on the board. For example:

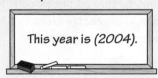

This year is (2004).

c. Based on what the year is, have students rephrase the sentences about the characters in Exercises 1, 2, 5, 6, 7, 8, and 11 on text pages 52 and 53. Have students either say or write their new sentences. For example:

Exercise 1: Tom and Janet have known each other for two years.
rephrased: They've known each other since (2002).

Exercise 2: Mr. and Mrs. Garcia have been married since 1985.
rephrased: They've been married for (19) years.

Exercise 5: Ms. Bennett has been a guidance counselor for 19 years.
rephrased: She's been a guidance counselor since (1985).

Exercise 6: There have been satellites in space since 1957.
rephrased: There have been satellites in space for (47) years.

Exercise 7: I've owned this car for three and a half years.
rephrased: I've owned this car since (2001).

Exercise 8: Bob has owned his own house since 1991.
rephrased: Bob has owned his own house for (13) years.

Exercise 11: I've been here since 1979.
rephrased: I've been here for (25) years.

d. Call on individual students to give their answers.

Variation: Do the activity as a game with competing teams. The team that writes the sentences in the shortest time is the winner.

3. Grammar Chain: How Long Have You Lived Here? ★★

a. Write the following conversation model on the board:

A. How long have you lived here?
B. I've lived here since _____.
A. Since _____? You've lived here for _____ years!
B. That's right. How long have YOU lived here?

b. Start the chain game by modeling the conversation with a student. Then have students continue the chain. For example:

Teacher: How long have you lived here?
Student A: I've lived here since (1991).
Teacher: Since (1991)? You've lived here for (13) years!
Student A: That's right. *[to Student B:]* How long have YOU lived here?
Student B: I've lived here since (2001).

Tell students they can use any date they wish to answer the first question.

4. Get to Know Your Classmates ★★★

a. Write the following on the board:

study
live in
be interested in
own
have
be
know

b. Divide the class into pairs and have students ask each other questions with *how long*, using the verbs on the board. For example:

A. How long have you studied English?
B. I've studied English for two years.

A. How long have you owned a bicycle?
B. I've owned a bicycle since 2000.

c. Have students tell the class about the person they interviewed.

(continued)

5. Find the Right Person! ★★★

a. From the prior activity, write down information about the students.

b. Put the information on a handout in the following form:

> Find someone who . . .
>
> 1. has lived here since 1986. _____
> 2. has studied English for _____
>   five years.
> 3. has owned a bicycle for _____
>   ten years.
> 4. has been interested in jazz _____
>   since he was a teenager.

c. Have students circulate around the room, asking each other questions to identify the above people.

d. The first student to find all the people, raise his or her hand, and correctly identify the people is the winner of the game.

6. Which One Isn't True? ★★★

a. Tell students to write two true statements and one false statement about themselves. For example:

> I've owned a car since 2001.
> I've been interested in ballet since I was ten.
> I've had a bad headache since last night.

b. Have students take turns reading their statements to the class, and have the class guess which statement isn't true.

READING *A Very Dedicated Doctor*

FOCUS

- Present Perfect Tense
- Since/For

NEW VOCABULARY

black and blue	more than *a week*
body	neck
dedicated	pain
dizzy	patient (n)
early this morning	stiff
feel dizzy	swollen
for the past *24 hours*	take time
high fever	waiting room

READING THE STORY

Optional: Preview the story by having students talk about the story title and/or illustrations. You may choose to introduce new vocabulary beforehand, or have students encounter the new vocabulary within the context of the reading.

1. Have students read silently, or follow along silently as the story is read aloud by you, by one or more students, or on the audio program.

2. Ask students if they have any questions. Check understanding of vocabulary.

3. Check students' comprehension, using some or all of the following questions:

   What's the matter with George?
   What's the matter with Martha?
   What's the matter with Lenny?
   What's the matter with Carol?
   What's the matter with Bob?
   What's the matter with Bill?

What's the matter with Tommy and Julie?
How long has Dr. Fernando been in his
   office?
What don't his patients know?
What's the matter with him?
Why hasn't he taken time to stay at home
   and rest?

✔ READING *CHECK-UP*

Q & A

1. Call on a pair of students to present the model.

2. Have students work in pairs to create new dialogs.

3. Call on pairs to present their new dialogs to the class.

CHOOSE

1. a	**5.** a
2. b	**6.** b
3. b	**7.** a
4. a	**8.** a

CHOOSE

1. b	**4.** a
2. a	**5.** b
3. b	**6.** b

READING EXTENSION

1. *Miming*

   a. Write on cards the symptoms from the reading. For example:

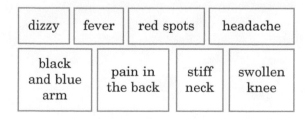

b. Have students take turns picking a card from the pile and pantomiming the symptom on the card.

c. The class must guess what symptom the person is miming and which character in the story has that symptom.

Variation: Do the activity as a game with competing teams.

2. **Class Discussion: A Good Doctor**

a. Write the following on the board:

A good doctor is dedicated.
A good doctor is _____ and
_____.
A good doctor doesn't think about
_____.
A good doctor always _____.
A good doctor never _____.

b. Have students complete the sentences and then compare their answers.

c. Follow up with a class discussion about what qualities make a good doctor.

FOCUS

- Present Perfect Tense:
    Contrast with the Present Tense
    Since Expressions

CLOSE UP

RULE: *Since* is used with past time phrases that describe a point in time in the past.

EXAMPLES: I've known how to ski **since I was a little girl**.
We've been engaged **since we finished college**.

GETTING READY

Contrast the simple present tense and the present perfect tense.

1. Put these cues on the board:

Lucy

speak English
interested/astronomy
married
own/house
work/restaurant

2. Make two statements about each cue: one in the present tense and one in the present perfect tense. For example:

   Lucy speaks English.
   She's spoken English since she was young.

   Lucy is interested in astronomy.
   She's been interested in astronomy for a long time.

3. Point to each cue and call on one or more students to tell about Lucy in the same way.

INTRODUCING THE MODELS

There are two model conversations. Introduce and practice each separately. For each model:

1. Have students look at the model illustration.

2. Set the scene:

   1st model: "Two friends are talking."
   2nd model: "A woman is talking to a young couple at a party."

3. Present the model.

4. Full-Class Repetition.

5. Ask students if they have any questions. Check understanding of the word *engaged* in the 2nd model.

   ### Culture Note

   In traditional U.S. culture, a couple who are planning to get married may announce their intentions by becoming *engaged* to be married. The man may also give the woman an engagement ring.

6. Group Choral Repetition.

7. Choral Conversation.

8. Call on one or two pairs of students to present the dialog.

   (For additional practice, do Choral Conversation in small groups or by rows.)

Examples

> 1. A. Does your sister Jennifer play the cello?
>   B. Yes. She's played the cello since she was eight years old.
>
> 2. A. Is your friend Michael a professional musician?
>   B. Yes. He's been a professional musician since he graduated from music school.

1. **Exercise 1:** Introduce the word *cello*. Call on two students to present the dialog. Then do Choral Repetition and Choral Conversation practice.

2. **Exercise 2:** Introduce the words *musician, graduate* (v), *music school*. Same as above.

3. **Exercises 3–12:** Either Full-Class Practice or Pair Practice.

> **New Vocabulary**
>
> 3. personal computer
> 4. modern art
>   Picasso
> 6. count (v)
> 10. termites
> 12. the birds and the bees
>   the facts of life

Culture Notes

Exercise 4: Pablo Picasso is a famous 20th-century artist.

Exercise 11: *Titanic* is the true story of a large ship that sank in the North Atlantic. Most of the ship's passengers died in the disaster.

Exercise 12: The euphemistic expression "the birds and the bees" is used in polite conversation to refer to the *facts of life* or *where babies come from*.

WORKBOOK

Pages 55–57

EXPANSION ACTIVITIES

1. Sense or Nonsense? ★★

   a. Divide the class into four groups.

   b. Make many sets of split sentence cards with beginnings and endings of sentences. For example:

   | She's had a stomachache since . . . | she ate a donut this morning. |

   | He's liked classical music since . . . | he heard his first concert. |

   | She's been interested in astronomy since . . . | she first saw the stars at night. |

   | He's studied Spanish since . . . | he went to Mexico on vacation. |

She's owned her own business since . . .	she graduated from business school.
They've had blue hair since . . .	they became rock stars.
She's been interested in photography since . . .	she bought a new camera.
He's had pain in his back since . . .	he worked in his garden yesterday.
My children have stayed in bed since . . .	they got the measles.
Her neck has been stiff since . . .	she was in a car accident.

c. Mix up the cards and distribute sets of cards to each group, keeping the beginning and ending cards in different piles.

d. Have students take turns picking up one card from each pile and reading the sentence to the group. For example:

She's been interested in photography since . . .	they got the measles.

e. That group decides if the sentence makes *sense* or is *nonsense*.

f. After all the cards have been picked, have the groups lay out all the cards and put together all the sentence combinations that make sense.

2. Change the Sentence! ★★

a. Write a sentence on the board, underlining and numbering different portions of the sentence. For example:

1	2
Paul	has been interested in
3	4
Russian history	since he visited Moscow.

b. Have students sit in a circle.

c. Tell them that when you say a number, the first student in the circle makes a change in that part of the sentence. For example:

Teacher: Two.
Student 1: Paul has wanted to study Russian history since he visited Moscow.

d. The second student keeps the first student's sentence, but changes it based on the next number you say. For example:

Teacher: Three.
Student 2: Paul has wanted to study Russian poetry since he visited Moscow.

e. Continue this way with the rest of the students in the circle. For example:

Teacher: Four.
Student 3: Paul has wanted to study Russian poetry since he met Anna.

3. Expand the Sentence! ★★

Tell students that the object of the activity is to build a long sentence on the board, one word at a time.

a. Call on a student to write a pronoun or someone's name on the far left side of the board. For example:

Barbara

b. Have another student come to the board and add a word. For example:

Barbara has

(continued)

c. Have a third student add a third word. For example:

> Barbara has been

d. Continue until each student in the class has had one or more turns to add a word to expand the sentence into the longest one they can think of. For example:

> Barbara has been interested in modern art since she found a wonderful book about Picasso in the library in the center of her city.

4. Class Discussion: Complete the Sentences ★★

a. Write on the board the following sentence beginnings:

> Since I was a child, I've known how to _____.
>
> Since I was a child, I've liked _____.
> Since I started English classes, I've _____.
> Since I read about _____, I've wanted to _____.

b. Have students complete the sentences individually and then share their sentences in small groups or as a class.

5. Sentence Cues ★★

a. On separate cards, write key words that can be put together to form sentences or questions. Clip together the cards for each sentence. For example:

you	speak	Spanish	since	go to Caracas

she	be interested	ballet	since	see Swan Lake

they	work	on the farm	since	leave New York City

b. Divide the class into small groups and give a clipped set of cards to each group.

c. Have each group write a sentence based on their set of cards.

d. Have one member of each group write that group's sentence on the board and compare everybody's sentences.

6. Guess Who! ★★★

a. Write on the board:

> I like _____.
> I'm interested in _____.
> I know how to _____
> I play _____.
> I'm a _____.
> I want to be a _____.
> I have _____.

b. Have each student write three sentences about himself or herself, using some of the cues on the board. For example:

> I'm interested in computers.
> I play the guitar.
> I have a pet bird.

c. Have students fold their papers and give them to you. Mix them up and give each student someone else's paper.

d. Call on students to read the sentences. Then have the class guess who wrote them.

e. After the class has identified the person who wrote the statements, have students ask that person any questions they wish, using how long.

7. Key Word Role Play: At a Party ★★★

a. Write the following on the board:

interested in?
live?
work?
how long?

b. Divide the class into pairs.

c. Tell each pair that they've just met at a party. Have them create a role play, using the key expressions on the board.

d. Call on pairs to present their role plays to the class.

8. What's Wrong? ★★★

a. Divide the class into pairs or small groups.

b. Write several sentences such as the following on the board or on a handout. Some of the sentences should be correct, and others incorrect. For example:

> I know them for a long time.
> He's been interested in computers since many years.
> She's played the piano since she was a child.
> They been married for fifty years.
> How long you own that car?
> I been sick since last Monday.
> You've had a backache for a week.
> How long there be problems at your company?

c. The object of the activity is for students to identify which sentences are incorrect and then correct them.

d. Have students compare their answers.

Variation: Do the activity as a game with competing teams. The team that successfully completes the task in the shortest time is the winner.

FOCUS

- Present Perfect Tense:
    Contrast with the Past Tense
    Review of Yes/No Questions

CLOSE UP

RULE: The present perfect describes an activity that began in the past and continues up to the present. The simple past describes an activity that began and ended in the past.

EXAMPLES: **I've taught** history for the past three years. *(I continue to teach history.)*
Before that, I **taught** geography. *(I don't teach geography now.)*

INTRODUCING THE MODELS

There are two model conversations. Introduce and practice each separately. For each model:

1. Have students look at the model illustration.

2. Set the scene.

    1st model: "A student is talking to his history professor."
    2nd model: "Two people are talking about Victor."

3. Present the model.

4. Full-Class Repetition.

5. Ask students if they have any questions. Check understanding of new vocabulary:

    1st model: *geography*
    2nd model: *immigrate, engineer*

6. Group Choral Repetition.

7. Choral Conversation.

8. Call on one or two pairs of students to present the dialog.

    (For additional practice, do Choral Conversation in small groups or by rows.)

SIDE BY SIDE EXERCISES

Examples

1. A. Have you always liked classical music?
   B. No. I've liked classical music for the past five years. Before that, I liked jazz.

2. A. Has Carlos always been the store manager?
   B. No. He's been the store manager since last January. Before that, he was a cashier.

1. **Exercise 1:** Call on two students to present the dialog. Then do Choral Repetition and Choral Conversation practice.

2. **Exercise 2:** Introduce the expression *store manager*. Same as above.

3. **Exercises 3–8:** Either Full-Class Practice or Pair Practice.

New Vocabulary

4. astronaut
5. southern accent
   New York accent
   Georgia
7. whole milk
8. lottery

How to Say It!

Reacting to Information: In spoken English, it is common to react to new information with any of these three phrases: "Oh. I didn't know that." "Oh. I didn't realize that." "Oh. I wasn't aware of that."

1. Present the expressions.
2. Full-Class Repetition.
3. Ask students if they have any questions.

4. Group Choral Repetition.
5. Have students practice the conversations in this lesson again, using any of these new expressions.
5. Call pairs of students to present their conversations to the class.

How About You?

1. Go over the questions before students do the activity.
2. Call on a few pairs of students to ask and answer the questions.
3. Divide the class into pairs, and have students ask and answer the questions. Remind students to use the expressions for *Reacting to Information* from the *How to Say It!* section above.

WORKBOOK

Pages 58–59

EXPANSION ACTIVITIES

1. Summarizing with the Present Perfect ★★

Have students listen as you read each of the situations below. Then call on a student to summarize what happened, using the present perfect. (There may be more than one way to summarize what happened.) For example:

Situation: Bill saw Jim this morning. He saw him again at lunch. Then he saw him again in the parking lot.

Summary: Bill has seen Jim three times today.
or
Bill has seen Jim several times/ a lot today.

Situations:

Gloria called her cousin this morning, and she called him again this afternoon.

Robert wrote two letters to the Kendall Company last week, and he wrote them another one this morning.

We saw Mr. and Mrs. Chen at a basketball game on Tuesday night and at a concert on Thursday night.

Alan studied French in high school. He studied Spanish in college. And last year he studied Japanese.

Mrs. Phillips went to Europe in 1995. She went to Europe again in 2000.

Larry is reading a lot this year in school. He read four books last semester. And he read two more books last month.

Joe came to class late yesterday. He came to class late again today.

Julie's aunt sent her a birthday gift this week. Her friend Eileen sent her one, too.

Veronica had a baby girl in 1998. In 2001 she had a baby boy.

Mrs. Garcia's students did well on their history tests last semester. They did well on their tests this semester, too.

(continued)

2. Find the Right Person! ★★

a. Write the following on the board:

> For the past six months I have _____.
> For the past few years I have _____.
> I have always _____.

b. Have students complete these sentences any way they wish and hand them in to you.

c. Put the information on a handout in the following form:

> Find someone who . . .
>
> 1. has been school president _____
>   for the past six months.
> 2. has studied piano for the _____
>   past few years.
> 3. has always wanted to fly _____
>   an airplane.

d. Have students circulate around the room, asking each other questions to identify the above people. For example:

> Student A: Have you ever been school president?
> Student B: Yes, I have. I've been school president for the past six months.

e. The first student to find all the people, raise his or her hand, and identify the people is the winner of the game.

3. Same and Different: Musical Tastes ★★★

a. Put the following on the board:

> I have _____.
> My partner has _____.
> We both have _____.

b. Write a list of questions about students' musical tastes such as the following on the board or on a handout for students:

> What kind of music do you like?
> How long have you liked/listened to _____?
> Do you play any musical instruments?
> How long have you studied _____?

c. Divide the class into pairs.

d. Have students interview each other and then report to the class about the ways in which they're *the same* and the ways in which they're *different*. For example:

> I have listened to jazz since I was young.
> My partner has studied the piano for ten years.
> We both have always liked classical music.

4. Sharing Histories ★★★

a. Write on the board:

> I've _____ since/for _____.
> Before that I _____.

b. Have students complete the sentences, using the model on the board. Have them write about their work histories, where they have lived, where they have gone to school, sports they have played, or general facts about themselves.

c. Divide the class into groups. Have students share their information with the class. Remind students that they can react using the expressions in the *How to Say It!* section on student text page 59.

READING *A Wonderful Family*

FOCUS

- Present Perfect vs. Present Tense

NEW VOCABULARY

bachelor	medical school
computer programmer	physician
fortunate	Singapore
guitarist	successful
happily married	

READING THE STORY

Optional: *Preview the story by having students talk about the story title and/or illustration. You may choose to introduce new vocabulary beforehand, or have students encounter the new vocabulary within the context of the reading.*

1. Have students read silently or follow along silently as the story is read aloud by you, by one or more students, or on the audio program.

2. Ask students if they have any questions. Check understanding of vocabulary.

3. Check students' comprehension, using some or all of the following questions:

   What does Ruth do?
   How long has she been an engineer?
   How long have Ruth and Pablo been married?
   What does Pablo do?
   How long has he known how to play the guitar?
   What does David do?
   How long has he been interested in computers?
   What does Rita do?

How long has she been a physician?
Is Herbert married?
What does Herbert do?
Have Mr. and Mrs. Patterson seen him recently?

✓ READING *CHECK-UP*

1. True
2. False
3. False
4. True
5. False
6. True
7. False

READING EXTENSION

Family Trees

1. Have students draw a family tree for the Patterson family in the reading. Have pairs of students compare their drawings.

2. Have students then draw their own family trees. Have students share their family trees in small groups. Have students ask and answer questions about each other's family. For example:

   Where does he/she live?
   How long has he/she lived there?
   What does he/she do?
   How long has he/she been a _____?

 LISTENING

Listen to the conversation and choose the answer that is true.

1. A. How long have you had a backache?
   B. For three days.

2. A. Has your father always been an engineer?
   B. No, he hasn't.

3. A. How long has your knee been swollen?
   B. For a week.

4. A. How long have you known how to ski?
   B. Since I was a teenager.

5. A. Did you live in Tokyo for a long time?
   B. Yes. Five years.

6. A. How long has Roger been interested in Egyptian history?
   B. Since he lived in Cairo.

7. A. Is Amy still in the hospital?
   B. Oh. I forgot to tell you. She's been home for two days.

8. A. Have you played hockey for a long time?
   B. Yes. I've played hockey since I moved to Toronto three years ago.

Answers

1. b
2. a
3. b
4. a
5. b
6. b
7. a
8. a

READING *Working Their Way to the Top*

FOCUS

* Present Perfect vs. Past Tense

NEW VOCABULARY

assistant manager
bottom
Dallas
department
start at the bottom
Texas
vice president
work *his* way up to the top

READING THE STORY

Optional: Preview the story by having students talk about the story title and/or illustrations. You may choose to introduce new vocabulary beforehand, or have students encounter the new vocabulary within the context of the reading.

1. Have students read silently or follow along silently as the story is read aloud by you, by one or more students, or on the audio program.

2. Ask students if they have any questions. Check understanding of vocabulary.

3. Check students' comprehension, using some or all of the following questions:

> How long has Louis been the store manager?
> How long was he a clerk?
> How long was he a cashier?
> How long was he an assistant manager?
> When did he become the manager?
> Why is everybody at the Big Value Supermarket proud of Louis?

How long has Kate been the president?
How long was she a salesperson?
How long was she the manager of the Women's Clothing Department?
How long was she the store manager?
What happened after that?
When did she become the president?
Why is everybody at the Marcy Department Store in Dallas proud of Kate?

✓ READING *CHECK-UP*

1. False
2. True
3. Maybe
4. False
5. Maybe
6. True

READING EXTENSION

1. *Tic Tac Question the Answer*

a. Draw a tic tac grid on the board and fill it in with short answers to questions:

For six years.	Two years ago.	Yes, he did.
For three years.	Yes, they have.	No, he didn't.
Yes, she has.	Yes, he has.	Yes, she did.

b. Divide the class into teams. Give each team a mark: *X* or *O*.

c. Have each team ask a question about the story on text page 61 for an answer in the grid. For example:

> X Team: Has Kate worked very hard to get where she is today?
> Yes, she has.

d. If an answer is appropriate and is stated correctly, that team may replace the answer with its team mark. For example:

For six years.	Two years ago.	Yes, he did.
For three years.	Yes, they have.	No, he didn't.
X	Yes, he has.	Yes, she did.

e. The first team to mark out three boxes in a straight line—either vertically, horizontally, or diagonally—wins.

2. *Time Lines*

a. Have students draw a time line for the two characters in the reading. Have pairs of students compare their time lines.

b. Have students then draw a time line of someone they know. Have students share their time lines with a partner. Have students ask and answer questions about each other's time line. For example:

When did he/she begin that job?
Where did he/she live?
How long did he/she work there?
What does he/she do now?

Writing

1. Make sure students understand the questions.

2. Have students ask you the questions and take notes based on your answers.

3. Have students write their stories about you at home, using a dictionary for any new words they wish to use.

4. Have students present and discuss what they have written in pairs, small groups, or as a class.

ROLE PLAY *It's Been a Long Time*

FOCUS

* Review: Present Perfect Tense

INTRODUCING THE MODEL

1. Have students look at the model illustration.

2. Set the scene: "Two old friends have just met on the street. They haven't seen each other in a long time."

3. Have students listen as you present the dialog or play the audio one or more times.

4. Ask students if they have any questions. Check understanding of new vocabulary: *barber, taxi driver, saxophone, Good idea, It's been a long time.*

   ### Language Note

   Good idea is a reduced form of the expression *That's a good idea.*

5. Divide the class into pairs. Have students practice the dialog.

6. Call on one or two pairs of students to present the dialog.

ROLE PLAY

1. Divide the class into pairs. Have students role play the dialog using the guide on text page 63 and any vocabulary they wish.

2. Call on pairs of students to present their role plays to the class without referring to the text.

EXPANSION ACTIVITY

Scrambled Dialog Game ★★

1. Divide the class into five teams.

2. Make five sets of the conversation from student text page 62, writing each line on a separate card.

3. Give each group one set of the cards, and have the group members reorder the conversations.

4. The first team to put the conversation in the correct order is the winner.

WORKBOOK

Pages 60–61

PRONUNCIATION Reduced *have & has*

> **Reduced *have & has:*** In spoken English, the pronunciation of the *h* in the auxiliaries *have* and *has* is often omitted. The reduced pronunciation of *have* is [ov] and of *has* is [az].

Focus on Listening

Practice the sentences in the left column. Say each sentence or play the audio one or more times. Have students listen carefully and repeat.

Focus on Pronunciation

Practice the sentences in the right column. Have students say each sentence and then listen carefully as you say it or play the audio.

If you wish, have students continue practicing the sentences to improve their pronunciation.

JOURNAL

Have students write their journal entries at home or in class. Encourage students to use a dictionary to look up words they would like to use. Students can share their written work with other students if appropriate. Have students discuss what they have written as a class, in pairs, or in small groups

GRAMMAR FOCUS

Answers

1. have known, since
2. has been sick, for
3. have you had
4. Are you
5. We've owned, for
6. She's had, since, she had
7. has been, since, he was
8. haven't seen, have
9. haven't lived, I live

MULTILEVEL VARIATION ★★★

Challenge *above-level* students to cover the grammar boxes as they complete the grammar exercises.

1 CONVERSATION
Describing Work Experience

1. Have students look at the photo. Ask: "What's the man doing?" (He's interviewing for a job.) Have students look at the job application forms next to the photos. Ask questions to get students oriented to the information. For example: "Where does this person work now? How long has he/she worked there? Where did he/she work before? How long did he/she work there?" Introduce the words *inn* and *discount store*.

2. Model Conversation 1 with a student volunteer. For example:

   A. Where do you work now?
   B. I work at Zenith Computer Company.
   A. How long have you worked there?
   B. I've worked there since June 2007.
   A. Where did you work before that?
   B. I worked at Carter Insurance.
   A. How long did you work there?
   B. I worked there for two years.

3. In pairs, have students practice the conversations as you circulate around the classroom.

4. Model the *open* conversation with a student. Play the role of Student B. Use your own information. For example:

   A. Where do you work now?
   B. I work at Springdale Learning Center.
   A. How long have you worked here?
   B. I've worked here since September 2004.
   A. Where did you work before that?
   B. I worked at Citywide Language School.
   A. How long did you work there?
   B. I worked there for two years.

5. In pairs, have students practice the open conversation as you circulate around the classroom.

6. Call on pairs of students to present their conversations to the class.

2 CONVERSATION
Asking for Clarification

1. Have students look at the photo. Ask: "What do you say when you don't understand what someone has said?" Write students' ideas on the board. Introduce the new words *incarcerated* and *terminated*.

2. Model Conversation 1 with a student volunteer. For example:

   A. Have you ever been terminated?
   B. I'm sorry. I don't understand what "terminated" means.
   A. Have you ever been fired from a job?
   B. I understand. No, I haven't.

3. In pairs, have students practice the conversations as you circulate around the classroom, helping students as necessary.

4. Call on students to present their conversations to the class.

TEAMWORK

1. In pairs, have students brainstorm questions, phrases, and situations they didn't understand.

2. Call on students to share their ideas with the class. Write a list of questions and phrases students were confused by. Call on other students to explain them. Clarify any items that students aren't able to explain.

LIFE SKILLS ENRICHMENT

Job Interview: Employment History

Life Skills Worksheet 13

Make copies of Life Skills Worksheet 13 and give one to each student. Have students complete the worksheet as homework. In the next class, have students compare their answers in pairs.

1. Scrambled Sentences ★

Activity Master 34

Divide the class into pairs. Make enough copies of Activity Master 34 for half the class. Cut them into cards and distribute one set to each pair of students. Have students take turns picking up a scrambled sentence prompt and then saying the sentence in the correct order. Then have students assemble the sentences into a dialog.

Variation: Students can write out their dialog and then compare their answers with other pairs.

2. Student Interview: Employment History ★★

Activity Master 35

a. Make multiple copies of Activity Master 35. Divide the class into pairs. Give one Activity Master to each student.

b. Tell students they have ten minutes each to conduct their interviews and write down their partners' information on the Activity Master.

c. As students are interviewing one another, circulate to help as necessary.

d. Have students show one another their completed forms to check the accuracy of their comprehension.

MULTILEVEL VARIATIONS

★ Allow *below-level* students to look at the questions at the bottom of the Activity Master.

★★ Challenge *above-level* students to fold the questions under the Activity Master and form their own questions to ask their partners.

3. Survey: What Do You Do? ★★

Activity Master 36

a. Make copies of Activity Master 36 and give one to each student.

b. Have students interview others in the class by asking: "What do you do?" For example:

    A. What do you do?
    B. I'm a cook.
    A. How long have you been a cook?
    B. For four years.
    A. [Write information on the form.]

c. When students have completed their surveys, have them share their information with the class. Follow-up with the question: "Who has had the same occupation the longest?"

4. Dictate and Discuss ★★★

Divide the class into pairs or small groups. Dictate sentences such as the following and have students discuss whether they agree or disagree with the statements.

You have to tell the truth in a job interview.
You have to write the truth on a job application.
The employer will find out if you were ever incarcerated.
The employer will find out if you were ever terminated.
It's good to stay at the same company for many years.
It's good to change your job every few years.

1. Point to the resume on student text page 64b. Ask: "What's this?" (A resume.) Point to the cover letter on student text page 64b. Ask: "What's this?" (A cover letter.) "Who wrote this letter?" (Linda Palermo.) "Why is she writing this letter?" (She's applying for a job at the Seaside Restaurant Company.) Point out the writing conventions, such as the return address and date in the upper right corner; the title, name, and address of the recipient; the salutation *Dear* _____, the closing *Sincerely,* _____; and the signature as well as the typed name.

2. Read the letter and resume aloud to the class or have students take turns reading them aloud. Introduce the new vocabulary: *arrange, clerk, complaint, cover letter, deli counter, family restaurant, handle* (v), *management, package* (v), *peel, salad plate, seafood, staff, supplies, takeout food, team, vegetable dish,* and *weigh.*

3. Have students do the comprehension exercises individually and then compare their answers in pairs.

Answers

1.	C	**4.**	A
2.	B	**5.**	D
3.	A	**6.**	B

WRITING

Have students complete Life Skills Worksheet 14 and then write their own cover letter. Life Skills Worksheet 15 provides a model for students to use to create their own resumes.

LIFE SKILLS ENRICHMENT

A Cover Letter

Life Skills Worksheet 14

Make copies of Life Skills Worksheet 14 and give one to each student. Have students complete the worksheet as homework. In the next class, have students compare their letters in pairs.

Write Your Resume

Life Skills Worksheet 15

Make copies of Life Skills Worksheet 15 and give one to each student. Write a sample resume on the board following the outline on Life Skills Worksheet 15. Have students write their own resumes as homework. In the next class, have students compare their resumes in pairs and then submit them to you for review.

EXPANSION ACTIVITIES

1. Guess the Word! ★

a. Divide the class into two teams. Choose a vocabulary word or phrase from the reading, and on the board, write a blank for each letter in the word or phrase. For example: (resume)

b. Give students a clue about the word or phrase. For example: "a description of an applicant's employment history, skills, and references."

c. The team that guesses the word gets a point. The team with the most points wins the guessing game.

2. True or False? ★★

Make statements about the resume on student text page 64b and have students decide whether the statements are true or false. If a statement is false, have students correct it. For example:

Linda's most recent job is as a chef. [False. Her most recent job is as a manager.]

Linda was a prep cook before she was a chef. [True.]

Linda had two different positions in the same company. [True. She was a deli counter clerk and then a prep cook at Health Food Markets in North Miami.]

Linda lives in North Miami. [False. She lives in Sunrise.]

Variation: Do the activity as a game with competing teams.

3. Role Play ★★

a. Divide the class into pairs. Have each pair write and then role play a job interview between Linda Palermo and Monica Jordan.

b. Call on a few pairs to perform their role plays for the class.

4. Dictate and Discuss ★★★

Divide the class into pairs or small groups. Dictate sentences such as the following and have students discuss whether they agree or disagree with the statements.

A cover letter is a way to introduce your resume.

Most office jobs and management jobs require a resume.

You should use nice paper for your cover letter and resume.

You should write your social security number on your resume.

You should write down all your work experience on your resume.

You should describe your family on your resume.

You should hand in your cover letter and resume in person.

1. Ask students: "What kind of information does a new employee need on the first day of work?" Write students' ideas on the board.

2. Introduce the new vocabulary: *direct deposit, form, get paid, hours of work, infect, lunch break, medical reason, necessary, paycheck, payment schedule, payroll office, punch in, punch out, record* (v), *save up, sick day, sick leave, sick time, sign up, tardiness, time clock, time sheet, unused, vacation day,* and *work shift.*

3. Have students work individually to complete the comprehension exercise and then compare answers in pairs, small groups, or as a class.

Answers

1. C	**4.** B
2. A	**5.** C
3. D	**6.** B

LIFE SKILLS ENRICHMENT

New Employee Manual Checklist

Life Skills Worksheet 16

Make copies of Life Skills Worksheet 16 and give one to each student. Have students complete the worksheet as homework. In the next class, have students compare their answers in pairs.

EXPANSION ACTIVITIES

1. Scrambled Words ★

   a. Choose words or phrases from student text page 64c and write them on the board or on a card with the letters scrambled out of order. For example:

   cedrti sipoted

   b. Have students take turns guessing what the word or phrase is. [direct deposit]

   Variation 1: Do the activity in pairs or small groups, with students taking turns scrambling words and phrases for others to guess.

   Variation 2: Do the activity as a class game with competing teams.

2. Mix and Match Words ★★

   Activity Master 37

   The employee manual on student text page 64c has many words that go together, but each word has a meaning by itself, too.

   a. Divide the class into groups of three. Make a copy of Activity Master 37 for each group. Cut the Activity Masters into two sets of cards, shuffle the cards, and place them face down in two piles—one for first words and the other for second words.

   Note: The small cards are for first words and the large cards are for second words.

   b. Distribute the two sets of cards to each group. Have students take turns picking up one card from each pile and reading the word combination to the group. For example:

time	office

   (continued)

The group decides if the word combination is in the reading on student text page 64c. If it is, they write it down on a piece of paper.

c. After all the cards have been chosen, have the group lay out all the cards and put together all the word combinations from the reading.

MULTILEVEL VARIATIONS

★ *Below-level* students can read through the two sets of cards all at once and then match them face up.

★★★ *Above-level* students can also generate other word combinations that make sense— for example: *work schedule, lunch schedule, vacation schedule.*

3. How Much Do You Remember? ★★

a. Write the following topics on the board:

> Hours of Work
> Time Clock and Time Sheets
> Payments Schedule
> Sick Time
> Vacation Time
> Absence and Tardiness

b. Divide the class into pairs. Have students close their books and retell to each other what they remember about the topics from the employee manual on student text page 64c. Then have them open their books and check to see how much they remembered.

4. True or False? ★★

Make statements about the employee manual on student text page 64c and have students decide whether the statements are true or false. If a statement is false, have students correct it. For example:

> Employees can pick up their checks at the payroll office. [True.]
> The employees get paid once a month. [False. They get paid once a week.]
> Employees must punch out before lunch every day. [True.]
> Employees get ten vacation days a year. [True.]
> Employees are allowed to save up vacation days to use in future years. [False. They can't save up vacation days.]

Variation: Do the activity as a game with competing teams.

5. Interview an Employee ★★★

Activity Master 38

Note: The activity is intended for students who have jobs. If many in your class are not working, have students interview others in the school who are currently employed.

a. Make multiple copies of Activity Master 38. Divide the class into pairs. Give one Activity Master to each student.

b. Tell students they have ten minutes each to conduct their interviews and write down their partners' information on the Activity Master.

c. As students are interviewing one another, circulate to help as necessary.

MULTILEVEL VARIATION ★★★

Challenge *above-level* students to write a summary paragraph of their interviews and submit it to you for your review.

CHECK-UP TEST

Have students do the check-up test and then review the answers as a class.

Answers

1. C	**6.** B
2. A	**7.** D
3. D	**8.** C
4. B	**9.** D
5. A	**10.** B

SKILLS CHECK ✔

Words:

Explain to students that this is a list of words they have learned in the unit. Have students take turns reading each item aloud to the class. Have students put a check next to the item if they feel they have learned it. Encourage students to get a small notebook where they can write down words that are difficult for them.

I can:

Explain to students that this is a list of skills they have learned in the unit. Read each item aloud to the class. Ask individual students or pairs of students to demonstrate the skill. For example:

> Teacher: I can ask and answer: How long have you been here?
> Student A: How long have you been here?
> Student B: I've been here for two and a half years.
>
> Teacher: I can ask for clarification.
> Student: I'm sorry. I don't understand. What does "incarcerate" mean?

Have students put a check next to the item if they feel they have learned it. Use this information to determine which lessons you may want to review or reinforce for the entire class or for particular students.

EXPANSION ACTIVITIES

1. Listen for the Verbs ★

   a. Have students make three columns on a piece of paper and write the following at the top of each column:

      Present
      Present Perfect
      Past

   b. Dictate the following sentences and have students write the verbs in the appropriate column.

      He's known how to paint for years.
      He knows how to paint.
      She's had a headache for two days.
      She has a headache.
      She had a headache for two days.
      They own their own business.
      They've owned their own business since 2004.
      They owned their own business in 2004.
      I've liked jazz for years.
      I like jazz.
      I liked jazz when I was younger.

   c. As a class, in pairs, or in small groups, have students check their work.

2. Associations ★

   a. Divide the class into small groups. Call out an occupation from the word list on student text page 64d and have the groups write down as many associations with that occupation as they can think of. For example:

      barber: [cut hair/scissors/shave/chair/greet customers]
      manager: [supervise/train employees/hire new employees]

   b. Have the groups call out their words and make a common list on the board.

3. Scrambled Sentences ★

   Activity Master 39

   Divide the class into pairs. Make enough copies of Activity Master 39 for half the class. Cut them

   (continued)

into cards and distribute one set of cards to each pair of students. Have students take turns picking up a scrambled sentence prompt and then saying the sentence in the correct order.

Variation: Students can write their sentences and then compare their answers with other pairs.

4. Board Game ★★

Activity Master 40

For this activity, you will need a die, markers, and a piece of paper. (If students use a coin as a die, the class should decide which side of the coin will indicate a move of one space and which will indicate a move of two spaces.)

a. Make multiple copies of Activity Master 40. Divide the class into small groups and give each group a copy of Activity Master 40 along with a die, markers, and a piece of paper.

b. Have students place their markers on *Start*. The group should decide who goes first. That student begins the game by rolling the die or flipping the coin and moving his or her marker. If the student responds to the question or task correctly, he or she may take one more turn. If the student doesn't respond correctly, the next student takes a turn. No one may take more than two turns at a time.

Option 1: The first person to reach *Finish* is the winner.

Option 2: The game continues until each student reaches *Finish*. This way everybody is a winner.

5. Question Game ★★

a. Write the following sentence on the board:

> Miguel has been interested in Japanese art since he went to Japan last year.

b. Underline different elements of the sentence and have students create a question based on that portion of the sentence. For example:

> Miguel has been interested in Japanese art <u>since he went to Japan last year.</u>

How long has Miguel been interested in Japanese art?

> Miguel has been interested <u>in Japanese art</u> since he went to Japan last year.

What has Miguel been interested in since he went to Japan?

c. Continue with other sentences.

6. What's Wrong? ★★★

a. Write several sentences such as the following on the board or on a handout that you give to students. Some of the sentences should be correct and others incorrect. For example:

> I've know him for twenty years.
> She's owned her own house since two
>   years.
> They've been interested in modern art for
>   last year.
> I've known how ski since five years ago.
> We've been tired when the baby was born.
> She's been president since three months.
> Before that, she was vice president.
> He's always wanted to be an astronaut.
> They've been on vacation since they won
>   the lottery.
> Before that, they've worked in San Diego.
> We've had a cat for 2007.
> How long you worked there?
> Where have you worked before that?

b. Divide the class into pairs. The object of the activity is for students to identify which sentences are incorrect and then correct them. Have students compare their answers in small groups.

Variation: Do the activity as a game with competing teams. For each team's turn, write one sentence on the board and have the team decide whether the sentence is correct or not. If it isn't correct, the team must correct it. Every time a team is right, that team receives one point. The team with the greatest number of points wins.

Multilevel Variation ★

For *below-level* students, underline the errors and have the below-level pairs focus only on correcting them.

Text Pages 65–68: *Side by Side Gazette*

 FEATURE ARTICLE
*"24/7"—24 Hours a Day/
7 Days a Week*

PREVIEWING THE ARTICLE

1. Have students talk about the title of the article and the accompanying photographs.

2. You may choose to introduce the following new vocabulary beforehand, or have students encounter it within the context of the article:

area
child-care center
communication
computer company
daytime
do business
factory worker
fax
firefighter
in the past
instant
late-night
local
manufacturing company
9 to 5
night shift
office worker
photocopy center
shift
stay open
switch
24/7
work schedule
World Wide Web
worldwide

READING THE ARTICLE

1. Have students read silently, or follow along silently as the article is read aloud by you, by one or more students, or on the audio program.

2. Ask students if they have any questions. Check understanding of new vocabulary.

3. Check students' comprehension by asking the following questions:

   Why are more and more companies operating "24/7"?
   What percentage of employees work the evening and night shifts?
   What kinds of jobs did traditional night-shift workers have?
   Who are the new night-shift workers?
   How have local businesses changed to serve these night-shift workers?

4. Have students discuss the questions in small groups or as a class.

EXPANSION ACTIVITIES

1. Dictate and Discuss ★★★

   a. Divide the class into pairs or small groups.

   b. Dictate sentences such as the following and then have students discuss them:

      People work more now than they did twenty years ago.
      Technology makes life easier.
      The 24/7 work schedule is good for families.
      Technology makes it possible for people to take longer vacations.

   c. Call on students to share their opinions with the rest of the class.

2. The Longest List ★★★

   a. Divide the class into several teams. Have students brainstorm the types of businesses that operate twenty-four hours a day.

   b. Have the teams share their lists with the class. The team with the longest list wins.

3. Advantages and Disadvantages ★★★

   a. Have students draw two columns on a piece of paper. At the top of one column, have students write Advantages. At the top of the other column, have them write Disadvantages.

b. Name one late-night activity—for example: *late-night shopping at a supermarket, working the 11:00 to 7:00 shift, or late-night shopping on the Internet.* Have students brainstorm the advantages and disadvantages of doing this at night instead of during the day. Write students' ideas in the columns and have students copy the sentences on their papers. For example:

<u>Late-Night Shopping at a Supermarket</u>

<u>Advantages</u>

There's no traffic, and there are no parking problems.

There's a short check-out lane because there are few shoppers.

<u>Disadvantages</u>

Tired drivers can make mistakes.

There are fewer employees to help customers.

---

4. Survey ★★★

Have students find out about their classmates' preferred schedules.

a. Brainstorm with the class questions students can ask each other about their preferences. For example:

> When are you most active—in the morning or at night?
> Do you like to stay up late at night?
> When do you do your shopping?
> When do you work?

b. Have each student choose one question to ask and then conduct a survey by circulating around the room, asking the others that question.

c. For homework, have students draw up the survey results in graph form (for example, a bar graph or pie chart). In class, have students share their graphs and report their results.

5. A Perfect Work Schedule ★★★

a. For homework, have students answer the following:

> In your opinion, what is a perfect work schedule? Why?

b. Have students share their writing in pairs.

AROUND THE WORLD
Unique Jobs

1. Have students read silently or follow along silently as the text is read aloud by you, by one or more students, or on the audio program.

2. Check understanding of the words *coffee plantation worker, dog day-care worker, exist, reindeer herder, safari guide, subway pusher, tulip farmer, unique.*

3. Bring a map to class and point out the locations referred to in the photographs.

4. Have students first work in pairs or small groups, responding to the question. Then have students tell the class what they talked about. Write any new vocabulary on the board.

EXPANSION ACTIVITIES

1. Ranking ★★

a. Ask students: "Which of these jobs would you like to have?"

b. Have students rank these jobs from the *most interesting* to the *least interesting*.

c. As a class, in pairs, or in small groups, have students compare their lists.

2. Unique Local Jobs ★★

a. Divide the class into groups. Call out a city, town, or region in your area and have students brainstorm unique jobs that can be done only in that location.

b. Have the teams share their lists with the class.

INTERVIEW

1. Have students read silently, or follow along silently as the interview is read aloud by you, by one or more students, or on the audio program.

2. Ask students if they have any questions. Check understanding of the words *asleep, awake, day shift, forever, normally, notes, put to bed.*

3. Check students' comprehension by asking the following questions:

> What is Mrs. Souza's work schedule?
> What is Mr. Souza's work schedule?
> Who helps them with the children?
> Do their children go to school yet?
> When do Mr. and Mrs. Souza usually see each other?
> How do Mr. and Mrs. Souza communicate during the week?
> What does Mr. Souza hope for in the future?

EXPANSION ACTIVITIES

1. The Kids' Schedule ★★

The interview describes the mother's and father's day. Have students read the interview again and write out a typical day for the Souza children.

2. Advantages and Disadvantages ★★★

a. Have students draw two columns on a piece of paper. At the top of one column, have students write Advantages. At the top of the other column, have them write Disadvantages.

b. Have students brainstorm the advantages and disadvantages of the Souzas' work schedules. Write students' ideas in the columns and have students copy the sentences on their papers. For example:

> Advantages
> They don't have to spend money on child care.
> The grandmother is able to spend time with her grandchildren.
>
> Disadvantages
> Mr. and Mrs. Souza don't get to see each other.
> It's difficult for the parents because they never have time off to relax.

3. Student Interviews ★★★

a. If possible, have students conduct an interview with parents of young children they know. Have students brainstorm the kinds of questions they want to ask.

b. Have students report their findings to the class and write up a report for homework.

FACT FILE *Vacation Time in Different Countries*

1. Before reading the Fact File, show the class a world map. Have students identify the locations of the following place names:

> Australia
> Denmark
> Germany
> Japan
> Sweden
> the United States

2. Have students rank the countries according to which ones they think would have the longest vacations. Write students' ideas on the board. Then have students read the table on text page 67 to check their predictions.

3. Read the table aloud as the class follows along. Ask students: "Is this list different from your list? How is your list different?"

EXPANSION ACTIVITY

Student Investigation ★★★

1. Have students conduct interviews with people from the previous generation. Have students ask:

> How much vacation time did you get thirty years ago?
> Do you think people today get more or less vacation time?
> How is vacation time different now?

2. Have students compare their notes. Ask: "Are people now getting more vacation time or less vacation time than in the past? How was vacation time different thirty years ago?"

LISTENING *Office Voice Mail*

1. Check understanding of the expression *voice mail*.

2. Set the scene: "Sam works for Ms. Rivera. These are phone messages they left for each other."

LISTENING SCRIPT

Listen to the voice-mail messages between Gloria Rivera and her office assistant, Sam. Has Sam done the things on Ms. Rivera's list? Check *Yes* or *No*.

You have one message. Tuesday, 8:15 A.M.

Hello, Sam? This is Ms. Rivera. I'll be out of the office all day today. I'm not feeling well. Here's a list of things you'll need to do while I'm not here. First, please write a note to Mrs. Wilson and tell her I'm sick. Then, please call Mr. Chen and change the time of our appointment. Also, send an e-mail to everybody in the office, and tell them about next week's meeting. Don't forget to speak to the custodian about my broken desk lamp. I hope he can fix it. Hmm. Let's see. I know there are a few more things. Oh, yes. Please make a list of all the employees and give it to Ms. Baxter. She asked me for the list last week. Okay, Sam. I think that's everything. Oh . . . one more thing. Please take the package on my desk to the post office if you have time. And that's it. Thanks, Sam. I'll see you tomorrow morning.

You have reached the voice mailbox of Gloria Rivera. Please leave a message after the tone.

Ms. Rivera? This is Sam. I'm sorry you aren't feeling well. I hope you feel better tomorrow. I'm calling to tell you what I've done today, and what I haven't done yet. It's been very busy here, so I haven't had time to do everything. I wrote a note to Mrs. Wilson. I called Mr. Chen and changed the time of your appointment. I also sent the e-mail about next week's meeting. I haven't spoken to the custodian. He's been sick all week. I made a list of all the employees, but I haven't given it to Ms. Baxter yet. I'll give it to her early tomorrow morning. Finally, I haven't taken the package to the post office yet. I haven't had time. I'm going to take it to the post office on my way home.

Again, I hope you're feeling better. I'll see you in the morning.

Answers

	Yes	No
1.	✔	___
2.	✔	___
3.	✔	___
4.	___	✔
5.	✔	___
6.	___	✔
7.	___	✔

 FUN WITH IDIOMS

> a couch potato
> a real ham
> a real peach
> a smart cookie
> chicken
> the top banana

INTRODUCTION AND PRACTICE

For each idiom, do the following:

1. Have students look at the illustration.

2. Present the idiom. Say the expression and have the class repeat it chorally and individually. Check students' pronunciation of the words.

DO YOU KNOW THESE EXPRESSIONS?

Have students match the expressions with their meanings.

Answers

1. d
2. f
3. a
4. e
5. c
6. b

EXPANSION ACTIVITIES

1. Line Prompts ★★

Call out one of the following line prompts and have students respond appropriately with "yes" and one of the idioms.

Is she an important person in the company.
(Yes. She's the top banana.)

Is he funny all the time?
(Yes. He's a real ham.)

Do you like your new co-worker?
(Yes. She's a real peach.)

Is he really lazy?
(Yes. He's a couch potato.)

Is she as intelligent as she looks?
(Yes. She's a smart cookie.)

Is he always afraid to try new things?
(Yes. He's chicken.)

2. Idiom Challenge! ★★★

a. Divide the class into pairs.

b. Have each pair create a conversation in which they use as many of the idioms from text page 67 as they can.

c. Have the pairs present their conversations to the class. Which pair used the most idioms?

 WE'VE GOT MAIL!

THE LETTER TO *SIDE BY SIDE*

1. Have students read silently, or follow along silently as the letter is read aloud by you, by one or more students, or on the audio program.

2. Ask students if they have any questions. Check understanding of the words *confused, past participle, perfectly.*

3. Check students' comprehension by having them decide whether these statements are true or false:

The writers are confused about the tense in the sentence "I have driven." *(True)*

The students have a similar tense in their own languages. *(False)*
The students don't know when to use the present perfect tense. *(True)*
The students think that part participles are easy to learn. *(False)*
The students don't understand why there are so many new verb forms in the present perfect. *(True)*

4. Ask students:

Did you ever have this question?
Do you have a tense similar to the present perfect in your language?
Can you explain how the present perfect is different from the present tense? How is it different from the past tense?

THE RESPONSE FROM *SIDE BY SIDE*

1. Have students read silently, or follow along silently as the letter is read aloud by you, by one or more students, or on the audio program.

2. Ask students if they have any questions. Check understanding of the words *exact, learner.*

3. Check students' comprehension by having them decide whether these statements are true or false:

People use the present perfect tense to talk about things that happened at a specific point in the past. *(False)*
It's correct to say in English "I have seen you yesterday morning." *(False)*
People use the present perfect to talk about things that happened several times in the past. *(True)*
It's correct to say in English "He's visited Tokyo three times." *(True)*
People use the present perfect to talk about things that began in the past and continue until now. *(True)*
It's correct to say in English "I worked here for the last two years." *(False)*

EXPANSION ACTIVITY

What's Wrong? ★★★

1. Divide the class into pairs or small groups.

2. Write several sentences such as the following on the board or on a handout. Some of the sentences should be correct, and others incorrect. For example:

   > I live here since 2001.
   > You've been here since last Sunday.
   > We tried that recipe last weekend.
   > She's never saw a rainbow.
   > He's read that book.
   > I've already gave you a key.
   > I drove a taxi for three years, and I still do.
   > She knows us since 2000.
   > They've went to Paris five times.
   > He teaches history for several years.

3. The object of the activity is for students to identify which sentences are incorrect and then correct them. For each incorrect statement, have students identify which rule on text page 68 it breaks.

4. Have students compare their answers.

   Variation: Do the activity as a game with competing teams. The team that successfully completes the task in the shortest time is the winner.

GLOBAL EXCHANGE

1. Set the scene: "Alex32 is writing to a keypal."

2. Have students read silently or follow along silently as the message is read aloud by you, by one or more students, or on the audio program.

3. Ask students if they have any questions. Check understanding of the expression *in a while.*

4. Options for additional practice:

   - Have students write a response to Alex32 and share their writing in pairs

   - Have students correspond with a keypal on the Internet and then share their experience with the class.

 ## WHAT ARE THEY SAYING?

FOCUS

- Accomplishing Tasks

Have students talk about the people and the situation, and then create role plays based on the scene. Students may refer back to previous lessons as a resource, but they should not simply reuse specific conversations.

Note: You may want to assign this exercise as written homework, having students prepare their role plays, practice them the next day with other students, and then present them to the class.

GRAMMAR

PRESENT PERFECT CONTINUOUS TENSE

(I have)	I've	
(We have)	We've	
(You have)	You've	
(They have)	They've	been working.
(He has)	He's	
(She has)	She's	
(It has)	It's	

Have	I we you they	been working?
Has	he she it	

Yes,	I we you they	have.
	he she it	has.

FUNCTIONS

ASKING FOR AND REPORTING INFORMATION

What have you been doing?
    I've been *writing letters*.
How many *letters* have you *written*?
    I've already *written fifteen letters*.

How long have you been *waiting*?
    I've been *waiting* for *two hours*.
    I've been *waiting* since *this morning*.

What *are your neighbors* doing?
    They're arguing.
Have *they* been *arguing* for a long time?
    Yes, *they* have. *They've been arguing all day*.

Where do you *live* now?
How long have you been *living* there?
Where else have you *lived*?
    I've also *lived* in _____.
How long did you *live* there?
    I *lived* there for _____.

What do you do there?
And where did you *work* before that?
    I *worked* at _____.
What did you do?

We're having a problem with *our bedroom ceiling*.
    Oh? What's the problem?
It's leaking.

Tell me, _____?

Why?

RESPONDING TO INFORMATION

Really?

INDICATING UNDERSTANDING

I see.

EXPRESSING SURPRISE–DISBELIEF

You're kidding!
No kidding!
You've got to be kidding!
I can't believe it!
That's incredible!
That's unbelievable!
That's amazing!

DESCRIBING FEELINGS–EMOTIONS

I'm nervous.

REASSURING

Don't worry!

Believe me, there's nothing to be nervous about!

PERSUADING

Believe me, . . .

EXPRESSING INTENTION

I'll *take care of it* as soon as I can.
We'll *call you* soon.

GREETING PEOPLE

Hello.
    Hello. This is *Mrs. Banks*.
Yes, *Mrs. Banks*. What can I do for you?

INITIATING A TOPIC

You look tired.

EXPRESSING GRATITUDE

Thank you.
Thank you very much.

I appreciate the opportunity to *meet with you*.

RESPONDING TO GRATITUDE

It's been a pleasure.

NEW VOCABULARY

Housing

building entrance
ceiling
dumpster
emergency maintenance
  number
fire hazard
hallway
heating system
maintenance request form
personal possessions
pest control company
premise
property
recycling bin
recycling collection site
recycling program
reduced waste
refuse
storage area
water heater

Utility Bills

account number
adjustments
balance information
billing
billing date
billing period
billing summary
credit rating
credits
current charges
customer assistance line
due date
full payment
kilowatt hour
late payment
late payment charge
local services
long distance
meter number
meter reading
minimum
past due
payment
payment due
payment received
power and light
power outage

remaining balance
service (n)
service address
service balance
statement
statement date
Therm
total amount due
total balance
unpaid balance
usage

Applying for a Job

opportunity
resume
work experience

Verbs

appreciate
date
deliver a baby
direct traffic
discover
do sit-ups
empty
give *piano* lessons
harbor
keep clear
leak
make noises
mend
peel
pick
respond
ring
rinse out
sign
stand in line

Time Expressions

as soon as
lately

Adjectives

exhausted
furious
jammed
leased
legal

metal
permitted
prohibited
routine (adj)
valuable

Miscellaneous

bones
cage
cardboard
chemistry
concert ticket
contract
downtown
hardwood floor
marathon
officer
P.O. Box
parking ticket
pits
pleasure
preparation
strictly
summary
ticket

EXPRESSIONS

all right
at once
believe me
for years
It's been a pleasure.
There's nothing to be nervous
  about!
What can I do for you?

You're kidding!
No kidding!
You've got to be kidding!
I can't believe it!
That's incredible!
That's unbelievable!
That's amazing!

VOCABULARY PREVIEW

You may want to present these words before beginning the unit, or you may choose to wait until they first occur in a specific lesson. If you choose to present them at this point, here are some suggestions:

1. Have students look at the illustrations on text page 69 and identify the words they already know.

2. Present the vocabulary. Say each word and have the class repeat it chorally and individually. Check students' understanding and pronunciation of the words.

3. Practice the vocabulary as a class, in pairs, or in small groups. Have students cover the word list and look at the pictures. Practice the words in the following ways:

   • Say a word and have students tell the number of the illustration.

   • Give the number of an illustration and have students say the word.

FOCUS

• Present Perfect Continuous Tense

CLOSE UP

RULE: The present perfect continuous tense is formed with the auxiliary verb *have* + *been* + the present participle (the *-ing* form of the verb). The auxiliary verb *have/has* is usually contracted in informal language.

EXAMPLES: **I've been working.**
You've been working.
He's been working.
She's been working.
It's been working.
We've been working.
They've been working.

RULE: Like the present perfect tense, the present perfect continuous tense is associated with a period of time beginning in the past and continuing up until the present.

EXAMPLES: **I've been waiting** for two hours. *(I'm still waiting.)*
It's been barking since this morning. *(It's still barking.)*

INTRODUCING THE MODELS

There are two model conversations. Introduce and practice each separately. For each model:

1. Have students look at the model illustration.

2. Set the scene:

   1st model: "Some people are waiting to see the doctor."
   2nd model: "One friend is asking the other about her neighbor's dog."

3. Present the model.

4. Full-Class Repetition.

Pronunciation Note

The pronunciation focus of Unit 6 is **Reduced *for*** (text page 80). You may wish to model this pronunciation at this point *(I've been waiting for two hours)* and encourage students to incorporate it into their language practice.

5. Ask students if they have any questions. Check understanding of new vocabulary:

   1st model: *have been waiting*
   2nd model: *has been barking*

6. Group Choral Repetition.

7. Choral Conversation.

8. Call on one or two pairs of students to present the dialog.

   (For additional practice, do Choral Conversation in small groups or by rows.)

9. Form sentences with the words in the box at the top of text page 70 and have students repeat chorally. For example:

   I've been working.
   We've been working.

10. Expand the first model with further practice by replacing *you* with *they, we, Mary*. For example:

    they
    A. How long have they been waiting?
    B. They've been waiting for two hours.

SIDE BY SIDE EXERCISES

Examples

1. A. How long has Yasmin been studying English?
   B. She's been studying English for eight months.

2. A. How long have Mr. and Mrs. Green been living on School Street?
   B. They've been living on School Street since 1994.

1. **Exercise 1:** Call on two students to present the dialog. Then do Choral Repetition and Choral Conversation practice.

2. **Exercise 2:** Same as above.

3. **Exercises 3–12:** Either Full Class Practice or Pair Practice.

New Vocabulary

3. ring (v)
9. date (v)

WORKBOOK

Pages 62–65

EXPANSION ACTIVITIES

1. Match the Conversations ★★

a. Make up matching cards such as the following:

How long have you been reading?	I've been reading for an hour.
How long have you been eating?	I've been eating for an hour.
How long has she been driving?	She's been driving since ten o'clock.

How long has she been riding?	She's been riding since ten o'clock.
How long has he been sitting?	He's been sitting for fifteen minutes.
How long has he been knitting?	He's been knitting for fifteen minutes.
How long have you been dating?	We've been dating since last month.

How long have you been waiting?	We've been waiting since last month.
How long have they been ringing?	They've been ringing for a long time.
How long have they been singing?	They've been singing for a long time.
How long have you been feeling bad?	I've been feeling bad since last Tuesday.
How long have you been feeling sad?	I've been feeling sad since last Tuesday.

b. Distribute a card to each student.

c. Have students memorize the sentences on their cards, and then have students walk around the room saying their sentences until they find their match.

d. Then have pairs of students say their matched sentences aloud to the class.

2. Create a Story ★★

Have students look at the illustration for Exercise 1 and use their imaginations to tell more about Yasmin.

a. Write the following on the board:

> study hard
> do her homework every _____
> come to class on time
> speak English with _____
> watch television programs
> see movies
> _____

b. Tell the class that Yasmin is going to take a very important English examination soon. She's been trying to get ready for the exam.

c. Have students use the cues on the board as well as ideas of their own to answer the question: "What has Yasmin been doing to get ready for the exam?" For example:

> She's been studying hard.

She's been doing her homework every day.
She's been coming to class on time.
She's been speaking English with other students.
She's been watching television programs in English.
She's been seeing American movies.
She's been listening to English language tapes.
She's been talking to the teacher after class.

d. Have students pretend to be Yasmin, and ask them: "Yasmin, what have you been doing to improve your English?"

> I've been studying very hard.
> I've been doing my homework every day.
>   etc.

3. Change the Sentence! ★★

a. Write a sentence on the board, underlining and numbering different portions of the sentence. For example:

> 1   2
> Paul   has been practicing
> 3   4
> the guitar   since this morning.

b. Have students sit in a circle.

c. Tell them that when you say a number, the first student in the circle makes a change in that part of the sentence. For example:

> Teacher: Two.
> Student 1: Paul *has been cleaning* the guitar since this morning.

d. The second student keeps the first student's sentence, but changes it based on the next number you say. For example:

> Teacher: Three.
> Student 2: Paul has been cleaning *the house* since this morning.

e. Continue this way with the rest of the students in the circle. For example:

> Teacher: Four.
> Student 3: Paul has been cleaning the house *for two hours.*

(continued)

4. Role Play: I've Been Very Busy ★★

a. Write the following conversation model on the board:

> A. Hi, _____. How are you?
> B. Okay. And you?
> A. Fine, thanks. I haven't spoken to you in a few days. What's new?
> B. Well, I've been very busy.
> A. Oh. What have you been doing?
> B. _____

b. Make up the following situation cards:

> You're having a big English test this week.
> You've been _____ing.
> You've been _____ing.
> You've been _____ing.

> You're having a big party this weekend.
> You've been _____ing.
> You've been _____ing.
> You've been _____ing.

> You're going on a vacation next week, and you've been very busy.
> You've been _____ing.
> You've been _____ing.
> You've been _____ing.

c. Divide the class into pairs and have them create role plays based on the model on the board. Give one member of the pair one of the situation cards as a cue for why he or she has been so busy. That person must tell about at least three things he or she has been doing.

d. Have students rehearse their role plays, and then call on various pairs to present them to the class.

5. Question the Answers! ★★

a. Dictate answers such as the following to the class:

For two hours.
Since last week.
For several years.
Since I was a child.
For twenty minutes.

b. Have students write questions for which these answers would be correct. For example:

| For two hours. | How long have you been waiting for the doctor? |
| Since last week. | How long has your back been hurting you? |

c. Have students compare their questions with each other.

Variation: Write the answers on cards. Divide the class into groups and give each group a set of cards.

6. Find the Right Person! ★★★

a. Write the questions below on the board. Have students write their responses and hand them in to you.

> Where do you live?
> How long have you been living there?
> What do you do?
> How long have you been doing that?
> What are your hobbies?
> How long have you been doing them?

b. Put the information in the following form:

> Find someone who . . .
> 1. has been living in Westville for 10 years. _____
> 2. has been skiing since first grade. _____
> 3. has been working at a bank for three months. _____
> 4. has been studying guitar for two years. _____

c. Have students circulate around the room, asking each other the original questions on the board to identify the above people.

d. The first student to find all the people, raise his or her hand, and identify the students is the winner of the game.

7. Barry's Boring Life ★★★

a. Write the following on the board:

Barry

He _____.

He's been _____ing every _____

{ for the last } _____.
{ since }

b. Set the scene: "Barry is a very nice person, but his life is a little boring. Barry's life never changes. He's been doing the same things for many, many years. For example: He works at the post office on Main Street. He's been working at the post office on Main Street since 1985."

c. Ask questions about Barry. Have students use the model on the board to tell about Barry's boring life, using any vocabulary they wish. For example:

Teacher: What does Barry eat for breakfast every morning?

Student: He eats scrambled eggs and two pieces of bread. He's been eating scrambled eggs and two pieces of bread for breakfast every morning for the past twenty years.

Possible questions:

What time does Barry get up every morning?
How does Barry get to work every day?
What does he have for lunch every day?
What does he do every evening after work?
What time does he go to bed at night?
When does he clean his apartment?
What does he do every Saturday night?
Where does he go on vacation every year?

d. Have students suggest ways in which Barry might change his life to make it less boring.

Text Page 72: They've Been Arguing All Day

FOCUS

- Present Perfect Continuous Tense: Yes/No Questions and Short Answers
- Contrast: Present Perfect Continuous and Present Continuous Tenses

INTRODUCING THE MODEL

1. Have students look at the model illustration.

2. Set the scene: "Two friends are talking. One of them is upset about his noisy neighbors."

3. Present the model.

4. Full-Class Repetition.

5. Ask students if they have any questions. Check understanding of vocabulary.

6. Group Choral Repetition.

7. Choral Conversation.

8. Call on one or two pairs of students to present the dialog. Have some of the students use the alternative expressions (shown under the model) in place of *all day*.

   (For additional practice, do Choral Conversation in small groups or by rows.)

SIDE BY SIDE EXERCISES

Students can use any time expressions they wish in the exercises.

Examples

1. A. What are you doing?
   B. I'm studying.
   A. Have you been studying for a long time?
   B. Yes, I have. I've been studying all *(morning)*.

2. A. What's Gary doing?
   B. He's exercising.
   A. Has he been exercising for a long time?
   B. Yes, he has. He's been exercising all *(afternoon)*.

1. **Exercise 1:** Call on two students to present the dialog. Then do Choral Repetition and Choral Conversation practice.

2. **Exercise 2:** Same as above.

3. **Exercises 3–8:** Either Full-Class Practice or Pair Practice.

New Vocabulary

5. make noises
6. direct traffic
8. stand in line
   tickets

4. **Exercise 9:** Have students use the model as a guide to create their own conversations, using vocabulary of their choice. Encourage students to use dictionaries to find new words they want to use. This exercise can be done orally in class or for written homework. If you assign it for homework, do one example in class to make sure students understand what's expected. Have students present their conversations in class the next day.

WORKBOOK

Page 66–68

1. Not Long at All! ★★

For this activity, use *Side by Side* Picture Cards for verbs (36–67, 88–90, 123–130, 158–162) or your own visuals that depict actions.

a. Write the following on the board:

A. Has/Have _____ been _____ing very long?

B. No. _____ hasn't/haven't been _____ing long at all. In fact, _____ just started _____ ing a few minutes ago.

b. Hold up a visual and call on a pair of students to create a conversation, using the model on the board. For example:

[visual: man reading]

A. Has he been reading very long?
B. No, he hasn't been reading long at all. In fact, he just started reading a few minutes ago.

[visual: couple dancing]

A. Have they been dancing very long?
B. No, they haven't been dancing long at all. In fact, they just started dancing a few minutes ago.

2. Tic Tac Question the Answer ★★

a. Draw a tic tac grid on the board and fill it in with short answers to questions:

Yes, she has.	Yes, she is.	Yes, they are.
No, they haven't.	Yes, we have.	No, we aren't.
Yes, it is.	No, it isn't.	Yes, it has.

b. Divide the class into teams. Give each team a mark: *X* or *O*.

c. Have each team ask a question for an answer in the grid. For example:

X Team: Have you been studying English for a long time?
Yes, we have.

d. If an answer is appropriate and is stated correctly, that team may replace the answer with its team mark. For example:

Yes, she has.	Yes, she is.	Yes, they are.
No, they haven't.	X	No, we aren't.
Yes, it is.	No, it isn't.	Yes, it has.

e. The first team to mark out three boxes in a straight line—either vertically, horizontally, or diagonally—wins.

3. Miming ★★

a. Write various activities on cards. For example:

exercising	crying	jogging
looking for your wallet	waiting for the train	standing in line
studying for a test	practicing the piano	watching people
lifting weights	repairing your bicycle	paying bills

b. Have students take turns picking a card from the pile and pantomiming the action on the card.

c. Students must guess what the person is doing. Once the action has been guessed, students may then ask: "How long have you been _____?" The person answers using any time expression he or she wishes.

(continued)

Variation: Do the activity as a game with competing teams.

4. Picture Clues ★★★

   a. Show the class a picture of an interesting scene.

   b. Divide the class into pairs. Have students answer the following questions:

   > What's happening?
   > What are the people doing?
   > How long have they been doing that?
   > What will happen next?

   c. Have students share their interpretations with the class.

5. Group Story ★★★

   a. Write on the board:

   > Today has been one of the worst days I can remember! _____ has/have been _____ing since/for _____.

   b. Divide the class into groups of 3 to 5 students.

   c. Begin the following story, using the model on the board:

   > Today has been one of the worst days I can remember! My upstairs neighbors have been arguing since nine o'clock this morning.

   d. Have each group continue the story by writing at least ten more things that have been happening. Encourage students to use their imaginations to tell the story of this person's terrible day.

   e. Have one person from each group present that group's story to the class.

   f. Have the class decide which group's story describes the *worst* day of all.

READING *Apartment Problems*

FOCUS

- Present Perfect Continuous Tense

NEW VOCABULARY

ceiling	leak (v)
furious	peel
hallway	water heater
heating system	

READING THE STORY

Optional: Preview the story by having students talk about the story title and/or illustration. You may choose to introduce new vocabulary beforehand, or have students encounter the new vocabulary within the context of the reading.

1. Have students read silently, or follow along silently as the story is read aloud by you, by one or more students, or on the audio program.

2. Ask students if they have any questions. Check understanding of vocabulary.

3. Check students' comprehension, using some or all of the following questions:

   What's wrong with the bedroom ceiling?
   What's wrong with the refrigerator?
   What's wrong with the paint in the hallway?
   Why have they been taking cold showers?
   Why haven't they been sleeping at night?
   Who have they been calling every day?
   What has he been promising?
   Has he fixed anything yet?

READING EXTENSION

Tic Tac Question the Answer

1. Draw a tic tac grid on the board and fill it in with the following short answers to questions:

For more than a week.	No, it hasn't.	Since last week.
No, he hasn't.	Every day.	Yes, it has.
Yes, they have.	For several weeks.	No, they haven't.

2. Divide the class into teams. Give each team a mark: *X* or *O*.

3. Have each team ask a question about the reading for an answer in the grid. For example:

   X Team: How often have Mr. and Mrs. Banks been calling their landlord? Every day.

4. If an answer is appropriate to the reading and is stated correctly, that team may replace the answer with its team mark.

5. The first team to mark out three boxes in a straight line—either vertically, horizontally, or diagonally—wins.

✓ READING *CHECK-UP*

Q & A

1. Call on a pair of students to present the model. Check understanding of the expressions *What can I do for you?*, *all right*, *as soon as I can.*

2. Have students work in pairs to create new dialogs.

3. Call on pairs to present their new dialogs to the class.

How About You?

Have students answer the question in pairs or as a class.

FOCUS

- Contrast: Present Perfect and Present Perfect Continuous Tenses

CLOSE UP

RULE: Unlike the present perfect, the present perfect continuous cannot be used to describe an event which has ended or has been completed.

EXAMPLES: **I've been writing** letters since nine o'clock this morning.
(I'm still writing.)
I've already **written** fifteen letters.
(I've completed fifteen letters.)

GETTING READY

Contrast the present perfect continuous and present perfect tenses.

1. Write the following on the board:

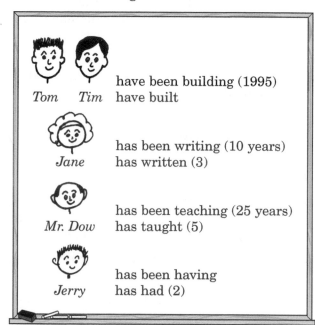

have been building (1995)
Tom   Tim   have built

Jane   has been writing (10 years)
has written (3)

Mr. Dow   has been teaching (25 years)
has taught (5)

Jerry   has been having
has had (2)

2. Have students listen as you tell the following, while pointing to the appropriate cues on the board:

Tom and his brother Tim have been building

houses since 1995. They've built twenty houses this year.

Jane has been writing books for ten years. She's written three novels.

Mr. Dow has been teaching languages for twenty-five years. He's taught five different languages.

Unfortunately, Jerry isn't a very good driver. He's been having accidents since he started driving. He's already had two accidents this year.

3. Check students' understanding of the two tenses.

4. Tell each situation again and ask questions after each. For example:

How long have Tom and Tim been building houses?
How many houses have they built this year?

INTRODUCING THE MODELS

There are two model conversations. Introduce and practice each separately. For each model:

1. Have students look at the model illustration.

2. Set the scene:

   1st model: "One friend is visiting another."

   2nd model: "Two people are talking about Anthony."

3. Present the model. (Note that the capitalized words indicate spoken emphasis.)

4. Full-Class Repetition.

5. Ask students if they have any questions. Check understanding of vocabulary.

6. Group Choral Repetition.

7. Choral Conversation.

8. Call on one or two pairs of students to present the dialog.

   (For additional practice, do Choral Conversation in small groups or by rows.)

SIDE BY SIDE EXERCISES

Students can use any time expressions and numbers they wish in the exercises.

Examples

1. A. You look tired. What have you been doing?
   B. I've been planting flowers since *(eight o'clock)* this morning.
   A. Really? How many flowers have you planted?
   B. Believe it or not, I've already planted *(fifty)* flowers.
   A. You're kidding! *(Fifty)* flowers?! NO WONDER you're tired!

2. A. Ms. Perkins looks tired. What has she been doing?
   B. She's been giving piano lessons since *(ten o'clock)* this morning.
   A. Really? How many piano lessons has she given?
   B. Believe it or not, she's already given *(seven)* piano lessons.
   A. You're kidding! *(Seven)* piano lessons?! NO WONDER she's tired!

1. **Exercise 1:** Call on two students to present the dialog. Then do Choral Repetition and Choral Conversation practice.

2. **Exercise 2:** Introduce the new expression *give piano lessons.* Same as above.

3. **Exercises 3–12:** Either Full Class Practice or Pair Practice.

New Vocabulary

   4. mend
   5. pick
   6. thank-you note
   10. cage
   11. do sit-ups
   12. deliver a baby

Culture Note

Exercise 6: It's polite to write a thank-you note after receiving a gift or after spending two or more days visiting at someone's home.

Language Note

Exercise 12: To *deliver a baby* is to help the mother give birth.

WORKBOOK

Pages 69–71

1. Complete the Sentence ★★

With books closed, read each of the sentences below and have students complete it with an appropriate verb.

How many thank-you notes have you . . . ?
(written)

How many flowers has she . . . ?
(planted)

How many photographs have they . . . ?
(taken)

How many sit-ups has he . . . ?
(done)

How many pictures have you . . . ?
(drawn)

How many patients has Dr. Green . . . ?
(seen)

How many lessons has your piano teacher . . . ?
(given)

How many socks has she . . . ?
(mended)

How many apples have you . . . ?
(picked)

How many apple pies have they . . . ?
(made/baked)

How many babies has Dr. Chen . . . ?
(delivered)

How many job interviews has she . . . ?
(gone to)

2. Match the Conversations ★★

a. Make up the following matching cards:

I've been writing all morning.	What have you written?
I've been riding all morning.	Where have you ridden?
I've been reading all morning.	What have you read?
I've been eating all morning.	What have you eaten?

I've been swimming all afternoon.	Where have you swum?
I've been singing all afternoon.	What have you sung?
I've been sweeping all afternoon.	What have you swept?
I've been sleeping all afternoon.	Where have you slept?
I've been chopping all day.	What have you chopped?
I've been shopping all day.	Where have you shopped?

b. Distribute a card to each student.

c. Have students memorize the sentences on their cards, and then have students walk around the room saying their sentences until they find their match.

d. Then have pairs of students say their matched sentences aloud to the class.

3. The Differences Between Steve and Bill ★★

a. Write the following on the board:

Steve   Bill

Bill has been _____ing for many years too, but he's never _____.

b. Tell about *Steve* by reading the statements below. After each one, call on a student to make a contrasting statement about *Bill*. For example:

Teacher: Steve has been driving for many years, and he's had a lot of accidents.

Student: Bill has been driving for many years too, but he's never had an accident.

Statements:

Steve has been studying French for many years, and he's traveled to France many times.

Steve has been working in Washington for many years, and he's seen the president several times.

Steve has been listening to jazz on the radio for many years, and he's gone to a lot of jazz concerts.

Steve has been playing baseball for many years, and his team has won all their games.

Steve has been visiting New York for many years, and he's seen the Statue of Liberty many times.

Steve has been going skiing every winter for many years, and he's broken his leg a few times.

Steve has been going sailing every summer for many years, and he's gotten seasick a few times.

Steve has been cooking delicious meals for many years, and he's had several dinner parties.

Steve has been giving blood at the hospital every year for a long time, and he's fainted a few times.

Steve has been singing opera for many years, and he's sung at the White House two or three times.

Steve has been swimming every day for many years, and he has swum in the Mediterranean several times.

Steve has been playing the piano for many years, and he's written several songs.

4. Begin the Sentence! ★★

Give students sentence endings and have them add appropriate beginnings, paying attention to the verb tenses. For example:

Teacher: fifteen lessons

Student: The teacher has given fifteen lessons.

Teacher: pizzas since eight o'clock

Student: He's been making pizzas since eight o'clock.

Variation: This activity may be done as a class, in pairs or small groups, or as a game with competing teams.

5. Surprise Situations ★★★

a. Put a skeletal framework of the model conversation on the board:

A. You look tired. What _____ doing?
B. I've been _____ since _____.
A. Really? How many _____?
B. Believe it or not, ____ already _____.
A. _____?! No wonder you're tired!

b. Ask for a pair of student volunteers to come to the front of the room.

c. Give them word cards such as the following and have them create a conversation based on the framework on the board, using the information on their cards. They should feel free to modify the conversation any way they wish.

Speaker A: Your friend looks tired.	Speaker B: You've been making cookies since _____.
Speaker A: Your friend looks tired.	Speaker B: You've been doing grammar exercises since _____.
Speaker A: Your friend looks tired.	Speaker B: You've been filling out job applications since _____.

(continued)

6. Interview: Students' Hobbies ★★★

a. Brainstorm with the class questions to ask each other about hobbies and sports interests. For example:

What hobbies do you have?
How long have you been _____?
Do you play any team sports?
How long have you been playing _____?
How many games have you played this season?
How many awards has your team won?
How often does your team practice?

b. Have students interview each other and then report to the class.

7. Number Facts ★★★

a. Have students complete the following sentences:

I've _____ three _____.
I've _____ four _____.
I've _____ five _____.
I've _____ ten _____.

b. Have students share their sentences in pairs or small groups. For example:

I've skied two times this year.
I've been to Paris four times.
I've read five books by Agatha Christie.
I've seen ten movies this year.

c. Have students report to the class any interesting facts they have learned about each other.

How to Say It!

Expressing Surprise: In informal spoken English, there are many ways to express surprise, such as the ones presented on text page 75.

1. Present the expressions.

2. Full-Class Repetition.

3. Ask students if they have any questions.

4. Have students practice the conversations in this lesson again, using any of these new expressions.

5. Call on pairs to present their conversations to the class.

FOCUS

- Contrast: Present Perfect and Present Perfect Continuous Tenses

INTRODUCING THE MODEL

1. Have students look at the model illustration.

2. Set the scene: "Two college roommates are talking. One of them is going on a trip tomorrow."

3. Present the model.

4. Full-Class Repetition.

5. Ask students if they have any questions. Check understanding of new vocabulary: *for years, believe me, There's nothing to be nervous about!*

6. Group Choral Repetition.

7. Choral Conversation.

8. Call on one or two pairs of students to present the dialog.

   (For additional practice, do Choral Conversation in small groups or by rows.)

SIDE BY SIDE EXERCISES

Examples

1. A. I'm nervous.
   B. Why?
   A. I'm going to drive downtown tomorrow, and I've never driven downtown before.
   B. Don't worry! I've been driving downtown for years. And believe me, there's nothing to be nervous about!

2. A. I'm nervous.
   B. Why?
   A. I'm going to give blood tomorrow, and I've never given blood before.
   B. Don't worry! I've been giving blood for years. And believe me, there's nothing to be nervous about!

1. **Exercise 1:** Introduce the word *downtown*. Call on two students to present the dialog. Then do Choral Repetition and Choral Conversation practice.

2. **Exercise 2:** Same as above.

3. **Exercises 3–11:** Either Full-Class Practice or Pair Practice.

> **New Vocabulary**
> 4. chemistry
> 5. marathon

Culture Notes

Exercise 5: Long-distance running and running in marathons for amateur athletes is very popular in the United States. Some U.S. cities, such as Boston and New York, sponsor annual marathons.

Exercise 10: It is common for U.S. employers to give their workers regular salary increases. Employees may also ask for additional increases in salary if they feel they deserve more money for the work they do.

After each exercise, have students tell about their own experiences. Encourage students to ask each other questions. For example, after doing Exercise 2:

> Have you ever given blood?
> Were you nervous?
> Tell about your experience.

4. **Exercise 12:** Have students use the model as a guide to create their own conversations, using vocabulary of their choice. Encourage students to use dictionaries to find new words they want to use. This exercise can be done orally in class or for written homework. If you assign it for homework, do one example in class to make sure students understand what's expected. Have students present their conversations in class the next day.

INTERVIEW *Have You Ever...?*

1. Check understanding of the word *valuable*.

2. Have students interview each other about their experiences and then report back to the class.

EXPANSION ACTIVITIES

1. Memory Chain ★★

a. Divide the class into groups of 5 or 6 students each.

b. Tell each student to think of something that he or she has never done.

c. One group at a time, have Student 1 begin. For example:

> I've never given blood.

d. Student 2 repeats what Student 1 said and adds a statement about himself or herself. For example:

> Marco has never given blood, and I've never run in a marathon.

e. Student 3 continues in the same way. For example:

> Marco has never given blood. Carol has never run in a marathon, and I've never ridden a motorcycle.

f. Continue until everyone has had a chance to play the *memory chain*.

2. Good Suggestions ★★

a. Write the following conversation model on the board:

> A. I've never _____ before. Do you have any suggestions?
> B. Yes. You should _____, you should _____, and most of all you should _____.
> A. Thanks. Those are good suggestions.

b. Have pairs of students talk about how to prepare for the situations on text pages 76 and 77, using the model on the board as a guide. For example:

> *Situation 2*
> A. I've never gone to a job interview before. Do you have any suggestions?
> B. Yes. You should prepare a resume, you should make a list of your qualifications, and most of all you should relax.
> A. Thanks. Those are good suggestions.

3. Grammar Chain ★★

a. Write the following conversation model and verbs on the board:

> A. Have you ever _____?
> B. Yes. I've been _____ for years!

> ride ____
> speak ____
> take a ____ lesson
> sing in front of ____
> ask for ____
> drive ____
> go out ____
> buy a used ____
> give ____
> fly ____

b. Start the chain game by saying:

Teacher *(to Student A)*: Have you ever *ridden a motorcycle*?

c. Student A answers according to the model on the board, and then asks a different question to Student B, and the chain continues. For example:

Student A: Yes. I've been riding motorcycles for years!
(to Student B): Have you ever *spoken at a meeting*?

Student B: Yes. I've been speaking at meetings for years!
(to Student A): Have you ever *taken a karate lesson*?

4. Surprise Situations ★★★

a. Put the following cues for the model conversation on the board:

> A. nervous
> B. Why?
> A. going to
>   never / before
> B. Don't worry!
>   for years
>   Believe me!

b. Ask for a pair of student volunteers to come to the front of the room.

c. Give them word cards such as the following and have them create a conversation based on the model conversation from the text, using the key words on the board and the information on their cards. They should feel free to modify the conversation any way they wish.

Speaker A:	Speaker B:
You're nervous! You're going to ride in a hot-air balloon.	Your friend is nervous. Give your friend some encouragement.

Speaker A:	Speaker B:
You're nervous! You're going to go water-skiing.	Your friend is nervous. Give your friend some encouragement.

Speaker A:	Speaker B:
You're nervous! You're going to sing in a karaoke club.	Your friend is nervous. Give your friend some encouragement.

5. Pantomime Role Play ★★★

This activity is similar to Activity 4. However, this activity is done through miming.

a. Make up role-play cards such as the following:

> You're nervous. You're going to fly in a helicopter, and you've never flown in a helicopter before. Your friend tells you not to worry.

> You're nervous. You're going to ride a horse, and you've never ridden a horse before. Your friend tells you not to worry.

> You're nervous. You're going to drive a truck, and you've never driven a truck before. Your friend tells you not to worry.

> You're nervous. You're going to go scuba diving, and you've never gone scuba diving before. Your friend tells you not to worry.

b. Have pairs of students pantomime their role plays. The class watches and guesses the situation and what the two characters are saying.

(continued)

6. Which One Isn't True? ★★

   a. Tell students to write three true statements and one false statement about themselves. For example:

> I've never given blood.
> I've run in several marathons.
> I called the president on the telephone last week.
> I've been studying Swahili for the past two years.

   b. Have students take turns reading their statements to the class, and have the class guess which statement isn't true.

ROLE PLAY *At a Job Interview*

FOCUS

- Review: Present Perfect, Present Perfect Continuous, Simple Past

INTRODUCING THE ROLE PLAY

1. Have students look at the model.
2. Set the scene: "Someone is at a job interview."
3. Present the model dialog, using any names, places, and time expressions you wish.
4. Ask students if they have any questions. Check understanding of new vocabulary: *resume, work experience, appreciate, opportunity, It's been a pleasure.*

ROLE PLAY

1. Call on two of your stronger students to role-play the conversation, using any names, places, and time expressions they wish.
2. Divide the class into pairs and have students practice the role play. Then call on pairs to present their role plays to the class.

EXPANSION ACTIVITY

Scrambled Interview ★★

1. Complete the first 6 lines of the dialog on text page 78 any way you wish, and write each line on a separate card.
2. Scramble the cards, and give a card to six different students.
3. Have those students work together to put the lines in the correct order.
4. Those students should then come to the front of the room and present their lines in the correct order.
5. Do the same with the next 6 lines, beginning with "Okay. I see here on your resume . . ."
6. Do the same with the next 12 lines, beginning with "Tell me about your work experience."

READING *It's Been a Long Day*

FOCUS

- Present Perfect Tense
- Present Perfect Continuous Tense

NEW VOCABULARY

exhausted
officer
parking ticket

READING THE STORY

Optional: *Preview the story by having students talk about the story title and/or illustrations. You may choose to introduce new vocabulary beforehand, or have students encounter the new vocabulary within the context of the reading.*

1. Have students read silently, or follow along silently as the story is read aloud by you, by one or more students, or on the audio program.

2. Ask students if they have any questions. Check understanding of vocabulary.

   ### Culture Note

   Parking is a problem in many U.S. cities. Public parking garages are expensive. Street parking is difficult to find. People have to put money into parking meters for street parking. Police officers give parking tickets to cars parked in illegal spaces and at meters that have run out of money.

3. Check students' comprehension, using some or all of the following questions:

What has Frank been doing since 7 A.M.?
How many cameras has he assembled?
Has he ever assembled that many cameras in one day before?
What does he have to do before he can go home?

What has Julie been doing since 9 A.M.?
How many letters has she typed?
Has she ever typed that many letters in one day before?
What does she have to do before she can go home?

What has Officer Jackson been doing since 8 A.M.?
How many parking tickets has he written?
Has he ever written that many parking tickets in one day before?
What does he have to do before he can go home?

✓ READING *CHECK-UP*

Q & A

1. Call on a pair of students to present the model.

2. Have students work in pairs to create new dialogs.

3. Call on pairs to present their new dialogs to the class.

READING EXTENSION

Tic Tac Question the Answer

1. Draw a tic tac grid on the board and fill it in with short answers to questions:

Yes, she has.	Yes, she is.	25.
No, she hasn't.	Yes, it has.	No, he hasn't.
19.	211.	Yes, he is.

2. Divide the class into teams. Give each team a mark: *X* or *O*.

3. Have each team ask a question for an answer in the grid. For example:

   > X Team: Has Julie been typing letters since 9 A.M.?
   >
   > Yes, she has.

4. If an answer is appropriate and is stated correctly, that team may replace the answer with its team mark.

5. The first team to mark out three boxes in a straight line—either vertically, horizontally, or diagonally—wins.

 **LISTENING**

WHICH WORD DO YOU HEAR?

Listen and choose the correct answer.

1. He's gone to the bank.

2. I've never written so many letters in one day before.

3. She's been seeing patients all day.

4. What courses have you taken this year?

5. Is Beverly giving blood?

6. Ben has driven all night.

Answers

1. a

2. a

3. b

4. a

5. b

6. a

WHO IS SPEAKING?

Listen and decide who is speaking.

1. What a day! All the tenants have been complaining that nothing is working.

2. I'm very tired. I've given six lessons today.

3. Thank you! You've been a wonderful audience!

4. I'm really tired. I've been watching them all day.

5. I'm very tired. I've been looking at paychecks since early this morning.

6. It's been a long day. I've been selling tickets since ten A.M.

Answers

1. a

2. b

3. a

4. b

5. b

6. a

PRONUNCIATION Reduced *for*

 GRAMMAR FOCUS

> **Reduced *for*:** When spoken in mid-sentence, the word *for* is commonly reduced to "fr."

Focus on Listening

Practice the sentences in the left column. Say each sentence or play the audio one or more times. Have students listen carefully and repeat.

Focus on Pronunciation

Practice the sentences in the right column. Have students say each sentence and then listen carefully as you say it or play the audio.

If you wish, have students continue practicing the sentences to improve their pronunciation.

 ## JOURNAL

Have students write their journal entries at home or in class. Encourage students to use a dictionary to look up words they would like to use. Students can share their written work with other students if appropriate. Have students discuss what they have written as a class, in pairs, or in small groups.

WORKBOOK

Check-Up Test: Pages 76–77

Answers

1. have, been living
   We've been living, for
2. has, been practicing
   She's been practicing, since
3. Have, been standing
   they have, They've been standing, for
4. has been taking, since
   She's, taken
5. I've been writing, for
   I've, written

MULTILEVEL VARIATIONS

★ Tell *below-level* students the verb for each exercise, so they can focus only on putting it in the correct form.

★★★ Challenge *above-level* students to cover the grammar boxes as they complete the grammar exercises.

❶ CONVERSATION *Inquiring about Lease Information*

1. Have students look at the photo. Ask: "Where are these people?" (In a building manager's office.) "What are they doing?" (They're reading through a lease.) Introduce the new vocabulary: *building entrance, contract, harbor* (v), *hardwood floor, leased* (adj), *legal, minimum, permitted, premise, prohibited, property, refuse, sign* (v), and *strictly*.

   Language Note: "Tenant shall *carpet* or *rug* a minimum of 80% of hardwood floor areas." In English, many nouns are also used as verbs—for example, *to carpet* (to put down carpet), *to rug* (to put down a rug). Other examples: the noun *water* and the verb *to water* (to put water on something); the noun *iron* and the verb *to iron* (to use an iron).

2. Model the conversation with a student volunteer. For example:

   A. I don't understand this line in the lease: No refuse or trash will be permitted to be left at the building entrance. What does it mean?
   B. You can't put garbage in front of the building.
   A. Oh. I understand.

3. In pairs, have students practice the conversations as you circulate around the classroom.

4. Call on pairs of students to present their conversations to the class.

THINK & SHARE

Have the class discuss the questions.

❷ TEAMWORK *Apartment Rules*

Have students work in pairs to write a list of rules for tenants and then share their ideas with the class. Write a master list on the board.

LIFE SKILLS ENRICHMENT

Lease Vocabulary

Life Skills Worksheet 17

Make copies of Life Skills Worksheet 17 and give one to each student. Have students complete the worksheet as homework. In the next class, have students compare their answers in pairs.

MULTILEVEL VARIATION ★★★

Challenge *above-level* students to fold the word box under the worksheet and find the words on their own.

1. Scrambled Words ★

a. Choose words or phrases from the lease on student text page 80a and write them on the board or on a card with the letters scrambled out of order. For example:

s d l e e a   r m s s i e e p

b. Have students take turns guessing what the word or phrase is. [leased premises]

Variation 1: Do the activity in pairs or small groups, with students taking turns scrambling words and phrases for others to guess.

Variation 2: Do the activity as a class game with competing teams.

2. Chain Story ★★

a. Begin the story by saying: "There are many rules in my apartment building. We're not allowed to hang anything on the balcony."

b. Student 1 repeats what you said and adds another rule—for example: "There are many rules in my apartment building. We're not allowed to hang anything on the balcony, and pets are not allowed." Student 2 repeats what you and Student 1 said and adds another rule—for example: "There are many rules in my apartment building. We're not allowed to hang anything on the balcony, pets are not allowed, and we're not allowed to keep our bikes in the hallway."

c. Continue around the room in this fashion, with each student repeating what the previous student said and adding another rule. Do the activity again, beginning and ending with different students.

3. Retell the Rental Agreement ★★

a. Write the following topics of the lease on the board:

Garbage
Parking Lot
Balcony
Pets
Floors

b. Divide the class into pairs. Have students close their books and retell to each other what they remember about the rules in the lease on student text page 80a. Then have them open their books and check to see how much they remembered.

4. True or False? ★★

Make statements about the lease on student text page 80a and have students decide whether the statements are true or false. If a statement is false, have students correct it. For example:

A lease includes information about rent, the numbers of tenants who can live in an apartment, and the rules of the building. [True.]
Tenants can work on their cars in the parking lot. [False. Tenants are not allowed to fix their cars in the parking lot.]
Tenants must cover all their hardwood floors with rugs. [False. Tenants must cover 80% of their floors.]

Variation: Do the activity as a game with competing teams.

5. Survey ★★

Activity Master 41

a. Make copies of Activity Master 41 and give one to each student. Have students add three questions of their own. For example:

> Are you allowed to have a washer and dryer in your apartment?
> Are you allowed to add locks to your door?
> Are you allowed to have people stay with you longer than one week?
> Are you allowed to paint the apartment?

b. Have students survey their classmates or other students in the school by asking the questions on the Activity Master along with their own questions.

c. When students have completed their surveys, have them share their information with the class.

6. Role Play: Sign the Lease! ★★★

a. Tell students the role-play situation:

> A tenant and a landlord are going over the building rules and regulations. The tenant has *many* questions, and the landlord has to explain everything.

b. Divide the class into pairs. Have students write a conversation between the new tenant and the landlord as they sign their lease. Circulate to help students as necessary.

c. Call on students to perform their role plays for the class.

1. Point to each of the three bills on student text pages 80b and 80c. Ask: "What is this bill for?" (Electricity. Gas. Phone.)

2. Have students look at the California Power and Light bill. Ask the following questions to orient students to the bill: "How much is the bill for?" ($89.91.) "When does Hector have to pay it?" (November 10.) "How much electricity did Hector use?" (572 kilowatt hours.) Introduce the new vocabulary: *account number, billing date, billing summary, current charges, customer assistance line, due date, full payment, kilowatt hour, meter number, P.O. Box, payment, payment due, payment received, power and light, power outage, statement, total balance, unpaid balance,* and *usage.*

   Note: A *kilowatt hour* is a measure of electricity for billing purposes. 100 kilowatt hours equals the amount of electricity a 100-watt bulb would use in 1000 hours. One kilowatt hour is the amount of electricity needed to dry medium length hair with a hair dryer 15 times, listen to 15 CDs, or use a small refrigerator for 24 hours.

3. Have students look at the Southern Energy bill. Ask the following questions to orient students to the bill: "How much is the bill for?" ($38.63.) "How much gas did Samira use?" (35 Therms.) Introduce the new vocabulary: *adjustments, billing period, credits, late payment charge, meter reading, past due, service address, service balance, statement date, Therm,* and *total amount due.*

   Note: A *Therm* is a unit of measure of natural gas.

4. Have students look at the Bell Telephone bill. Ask the following questions to orient students to the bill: "How much is the bill for?" ($131.22.) "Did Lena pay her last bill?" (No.) Introduce the new vocabulary: *late payment, local services, long distance, remaining balance,* and *summary.*

5. Have students do the comprehension exercises individually and then compare their answers in pairs.

MULTILEVEL VARIATION ★

Have *below-level* students work on the reading and questions in pairs to provide each other with more support.

Answers

1. C	**5.** D
2. B	**6.** C
3. D	**7.** C
4. A	**8.** B

CONSUMER TIP

1. Write the word *credit rating* on the board. Ask students: "What do you think a credit rating is?" Write their ideas on the board.

2. Have students read the paragraph. Ask: "Were your ideas about *credit rating* correct?"

3. Then have the class discuss the following questions:

   • What kinds of businesses and agencies want to know your credit rating? (Banks, mortgage lenders, credit card companies.)

   • How do they find out your credit rating? (They contact a credit rating agency, tell them your name and social security number, and pay a fee for the information.)

   • How can you find out your own credit rating? (You can contact a credit rating company.)

LIFE SKILLS ENRICHMENT

The following Life Skills Worksheets provide students with important banking and bill paying practice: paying bills, making bank deposits and withdrawals, balancing a checkbook, and applying for a checking account.

Make copies of each of the worksheets and give one to each student. Have students complete the worksheet as homework. In the next class, have students compare their answers in pairs.

EXPANSION ACTIVITIES

1. Guess the Word! ★

a. Divide the class into two teams. Choose a vocabulary word or phrase from student text pages 80b or 80c, and on the board, write a blank for each letter in the word or phrase. For example: [*current charges*]

b. Give students a clue about the word or phrase. For example: "the cost of your usage this billing period."

c. The team that guesses the word gets a point. The team with the most points wins the guessing game.

2. Billing Bingo ★★★

Activity Master 42

a. Make multiple copies of Activity Master 42 and give one to each student.

b. Have students write any nine words or phrases from the box onto their grid.

c. Randomly define the words or phrases in the word choice box using the following definitions. Tell students to identify that word and look for it on their grids. If they have that word on their grids, they should cross it out.

billing period—the weeks or months covered in this bill

credits—money the customer has already paid, or money that is returned to the customer

current charges—the amount of money the customer has to pay for using the services during this billing period

due date—the final day when the customer has to pay the bill

full payment—when the customer pays the whole bill (the total balance)

late payment charge—the extra fee the customer pays when he or she pays the bill late

meter—a machine that measures how much electricity, gas, or water the customer uses

past due—a payment that is late (it is past the *due date*)

remaining balance—the amount the customer still needs to pay after counting credits and other previous payments

service address—the place the utility is delivered to

statement—bill

usage—how much of the utility the customer uses

d. The first student to mark out three boxes in a straight line—vertically, horizontally, or diagonally—wins.

3. True or False? ★★

Make statements about the bills on student text pages 80b and 80c and have students decide whether the statements are true or false. If a statement is false, have students correct it. For example:

California Power and Light Bill
Hector used 572 kilowatt hours of electricity between September 14 and October 14th. [True.]
Hector's payment is due on October 11th. [False. It's due on November 10th.]

Southern Energy Bill
Samira didn't pay her last bill. [False. She paid it on September 4, 2010.]
Samira used 35 Therms of gas between July 23rd and August 23rd. [True.]

(continued)

Bell Telephone Bill
Lena didn't pay her last bill. [True.]
Lena's last bill was for $131.22. [False. Her
    last bill was for $87.32.]

Variation: Do the activity as a game with
competing teams.

4. Ranking ★★

Have students brainstorm all the bills they pay
in a month—for example: gas, electricity, phone,
cell phone, rent, cable, car payments, and water.
Have students look at the words listed in the
lesson and rank them according to cost, with one
being the most expensive. For example:

1. rent
2. car payment
3. gas
4. cable
5. phone
6. cell phone
7. electricity
8. water

5. Role Play: Customer Service! ★★★

Activity Master 43

a. Make multiple copies of Activity Master 43.
   Cut the role-play cards into A cards and B
   cards and clip each role play (1, 2, or 3)
   together.

b. Divide the class into pairs. Give each partner
   one set of role-play cards—A or B. Tell
   students they have five minutes to act out
   the role play.

c. As students are acting out their role plays,
   circulate to help as necessary.

d. After five minutes, call on a few pairs to
   perform their role plays for the class.

MULTILEVEL VARIATIONS ★/★★/★★★

Allow *below-level* students to look at each other's
cards. If *at-level* or *above-level* students finish
their role plays quickly, give them another set of
role-play cards.

1. Ask students: "What kind of information does a building manager need to tell a new tenant?" Write students' ideas on the board.

2. Introduce the new vocabulary: *at once, bones, cardboard, discover, dumpster, emergency maintenance number, empty* (v), *fire hazard, jammed* (adj), *keep clear, maintenance request form, metal, personal possessions, pest control company, pits, preparation, recycling bin, recycling collection site, recycling program, reduced waste, respond, rinse out, routine* (adj), *service* (n), *smoothly,* and *storage area.*

3. Have students work individually to complete the comprehension exercise and then compare answers in pairs, small groups, or as a class.

MULTILEVEL VARIATION ★

Have *below-level* students work on the reading and questions in pairs to provide each other with more support.

Answers

1.	D	**4.**	C
2.	C	**5.**	A
3.	B	**6.**	D

LIFE SKILLS ENRICHMENT

Rental Apartment Acceptance Form

Life Skills Worksheet 22

Make copies of Life Skills Worksheet 22 and give one to each student. Have students complete the worksheet as homework. In the next class, have students compare their answers in pairs.

Note: A Rental Apartment Acceptance Form is a form tenants fill out soon after they move into an apartment. They write down problems they find in the apartment.

EXPANSION ACTIVITIES

1. Scrambled Words ★

a. Choose words or phrases from student text page 80d and write them on the board or on a card with the letters scrambled out of order. For example:

```
g i n y l r e c c   i n b
```

b. Have students take turns guessing what the word or phrase is. [recycling bin]

Variation 1: Do the activity in pairs or small groups, with students taking turns scrambling words and phrases for others to guess.

Variation 2: Do the activity as a class game with competing teams.

2. How Much Do You Remember? ★★

a. Write the following topics on the board:

```
Common Areas
Trash and Recycling
Pest Control
Routine Maintenance
Emergency Maintenance
```

b. Divide the class into pairs. Have students close their books and retell to each other what they remember about the topics from the letter to tenants on student text page 80d. Then have them open their books and check to see how much they remembered.

3. True or False? ★★

Make statements about the letter to tenants on student text page 80d and have students decide whether the statements are true or false. If a statement is false, have students correct it. For example:

Tenants must rinse out all glass and cans before they recycle them. [True.]
There are dumpsters outside of every building. [False. There are dumpsters outside of Buildings A, C, and E.]
There's a phone line for emergency maintenance requests. [True.]
The most common maintenance problem in Hillside Apartments is recycling. [False. The most common problem is jammed garbage disposals.]
Tenants have a storage area in the basement. [True.]

Variation: Do the activity as a game with competing teams.

4. Category Dictation ★

a. Have students make two columns on a piece of paper and write the following at the top of each column:

Emergency Maintenance
Routine Maintenance

b. Dictate maintenance problems such as the following and have students write them in the appropriate column:

My garbage disposal is jammed.
The lock on my front door doesn't work.
The toilet won't flush.
The light in my kitchen doesn't turn on.
The window in my bedroom is jammed.
The bathroom faucet is leaking.

c. As a class, in pairs, or in small groups, have students check their work.

5. Tic Tac Question ★★★

a. Draw a tic tac grid on the board and write the following answers in random order on the grid:

On the second Monday of each month.	Behind Buildings A, C, and E.	3700 East 25th Avenue.
Fill out a maintenance request form.	In your storage area in the basement.	Call (310) 278-1489.
Call (310) 457-8923.	By 10%.	Anytime.

b. Divide the class into two teams. Give each team a mark: X or O.

c. Give the teams five minutes to write the questions for each of the answers on the grid. Then have the teams take turns calling out an answer and the corresponding question. If the question is correct, the team gets to put its mark in that space. For example:

   X Team: 3700 East 25th Avenue. What is the address of Hillside Apartments?

d. The first team to mark out three boxes in a straight line—vertically, horizontally, or diagonally—wins.

YELLOW PAGE LISTINGS

1. Have students look at the yellow pages. Ask: "Are these names of businesses or people?" (Businesses.) "What information do you see in the yellow pages?" (Advertisements, names, addresses, and phone numbers of businesses in the community.)

2. Familiarize students with the yellow pages. Point to the category headings. Say: "All the information under each category is arranged alphabetically."

3. Have students work individually to read the text and complete the comprehension exercise. Have them compare answers in pairs, small groups, or as a class.

MULTILEVEL VARIATION ★

Have *below-level* students work on the reading and questions in pairs to provide each other with more support.

Answers

1.	B	4.	C
2.	D	5.	B
3.	A	6.	D

LIFE SKILLS ENRICHMENT

Reading the Yellow Pages

Life Skills Worksheet 23

Make copies of Life Skills Worksheet 23 and give one to each student. Have students complete the worksheet as homework. In the next class, have students compare their answers in pairs.

EXPANSION ACTIVITIES

1. Put in Order ★

Activity Master 44

Divide the class into pairs. Make multiple copies of Activity Master 44, cut them into cards, and distribute one set to each pair. Have the pairs work together to put the business names in alphabetical order. Call on a pair to read their list and have the class decide whether or not the order is correct.

Note: Tell students to alphabetize the categories first and then alphabetize the businesses within each category.

2. True or False? ★★

Make statements about the information in the directories on student text page 80e and have students decide whether the statements are true or false. If a statement is false, have students correct it. For example:

There are two Pest Control Specialists. [True.]
Mike's Painting has a website. [True.]
There are four ads on this page. [False. There are three ads.]
Harmony Painters and Ramirez Painting are in the same towns. [False. They're in different towns.]

Variation: Do the activity as a game with competing teams.

3. Survey ★★★

Activity Master 45

a. Make copies of Activity Master 45 and give one to each student.

b. Have students interview others in the class by asking: "How have you found repairpeople?" Tell students they may give as many ways as they wish. For example:

A. How have you found repairpeople?
B. I've looked in the Yellow Pages and I've asked friends.

c. The interviewer should write a check next to the appropriate response(s).

d. When students have completed their surveys, have them add up the number of checks for each response. Talk as a class about the results.

Option: Have students create a bar graph illustrating their survey findings.

CHECK-UP TEST Ⓐ Ⓑ Ⓒ Ⓓ

Have students do the check-up test and then review the answers as a class.

Answers

1. C	**6.** B
2. B	**7.** D
3. D	**8.** C
4. A	**9.** B
5. C	**10.** A

SKILLS CHECK

Words:

Explain to students that this is a list of words they have learned in the unit. Have students take turns reading each item aloud to the class. Have students put a check next to the item if they feel they have learned it. Encourage students to get a small notebook where they can write down words that are difficult for them.

I can:

Explain to students that this is a list of skills they have learned in the unit. Read each item aloud to the class. Ask individual students or pairs of students to demonstrate the skill. For example:

Teacher: I can ask and answer: How long
have you been waiting?
Student A: How long have you been waiting?
Student B: I've been waiting for two and a half
hours.

Teacher: I can express surprise.
Student: You've got to be kidding!

Have students put a check next to the item if they feel they have learned it. Use this information to determine which lessons you may want to review or reinforce for the entire class or for particular students.

EXPANSION ACTIVITIES

1. Category Dictation ★

   a. Have students make two columns on a piece of paper and write the following at the top of each column:

      Billing Vocabulary
      Housing Vocabulary

   b. Dictate words from the list on student text page 80f and have students write the words in the appropriate column. For example:

<u>Billing Vocabulary</u>	<u>Housing Vocabulary</u>
balance	recycling bin
current charges	smoke detector

   c. As a class, in pairs, or in small groups, have students check their work.

2. Sentence Prompts ★

   Activity Master 46

   Divide the class into pairs. Make enough copies of Activity Master 46 for half the class, cut them into cards, and distribute one set to each pair. Have students take turns picking up a sentence prompt and then saying the sentence in the correct tense.

   Variation: Students can write out their sentences and arrange them into three different dialogs and then compare their answers with other pairs.

3. Finish the Sentence! ★★

   Begin a sentence using verbs from the unit and have students repeat what you said and add appropriate endings. For example:

   Teacher: She's been drawing . . .
   Student: She's been drawing pictures all day.

   Teacher: He's peeled . . .
   Student: He's peeled ten apples.

   Teacher: They've been standing in . . .
   Student: They've been standing in line for an
   hour.

4. Board Game ★★

Activity Master 47

For this activity, you will need a die, markers, and a piece of paper. (If students use a coin as a die, the class should decide which side of the coin will indicate a move of one space and which will indicate a move of two spaces.)

a. Make multiple copies of Activity Master 47. Divide the class into small groups and give each group a copy of Activity Master 47 along with a die, markers, and a piece of paper.

b. Have students place their markers on *Start*. The group should decide who goes first. That student begins the game by rolling the die or flipping the coin and moving his or her marker. If the student responds to the question or task correctly, he or she may take one more turn. If the student doesn't respond correctly, the next student takes a turn. No one may take more than two turns at a time.

Option 1: The first person to reach *Finish* is the winner.

Option 2: The game continues until each student reaches *Finish*. This way everybody is a winner.

5. Dialog Builder! ★★★

a. Divide the class into pairs. Write a line on the board from a conversation such as the following:

That's incredible!

Other possible lines are:

Don't worry.
Believe it or not . . .
I'm nervous.
You're kidding!
What does it mean?

b. Have each pair create a conversation incorporating that line. Students can begin and end their conversations any way they wish, but they must include that line in their dialogs.

c. Call on students to present their conversations to the class.

6. What's Wrong? ★★★

a. Write several sentences such as the following on the board or on a handout that you give to students. Some of the sentences should be correct and others incorrect. For example:

> We've been arguing all day.
> They've been living on this street for 2007.
> It's been leaking all morning.
> She has been doing twenty sit-ups.
> I've been feeling bad since five hours ago.
> It been making strange noises all day.
> We've been hanging our clothes on the balcony since we moved into this apartment.
> He's already been paying five bills this evening.
> I've never been buying a used car.
> She's sung in front of an audience before.
> The tenants have been recycling paper for two years.

b. Divide the class into pairs. The object of the activity is for students to identify which sentences are incorrect and then correct them. Have students compare their answers in small groups.

Variation: Do the activity as a game with competing teams. For each team's turn, write one sentence on the board and have the team decide whether the sentence is correct or not. If it isn't correct, the team must correct it. Every time a team is right, that team receives one point. The team with the greatest number of points wins.

MULTILEVEL VARIATION ★

For *below-level* students, underline the errors and have the below-level pairs focus only on correcting them.

GRAMMAR

VERB + INFINITIVE

| decide
learn | to _____ |

VERB + GERUND

| avoid
consider
enjoy
keep on
practice
quit
stop
think about | _____ing |

VERB + INFINITIVE / GERUND

| begin
can't stand
continue
hate
like
start | to _____
_____ing |

GERUND AS SUBJECT

Watching TV is my favorite way to relax.

GERUND AS OBJECT

I'm thinking about **getting married**.

FUNCTIONS

INQUIRING ABOUT LIKES/DISLIKES

Do you like to *watch TV*?

What do you like to *read*?

EXPRESSING LIKES

I enjoy *reading short stories*.
I enjoy *watching TV* very much.
I like to *read books about famous people*.

Watching TV is my favorite way to relax.

EXPRESSING DISLIKES

I can't stand to *drive downtown*.
I can't stand *driving downtown*.

I avoid *going to the mall* whenever I can.

INQUIRING ABOUT SATISFACTION

Are you enjoying the *party*?

EXPRESSING PREFERENCE

I'd rather be *reading*.

OFFERING ADVICE

I don't mean to be critical, but I really think
  you should *stop eating junk food*.

Getting married is a great idea.

INITIATING A TOPIC

Guess what I've decided to do!

I've made a decision.

ASKING FOR AND REPORTING INFORMATION

How about you?

I've never *swum* before.

I've decided to *get married*.

I considered *getting married* a few years ago,
  but never did.

How long have you been thinking about
  getting married?

How did you learn to *swim* so well?
    I started to *swim* when I was *young*, and
      I've been *swimming* ever since.

Have you ever tried to *stop eating junk food*
  before?

RESPONDING TO INFORMATION

I hope you're successful this time.

FOCUSING ATTENTION

In fact, . . .

After all, . . .

ADMITTING

To tell you the truth, . . .

The truth is . . .

CONGRATULATING

That's wonderful!
That's great!

EXPRESSING AGREEMENT

You're right.

EXPRESSING GRATITUDE

Thank you.
Thanks.

EXPRESSING APPRECIATION

Thank you.
I appreciate that.
That's very kind of you.
That's very nice of you.

LEAVE TAKING

Well, please excuse me.

I have to go now.

It was nice meeting you.
    Nice meeting you, too.

DESCRIBING FEELINGS—EMOTIONS

I envy you.

HESITATING

You know, . . .

ATTRACTING ATTENTION

Nancy?

NEW VOCABULARY

Verbs

avoid
box
break a habit
can't stand
consider
continue
enroll
envy
figure skate
go on a diet
go out of business
gossip
guess
hate
have trouble
interrupt
keep on
make a decision
make conversation
make small talk
quit
share
surf
tap dance
tease

Miscellaneous

beginning (n)
celebrities
chart
critical
dentist's appointment
doctor's appointment
engineering
ever since
example
fast-food restaurant
fundraising letter
habit
illness
junk food
listening (n)
lunch tray
network programming
part
practice (n)
progress
rather
religion
reporter
rest
technical school

topic
vegetarian

Work

assembly line
copy machine
day off
monthly report
PowerPoint presentation
small talk
training session

EXPRESSIONS

after all
I don't mean to be critical.
I hope so.
It was nice meeting you.
Nice meeting you, too
Not at all.
the rest of
the truth is
to tell you the truth

Text Page 81: Unit Opening Page

VOCABULARY PREVIEW

You may want to present these words before beginning the unit, or you may choose to wait until they first occur in a specific lesson. If you choose to present them at this point, here are some suggestions:

1. Have students look at the illustrations on text page 81 and identify the words they already know.

2. Present the vocabulary. Say each word and have the class repeat it chorally and individually. Check students' understanding and pronunciation of the words.

3. Practice the vocabulary as a class, in pairs, or in small groups. Have students cover the word list and look at the pictures. Practice the words in the following ways:

    • Say a word and have students tell the number of the illustration.

    • Give the number of an illustration and have students say the word.

Text Page 82: My Favorite Way to Relax

FOCUS

- Like to _____
- Enjoy _____ ing
- Gerunds as Subject of a Sentence

CLOSE UP

RULE:	Gerunds are formed by adding *-ing* to the base form of the verb.
EXAMPLES:	watch **watching** paint **painting** swim **swimming**
RULE:	Gerunds perform the same function as nouns. They can act as subjects and as objects.
EXAMPLES:	I enjoy **watching TV**. **Watching TV** is my favorite way to relax.
RULE:	Some verbs are followed only by gerunds and others only by infinitives. Some verbs are followed by either gerunds or infinitives with no change in meaning. For a comprehensive list of each category, see text page 94.
EXAMPLES:	**like to** watch **like** watch**ing** **enjoy** watch**ing**

GETTING READY

Introduce *like* with infinitives and *enjoy* with gerunds.

1. Write on the board:

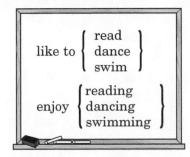

```
          ⎧ read  ⎫
like to   ⎨ dance ⎬
          ⎩ swim  ⎭

          ⎧ reading   ⎫
enjoy     ⎨ dancing   ⎬
          ⎩ swimming  ⎭
```

2. Form sentences with the words on the board and have students repeat chorally. For example:

> I like to read.
> I enjoy reading.

> *(George)* likes to dance.
> He enjoys dancing.

> *(Jane)* likes to swim.
> She enjoys swimming.

3. Ask students questions in order to have them practice making statements about themselves, using these verbs. For example:

> Teacher: What do you like to do?
> Student: I like to swim.

Teacher: What do you enjoy doing?
Student: I enjoy playing baseball.

INTRODUCING THE MODEL

1. Have students look at the model illustration.

2. Set the scene: "Two co-workers are talking during a break at work."

3. Present the model.

4. Full-Class Repetition.

   ### Pronunciation Note

   The pronunciation focus of Unit 7 is **Reduced *to*** (text page 94). You may wish to model this pronunciation at this point and encourage students to incorporate it into their language practice.

5. Ask students if they have any questions. Check understanding of vocabulary.

6. Group Choral Repetition.

7. Choral Conversation.

8. Call on one or two pairs of students to present the dialog.

9. Expand the model with further practice by replacing *she, he,* and *they* with names of students in the class. For example:

   Does (Anna) like to watch TV?
   Yes. She enjoys watching TV very much.
   Watching TV is her favorite way to relax.

   (For additional practice, do Choral Conversation in small groups or by rows.)

SIDE BY SIDE EXERCISES

Examples

1. A. Do you like to paint?
   B. Yes. I enjoy painting very much.
      Painting is my favorite way to relax.

2. A. Does Beverly like to knit?
   B. Yes. She enjoys knitting very much.
      Knitting is her favorite way to relax.

1. **Exercise 1:** Call on two students to present the dialog. Then do Choral Repetition and Choral Conversation practice.

2. **Exercise 2:** Same as above.

3. **Exercises 3–8:** Either Full-Class or Pair Practice.

   Whenever possible, after doing each exercise ask students about their own likes and dislikes. For example:

   Do you like to swim?
   Do you enjoy dancing?

4. **Exercise 9:** Have students use the model as a guide to create their own conversations, using vocabulary of their own choice. Encourage students to use dictionaries to find new words they want to use. This exercise can be done orally in class or for written homework. If you assign it for homework, do one example in class to make sure students understand what's expected. Have students present their conversations in class the next day.

WORKBOOK

Pages 78–79

EXPANSION ACTIVITIES

1. Grammar Chain ★★

a. Write the following conversation model on the board:

> A. Do you like to _____?
> B. Yes. I enjoy _____ a lot. As a matter of fact, I've been _____ for years!

b. Start the chain game by saying:

> Teacher (to Student A): Do you like to skate?

c. Student A answers according to the model on the board and then asks Student B a different question, and the chain continues. For example:

> Student A: Yes. I enjoy skating a lot. As a matter of fact, I've been skating for years!
> (to Student B): Do you like to run?
>
> Student B: Yes. I enjoy running a lot. As a matter of fact, I've been running for years!
> (to Student C): Do you like to knit?
> Etc.

2. Memory Chain ★★

a. Divide the class into groups of 5 or 6 students each.

b. Have each student tell what he or she enjoys doing to relax.

c. One group at a time, have Student 1 begin. For example:

> I enjoy sitting in the park.

d. Student 2 repeats what Student 1 said and adds a statement about himself or herself. For example:

> Susan enjoys sitting in the park, and I enjoy reading.

e. Student 3 continues in the same way. For example:

> Susan enjoys sitting in the park, Robert enjoys reading, and I enjoy playing chess.

f. Continue until everyone has had a chance to play the memory chain.

3. Find the Right Person ★★

a. Write the following on the board:

> I like to _____.
> I enjoy _____ing.
> _____ing is my favorite way to relax.

b. Have students complete these sentences on a separate piece of paper with real information about themselves.

c. Collect the papers and distribute them randomly to everyone in the class.

d. Have students interview each other in order to find the correct person to match the information they have. For example:

> Do you like to (ski)?
> Do you enjoy (going to movies)?
> Is (reading) your favorite way to relax?

e. Have students report back to the class.

Variation: This activity can be done as a game in which the first student to identify the correct person is the winner.

4. Places Around Town ★★

a. Write the following on the board:

> A. Have you ever gone to _____?
> B. Yes. I really enjoy _____ing there.

b. The object of the activity is for students to tell things people enjoy doing in different places in their community. Present the dialog with one of your students. Begin by asking about a place such as a park, a restaurant, a cafe, or a museum. For example:

> A. Have you ever gone to (The Europa Cafe)?
> B. Yes. I really enjoy eating there.

(continued)

A. Have you ever gone to (Central Park)?
B. Yes. I really enjoy flying my kite there.

c. In pairs or as a class, have students talk about other places around town, using the model on the board.

5. Survey ★★

a. Have the class brainstorm the different things people do to relax, and have students write down these activities on a sheet of paper with columns for *yes* and *no* responses. For example:

Ways to Relax	Yes	No
go to the movies listen to music read rent videos go to the mall plant flowers		

b. Have students circulate around the room interviewing each other about their preferred relaxation activities. For example:

Student 1: Do you like to go to the movies?
Student 2: No, I don't.
Student 1: Do you enjoy listening to music?
Student 2: Yes, I do. How about you? Do you enjoy going to the movies?
    Etc.

c. Have students report their findings to the class.

Variation: ★★ Have students also interview friends and family members and report to the class.

Option: ★★★ Have students put the results of their surveys in chart or graph form.

6. Complete the Sentences ★★★

a. Write the following on the board or on a handout:

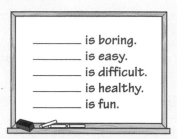

_____ is boring.
_____ is easy.
_____ is difficult.
_____ is healthy.
_____ is fun.

b. Divide the class into pairs or small groups.

c. Have students complete each sentence with 5 examples.

d. Have students compare their lists.

7. Dictate and Discuss ★★★

a. Divide the class into pairs or small groups.

b. Dictate sentences such as the following, and then have students discuss whether they agree or disagree:

Watching TV is a good way to relax.
Running is not good for you.
Drinking coffee is a good way to stay awake.
Swimming is healthier than jogging.
Skiing is easier than skating.
Going to the movies is more fun than renting videos.
Knitting is only for women.
Browsing the web is boring.
Going to English movies is a good way to learn the language.
Playing golf is only for men.

c. Call on students to share their opinions with the rest of the class.

Variation: Divide the class into small groups, and have the groups create statements for others in the class to react to.

READING *Enjoying Life*

FOCUS

- Gerunds

NEW VOCABULARY

part

READING THE STORY

Optional: Preview the story by having students talk about the story title and/or illustrations. You may choose to introduce new vocabulary beforehand, or have students encounter the new vocabulary within the context of the reading.

1. Have students read silently, or follow along silently as the story is read aloud by you, by one or more students, or on the audio program.

2. Ask students if they have any questions. Check understanding of vocabulary.

3. Check students' comprehension, using some or all of the following questions:

   What does Howard enjoy doing?
   Where does he like to read?

   What does Patty enjoy doing?
   Where does she like to sing?

   What does Brenda enjoy doing?
   Where does she like to watch TV?

   What does Tom enjoy doing?
   Who does Tom like to talk about politics with?

✓ READING *CHECK-UP*

Q & A

1. Call on a pair of students to present the model.

2. Introduce the following expressions: *to tell you the truth, It was nice meeting you. Nice meeting you, too.*

3. Have students work in pairs to create new dialogs.

4. Call on pairs to present their new dialogs to the class.

READING EXTENSION

Guess Who!

1. Have each student think of a famous person.

2. Have a volunteer come to the front of the classroom and pretend to *be* that person.

3. The other students in the class then try to guess the person's identity by asking questions. For example:

   [thinking of Andrea Bocelli]

   Student 1: I'm a famous person.

   Student 2: What do you like to do?
   Student 1: I like to sing.

   Student 3: What kind of music do you enjoy singing?
   Student 1: I enjoy singing opera.

   Student 4: What language do you usually sing in?
   Student 1: I usually sing in Italian.

   Student 2: Are you Andrea Bocelli?
   Student 1: Yes, I am!

4. Have other students take a turn thinking of a celebrity for the others to guess.

FOCUS

- { Like to _____
  { Like _____ing

- { Hate to _____
  { Hate _____ing

- Avoid _____ing

CLOSE UP

RULE:	The verbs *like* and *hate* are followed by either gerunds or infinitives with no change in meaning.
EXAMPLES:	**like to** work **like** work**ing** **hate to** work **hate** work**ing**
RULE:	The verb *avoid* is followed only by a gerund.
EXAMPLE:	**avoid** driv**ing**

GETTING READY

Introduce *like*, *hate*, and *avoid*.

1. Write the following on the board:

likes to _____   hates to _____
likes _____ing   hates _____ing
                      avoids _____ing

2. Tell the following story about *Richard*. Point to the appropriate verb on the board as you tell each part of the story.

> Richard likes to study languages.
> He also likes meeting people from other countries.

Unfortunately, he doesn't like to travel.
    In fact, he HATES to travel.
He hates riding in airplanes.
He also hates driving long distances.
It's too bad that Richard avoids traveling.
He could meet a lot of interesting people.

3. Point to each verb on the board as you say each sentence again. Call on students to retell that sentence.

INTRODUCING THE MODEL

In this model conversation, the verbs *like* and *hate* can be used with the infinitives *to drive* or the gerund *driving*. Present the model first with the infinitive. Then present it again with the gerund.

1. Have students look at the model illustration.

2. Set the scene: "Two people are talking about Helen."

3. Present the model.

4. Full-Class Repetition.

5. Ask students if they have any questions. Check understanding of the verbs *hate* and *avoid*.

6. Group Choral Repetition.

7. Choral Conversation.

8. Call on several pairs of students to present the dialog.

9. Introduce the expression *can't stand to* _____ / *can't stand* _____ *ing*.

Call on pairs of students to present the dialog again, using *can't stand* in place of *hate*.

(For additional practice, do Choral Conversation in small groups or by rows.)

SIDE BY SIDE EXERCISES

Examples

1. A. Does Albert like to travel/traveling by plane?
   B. No. He hates to travel/traveling by plane. He avoids traveling by plane whenever he can.

2. A. Do you like to go/going to the mall?
   B. No. I hate to go/going to the mall. I avoid going to the mall whenever I can.

1. **Exercise 1:** Call on two students to present the dialog. Then do Choral Repetition and Choral Conversation practice.

2. **Exercise 2:** Same as above.

3. **Exercises 3–8:** Either Full-Class Practice or Pair Practice.

   Whenever possible, after doing each exercise ask students about their own likes and dislikes. For example:

   Do you like driving downtown?
   Do you like to travel by plane?

> **New Vocabulary**
> 3. fast-food restaurant
> 8. reporter

Culture Note

Exercise 3: *Fast-food restaurants* serve food that is already prepared and can be served immediately. Examples of this kind of food include hamburgers, hot dogs, french fries, sandwiches, and pizza.

4. **Exercise 9:** Have students use the model as a guide to create their own conversations, using vocabulary of their own choice. Encourage students to use dictionaries to find new words they want to use. This exercise can be done orally in class or for written homework. If you assign it for homework, do one example in class to make sure students understand what's expected. Have students present their conversations in class the next day.

How About You?

Have students answer the questions in pairs or as a class.

WORKBOOK

Pages 80–81

EXPANSION ACTIVITIES

1. Memory Chain ★★

a. Divide the class into groups of 5 or 6 students each.

b. Tell each student to name something he or she *hates* or *can't stand* to do.

c. One group at a time, have Student 1 begin. For example:

    I hate going to the mall.

d. Student 2 repeats what Student 1 said and adds a statement about himself or herself. For example:

    Marco hates going to the mall, and I can't stand driving downtown.

e. Student 3 continues in the same way. For example:

    Marco hates going to the mall, Nancy can't stand driving downtown, and I hate to wear a tie.

f. Continue until everyone has had a chance to play the *memory chain*.

2. Sense or Nonsense? ★★

a. Divide the class into four groups.

b. Make many sets of split sentence cards with beginnings and endings of sentences. For example:

I can't stand talking on . . .	the phone.
I don't like to talk . . .	about politics.
I try to avoid eating in . . .	expensive restaurants.
I can't stand eating . . .	fish.
I don't like taking . . .	tests.

I try to avoid taking a . . .	taxi to the office.
I can't stand traveling . . .	by bus.
I avoid shopping . . .	on the Internet.
I avoid sitting . . .	in the sun.
I really like to sit on . . .	my new living room couch.

c. Mix up the cards and distribute sets of cards to each group, keeping the beginning and ending cards in different piles.

d. Have students take turns picking up one card from each pile and reading the sentence to the group. For example:

I can't stand traveling . . .	about politics.

e. The group decides if the sentence makes *sense* or is *nonsense*.

f. After all the cards have been picked, have the groups lay out all the cards and put together all the sentence combinations that make sense.

3. Miming ★★

a. Write the following on cards:

travel by plane	sit in the sun	talk on a cell phone
wear a suit and tie	eat with chopsticks	iron shirts
work overtime	baby-sit	do sit-ups

go water-skiing	browse the web	give blood

b. Have students take turns picking a card from the pile and pantomiming the action or situation on the card. The student should decide whether he or she *likes* to do that thing or *hates* to do that thing, and mime accordingly.

c. The class must guess how the person feels about what he or she is doing. For example:

> Maria likes doing sit-ups.
> Anthony hates wearing a suit and tie.

Variation: This can be done as a game with competing teams.

4. Change the Sentence! ★★

a. Write a sentence on the board, underlining and numbering different portions of the sentence. For example:

1	2	3	4
She	can't stand	to use	a cell phone.

b. Have students sit in a circle.

c. Tell them that when you say a number, the first student in the circle makes a change in that part of the sentence. For example:

> Teacher: Two.
> Student 1: She <u>likes</u> to use a cell phone.

d. The second student keeps the first student's sentence, but changes it based on the next number you say. For example:

> Teacher: Three.
> Student 2: She likes <u>to talk on</u> a cell phone.

e. Continue this way with the rest of the students in the circle. For example:

> Teacher: Four.
> Student 3: She likes to talk on <u>the Internet</u>.

5. Expand the Sentence! ★★

Tell students that the object of the activity is

to build a long sentence on the board, one word at a time.

a. Call on a student to write a pronoun or someone's name on the far left side of the board. For example:

b. Have another student come to the board and add a word. For example:

c. Have a third student add a third word. For example:

d. Continue until each student in the class has had one or more turns to add a word to expand the sentence into the longest one they can think of. For example:

> Carmen enjoys going to the movies on the weekend because she wants to become a movie star when she grows up.

6. Category Dictation: What We Share in Common ★★★

a. Have students draw two columns on a piece of paper. At the top of one column, have students write <u>I like</u>. At the top of the other column, have them write <u>I hate</u>.

b. Dictate various activities introduced in previous chapters. For example:

speaking English	going to the bank
writing letters	using the Internet
driving in the city	swimming
doing the laundry	eating with chopsticks

(continued)

giving blood
mending clothes
doing sit-ups
waiting for the bus

exercising
standing in line
running
watching the news

Have students write the activities in the appropriate column. For example:

<u>I like</u>
speaking English
watching the news

<u>I hate</u>
driving in the city
doing sit-ups

c. Divide the class into groups of four. Have students compare their lists and find at least three activities they share in common. Have each group share their common interests with the class.

7. Which One Isn't True? ★★

a. Tell students to write three true statements and one false statement about themselves, using *like, hate,* and *avoid.* For example:

I like going to the movies.
I hate to run in marathons.
I avoid eating in fast-food restaurants.

b. Have students take turns reading their statements to the class, and have the class guess which statement isn't true.

8. Pair Conversations ★★★

a. Write the following verbs and conversation model on the board:

watch   talk about
eat   listen to
do   talk to
play   go to
read   practice

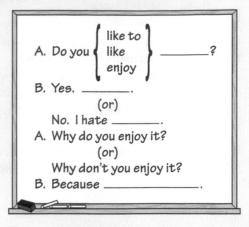

A. Do you { like to / like / enjoy } _____ ?
B. Yes. _____.
            (or)
   No. I hate _____.
A. Why do you enjoy it?
            (or)
   Why don't you enjoy it?
B. Because _____.

b. Have pairs of students create conversations based on the verbs and the model on the board. For example:

A. Do you enjoy talking about world politics?
B. Yes. I like it a lot.
A. Why do you enjoy it?
B. Because I think it's interesting to hear other people's opinions.

A. Do you like to practice the piano?
B. No. I can't stand practicing the piano.
A. Why don't you enjoy it?
B. Because it's boring, and it takes a lot of time.

READING *Bad Habits*

FOCUS

- Gerunds

NEW VOCABULARY

break a habit	interrupt
gossip (v)	junk food
habit	keep on

READING THE STORY

Optional: Preview the story by having students talk about the story title and/or illustrations. You may choose to introduce new vocabulary beforehand, or have students encounter the new vocabulary within the context of the reading.

1. Have students read silently, or follow along silently as the story is read aloud by you, by one or more students, or on the audio program.

2. Ask students if they have any questions. Check understanding of vocabulary.

   #### Culture Note

   Junk food refers to packaged snack foods such as soft drinks, potato chips, and candy.

3. Check students' comprehension, using some or all of the following questions:

   What do Jill's friends tell her?
   Why?
   Has Jill stopped eating junk food?
   Why can't she stop?

   What do Vincent's friends tell him?
   Why?

Has Vincent stopped gossiping?
Why can't he stop?

What do Jennifer's parents tell her?
Why?
Has Jennifer stopped interrupting people while they're talking?
Why can't she stop?

What does Walter's wife tell him?
Why?
Has Walter stopped talking about business?
Why can't he stop?

✓ READING *CHECK-UP*

Q & A

1. Call on a pair of students to present the model.

2. Introduce the following new expressions: *I don't mean to be critical, the truth is.*

3. Have students work in pairs to create new dialogs.

4. Call on pairs to present their new dialogs to the class.

READING EXTENSION

Giving Advice

1. Have groups of students create lists of advice for breaking one of the four bad habits in the reading. Their sentences can begin with:

   Avoid _____.
   Keep on _____.

2. Have students work in small groups to develop their lists of advice and then share their ideas with the class.

How About You?

Have students do the activity in pairs or as a class.

FOCUS

- { Start to _____
  Start _____ing
- { Learn to _____
  Practice _____ing
- Review of Tenses

CLOSE UP

RULE:	The verb *start* is followed by either a gerund or an infinitive with no change in meaning.
EXAMPLES:	**start to** swim **start** swimm**ing**
RULE:	The verb *practice* is followed only by a gerund.
EXAMPLE:	**practice** swimm**ing**
RULE:	The verb *learn* is followed only by an infinitive.
EXAMPLE:	**learn to** swim

GETTING READY

Introduce *start, learn,* and *practice.*

1. Write on the board:

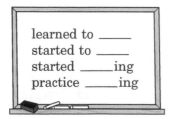

> learned to _____
> started to _____
> started _____ing
> practice _____ing

2. Tell the story below about *Bruno* one or two times. Point to the appropriate verb on the board as you tell each part of the story.

> Bruno *learned to swim* at the beach a long time ago.

His family *started to go* to the beach every summer when he was five years old.

And that's when Bruno *started swimming*.

Now he *practices swimming* in the pool at school whenever he can.

3. Point to each verb on the board as you say each sentence again. Call on students to retell that sentence.

INTRODUCING THE MODEL

1. Have students look at the model illustration.

2. Set the scene: "Someone is talking to a girl who is swimming."

3. Present the model. In line 2, first say the sentence with *started to swim*. Present the sentence again, using *started swimming*.

4. Full-Class Repetition.

5. Ask students if they have any questions. Check understanding of new vocabulary: *ever since, envy, Not at all.*

6. Group Choral Repetition.

7. Choral Conversation.

8. Call on two pairs of students to present the dialog. Have one pair use *started to swim* and have the other use *started swimming.*

   (For additional practice, do Choral Conversation in small groups or by rows.)

SIDE BY SIDE EXERCISES

Examples

1. A. How did you learn to draw so well?
   B. Well, I started to draw/drawing when I was young, and I've been drawing ever since.
   A. I envy you. I've never drawn before.
   B. I'll be glad to teach you how.
   A. Thank you. But isn't drawing very difficult?
   B. Not at all. After you practice drawing a few times, you'll probably draw as well as I do.

2. A. How did you learn to box so well?
   B. Well, I started to box/boxing when I was young, and I've been boxing ever since.
   A. I envy you. I've never boxed before.
   B. I'll be glad to teach you how.
   A. Thank you. But isn't boxing very difficult?
   B. Not at all. After you practice boxing a few times, you'll probably box as well as I do.

1. **Exercise 1:** Call on two students to present the dialog. Then do Choral Repetition and Choral Conversation practice.

2. **Exercise 2:** Introduce the word *box.*

3. **Exercises 3–5:** Either Full-Class Practice or Pair Practice.

New Vocabulary

3. surf
4. figure skate
5. tap dance

---

4. **Exercise 6:** Have students use the model as a guide to create their own conversations, using vocabulary of their own choice. Encourage students to use dictionaries to find new words they want to use. This exercise can be done orally in class or for written homework. If you assign it for homework, do one example in class to make sure students understand what's expected. Have students present their conversations in class the next day.

How to Say It!

Expressing Appreciation: In spoken English there are many ways to express appreciation to someone. These are the most common phrases: "Thank you." "I appreciate that." "That's very kind of you." and "That's very nice of you."

1. Present the expressions.

2. Full-Class Repetition.

3. Ask students if they have any questions. Check understanding of the expressions.

4. Group Choral Repetition.

5. Have students practice the conversations in this lesson again, using any of these new expressions.

6. Have pairs of students present conversations to the class.

WORKBOOK

Page 82

EXPANSION ACTIVITIES

1. Sentence Cues ★★

a. On separate cards, write key words that can be put together to form sentences or questions. Clip together the cards for each sentence. For example:

how	you	learn	do karate	so well
I	start	do karate	in 2000	
I	do karate		ever since	
I	never	tap dance	before	

After	you	practice	tap dance	you	tap dance very well

b. Divide the class into small groups and give a clipped set of cards to each group.

c. Have each group write a sentence based on their set of cards.

d. Have one member of each group write that group's sentence on the board and compare everybody's sentences. Did they choose the correct tense? What words helped them choose the correct verb form?

2. Scrambled Dialogs ★

a. Divide the class into pairs or small groups.

b. Write each line of the model conversation on text page 86 and the exercises on text page 87 on separate cards.

c. Give each pair or group a clipped set of cards for one conversation.

d. Have students unscramble the lines to put together their conversation.

e. Call on pairs to read their unscrambled dialogs.

3. Class Interviews ★★

a. Write on the board:

> I can _____ very well.

b. Call on students to tell about something they're good at. For example:

> I can skate very well.
> I can fix cars very well.

c. Ask students the following questions:

> When did you start to _____?
> or
> When did you start _____ing?
>
> Is _____ing very difficult?
> Why? / Why not?
>
> How often do you practice _____ing?

Encourage others in the class to ask additional questions.

Variation: ★★★ Divide the class into pairs, and have students interview each other about their skills and then report back to the class.

4. Role Play: Welcome to School! ★★★

a. Write on the board:

> A. Welcome to _____ School! We're very glad you're going to be studying here with us. Do you have any questions?
> B. Yes. What will we be learning first?
> A. First, we'll learn to _____, and we'll practice _____.
> B. And what will we be learning after that?
> A. Next, we'll practice _____, and we'll learn how to _____.
> B. And when will we start studying _____?
> A. _____.
> B. Oh, that'll be great! I'm really looking forward to starting school.

b. Divide the class into pairs. Have each pair choose or make up the name of a training school. For example:

> The (*Speedy*) Secretarial School
> The (*Ace*) Driving School
> The (*Chen*) Cooking School
> (*Charlie's*) Auto Repair School
> The (*Century*) Computer Programming School
> The (*Ajax*) Accounting School

Have each pair create a role play about the school, using the model on the board. Speaker A is the director or a teacher. Speaker B is a new student. Have students use dictionaries to find new vocabulary for skills one might learn at that school.

c. Have students present their role plays to the class. For example:

> A. Welcome to (*The Speedy Secretarial School*)! We're very glad you're going to be studying here with us. Do you have any questions?
> B. Yes. What will we be learning first?
> A. First we'll learn to (*file*), and we'll practice (*filing letters*).
> B. And what will we be learning after that?
> A. Next, we'll practice (*typing*), and we'll learn how to (*type business letters*).
> B. And when will we start studying (*accounting*)?
> A. (*We'll start studying accounting in a few weeks.*)
> B. Oh, that'll be great! I'm really looking forward to starting school.

5. Mystery People! ★★

a. Write the following on the board:

> I can _____.
> I started _____ when I was _____.
> I practice _____ every _____.
> I enjoy _____ because _____.

b. Have students complete the sentences about themselves and then return them to you. For example:

> I can ski.
> I started skiing when I was twelve.
> I practice skiing every winter.
> I enjoy skiing because I think it's good exercise.

c. Distribute students' sentences to others in the class, and call on students to read them. See if the class can guess who the *mystery people* are.

6. Group Conversations ★★★

a. Write on the board:

> I like _____.
> I learned to _____ when I was young.
> I've been _____ since _____.

b. Have students complete the sentences about their hobbies and special interests, using the model on the board.

c. Divide the class into groups. Have students share their information with one another.

Text Pages 88–89: Guess What I've Decided to Do!

FOCUS

- Decide to _____
- Consider _____ing
- Think about _____ing

CLOSE UP

RULE:	The verbs *consider* and *think about* are followed by gerunds.
EXAMPLES:	**consider** buy**ing** **think about** buy**ing**

RULE:	The verb *decide* is followed by an infinitive.
EXAMPLE:	**decide to** buy

GETTING READY

Introduce the new expressions *consider _____ing, think about _____ing,* and *decide to _____.*

1. Write on the board:

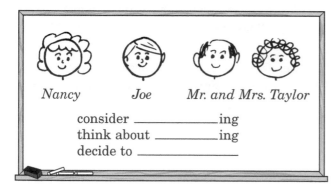

Nancy   Joe   Mr. and Mrs. Taylor

consider _____ing
think about _____ing
decide to _____

2. Have students listen for the new verbs as you tell about the people on the board one or more times:

   Nancy recently moved into a new apartment. She's *considering buying* a new TV. She saw a nice TV in a store downtown, and she's *thinking about buying* it.

Joe graduated from high school recently. He's looking for a job. He *considered going* to college. And for a while he *was thinking about* visiting some schools. But he's *decided to work* for a few years first.

Mr. and Mrs. Taylor are going to retire next year. They're *considering moving* after that. They're *thinking about selling* their house in the suburbs and *buying* an apartment in the city. They aren't sure what they'll do.

3. Check students' understanding of the new verbs by asking questions about each person. Have students retell as much of each story as they can. For example, after telling about Nancy, you can ask:

   What did Nancy do recently?
   What's she considering doing?

INTRODUCING THE MODEL

1. Have students look at the model illustration.

2. Set the scene: "Two co-workers are having lunch in the company cafeteria. One of them has some exciting news."

3. Present the model.

 268   UNIT 7

4. Full-Class Repetition.

5. Ask students if they have any questions. Check understanding of new vocabulary: *guess, consider, make a decision.*

6. Group Choral Repetition.

7. Choral Conversation.

8. Call on one or two pairs of students to present the dialog.

    (For additional practice, do Choral Conversation in small groups or by rows.)

SIDE BY SIDE EXERCISES

Examples

1. A. Guess what I've decided to do!
   B. What?
   A. I've decided to get a dog.
   B. That's wonderful! How long have you been thinking about getting a dog?
   A. For a long time, actually. I considered getting a dog a few years ago, but never did.
   B. Well, I think you're making the right decision. Getting a dog is a great idea.

2. A. Guess what I've decided to do!
   B. What?
   A. I've decided to buy a new car.
   B. That's wonderful! How long have you been thinking about getting a new car?
   A. For a long time, actually. I considered getting a new car a few years ago, but never did.
   B. Well, I think you're making the right decision. Getting a new car is a great idea.

1. **Exercise 1:** Call on two students to present the dialog. Then do Choral Repetition and Choral Conversation practice.

2. **Exercise 2:** Same as above.

3. **Exercises 3–8:** Either Full-Class Practice or Pair Practice.

New Vocabulary

5. go back
8. vegetarian

As a follow-up after each pair has presented its conversation about an important decision someone has made, interview that person and ask what the reasons were for making that decision.

4. **Exercise 9:** Have students use the model as a guide to create their own conversations, using vocabulary of their own choice. Encourage students to use dictionaries to find new words they want to use. This exercise can be done orally in class or for written homework. If you assign it for homework, do one example in class to make sure students understand what's expected. Have students present their conversations in class the next day.

WORKBOOK

Pages 83–84

EXPANSION ACTIVITIES

1. Our Future Plans ★★

a. Write on the board:

> A. What are you going to do after _____?
> B. I've been { thinking about } _____.
>   { considering }
>   How about you? What do YOU plan to do after _____?

b. Have pairs of students create conversations about their future plans. Encourage students to expand and vary the dialog any way they wish.

2. Advantages and Disadvantages ★★★

a. Have students draw two columns on a piece of paper. At the top of one column, have students write Advantages. At the top of the other column, have them write Disadvantages.

b. Say one of the decisions on student text page 89, and have students brainstorm its advantages and disadvantages. Write their ideas in the columns, and have students copy them on their papers. For example:

buy a new car

Advantages	Disadvantages
The car will last a long time.	The insurance is more expensive.
New cars have new technology.	You don't know if the car is reliable.

c. For homework, have students write two paragraphs: one about the advantages of a particular decision discussed in class and another about the disadvantages of that decision.

3. Role Play: Giving Advice ★★★

After doing the above activity of advantages and disadvantages, have students create role plays in which they give advice to the various characters on student text page 89.

a. Write on the board:

> Have you ever considered _____?
> You should avoid _____.
> You should start _____.

b. In pairs, have students develop a conversation with a character in the lesson based on the advantages and disadvantages identified in Activity 2. Students may wish to use the phrases on the board in their role plays.

c. Call on pairs to present their role plays to the class.

4. Role Play: That's Too Bad! ★★★

a. Write the following conversation model on the board:

> A. I'm having problems with my _____.
> B. What's the matter?
> A. _____.
> B. That's too bad.
>   { Have you considered _____?
>   { Have you thought about _____?
> A. That's a good idea.

b. Divide the class into pairs. Give one member of the pair a cue card with one of the following:

car	bicycle	cell phone
son	daughter	dog
cat	roof	feet
computer	back	boss
girlfriend	boyfriend	kitchen sink

c. Have pairs of students create conversations based on the cue cards and the conversation model on the board.

d. Call on pairs of students to present their conversations to the class. For example:

    A. I'm having problems with my back.
    B. What's the matter?
    A. It hurts after I sit at my desk all day.
    B. That's too bad. Have you thought about doing back exercises?
    A. That's a good idea.

5. Big Decisions ★★★

a. Individually, have students make a list of big decisions they have made in their lives. For example:

    I decided to go to this university.
    I decided to major in astronomy.
    I decided to live on campus.
    I decided to quit my job.

b. Divide the class into small groups, and have students share their lists with each other and tell whether they think they made the right decisions.

c. Call on students to report back to the class.

6. Dialog Builder! ★★★

a. Divide the class into pairs.

b. Write the following on the board:

I think you're making the wrong decision!

c. Have each pair create a conversation incorporating that line. Students can begin and end their conversations any way they wish, but they must include that line in their dialogs.

d. Call on students to present their conversations to the class.

Text Pages 90–91: I've Made a Decision

FOCUS

- Review: Start to _____
  Keep on _____ing
  Stop _____ing
- Introduction of New Expressions:

  {
  Begin to _____
  Begin _____ing

  {
  Continue to _____
  Continue _____ing

  Quit _____ing

CLOSE UP

RULE:	The verbs *begin* and *continue* are followed by either infinitives or gerunds, with no change in meaning.
EXAMPLES:	**begin to** eat **begin** eat**ing** **continue to** eat **continue** eat**ing**
RULE:	The verbs *keep on, quit,* and *stop* are followed by gerunds.
EXAMPLES:	**keep on** eat**ing** **quit** eat**ing** **stop** eat**ing**
RULE:	*Begin* and *start* are synonyms, *keep on* and *continue* are synonyms, and *quit* and *stop* are synonyms.
EXAMPLES:	begin to eat/begin eating = start to eat/start eating keep on eating = continue to eat/continue eating quit eating = stop eating

GETTING READY

1. Write the following on the board:

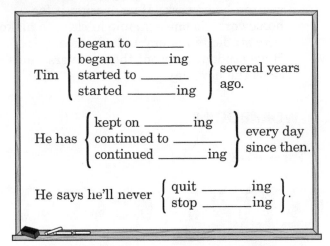

Tim { began to _____ / began _____ing / started to _____ / started _____ing } several years ago.

He has { kept on _____ing / continued to _____ / continued _____ing } every day since then.

He says he'll never { quit _____ing / stop _____ing }.

2. Tell the following story about *Tim*, pointing to the appropriate verbs on the board as you tell the story:

Tim began to ride his bicycle to work several years ago.

He has kept on riding his bicycle to work every day since then.

He says he'll never quit riding his bicycle to work.

Tell the story again, and then call on individual students to repeat each line.

3. Point to other verb forms on the board, and call on students to retell the story, using those verbs. For example:

Tim started riding his bicycle to work several years ago.

He has continued to ride his bicycle to work every day since then.

He says he'll never stop riding it to work.

INTRODUCING THE MODEL

1. Have students look at the model illustration.

2. Set the scene: "Two friends are talking. One of them has made a decision."

3. Present the model.

4. Full Class Repetition.

5. Ask students if they have any questions. Check understanding of new vocabulary: *begun, I hope so, after all, the rest of.*

6. Group Choral Repetition.

7. Choral Conversation.

8. Call on one or two pairs of students to present the dialog.

9. Call on pairs of students to present the model again, using the synonyms given below the grammar boxes as replacements for the boldface verbs in the model dialog.

(For additional practice, do Choral Conversation in small groups or by rows.)

SIDE BY SIDE EXERCISES

Examples

1. A I've made a decision.
   B. What is it?
   A. I've decided to quit biting my nails.
   B. That's great! Have you ever tried to stop biting your nails before?
   A. Yes. Many times. But every time I've stopped biting them, I've begun to bite/begun biting them again after a few days.
   B. Well, I hope you're successful this time.
   A. I hope so, too. After all, I can't keep on biting my nails for the rest of my life.

2. A. I've made a decision.
   B. What is it?
   A. I've decided to quit teasing my little sister.
   B. That's great! Have you ever tried to stop teasing your little sister before?
   A. Yes. Many times. But every time I've stopped teasing her, I've begun to tease/begun teasing her again after a few days.
   B. Well, I hope you're successful this time.
   A. I hope so, too. After all, I can't keep on teasing my little sister for the rest of my life.

1. **Exercise 1:** Call on two students to present the dialog. Then do Choral Repetition and Choral Conversation practice.

2. **Exercise 2:** Introduce the word *tease*. Same as above.

3. **Exercises 3–5:** Either Full-Class Practice or Pair Practice.

   As a follow-up after each pair has presented its conversation, ask Speaker A: "What things are you going to do to help you quit?"

4. **Exercise 6:** Have students use the model as a guide to create their own conversations, using vocabulary of their own choice. Encourage students to use dictionaries to find new words they want to use. This exercise can be done orally in class or for written homework. If you assign it for homework, do one example in class to make sure students understand what's expected. Have students present their conversations in class the next day.

WORKBOOK

Pages 85–87

EXPANSION ACTIVITIES

1. Scrambled Dialog ★

a. Divide the class into five groups.

b. Make five sets of the model conversation from text page 90, writing each line on a separate card.

c. Give each group one set of the cards, and have the group members reorder the conversations.

d. Have one group read the conversation aloud while the others listen to check for accuracy.

2. Grammar Chain ★★

a. Write the following conversation model on the board:

> A. When did you start _____?
> B. I began _____.
>   I've continued _____.
>   In fact, I'll never quit _____.
>
>   How about you?
>   When did you start _____?

b. Start the chain game by saying:

   Teacher (to Student A): When did you start studying English?

c. Student A answers according to the model and then asks a different question to Student B, and the chain continues. For example:

   Student A: I began studying two years ago. I've continued to study English. In fact, I'll never quit studying English.
   (to Student B): How about you? When did you start to *use a cell phone*?
   Student B: I began using a cell phone last year. I've continued to use a cell phone. In fact, I'll never quit using a cell phone.
   (to Student C): How about you? When did you start *jogging every day*?
   Etc.

d. Continue until everyone has had a chance to answer and ask a question.

3. In Common ★★★

a. Divide the class into pairs.

b. The object is for pairs of students to find one habit they have in common that they would like to break, and then report back to the class. For example:

   We both can't stop worrying about school.

c. Have students switch partners and again find a common habit they would like to break.

d. Continue until each student has talked with four other students. Ask the class: "What is the most common habit that people would like to break? What are ways to stop this habit?"

4. What Should You Do? ★★★

a. Write the following on the board:

start
begin
continue
keep on
stop
quit

b. Present situations such as the following and have students respond, using appropriate verbs from the list on the board:

You're driving along a street, and you see a red traffic light. What should you do?

You're driving down the street, and you see a green traffic light. What should you do?

You're driving down the street, and you see a yellow traffic light. What should you do?

You've been eating dinner, and now you're feeling full. (There's still a lot of food on your plate.) What should you do?

You have an exam tomorrow, and you haven't opened a book yet. What should you?

You have an exam tomorrow. You've studied for an hour, and now your friends want to go to a movie. What should you do?

Your doctor is concerned about your blood pressure. What should you do?

You don't think your supervisor is pleased with your work. What should you do?

You think your neighbors are going to complain to the landlord about you. What should you do?

c. Divide the class into small groups, and have students think of other situations.

d. Have each group present its situations to the class, and have students respond, using the verbs on the board.

5. Chain Story ★★

a. Begin by saying: "John made an important decision yesterday."

b. Student 1 repeats what you said and adds another item. For example: "John made an important decision yesterday. He decided to quit worrying about his health."

c. Continue around the room in this fashion, with each student repeating what the previous one said and adding another sentence.

d. You can do the activity again, beginning and ending with different students.

If the class is large, you may want to divide students into groups to give students more practice.

READING *Important Decisions*

FOCUS

- Gerunds
- Infinitives

NEW VOCABULARY

engineering
go out of business
network programming
technical school

READING THE STORY

Optional: *Preview the story by having students talk about the story title and/or illustrations. You may choose to introduce new vocabulary beforehand, or have students encounter the new vocabulary within the context of the reading.*

1. Have students read silently, or follow along silently as the story is read aloud by you, by one or more students, or on the audio program.

2. Ask students if they have any questions. Check understanding of vocabulary.

    Language Note

    Network programming is the development of computer programs for computer networks that are most commonly used in businesses and schools.

3. Check students' comprehension, using some or all of the following questions:

    Why did Jim have to make an important decision recently?

What did he consider doing first?
Then what did he think about doing?
What did he finally decide to do?
How does Jim feel about his decision?

Why did Emily have to make an important decision recently?
What did she consider doing first?
Then what did she think about doing?
What did she finally decide to do?
How does Emily feel about her decision?

Why did Nick have to make an important decision recently?
What did he consider doing first?
Then what did he think about doing?
What did he finally decide to do?
How does Nick feel about his decision?

Why did Maria have to make an important decision recently?
What did she consider doing first?
Then what did she think about doing?
What did she finally decide to do?
How does Maria feel about her decision?

✓ READING *CHECK-UP*

1. True
2. Maybe
3. True
4. False
5. Maybe
6. False
7. Maybe
8. Maybe
9. False
10. True

READING EXTENSION

1. ***Tic Tac Question the Answer***

    a. Draw a tic tac grid on the board and fill it in with short answers to questions about one of the stories on text pages 92–93. For example:

Wear a sweater.	Wearing a sports jacket.	A suit and tie.
Yes, he does.	The Tektron Internet Co.	Yes, he is.
Because it was the best thing to do.	Recently.	No, he didn't.

b. Divide the class into teams. Give each team a mark: *X* or *O*.

c. Have each team ask a question about the story for an answer in the grid. For example:

Story One

X Team: Why did Jim wear a suit and tie to the interview?
            Because it was the best thing to do.

d. If an answer is appropriate and is stated correctly, that team may replace the answer with its team mark.

e. The first team to mark out three boxes in a straight line—either vertically, horizontally, or diagonally—wins.

f. Do the same for the other stories.

2. *Interview the Characters*

a. Divide the class into pairs.

b. One member of the pair is *Jim, Emily, Nick,* or *Maria* from the story. The other is a friend. The friend wants to know why that person thought his or her decision was *the best thing to do.*

c. Have students report back to the class about their conversations, and compare everybody's reasons.

 **LISTENING**

Listen and choose the correct answer.

1. A. I avoid going to the mall whenever I can.
   B. Me, too.

2. A. I've decided to sell my car.
   B. Your beautiful car?

3. A. Please try to quit biting your nails.
   B. Okay, Mom.

4. A. Do you enjoy traveling by plane?
   B. Very much.

5. A. We're thinking about moving to Florida.
   B. Oh. That's interesting.

6. A. I've been considering getting married for a long time.
   B. Oh, really? I didn't know that.

7. A. Don't stop practicing.
   B. Okay.

8. A. Interrupting people is a habit I just can't break.
   B. That's too bad.

Answers

1. b
2. b
3. a
4. a
5. b
6. b
7. a
8. a

PRONUNCIATION Reduced *to*

> **Reduced *to*:** In spoken English, the pronunciation of *to* is often reduced to [tə].

Focus on Listening

Practice the sentences in the left column. Say each sentence or play the audio one or more times. Have students listen carefully and repeat.

Focus on Pronunciation

Practice the sentences in the right column. Have students say each sentence and then listen carefully as you say it or play the audio.

If you wish, have students continue practicing the sentences to improve their pronunciation.

 JOURNAL

Have students write their journal entries at home or in class. Encourage students to use a dictionary to look up words they would like to use. Students can share their written work with other students if appropriate. Have students discuss what they have written as a class, in pairs, or in small groups

 GRAMMAR FOCUS

Answers

1. listening
2. skating
3. to move
4. talking
5. biting
6. worrying
7. to draw
8. eating

MULTILEVEL VARIATION ★★★

Challenge *above-level* students to cover the grammar boxes as they complete the grammar exercises.

① CONVERSATION
Requests at Work

1. Have two student volunteers act out the model conversations for the class. Have them use the prop of a pencil so that the class can see the difference between *lending* (giving temporarily) and *borrowing* (taking temporarily). Then have students practice the conversation in pairs.

2. Have students look at the six photos. Ask: "Where are the people?" (At work.) Introduce the word *lunch tray*.

3. Model the conversations with a student volunteer using Exercise 1:

   A. Would you please clean table six?
   B. Sure. I'll be happy to.

   A. Thank you for cleaning table six.
   B. You're welcome.

4. In pairs, have students practice the conversations as you circulate around the classroom. Have students alternate the A and B roles. If you wish, rather than having students remain with the same partner, you can have students circulate around the room, practicing each conversation pair with a different partner.

5. Call on pairs of students to present their conversations to the class.

② TEAMWORK *Asking to Borrow Something*

1. Have students brainstorm a list of items they might borrow from their classmates during class. Write students' ideas on the board. For example:

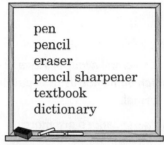

pen
pencil
eraser
pencil sharpener
textbook
dictionary

2. Have students work in small groups to practice the conversations. Or, if you wish, you can have students circulate around the classroom, practicing the conversations with different classmates.

LIFE SKILLS ENRICHMENT

Making and Responding to Requests

Life Skills Worksheet 24

Make copies of Life Skills Worksheet 24 and give one to each student. Have students complete the worksheet as homework. In the next class, have students compare their answers in pairs.

EXPANSION ACTIVITIES

1. Which Is More Formal? ★

a. Dictate the following pairs of sentences:

Could I possibly borrow a pencil?
Could I borrow a pencil?

Please take this report to Room 115.
Would you please take this report to
    Room 115?

No problem.
Sure. I'll be happy to.

b. Divide the class into small groups. Have the groups decide which sentence in each pair is more polite and formal.

Note: The following sentences are more formal.

Could I possibly borrow a pencil?
Would you please take this report to
    Room 115?
Sure. I'll be happy too.

2. Would You Please? ★★

a. Call out requests of individual students and have them perform them only when you say *please*. For example:

Teacher: Johanna, would you please open
            the door?
Johanna: Sure. I'll be happy to.

Teacher: Richard, would you close the door?
Richard: [doesn't get up to close the door]
            You didn't say "please!"

b. Have students continue the game. For example:

Student A: Ping, would you please open the
            door?
Student B: Sure. I'll be happy to. Maria,
            would you lend me a pencil?
Student C: You didn't say "please!" Alan,
            would you please . . .?

3. Finish the Sentence! ★★

Begin a sentence using the verbs from student text page 94a and have students repeat what you said and add appropriate endings. For example:

Teacher: Would you please set up . . .?
Student 1: Would you please set up the tables?
Student 2: Would you please set up the chairs?
Student 3: Would you please set up the game?

4. Find the Errors! ★★

Write the following four-line dialog on the board. In pairs, have students identify and correct the four errors.

A. Would you please to lend me your book?
B. I'll be happy for.
A. Thank you for borrowing me your book.
B. Your welcome.

5. Dictate and Discuss ★★★

Divide the class into pairs. Dictate sentences such as the following and have students discuss whether they agree or disagree with the statements.

Always say "please" when you make a request.
Always say "you're welcome" when someone
    thanks you.
It's okay to borrow pens and pencils from
    classmates.
It's okay to borrow money from classmates.
Americans say "thank you" too often.

1. Point to the three texts on student text page 94b. Ask: "Which are notes? Which is an e-mail message?"

2. Read the notes and messages aloud to the class or have students take turns reading them aloud. Introduce the new vocabulary: *assembly line, beginning* (n), *chart, copy machine, day off, dentist's appointment, doctor's appointment, fundraising letter, have trouble, monthly report, PowerPoint presentation, progress,* and *training session.*

3. Have students do the comprehension exercises individually and then compare their answers in pairs.

Answers

1. C	**4.** A
2. D	**5.** D
3. B	**6.** C

LIFE SKILLS ENRICHMENT

Writing Workplace Notes

Life Skills Worksheet 25

LIFE SKILLS WORKSHEETS 26–28

The following three worksheets deal with paychecks and earnings statements. Make copies of each of these worksheets and give one to each student. Have students complete the worksheets as homework. In the next class, have students compare their answers in pairs.

W-4 Form

Life Skills Worksheet 26 (two pages)

Note: Employees fill out a W-4 Form to determine the correct amount of federal income tax the employer needs to withhold from their paychecks.

Reading a Paycheck and Pay Stub

Life Skills Worksheet 27

W-2 Wage and Tax Statement

Life Skills Worksheet 28

Note: The W-2 Wage and Tax Statement is a wage and tax form that employers use to report income that employees have received and taxes they have paid.

1. Listen for the Verbs ★

a. Read the notes and messages on student text page 94b to the class and have students write down all the gerunds and infinitives they hear. For example:

Gerunds	Infinitives
making	to help
	to give
	to say
	to meet

b. Have pairs of students check each others' answers.

2. Trouble! ★

Write the following on the board. Have students complete the sentences and then share them with a partner.

I (sometimes) have trouble __(gerund)__.

I (sometimes) have trouble with __(noun)__.

For example:

I sometimes have trouble using PowerPoint.
I have trouble fixing things at home.
I have trouble with copy machines.
I sometimes have trouble with my neighbors.

3. True and False Definitions ★★

Define the new vocabulary and terms used on student text page 94b and have students decide whether the definitions are true or false. If a definition is false, have students provide a correct one. For example:

A PowerPoint presentation is a presentation using a computer. [True.]
A fundraising letter asks people to give money. [True.]
To make progress means to learn how to do something fast. [False. It means to learn how to do something well.]
A training session is when people have a meeting on a train. [False. It's a workplace class.]

Variation: Do the activity as a game with competing teams.

4. Retell the Notes ★★

Divide the class into pairs. Have students close their books and retell to each other the information in the notes on student text page 94b. Then have them open their books and check to see how much they remembered.

5. Writing a Thank-You Note ★★★

On student text page 94b, Joe asks Emily to help him with his PowerPoint presentation. Have students write the thank-you Joe writes to Emily after she helps him. Then have students compare their notes.

1. Ask students: "What's small talk?" Write their ideas on the board. Have students read the first paragraph of the article on student text page 94c. Ask: "Was your definition of small talk correct?"

2. Introduce the new vocabulary: *celebrities, example, gossip* (v), *illness, listening, make conversation, make small talk, practice* (n), *religion, share, small talk,* and *topic.*

3. Have students work individually to complete the comprehension exercise and then compare answers in pairs, small groups, or as a class.

Answers

1. C	**4.** A
2. B	**5.** D
3. C	**6.** B

TEAMWORK

Divide the class into pairs. Have each pair make a list of additional topics for small talk. Call on pairs to present their ideas to the class and have the class vote on the best topics.

EXPANSION ACTIVITIES

1. Question Dictation ★

a. Have students make two columns on a piece of paper and write the following at the top of each column:

> Good Small Talk Questions
> Bad Small Talk Questions

b. Dictate the following questions and have students write them in the appropriate column. For example:

> Are you married?
> Did you see the game last night?
> Do you like to ski?
> How did you learn to swim so well?
> How old are you?
> How was your weekend?
> What are you going to do this weekend?
> What did you think of the president's speech last night?
> What's your salary?

c. As a class, in pairs, or in small groups, have students check their work.

2. Small Talk Quiz ★★

Activity Master 48

a. Make a copy of Activity Master 48. Cut it into cards, and put the cards in a pile on a table or desk in the front of the classroom face down.

b. Divide the class into teams. Have students from each team take turns coming up to the front of the class, picking up a card, and reading it to the team. The team must decide whether the statement is true or false in one minute. For every correct decision, the team gets one point. The team with the most points wins.

Variation: Make multiple copies of the cards and have students work in pairs to decide whether the statements are true or false.

(continued)

3. Tic Tac Small Talk ★★★

a. Draw a tic tac grid on the board and write the following topics in random order on the grid:

weather	sports	hobbies
vacations	movies	celebrities
TV programs	news	family

b. Divide the class into two teams. Give each team a mark: X or O.

c. Give the teams five minutes to write appropriate small talk questions for each of the topics on the grid. Then have the teams take turns calling out a topic and a question. If the question is appropriate for small talk, the team gets to put its mark in that space. For example:

> X Team: sports
> Did you see the game last night?

d. The first team to mark out three boxes in a straight line—either vertically, horizontally, or diagonally—wins.

4. Small Talk Dialog Builder! ★★★

a. Divide the class into pairs. Write a line on the board from a conversation such as the following:

Oh, really?

Other possible lines are:

> That's wonderful!
> It was awesome!
> It was excellent!
> Oh! I didn't know that!
> You're kidding!
> I can't believe it!

b. Have each pair create a small talk conversation incorporating that line. Students can begin and end their conversations any way they wish, but they must include that line in their dialogs.

c. Call on students to present their small talk conversations to the class.

CHECK-UP TEST

Have students do the check-up test and then review the answers as a class.

Answers

1.	B	**6.**	B
2.	C	**7.**	A
3.	A	**8.**	D
4.	D	**9.**	C
5.	C	**10.**	B

SKILLS CHECK ✔

Words:

Explain to students that this is a list of verbs they have learned in the unit. Have students take turns reading each verb aloud to the class and say whether it is followed by a gerund, infinitive, or both. Have students put a check next to the item if they feel they have learned it. Encourage students to get a small notebook where they can write down words that are difficult for them.

I can:

Explain to students that this is a list of skills they have learned in the unit. Read each item aloud to the class. Ask individual students or pairs of students to demonstrate the skill. For example:

> Teacher: How did you learn to speak English so well?
> Student A: How did you learn to speak English so well?
> Student B: I started studying when I was a teenager.
>
> Teacher: I can express appreciation.
> Student: That's very kind of you.

Have students put a check next to the item if they feel they have learned it. Use this information to determine which lessons you may want to review or reinforce for the entire class or for particular students.

EXPANSION ACTIVITIES

1. Category Dictation ★

   a. Have students make two columns on a piece of paper and write the following at the top of each column:

   To swim
   Swimming

   b. Dictate verbs from the unit and have students write them in the appropriate column. For example:

To swim	Swimming
begin	begin
decide	can't stand
continue	continue
like	like
learn	enjoy

   c. As a class, in pairs, or in small groups, have students check their work.

2. Associations ★

   a. Divide the class into small groups. Call out a category such as the following and have the groups write down as many associations as they can think of. For example:

   things you avoid doing: [paying the bills/washing the curtains/calling the doctor]
   things you enjoy doing: [watching movies/reading/coming to English class]
   things you think about doing someday: [getting married/going to Hawaii]

   b. Have the groups call out their ideas and make a common list on the board.

3. Sentence Prompts ★

   Activity Master 49

   Divide the class into pairs. Make enough copies of Activity Master 49 for half the class, cut them into cards, and distribute one set of cards to each pair of students. Have students take turns picking up a sentence prompt and completing the sentence.

   (continued)

Variation: Students can write out their sentences and then share their sentences with other pairs.

4. Board Game ★★

Activity Master 50

For this activity, you will need a die, markers, and a piece of paper. (If students use a coin as a die, the class should decide which side of the coin will indicate a move of one space and which will indicate a move of two spaces.)

a. Make multiple copies of Activity Master 50. Divide the class into small groups and give each group a copy of Activity Master 50 along with a die, markers, and a piece of paper.

b. Have students place their markers on *Start.* The group should decide who goes first. That student begins the game by rolling the die or flipping the coin and moving his or her marker. If the student responds to the question or task correctly, he or she may take one more turn. If the student doesn't respond correctly, the next student takes a turn. No one may take more than two turns at a time.

Option 1: The first person to reach *Finish* is the winner.

Option 2: The game continues until each student reaches *Finish.* This way everybody is a winner.

5. Change the Sentence! ★★★

a. Write several sentences such as the following on the board, underlining and numbering portions of the sentence. For example:

> 1 2
> Vincent is considering going   on a diet
>   3
> after he retires.

b. Explain that when you say a number, the first student makes a change in that part of the sentence. Write the change on the board. For example:

> Teacher: Two.
> Student 1: Vincent is considering going to Brazil after he retires.
> [Teacher erases *on a diet* and writes *to Brazil.*]

c. Other students keep the first students' sentence, but change it based on the next number you say. For example:

> Teacher: Three.
> Student 2: Vincent is considering going to Brazil this summer.

> Teacher: One.
> Student 3: Nancy has decided to go to Brazil this summer.

d. Continue this way with the other sentences you have put on the board.

6. Class Discussion: Giving Advice ★★★

a. Write the following on the board:

> avoid   begin
> consider   stop
> think about   learn
> continue   practice
> keep on   decide
> start

b. Have small groups of students create lists of advice for the following topics, using any of the verbs on the board they wish.

> saving money
> driving downtown
> buying a computer
> buying a car
> studying English
> planning a trip
> going to an interview
> making small talk at work

c. Have students share their ideas with the class.

7. 30-Second Talks! ★★★

Activity Master 51

a. Divide the class into small groups. Make multiple copies of Activity Master 51 and cut them into cards. Give one set of cards to each group.

b. Have students take turns picking up a card and then spontaneously talking about the topic on the card for thirty seconds.

8. What's Wrong? ★★★

a. Write several sentences such as the following on the board or on a handout that you give to students. Some of the sentences should be correct and others incorrect. For example:

He enjoys to browse the web.
To watch TV is her favorite way to relax.
They hate to travel by plane.
He always tells me to stop biting my nails.
She started play the piano when she was
  five years old.
They decided getting married.
How long have you been thinking about to
  change jobs?
We're considering to get a dog.
Thank you for cleaning the room.
When did you start to tap dance?
Would you please to change the oil?

b. Divide the class into pairs. The object of the activity is for students to identify which sentences are incorrect and then correct them. Have students compare their answers in small groups.

Variation: Do the activity as a game with competing teams. For each team's turn, write one sentence on the board and have the team decide whether the sentence is correct or not. If it isn't correct, the team must correct it. Every time a team is right, that team receives one point. The team with the greatest number of points wins.

MULTILEVEL VARIATION ★

For *below-level* students, underline the errors and have the below-level pairs focus only on correcting them.

GRAMMAR

PAST PERFECT TENSE

I He She It We You They	had eaten.

I He She It We You They	hadn't eaten.

PAST PERFECT CONTINUOUS TENSE

I He She It We You They	had been eating.

FUNCTIONS

ASKING FOR AND REPORTING INFORMATION

I heard that *Arnold failed his driver's test*.

What happened?
What went wrong?

He *broke* his *leg*.
She *sprained* her *wrist*.

How did *he* do that?

He was *roller-skating* . . . and he had never *roller-skated before*.

I hadn't *swum in the ocean* in a long time.

Why didn't *Mr. and Mrs. Henderson see a movie last weekend*?
They didn't want to. *They* had *seen a movie the weekend before*.

Did you *get to the plane* on time?
No I didn't. By the time *I got to the plane, it* had already *taken off*.

What were you preparing for?
What had you done?

What had you forgotten to do?
What had you planned to do?
What had you done beforehand?
How long had you been planning to do it?
How long had you been preparing for that?
What did you accomplish?

Is it true?
  Yes, it is.

SHARING NEWS ABOUT SOMEONE

Have you heard about *Harry*?
Have you heard the news about *Harry*?
Have you heard what happened to *Harry*?

RESPONDING TO INFORMATION

That's terrible!

SYMPATHIZING

Poor *Harry*!

EXPRESSING REGRET

It's really a shame.

EXPRESSING HOPE

I hope *he feels better soon*.

INQUIRING ABOUT FEELINGS–EMOTIONS

Were you upset?
Were you disappointed?

DESCRIBING FEELINGS–EMOTIONS

I feel nostalgic when _____.
I felt foolish when _____.
I was furious when _____.
I was heartbroken when _____.

INQUIRING ABOUT SATISFACTION

Did you enjoy *swimming last weekend*?

EXPRESSING WANT–DESIRE

They didn't want to.

EXPRESSING APPRECIATION

I appreciate that.
That's very kind of you.
That's very nice of you.

NEW VOCABULARY

Illnesses, Diseases, and Other Health Problems

AIDS
asthma
back problem
bee sting
broken leg
cancer
chicken pox
colon cancer
depression
diabetes
diphtheria
heart disease
hepatitis
high blood
  pressure
influenza
kidney disease

liver disease
loss of
  appetite
mumps
pertussis
pneumonia
polio
rubella
severe
  headaches
stomach
  problems
tuberculosis
varicella
whooping
  cough

Parts of the Body

bones
gall bladder
heart

kidney
liver
wrist

Medical Treatments

drug
immunization
insulin
medication
multivitamin
non-prescription
  drug

prescription
  drug
tetanus shot
tuberculosis
  test
vaccination

Health Care

blood cholesterol
childhood disease
colonoscopy
dental examination
drop-in-clinic
emergency care
emergency room
eye care
eye examination
family clinic
family history
flu shot
health care

health center
health plan
health problem
hearing test
medical care
medical clinic
medical history
medical problem
medical services
medication
pneumonia vaccination
prescription drug
preventive care
public health department
screening test
skin examination
tetanus shot
vaccination

Foods

bean group
brownies
corn
cream
cream cheese
dairy food
dairy group
dairy products
dark green vegetables
dry beans
fiber
food pyramid
foods
fruit group
fruit juice
grain group
grains
health food
milk group
milk product
popcorn
starchy vegetables
steak bone
strawberry shortcake
vegetable group

Time Expressions

ahead of time
beforehand
by the time

end
in advance

Verbs

accomplish
afford
break up
bring along
bring back
bump into
cancel
check for
chew
choose
confirm
consist
deserve
discuss
dislocate
do card tricks
do poorly
earn
eat out
fail
fall through
fly a kite
get ready (for)
get to
give a party
go by
go canoeing

go together
injure
look through
lose *his* voice
memorize
move out
pass a test
pass by
perform
plan
play squash
purchase
rehearse
represent
reschedule
roller-skate
sail away
say hello
shine
shovel
take a course
take off
train
twist *her* wrist
water
wrestle

Adjectives

24-hour
average
colored
fat-free
following
foolish
frequent
full-service
heartbroken
homemade

imported
multilingual
narrow
nostalgic
outstanding
routine
scheduled
severe
tenth-grade
up-to-date

Performing Arts

curtain
movie hero
opera

recital
tango
voice

Entertaining

dinner party
dinner table

invitation
visit (n)

Leisure

card tricks kite
"hide and seek" window-
shopping

Travel

plane ticket traveler's checks

Getting a Driver's License

driver's test "rules of
driving school the road"

Miscellaneous

accomplishment full range
advance notice guide
appetite guidelines
aspect gymnastics
balcony heart attack
candy store home town
ceremony interpreter
childhood item
community fair kindly
computer lap
  programming lecture
danger loss
driveway love letter
dust memories
extra notice (n)
field notification
front teeth opening (n)

outskirts siblings
oven sliding scale
parade source
part staff
perfectly staircase
promotion street festival
risk stripes
rules translation
science teacher true

EXPRESSIONS

days gone by
from beginning to end
"get cold feet"
in advance
It's really a shame.
Poor *Harry*!

Text Page 95: Unit Opening Page

You may want to present these words before beginning the unit, or you may choose to wait until they first occur in a specific lesson. If you choose to present them at this point, here are some suggestions:

1. Have students look at the illustrations on text page 95 and identify the words they already know.

2. Present the vocabulary. Say each word and have the class repeat it chorally and individually. Check students' understanding and pronunciation of the words.

3. Practice the vocabulary as a class, in pairs, or in small groups. Have students cover the word list and look at the pictures. Practice the words in the following ways:

   • Say a word and have students tell the number of the illustration.

   • Give the number of an illustration and have students say the word.

FOCUS

* Past Perfect Tense

CLOSE UP

RULE:	The past perfect tense is formed with *had* plus the past participle of the verb.
EXAMPLES:	I **had eaten**. They **had driven**. He **had gone**.

RULE:	The past perfect is used to refer to actions or events that occurred before a particular point in the past.
EXAMPLES:	They **had seen** a movie the weekend before. She **had made** eggs the morning before.

INTRODUCING THE MODEL

1. Have students look at the model illustration.

2. Set the scene:

   a. Put the following time line on the board:

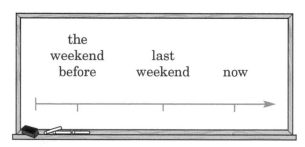

   the
   weekend   last
   before   weekend   now

   b. "Two people are talking about Mr. and Mrs. Henderson. One of them wants to know why the Hendersons didn't see a movie last weekend."

3. Present the model. Point to the appropriate time expression on the board as you present each line of the model.

4. Full-Class Repetition.

Pronunciation Note

The pronunciation focus of Unit 8 is **Reduced *had*** (text page 110). You may wish to model this pronunciation at this point and encourage students to incorporate it into their language practice.

5. Ask students if they have any questions. Check understanding of the expression *the weekend before*.

6. Group Choral Repetition.

7. Choral Conversation.

8. Call on one or two pairs of students to present the dialog.

   (For additional practice, do Choral Conversation in small groups or by rows.)

9. Practice other verbs in the past perfect tense.

   a. Practice verbs whose past participles are the same as the past tense forms.

1.) Write on the board:

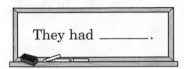

They had _____.

2.) Say the simple form of each verb and have students make a sentence with that verb in the past perfect tense, using the model on the board. For example:

Teacher: walk to school
Student: They had walked to school.

listen to music	watch TV
talk about politics	have a party
work late	wait for the bus
buy a car	visit some friends
read the newspaper	review their lessons

b. Practice verbs whose past participles differ from the past tense forms.

1.) Write on the board:

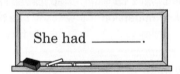

She had _____.

2.) Have students make sentences as above.

eat dinner	do well on the test
take the bus	fly to London
go to school	write a letter
have dinner	make pizza
give a party	drive to the airport

SIDE BY SIDE EXERCISES

Examples

1. A. Why didn't your parents eat out yesterday evening?
   B. They didn't want to. They had eaten out the evening before.

2. A. Why didn't Barry go canoeing last Saturday?
   B. He didn't want to. He had gone canoeing the Saturday before.

1. **Exercise 1:** Introduce the expression *eat out.* Call on two students to present the dialog. Then do Choral Repetition and Choral Conversation practice.

2. **Exercise 2:** Introduce the expression *go canoeing.* Same as above.

3. **Exercises 3–13:** Either Full-Class Practice or Pair Practice.

> **New Vocabulary**
>
> 9. opera
> 10. window-shopping
> 11. kite
> 12. discuss
>   dinner table
> 13. card tricks

Language Note

Exercise 10: *Go window-shopping* is an idiomatic expression that means *just looking around stores, store windows, and displays,* or *shopping without buying anything.*

4. **Exercise 14:** Have students use the model as a guide to create their own conversations, using vocabulary of their choice. Encourage students to use dictionaries to find new words they want to use. This exercise can be done orally in class or for written homework. If you assign it for homework, do one example in class to make sure students understand what's expected. Have students present their conversations in class the next day.

WORKBOOK

Pages 88–89

1. Grammar Chain ★★

a. Write the following conversation model on the board:

> A. Did you _____ last night?
> B. No, I didn't. I had _____ the night before.

b. Start the chain game by saying:

Teacher (to Student A): Did you *go out to eat* last night?

c. Student A answers according to the model on the board and then asks a different question to Student B, and the chain continues. For example

Student A: No, I didn't. I had *gone out to eat* the night before.

(to Student B): Did you *wear your suit* last night?

Student B: No, I didn't. I had *worn my suit* the night before.

(to Student C): Did you *drive downtown* last night?

2. Match the Sentences ★★

a. Make a set of split sentence cards such as the following:

I didn't want to have a sandwich for lunch today . . .	because I had had one yesterday.
I didn't want to wear a suit yesterday . . .	because I had worn one the day before.
I didn't want to fly a kite last weekend . . .	because I had flown one the weekend before.
I didn't want to take an astronomy course last semester . . .	because I had taken one the semester before.

I didn't want to make an omelet yesterday morning . . .	because I had made one the morning before.
I didn't want to see a play last weekend . . .	because I had seen one the weekend before.
I didn't want to drive to the beach last Sunday . . .	because I had driven there the Sunday before.
I didn't want to give a party last night . . .	because I had given one the night before.
I didn't want to write a composition yesterday . . .	because I had written one the day before.
I didn't want to ride a motorcycle last weekend . . .	because I had ridden one the weekend before.

b. Distribute a card to each student.

c. Have students memorize the sentence portion on their cards, then walk around the room trying to find their corresponding match.

d. Then have pairs of students say their completed sentences aloud to the class.

3. Concentration ★

a. Using the cards from the previous expansion activity, shuffle them and place them in five rows of four each.

b. Divide the class into two teams. The object of the game is for students to find the matching cards. Both teams should be able to see all the cards, since *concentrating* on their location is an important part of playing the game.

c. A student from Team 1 turns over two cards. If they match, the student picks up the cards, that team gets a point, and the student takes another turn. If the cards don't match, the student turns them face down, and a member of Team 2 takes a turn.

d. The game continues until all the cards have been matched. The team with the most correct matches wins the game.

Variation: This game can also be played in groups and pairs.

4. Sense or Nonsense? ★★

a. Divide the class into four groups.

b. Using the cards from Expansion Activity 2, mix up the cards and distribute sets of cards to each group, keeping the beginning and ending cards in different piles.

c. Have students take turns picking up one card from each pile and reading the sentence to the group. For example:

I didn't want to have a sandwich for lunch today . . .	because I had given one the night before.

d. That group decides if the sentence makes sense or is *nonsense.*

e. After all the cards have been picked, have the groups lay out all the cards and put together all the sentence combinations that make sense.

5. Student Interviews ★★★

a. Divide the class into pairs. Have students interview each other about what they did last weekend.

b. Have students report back to the class explaining what their classmate *had done* last weekend. Remind students to use the past perfect tense.

6. Where's Martha? ★★★

a. Write the following on the board or on a handout for students:

Martha

Morning
get up
wash her hair
meet a friend for breakfast
borrow some books from the library
take a math test

Afternoon
eat lunch with a friend
walk to the post office to get her mail
go to history class
talk to her English teacher about her exam
do her laundry
buy some things

A. Have you seen Martha today?

B. Yes. I saw her this $\begin{Bmatrix} \text{morning} \\ \text{afternoon} \end{Bmatrix}$.
She had just _____, and she was getting ready to _____.

b. Set the scene: "Martha and Sally are college students. They're roommates in a dormitory at the college. It's evening now. Sally is in her room, and she's worried because Martha isn't there. She's asking other people in the dormitory if they have seen Martha." For example, she asked Bill: "Have you seen Martha today?" And Bill said:

"Yes. I saw her this afternoon. She had just eaten lunch with a friend, and she was getting ready to walk to the post office to get her mail."

(continued)

c. Role play the conversation with a few of your students. Then call on pairs of students to role play. (Speaker B decides which cue to use in the answer.)

7. What's First? ★★

a. Divide the class into pairs.

b. On a handout, write pairs of sentences such as the following:

> She studied hard.
> She took the test.
>
> He made dinner.
> He bought the food.
>
> She went to work.
> She brushed her teeth.
>
> He started to cook on the barbecue.
> He made a fire.
>
> They practiced a lot.
> They ran in the race.
>
> My parents came to visit.
> I cleaned the house
>
> She returned it to the library.
> She read the book.
>
> We put on our coats.
> We went outside.
>
> She went to bed.
> She ate dinner.

c. Have students in each pair decide which sentence happened first, and then combine the sentences using the word *before*. For example:

> She had studied hard before she took the test.
> He had bought the food before he made dinner.

d. Have the pairs compare their sentences.

READING *The Most Important Thing*

FOCUS

- Past Perfect Tense

NEW VOCABULARY

ahead of time	look through
bring along	memorize
curtain	oven
dinner party	perfectly
driveway	plane ticket
end (n)	purchase (v)
foolish	rehearse
from beginning to end	shine
heartbroken	shovel
imported (adj)	traveler's checks
in advance	water (v)
invitation	

READING THE STORY

Optional: *Preview the story by having students talk about the story title and/or illustrations. You may choose to introduce new vocabulary beforehand, or have students encounter the new vocabulary within the context of the reading.*

1. Have students read silently, or follow along silently as the story is read aloud by you, by one or more students, or on the audio program.

2. Ask students if they have any questions. Check understanding of vocabulary.

3. Check students' comprehension, using some or all of the following questions:

What had Roger done to prepare for his dinner party?
What had he forgotten to do?
Why did Roger feel foolish?

What had Mr. and Mrs. Jenkins done to prepare for their vacation?
What had they forgotten to do?
Why were they heartbroken?

What had Harold done to prepare for his job interview?
What had he forgotten?
Why was Harold furious with himself?

What had Janet done to prepare for the play?
What had she forgotten to do?
Why was she embarrassed?

✓ READING *CHECK-UP*

TRUE, FALSE, OR MAYBE?

1. True
2. True
3. Maybe
4. False
5. True
6. True
7. Maybe
8. False
9. True

WHICH IS CORRECT?

Before doing the exercise, introduce the word *laptop.*

1. traveler's checks
2. an invitation
3. borrowed
4. heartbroken
5. important, imported

READING EXTENSION

1. *Time Lines*

Have students draw a time line for the each of the characters in the four readings. In pairs, have students compare their time lines.

2. *Chain Story*

a. Begin by saying, "Henry was all prepared for his first interview. He had bought a new suit."

b. Student 1 repeats what you said and adds another item. For example: "Henry was all prepared for his first interview. He had bought a new suit, and he had practiced the interview questions."

c. Continue around the room in this fashion, with each student repeating what the previous one said and adding another sentence.

d. You can do the activity again, beginning and ending with different students.

If the class is large, you may want to divide students into groups to give students more practice. Here are some additional story lines:

Martha was all prepared for the move to a new apartment.
Barry and Paul were all prepared for their car trip.
Our neighbors were all prepared for the rainstorm.
Jim was all prepared for the first day of school.

How About You?

Have students answer the questions in pairs or as a class.

FOCUS

- Past Perfect Tense

CLOSE UP

RULE: The time expression *by the time* establishes a point in time before which something occurred.

EXAMPLES: **By the time** I got to the concert, it had already begun.
By the time I got to the plane, it had already taken off.

INTRODUCING THE MODEL

1. Have students look at the model illustration.
2. Put the following time line on the board:

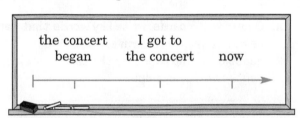

```
the concert      I got to
  began         the concert      now
```

3. Set the scene: "Two friends are talking. One was late for a concert."
4. Present the model while pointing to the appropriate cues on the time line on the board.
5. Full-Class Repetition.
6. Ask students if they have any questions. Check understanding of the expressions *by the time, get to.*
7. Group Choral Repetition.
8. Choral Conversation.
9. Call on one or two pairs of students to present the dialog.

   (For additional practice, do Choral Conversation in small groups or by rows.)

SIDE BY SIDE EXERCISES

Examples

1. A. Did you get to the post office on time?
   B. No, I didn't. By the time I got to the post office, it had already closed.
2. A. Did you get to the plane on time?
   B. No, I didn't. By the time I got to the plane, it had already taken off.

1. **Exercise 1:** Call on two students to present the dialog. Then do Choral Repetition and Choral Conversation practice.
2. **Exercise 2:** Introduce the expression *take off.* Same as above.
3. **Exercises 3–9:** Either Full-Class Practice or Pair Practice.

New Vocabulary	
5. lecture	9. parade
8. sail away	go by

WORKBOOK

Page 90

EXPANSION ACTIVITIES

1. Grammar Chain ★★

a. Write the following conversation model and verbs on the board:

> A. Did you _____?
> B. No. By the time I got to _____,
> _____ had already _____.

> catch your plane   mail the letter
> cash the check   talk to the mechanic
> buy the milk   take the train
> see the play   enjoy the lecture
> return the book   see the doctor

b. Start the chain game by saying:

> Teacher (to Student A): Did you *catch your plane?*

c. Student A answers according to the model on the board and then asks a different question to Student B, and the chain continues. For example

> Student A: No. By the time I got to the airport, the plane had already taken off.
> (to Student B): Did you *mail the letter?*
> Student B: No. By the time I got to the post office, it had already closed.
> (to Student C): Did you *cash the check?*
> Etc.

2. Change the Sentence! ★★

a. Write a sentence on the board, underlining and numbering different portions of the sentence. For example:

>   1   2
> By the time   I got to   the concert,
>   3
>   it had already begun.

b. Have students sit in a circle.

c. Tell them that when you say a number, the first student in the circle makes a change in that part of the sentence. For example:

> Teacher: Two.
> Student 1: By the time I got to <u>the movie</u>, it had already begun.

d. The second student keeps the first student's sentence, but changes it based on the next number you say. For example:

> Teacher: Three.
> Student 2: By the time I got to the movie, <u>it had already ended</u>.

e. Continue this way with the rest of the students in the circle. For example:

> Teacher: One.
> Student 3: By the time <u>we decided to see</u> the movie, it had already ended.

3. Sentence Cues ★★

a. On separate cards, write key words that can be put together to form sentences or questions. Clip together the cards for each sentence. For example:

by the time	she / it	get to class	already	begin
they	paint the house	before / they		sell it
he	travel	around the world	before / he	get married
she	by the time	arrive	it / end	already
by the time	we / it	get there	take off	already

b. Divide the class into small groups and give a clipped set of cards to each group.

c. Have each group write a sentence based on their set of cards.

d. Have one member of each group write that group's sentence on the board and compare everybody's sentences. Did they choose the correct tense? What words helped them choose the correct verb form?

4. Finish the Sentence! ★★

Begin sentences with "By the time, . . ." and call on students to repeat what you said and then complete the sentence any way they wish. For example:

Teacher: By the time I got to the party, . . .
Student: By the time I got to the party, everybody had already left.

Teacher: By the time I got to the parade, . . .
Student: By the time I got to the parade, it had already gone by.

5. No Wonder! ★★★

a. Write the following conversation framework on the board:

A. I saw _____ at _____ yesterday, and (he/she) looked very upset/sad/excited/happy.

B. I know. (He/She) had just _____.

A. No wonder (he/she) looked so _____!

b. Divide the class into pairs.

c. Have students create conversations based on the model on the board and then present them to the class. For example:

A. I saw your uncle at the supermarket yesterday, and he looked very upset.
B. I know. He had just lost his wallet.
A. No wonder he looked so upset!

A. I saw Gloria at the bank yesterday, and she looked very excited.

B. I know. She had just gotten a raise.
A. No wonder she looked so excited!

6. Class Quiz ★★★

a. Divide the class into pairs or small groups.

b. Dictate sentences about history (local, national, entertainment, or sports history) and then have students discuss whether they agree or disagree. For example:

By the time the French Revolution began, the American Revolutionary War had already ended.

c. Call on students to respond. For example:

I agree. The American Revolutionary War ended in 1783, and the French Revolution didn't begin until 1789.

7. Memory Game ★★

a. Write the following on a handout.

8:00–9:00	Alice took the bus to work.
9:00–12:00	She wrote a report.
12:00–1:00	She had lunch with a friend.
1:00–2:00	She went to the clinic for a check-up.
2:00–5:00	She gave a presentation at work.
5:00–6:00	She took the bus to the museum.
6:00–9:00	She looked at the paintings.
10:00	She came home.

b. Give the handout to students and tell them they have 30 seconds to look at it and try to remember as much information as they can.

c. Have students put the handout aside.

d. Write the following beginning of a sentence on the board:

By 2:00, Alice had already _____.

(continued)

Have students write down as many sentences as they can remember about Alice's day, using the past perfect.

e. Have students share their sentences with the class.

f. Let students look at the schedule for another 30 seconds, and then write the following sentence on the board:

By 10:00 P.M. she had already _____.

See how many students can write down all the things Alice had done that day.

Variation: You can do this activity as a game with competing teams. The first team to write the most number of correct statements about Alice's day is the winner.

FOCUS

- Past Perfect: Negatives

CLOSE UP

RULE:	To form the negative of the past perfect tense, *not* is added. The word *not* contracts with the auxiliary *had*.
EXAMPLES:	I **had not** gone. I **hadn't** gone.
	You **had not** gone. You **hadn't** gone.
	She **had not** gone. She **hadn't** gone.
	He **had not** gone. He **hadn't** gone.
	We **had not** gone. We **hadn't** gone.
	They **had not** gone. They **hadn't** gone.

INTRODUCING THE MODEL

1. Have students look at the model illustration.

2. Set the scene: "Two people are talking about their grandfather."

3. Present the model.

4. Full-Class Repetition.

5. Ask students if they have any questions. Check understanding of vocabulary.

6. Group Choral Repetition.

7. Choral Conversation.

8. Call on one or two pairs of students to present the dialog.

   (For additional practice, do Choral Conversation in small groups or by rows.)

SIDE BY SIDE EXERCISES

Examples

1. A. Did Natalie enjoy swimming in the ocean last weekend?
   B. Yes, she did. She hadn't swum in the ocean in a long time.

2. A. Did you enjoy seeing a movie yesterday evening?
   B. Yes, I did. I hadn't seen a movie in a long time.

1. **Exercise 1:** Call on two students to present the dialog. Then do Choral Repetition and Choral Conversation practice.

2. **Exercise 2:** Same as above.

3. Exercises 3–9: Either Full-Class Practice or Pair Practice.

New Vocabulary

6. strawberry shortcake
8. hide and seek
9. love letter

Culture Note

Hide and seek is a favorite game of young children in which one person *hides* and the others *seek* (look for) the person who is hiding.

WORKBOOK

Page 91

EXPANSION ACTIVITIES

1. Match the Sentences ★★

a. Make a set of split sentence cards such as the following:

I enjoyed looking at the paintings because . . .	I hadn't gone to a museum in a long time.
I enjoyed going to the beach last weekend because . . .	I hadn't gone swimming in a long time.
I enjoyed going out for dinner last Friday because . . .	I hadn't eaten in a restaurant in a long time.
I enjoyed going to the symphony last night because . . .	I hadn't listened to classical music in a long time.
I enjoyed relaxing in my yard last Saturday because . . .	I hadn't stayed home on the weekend in a long time.
I enjoyed making an apple pie yesterday because . . .	I hadn't baked anything in a long time.

I enjoyed working in my garden on Sunday because . . .	I hadn't planted flowers in a long time.
I enjoyed my flight to Denver last week because . . .	I hadn't flown anywhere in a long time.

b. Distribute a card to each student.

c. Have students memorize the sentence portion on their cards, then walk around the room trying to find their corresponding match.

d. Then have pairs of students say their completed sentences aloud to the class.

2. Concentration ★

a. Using the cards from the previous expansion activity, shuffle them and place them in four rows of four each.

b. Divide the class into two teams. The object of the game is for students to find the matching cards. Both teams should be able to see all the cards, since *concentrating* on their location is an important part of playing the game.

c. A student from Team 1 turns over two cards. If they match, the student picks up the cards, that team gets a point, and the student takes another turn. If the cards don't match, the student turns them face down, and a member of Team 2 takes a turn.

d. The game continues until all the cards have been matched. The team with the most correct matches wins the game.

Variation: This game can also be played in groups and pairs.

3. Sense or Nonsense? ★★

a. Divide the class into four groups.

b. Using the cards from Expansion Activity 2, mix up the cards and distribute sets of cards to each group, keeping the beginning and ending cards in different piles.

c. Have students take turns picking up one card from each pile and reading the sentence to the group. For example:

I enjoyed going out for dinner last Friday because . . .	I hadn't gone swimming in a long time.

d. That group decides if the sentence makes *sense* or is *nonsense.*

e. After all the cards have been picked, have the groups lay out all the cards and put together all the sentence combinations that make sense.

4. What's the Reason? ★★

a. Write the following list of verbs and conversation framework on the board:

drive	ride
eat	run
fly	sing
give	speak

That's because ____ hadn't _____ in a long time.

b. Present the situations below and have students respond, using an appropriate verb and the sentence framework on the board. For example:

Teacher: Tom had too much pizza last night.

Student: That's because he hadn't eaten pizza in a long time.

Situations:

Tom had too much pizza last night.
Barbara was very nervous before her flight to Florida yesterday.
Richard was afraid to take his car into New York City last weekend.
Kathy was very nervous before the marathon race last Saturday.
Alan was feeling nervous before choir practice yesterday.
Gloria almost fainted yesterday when the nurse at the hospital started taking her blood.
The president practiced Spanish all weekend before the president of Colombia arrived in Washington.
Tim Flynn, the movie actor, wasn't looking forward to making a western movie last year.

5. Have You Seen Them? ★★★

a. Write the following on the board:

A. Have you seen _____ since
   (he/she/they) _____?
B. No, I haven't. The last time I saw ____,
   (he/she/they) hadn't _____ yet.

b. Write the following cues on cards:

Betty have her baby	Bill move into his new apartment
Julie run in the marathon	George take his English exam
Jane win the lottery	Ted begin studying French

(continued)

Gloria become a movie star	Ron meet his new girlfriend
Sally speak to her supervisor about a raise	Brian decide to move to South America
Mr. and Mrs. Lopez buy a sports car	Judy and Tim get married
Walter had an operation on his knee	Nancy quit her job
Howard lose fifty pounds	Rita start lifting weights

c. Call on pairs of students to come to the front of the room. Have each pair pick a card and create a conversation based on that situation and the model on the board. For example:

A. Have you seen Betty since she had her baby?
B. No, I haven't. The last time I saw her, she hadn't had her baby yet.

A. Have you seen Bill since he moved into his new apartment?
B. No, I haven't. The last time I saw him, he hadn't moved into his new apartment yet.

6. What's Wrong? ★★★

a. Divide the class into pairs or small groups.

b. Write several sentences such as the following on the board or on a handout. Some of the sentences should be correct, and others incorrect. For example:

I hadn't see them in a long time.
I enjoyed swim at the beach last weekend.
She hadn't ate there in a long time.
By the time we got to the theater, the play had already started.
Did you seen your friends at the party?
They had took that course before.
By the time they got to the meeting, it already began.
Did they get to the airport on time?
Why didn't he gone to class last week?
He had ridden on a roller coaster in a long time.

c. The object of the activity is for students to identify which sentences are incorrect and then correct them.

d. Have students compare their answers.

Variation: Do the activity as a game with competing teams. The team that successfully completes the task in the shortest time is the winner.

READING *Days Gone By*

FOCUS

- Past Perfect Tense

NEW VOCABULARY

balcony	move out
bring back	movie hero
bump into	nostalgic
candy store	outskirts
childhood	pass by
days gone by	popcorn
field	say hello
homemade	science teacher
home town	tenth-grade
memories	visit (n)

READING THE STORY

Optional: Preview the story by having students talk about the story title and/or illustrations. You may choose to introduce new vocabulary beforehand, or have students encounter the new vocabulary within the context of the reading.

1. Have students read silently, or follow along silently as the story is read aloud by you, by one or more students, or on the audio program.

2. Ask students if they have any questions. Check understanding of vocabulary.

3. Check students' comprehension, using some or all of the following questions:

   What did Michael do last month?
   Why was Michael's visit to Fullerton very special to him?

Where did he walk, and what did he remember?
What did he pass by?
Where did he stand for a while, and what did he think about?
What did he have at the ice cream shop?
What did he do in the park?
Where did he go fishing?
Why did Michael feel like a kid again?
Who did Michael visit?
Who did he say hello to?
Who did he bump into?
What did Michael remember during his visit to his home town?
Why was his trip back to Fullerton a very nostalgic experience for him?

✓ READING *CHECK-UP*

TRUE, FALSE, OR MAYBE?

1. False
2. True
3. False
4. True
5. Maybe
6. True
7. True
8. Maybe

WHICH WORD IS CORRECT?

Before doing the exercise, introduce the word *located*.

1. homemade
2. outskirts
3. spent
4. into
5. back
6. nostalgic

READING EXTENSION

1. Michael's Childhood

Have students compose a short paragraph describing Michael's childhood based on the information in the reading.

2. Childhood Memories

a. Have students individually make a list of activities they enjoyed in their childhood.

b. Divide the class into pairs and have students share their lists. As they talk, have them find common childhood hobbies or activities.

c. Have students report to the class about their partners.

 LISTENING

Listen and choose the correct answer.

1. Did your parents enjoy eating at Joe's Restaurant last night?

2. Why don't you want to see the new James Bond movie with us next weekend?

3. Did you get to the play on time last night?

4. Michael, please go upstairs and do your homework.

5. Why did Carmen do so well on the history test?

6. We really enjoyed our vacation at the Ritz Hotel.

Answers

1. b

2. b

3. a

4. b

5. a

6. b

 THINK ABOUT IT! *Feelings and Experiences*

Have students complete the sentences and then share their responses in pairs or as a class.

FOCUS

• Contrast: Past Perfect vs. Past Continuous

INTRODUCING THE MODEL

1. Have students look at the model illustration.

2. Set the scene: "Harry had an accident recently. Two of his friends are talking about him."

3. Present the model.

4. Full-Class Repetition.

5. Ask students if they have any questions. Check understanding of the word *roller-skate*.

6. Group Choral Repetition.

7. Choral Conversation.

8. Call on one or two pairs of students to present the dialog.

   (For additional practice, do Choral Conversation in small groups or by rows.)

SIDE BY SIDE EXERCISES

Examples

1. A. Have you heard about Tom?
   B. No, I haven't. What happened?
   A. He twisted his ankle last week.
   B. That's terrible! How did he do THAT?
   A. He was flying a kite . . . and he had never flown a kite before.
   B. Poor Tom! I hope he feels better soon.

2. A. Have you heard about Peggy?
   B. No, I haven't. What happened?
   A. She injured her knee last week.
   B. That's terrible! How did she do THAT?
   A. She was skiing . . . and she had never skied before.
   B. Poor Peggy! I hope she feels better soon.

1. **Exercise 1:** Introduce the word *twist*. Call on two students to present the dialog. Then do Choral Repetition and Choral Conversation practice.

2. **Exercise 2:** Introduce the word *injure*. Same as above.

3. **Exercises 3–11:** Either Full-Class Practice or Pair Practice.

> **New Vocabulary**
>
> 3. brownies
> 4. wrist
>   play squash
> 6. wrestle
> 7. lose his voice
> 8. dislocate
>   gymnastics
> 10. tango
> 11. front teeth
>   chew
>   steak bone

4. **Exercise 12:** Have students use the model as a guide to create their own conversations, using vocabulary of their own choice. Encourage students to use dictionaries to find new words they want to use. This exercise can be done orally in class or for written homework. If you assign it for homework, do one example in class to make sure students understand what's expected. Have students present their conversations in class the next day.

How to Say It!

Sharing News About Someone: The present perfect is used to talk about a recent event. Three common opening questions to share some news about someone are: "Have you heard about _____?" "Have you heard the news about _____?" and "Have you heard what happened to _____?"

1. Present the expressions.

2. Full-Class Repetition.

3. Ask students if they have any questions. Check understanding of the expressions.

4. Group Choral Repetition.

5. Have students practice the conversations in this lesson again, beginning with any of these new expressions.

6. Call on pairs to present their conversations to the class.

WORKBOOK

Pages 92–93

EXPANSION ACTIVITIES

1. Can You Hear the Difference? ★

a. Write on the board:

Present Perfect	Past Perfect
I have seen that.	I had seen that.
You have been there.	You had been there.
We have had those.	We had had those.
They have gone.	They had gone.

b. Choose a sentence randomly from one of the two columns and say it to the class. Have the class listen and identify whether the sentence is in the *present perfect* or in the *past perfect*.

c. Have students continue the activity in pairs. One student pronounces a sentence and the other identifies the tense. Then have them reverse roles.

d. Write other similar sentences on the board and continue the practice.

2. Scrambled Dialogs ★

a. Write each line of Exercise 1 and Exercise 2 from text page 104 on a separate card. Scramble the cards.

b. Give the cards to 12 students. Have them unscramble the lines and put together the two conversations.

[Variation]

a. Divide the class into three groups.

b. Make three sets of Exercises 1 and 2, writing each line on a separate card.

c. Give each group one set of the cards, and have the group members reorder the conversations.

d. Have each group read one of the conversations aloud while the others listen to check for accuracy.

3. Concentration ★

a. Write the following sentences on separate cards:

She was roller-skating . . .	and she had never roller-skated before.
He was flying a kite . . .	and he had never flown a kite before.
She was skiing . . .	and she had never skied before.
He was singing opera . . .	and he had never sung opera before.
She was doing gymnastics . . .	and she had never done gymnastics before.
He was doing the tango . . .	and he had never done the tango before.

She was riding a motorcycle . . .	and she had never ridden a motorcycle before.
He was boxing . . .	and he had never boxed before.

b. Shuffle the cards and place them face down in four rows of four each.

c. Divide the class into two teams. The object of the game is for students to find the matching cards. Both teams should be able to see all the cards, since *concentrating* on their location is an important part of playing the game.

d. A student from Team 1 turns over two cards. If they match, the student picks up the cards, that team gets a point, and the student takes another turn. If the cards don't match, the student turns them face down, and a member of Team 2 takes a turn.

e. The game continues until all the cards have been matched. The team with the most correct matches wins the game.

Variation: This game can also be played in groups and pairs.

4. Telephone: Have You Heard the News? ★

a. Divide the class into large groups. Have each group sit in a circle.

b. Whisper some news to one student. For example:

"Have you heard the news? David sprained his right ankle and broke his left arm last week. He was ice-skating and he had never ice-skated before!"

c. The first student whispers the news to the second student, and so forth around the circle.

d. When the message gets to the last student, that person says it aloud. Is it the same message you started with? The group with the most accurate message wins.

5. Do You Remember? ★★

a. Have students close their books.

b. Ask questions about the things that happened to the people on text pages 104 and 105. See if students can remember who they are and what happened to them. For example:

Teacher: Who lost his voice?
Student: Victor.
Teacher: How did it happen?
Student: He was singing opera . . . and he had never sung opera before.

Teacher: Who got hurt in an accident?
Student: Ann.
Teacher: How did it happen?
Student: She was riding a motorcycle . . . and she had never ridden a motorcycle before.

Variation: Do the activity as a game with competing teams.

6. Finish the Sentence! ★★

a. Write on the board:

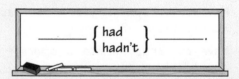

b. Begin each of the sentences below and call on different students to finish the sentence, using verbs in the past perfect. For example:

Teacher: Martha was very tired yesterday morning because . . .
Student 1: she had studied until midnight.
Student 2: she hadn't slept well.
Student 3: her neighbor's dog had barked until 2 A.M.

Sentences:

Martha was very tired yesterday morning because . . .

Joe was very hungry at dinner last night because . . .

Richard didn't have any clean clothes to wear last weekend because . . .

(continued)

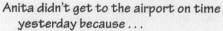

Anita didn't get to the airport on time
yesterday because . . .

Tom didn't get the job as a secretary last
week because . . .

Betty was very nervous before her job
interview yesterday because . . .

Brian was really excited about visiting Mexico
last summer because . . .

My parents didn't go to a movie last night
because . . .

7. How Did It Happen? ★★★

Text pages 104 and 105 deal with accidents or
unfortunate things that happened to various
people. Have students tell about similar
experiences they have had.

a. Write the following questions on the board or
on a handout for students:

Have you ever broken your leg or arm?
How did it happen?

Have you ever twisted your ankle?
How did it happen?

Have you ever sprained your wrist or back?
How did it happen?

Have you ever gotten into an accident?
How did it happen?

Have you ever lost your voice?
Tell about it.

b. Divide the class into pairs or small groups.

c. Have students ask each other the questions
and then report to the class about the other
person.

Variation: ★★★ For homework, have students
write about an unfortunate experience they have
had. Collect the papers and distribute them
randomly to students in the class. Have those
students read the papers to the class and have
others try to guess who this unfortunate event
happened to.

FOCUS

- Past Perfect Continuous Tense

CLOSE UP

RULE: The past perfect continuous tense is formed with *had been* plus the
present participle (*-ing* form) of the verb.

EXAMPLES: I **had been eating**
you **had been working**
he **had been going**
we **had been feeling**
they **had been studying**

RULE: Like the past perfect tense, the past perfect continuous refers to events or
actions that occurred before a particular point in the past. Like other
continuous tenses, the past perfect continuous focuses on the duration of
activity.

EXAMPLE: He **failed** his driver's test.
(*past event*)
He **had been practicing** for a long time.
(*activity that lasted for a long time*)

GETTING READY

Introduce the past perfect continuous tense.

1. Write on the board:

had been working

Bill
had been typing

Sally
had been talking

Frank and Susan
had been hiring

2. Point to the appropriate cues on the board as you tell the following story: "I went to see some of my old friends at the Presto Company yesterday afternoon. Everybody was happy to see me, but they were all very tired."

They *had been working* very hard all day.
Bill *had been typing* all day.
Sally *had been talking* on the telephone all day.
And Frank and Susan *had been hiring* new employees all day.

3. Have students repeat the sentences chorally and individually.

4. Form sentences with the words in the box at the top of text page 106. Have students repeat chorally. For example:

I had been eating.
He had been eating.

INTRODUCING THE MODEL

1. Have students look at the model illustration.

2. Set the scene: "Arnold took his driver's test last week, but he didn't do very well. Two of his friends are talking about what happened."

3. Present the model.

4. Full-Class Repetition.

5. Ask students if they have any questions. Check understanding of the words *fail, driver's test, true,* and the expression *it's really a shame.*

6. Group Choral Repetition.

7. Choral Conversation.

8. Call on one or two pairs of students to present the dialog.

   (For additional practice, do Choral Conversation in small groups or by rows.)

SIDE BY SIDE EXERCISES

Examples

1. A. I heard that Fred lost his job at the factory last week. Is it true?
   B. Yes, it is . . . and it's really a shame. He had been working there for a long time.

2. A. I heard that Larry and Jane broke up last week. Is it true?
   B. Yes, it is . . . and it's really a shame. They had been going together for a long time.

1. **Exercise 1:** Call on two students to present the dialog. Then do Choral Repetition and Choral Conversation practice.

2. **Exercise 2:** Introduce the words *break up, go together.* Same as above.

   ### Culture Note

   The expressions *go together* and *break up* are associated with dating customs in the United States. When two people date each other exclusively, they are *going together*. When this type of relationship ends, they *break up.*

3. **Exercises 3–10:** Either Full-Class Practice or Pair Practice.

   New Vocabulary
   3. cancel
      plan
   6. heart attack
   7. do poorly
   8. train
   9. perform
      recital

WORKBOOK

Pages 94–96

EXPANSION ACTIVITIES

1. Who Is It? ★

Make statements about the people in the exercises. Have students respond by telling who you're talking about. For example:

> They had been arguing a lot.
> *Larry and Jane [Exercise 2]*

> He had been trying to lose weight.
> *Walter [Exercise 6]*

> She had been studying French.
> *Mona [Exercise 3]*

> He hadn't studied enough.
> *Alex [Exercise 7]*

> She hadn't been wearing good shoes.
> *Penny [Exercise 8]*

> He had been a good employee.
> *Fred [Exercise 1]*

> She had fallen in love with someone else.
> *Pam [Exercise 4]*

> They had found a nice house in a different city.
> *Mr. and Mrs. Williams [Exercise 5]*

2. Jigsaw Story ★★★

a. Divide the class into groups of six. Give each member of the group one of these cards:

• John had been feeling very nervous.
• Alice had been looking for a dress.
• John's mother had been writing invitations.
• Alice's father had been trying on new tuxedos.
• John's father had been talking to bakers about special cakes.
• Alice's mother had been looking at different churches.

b. Have students share their information to create a story. Have them answer these two questions: *What had they been preparing for? What happened?*

c. Have each group tell its story and explain its logic to the class.

3. For a Long Time ★★

a. Write the following on the board:

> Yes. _____ had been _____ing for a long time.

b. Ask students the questions below and have them answer according to the model on the board. For example:

> Teacher: Was it raining when you got up this morning?
> Student: Yes. It had been raining for a long time.

Questions:

Was it raining when you got up this morning?
Were the musicians playing when you arrived at the concert?
Had Bob started working at the bank when you met him?
Was Professor Lopez already teaching when you came to class?
Had Nancy started driving trucks for a living when you met her?
Had Peter started to study astronomy when he went to college?
Had Mr. and Mrs. Miller already started to paint their house when you saw them last week?
Did Maria speak English when she moved to Canada?
Did you play baseball before you went to high school?
Were your friends eating when you got to the restaurant last night?
Were people dancing when you got to the party?

4. Chain Story ★★

a. Begin by saying, "It's really a shame Roger didn't get a raise. He had been working very hard."

b. Student 1 repeats what you said and adds another item. For example: "It's really a shame Roger didn't get the raise. He had been working very hard. He had been staying late at the office."

(continued)

c. Continue around the room in this fashion, with each student repeating what the previous one said and adding another sentence.

d. You can do the activity again, beginning and ending with different students.

   If the class is large, you may want to divide students into groups to give students more practice. Here are some additional story lines:

   Herbert failed his English exam and couldn't graduate.
   Mary lost her voice and couldn't perform in the Broadway show.
   There was a bad fire at the Smiths' new house.

5. Good News/Bad News ★★★

a. Write the following conversation model on the board:

   A. Hi, _____. What's new?
   B. _____.
   A. That's great! ____ had been _____ing.
      or
      That's a shame! ____ had been _____ing.

b. Write the following situations on cards:

   | You finally passed your driver's test. |

   | Your wife/husband just lost his/her job. |

   | Your wife/husband just got promoted. |

   | You just broke up with your boyfriend/girlfriend. |

   | You just got engaged. |

   | You did very badly on your (English) exam. |

   | You did very well on your (English) exam. |

   | You hurt your back and couldn't be in the school play last weekend. |

   | You had to cancel your trip to (Mexico) because you sprained your ankle. |

c. Have pairs of students pick a card and create conversations based on the model on the board. Encourage them to then expand the conversation any way they wish. For example:

   A. Hi, Joe. What's new?
   B. I finally passed by driver's test.
   A. That's great! You had been preparing for it for a long time.
   B. You're right.
   A. How are you going to celebrate?
   B. I'm going to drive to the beach this weekend with my friends.

   A. Hi, Barbara. What's new?
   B. My husband just lost his job at Green's Supermarket.
   A. That's a shame! He had been working there for a long time.
   B. I know.
   A. What's he going to do?
   B. He's going to look for a job at another supermarket.
   A. I hope he finds one.

6. When Your Parents Were Young ★★★

a. Write the following on the board:

   A. Did _____ when your parents were young?
   B. Yes. _____ had been _____ing for a long time.
      or
      No. _____ hadn't started _____ yet.

b. Use cues such as the following to create conversations about how things have changed since your students' parents were young. Write these cues on the board or on a handout for students:

Did people . . .
    wear jeans?
    watch TV?
    drive cars?
    travel by airplane?
    listen to rock music?
    eat frozen food?
    eat a lot of junk food?
    use computers?
    use fax machines?
    talk on cell phones?
    use the Internet?
    send e-mail?

Did women . . .
    work?
    wear pants?
    wear suits?

Did men . . .
    stay home and take care of their children?
    wear their hair long?
    wear earrings?

c. Have students think of other questions to
    ask and continue the activity.

READING *Their Plans "Fell Through"*

FOCUS

- Past Perfect
- Past Perfect Continuous

NEW VOCABULARY

ceremony
fall through
"get cold feet"
get ready (for)

READING THE STORY

Optional: *Preview the story by having students talk about the story title and/or illustrations. You may choose to introduce new vocabulary beforehand, or have students encounter the new vocabulary within the context of the reading.*

1. Have students read silently, or follow along silently as the story is read aloud by you, by one or more students, or on the audio program.

2. Ask students if they have any questions. Check understanding of vocabulary.

    ### Language Note

    The expression *get cold feet* is most often used when someone fails to follow through with an important plan, such as a wedding, asking someone out on a date, or applying for an important job.

3. Check students' comprehension, using some or all of the following questions:

    What had Patty planned to do last weekend?

What had she done before the party?
Why did she have to cancel the party?

What had Michael planned to do last weekend?
How had he been preparing to ask for a raise?
Did he get the raise? Why not?

What had John and Julia planned to do last month?
What had they done before the wedding?
Did they get married? Why not?

READING EXTENSION

Role Play

1. Divide the class into pairs.

2. Have students role-play a conversation between a friend and one of the characters in the three stories. For example:

    A. Patty, how are you?
    B. I'm sick. And I'm so disappointed! I had to cancel my party!
    A. That's a shame. You had been preparing for the party for so long.
    B. I know. I had invited everyone, I had cleaned the house, and I had cooked my favorite food. But then I got sick!
    A. Well, maybe you can have another party soon.

3. Have students present their role plays to the class.

 ## IN YOUR OWN WORDS

1. Make sure students understand the instructions. Check understanding of the word *beforehand*.

2. Have students do the activity as written homework, using a dictionary for any new words they wish to use.

3. Have students present and discuss what they have written, in pairs or as a class.

ON YOUR OWN
Accomplishments

FOCUS

* Past Perfect Continuous Tense

ON YOUR OWN ACTIVITY

1. Set the scene: "These are situations about people who worked very hard to get something." Check understanding of the title, *Accomplishments*.

2. Have students read each situation silently, or follow along silently as the situation is read aloud by you, by one or more students, or on the audio program.

3. Ask students if they have any questions. Check understanding of new vocabulary:

   Situation 1: *health food, deserve*
   Situation 2: *pass a test, driving school, rules of the road*
   Situation 3: *computer programming, extra, earn*

4. Check students' comprehension with the following questions:

   Situation 1:
   What did Stella Karp win last week?
   What had she been doing every morning?
   What had she been doing several months?
   What had she been doing every day after work?
   Why did she deserve to win?

   Situation 2:
   What did Stuart pass the other day?
   What had he been doing for several months?
   What had he been doing the past several weeks?

   What had he been studying since he was a little boy?
   Why did he deserve to pass his driver's test?

   Situation 3:
   What did Sally Compton get last week?
   What had she been doing for several months?
   What had she been studying in the evening?
   What had she been doing on the weekends?
   Why did she deserve to get a promotion?

5. In pairs, small groups, or as a class, have students tell about their own accomplishments.

WORKBOOK

Page 97

JOURNAL

Have students write their journal entries at home or in class. Encourage students to use a dictionary to look up words they would like to use. Students can share their written work with other students if appropriate. Have students discuss what they have written as a class, in pairs, or in small groups.

PRONUNCIATION Reduced
had

 GRAMMAR FOCUS

> **Reduced *had*:** In spoken English, the pronunciation of *had* in the past perfect and past perfect continuous tenses is often reduced to [həd].

Focus on Listening

Practice the sentences in the left column. Say each sentence or play the audio one or more times. Have students listen carefully and repeat.

Focus on Pronunciation

Practice the sentences in the right column. Have students say each sentence and then listen carefully as you say it or play the audio.

If you wish, have students continue practicing the sentences to improve their pronunciation.

WORKBOOK

Check-Up Test: Pages 98–99

Answers

1. I had seen
2. He had forgotten
3. She hadn't had
4. had, taken off
5. They had gone
6. riding, she had, ridden
7. They had been planning
8. He had been working
9. We hadn't played
10. She had been living

MULTILEVEL VARIATIONS

★ Tell *below-level* students the verb for each exercise, so they can focus only on putting it in the correct form.

★★★ Challenge *above-level* students to cover the grammar boxes as they complete the grammar exercises.

1 **CONVERSATION** *Making, Confirming, Rescheduling, & Canceling Appointments*

1. Review saying dates by going over days of the week, months of the year, and the pronunciation of ordinal numbers from 1st to 31st.

2. Have students look at the photos. Ask: "What are these people looking at?" (Calendars.) "What are they doing?" (They're scheduling an appointment.) Have students look at the appointment cards. Ask questions to get students oriented to the cards—for example: "When is Ana Ramirez's appointment? What doctor's office is it?" Introduce the new words: *advance notice, cancel, confirm, health center, in advance, kindly, medical clinic, notice* (n), *notification, opening* (n), *reschedule,* and *scheduled* (adj).

3. Model the *Making an Appointment* conversation with a student volunteer. Have the student select one of the completed appointment cards for the conversation. For example (using appointment card 2):

   A. Hello. This is Abdul Asmal. I'd like to make an appointment.
   B. All right. Can you come in on Monday, February 4 at 11:30?
   A. Monday, February 4 at 11:30? Yes. That would be fine. Thank you.

4. In pairs, have students practice the conversation using the information from different cards as you circulate around the classroom. As students gain confidence, have them make up their own appointment dates as they practice the conversation.

5. Repeat steps 3 and 4 with the other model conversations: *Confirming an Appointment, Rescheduling an Appointment,* and *Canceling an Appointment.*

6. Call on pairs of students to present their own conversations with original dates to the class. As the class listens, have students complete the final *empty* appointment card with the date information.

2 **COMMUNITY CONNECTIONS** *Medical Care*

Call on a student volunteer to read the question aloud. Have students share their ideas with the class. Write students' ideas on the board.

LIFE SKILLS ENRICHMENT

Telephone Skills: Scheduling Medical Appointments

Life Skills Worksheet 29

Make copies of Life Skills Worksheet 29 and give one to each student. Have students complete the worksheet as homework. In the next class, have students compare their answers in pairs.

EXPANSION ACTIVITIES

1. Scrambled Dialogs: Scheduling a Medical Appointment ★

Activity Master 52

Divide the class into pairs. Make multiple copies of Activity Master 52, cut them into cards, and give one set of cards to each pair of students. Have the partners sort and reorder the three conversations. Have three different pairs read a conversation aloud while the others listen to check for accuracy.

2. Disappearing Dialog ★★

Write one of the model conversations from student text page 110a on the board and ask for two student volunteers to read the conversation. Erase a few of the words from the dialog and have two different students read the conversation. Erase more words and call on two more students to read the conversation. Continue erasing words and calling on pairs of students until everyone has had a turn and the dialog has *disappeared*.

3. Appointment Confirmation Match Game ★★

Activity Master 53

a. Make two copies of Activity Master 53 and cut them into cards. (If you have fewer than twelve students, make one copy.) Distribute the appointment cards randomly, one to each student.

b. Write on the board:

> A. I'd like to confirm my appointment.
> B. When are you scheduled to come in?
> A. On (day)   (date) at (time) .

Note: Either student can begin the conversation since all students are carrying appointment cards.

c. Have students circulate around the room *confirming* their appointments until they find their match. Make sure students don't show their cards to their classmates since this is a listening and speaking exercise.

d. When students have found their match, have them *compare* their cards and then come show you.

4. Role Play ★★★

Activity Master 54

a. Make multiple copies of Activity Master 54. Cut the role-play cards into A cards and B cards and clip each role play (1 or 2) together.

b. Divide the class into pairs. Give each partner one set of role-play cards—A or B. Tell students they have five minutes to act out the role play.

c. As students are acting out their role plays, circulate to help as necessary.

d. After five minutes, call on a few pairs to perform their role plays for the class.

MULTILEVEL VARIATION ★★/★★★

If *at-level* or *above-level* students finish their role plays quickly, give them the other set of role-play cards.

5. Dictate and Discuss ★★★

Divide the class into pairs. Dictate sentences such as the following and have students discuss whether they agree or disagree with the statements.

> In the U.S., you have to make an appointment if you want to see a doctor.
> In the U.S., you have to wait a long time before you can see a doctor.
> You have to pay for a doctor's appointment if you don't come.
> You should always confirm your doctors' appointments.
> You should always arrive at least fifteen minutes before your doctor's appointment.

1. Introduce the names of internal organs with Life Skills Worksheet 30.

2. Point to the medical history form on student text page 110b. Ask: "What's this?" (A medical history form.) "Where do you get one of these?" (At a doctor's office.)

3. Read the medical history aloud to the class. Introduce the new words: *family history, medical history,* and *siblings.* Then introduce the following medical vocabulary as necessary. Students may find looking up the words in a bilingual dictionary helpful.

Illnesses and Diseases

AIDS (Acquired Immunodeficiency Syndrome)—a contagious disease that makes a person unable to fight off any other viruses or diseases.

asthma—a chronic inflammation of the airways that causes swelling and constriction of the airways. It results in difficulty breathing.

cancer—an abnormal growth of cells that, in some cases, spread (metastasize). Cancer is *malignant.*

chicken pox (also known as *varicella-zoster*)—a common contagious childhood disease in which the patient gets small blisters and a mild fever.

depression—a feeling of uncontrollable sadness.

diabetes—a chronic disease in which the body cannot control the levels of blood sugar.

heart disease—any disease that hurts the heart.

hepatitis—a virus that causes inflammation of the liver.

high blood pressure—high pressure in the arteries measured above 140/90 (140 "over" 90).

influenza (also known as *the flu*)—a contagious virus that infects the respiratory system.

kidney disease—damage to the kidneys caused by different diseases, including high blood pressure.

liver disease—damage to the liver caused by different viruses, including hepatitis.

mumps—a childhood virus that infects the salivary glands. The glands swell and are very tender.

pneumonia—an infection of the lungs caused by a virus, bacteria, or fungus.

tuberculosis—a contagious disease that affects the lungs and other organs in the body.

Other Health Problems
back problems
bee sting
broken leg
loss of appetite
severe headaches

Parts of the Body
gall bladder
kidney
liver
heart

Medical Treatments
drug
immunization
insulin
medication
multivitamins
non-prescription drug
preventive care
tetanus (shot)
tuberculosis test
vaccination

4. Read the Preventive Care Guidelines aloud to the class. Introduce the new vocabulary: *aspect, check for, childhood disease, colon cancer, community fair, following* (adj), *guidelines, health plan, medical problem, prescription drug, risk,* and *street festival.* Then introduce the following medical vocabulary as necessary. Students may find

looking up the words in a bilingual dictionary helpful.

Preventive Care
colonoscopy
dental examination
eye examination
flu shot
hearing test
pneumonia vaccination
screening test
skin examination
tetanus shot

5. Have students work individually to complete the comprehension exercise and then compare answers in pairs, small groups, or as a class.

MULTILEVEL VARIATION ★

Have *below-level* students work on the reading and questions in pairs to provide each other with more support.

Answers

1. Strawberries, cats, dogs, dust, and bee stings.
2. Insulin, aspirin, multivitamins, and calcium.
3. Yes. 2003 —surgery for a broken leg and 2007—gall bladder surgery.
4. Chicken pox, measles, and mumps.
5. High blood pressure, diabetes, and severe headaches.
6. Heart disease, high blood pressure, and diabetes.
7. In 2008.

8. In 2008.
9. In 2018
10. Every one to two years.
11. Every five years.
12. At age 50 and older.
13. One to two times a year.
14. Every ten years.
15. Every ten years.
16. If the doctor advises it.

COMMUNITY CONNECTIONS

Have students read the text silently and then share their thoughts with the class. Write students' ideas on the board.

LIFE SKILLS ENRICHMENT

Medical History

Life Skills Worksheet 31

Make copies of Life Skills Worksheet 31 and give one to each student. Have students complete the worksheet as homework. In the next class, have students ask any questions they may have about the form. (*Note*: This information should be confidential. Therefore, students should not show this to the teacher or to others in the class.)

1. Guess the Word! ★

a. Divide the class into two teams. Choose a vocabulary word or phrase from the readings, and on the board, write a blank for each letter in the word or phrase. For example: (*hepatitis*)

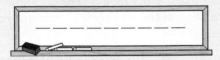

b. Give students a clue about the word or phrase. For example: "a liver disease."

c. The team that guesses the word gets a point. The team with the most points wins the guessing game.

2. Mix and Match Words ★★

Activity Master 55

The medical history form and the preventive health guidelines on student text pages 110b and 110c have many nouns that go together.

a. Divide the class into groups of three. Make a copy of Activity Master 55 for each group. Cut the Activity Masters into cards and place them in two piles face down.

Note: The large cards are for first words and the small cards are for second words.

b. Distribute the two sets of cards to each group. Have students take turns picking up one card from each pile and reading the word combination to the group. For example:

heart	shot

The group decides if the word combination is in the readings on student text pages 110b and 110c. If it is, they write it down on a piece of paper.

c. After all the cards have been chosen, have the group lay out all the cards and put together all the word combinations from the reading.

MULTILEVEL VARIATIONS

★ *Below-level* students can read through the two sets of cards all at once and then match them face up.

★★★ *Above-level* students can also generate other word combinations that make sense— for example: *blood disease, clinic history.*

3. True or False Medical History ★★

Make statements about Lena Kosta's medical history on student text page 110b and have students decide whether the statements are true or false. If a statement is false, have students correct it. For example:

> Lena has diabetes. [True.]
> Lena has had back problems. [False. Lena hasn't had back problems.]
> Someone in Lena's family has had high blood pressure. [True.]
> Lena got a measles vaccination in 2008. [False. She's never had one.]

Variation: Do the activity as a game with competing teams.

4. True or False Preventive Care Guidelines ★★

Make statements about the Preventive Care Guidelines on student text page 110c and have students decide whether the statements are true or false. If a statement is false, have students correct it. For example:

> Everybody should see a dentist once a year. [True.]
> If you're 60 years old, you should have a cholesterol blood test every two years. [False. You should have one every five years.]
> If you're 21 years old, you should see a dentist twice a year. [True.]
> Young adults need to get flu shots. [False. Only adults over the age of 50 need to get flu shots.]
> The risk of colon cancer increases with age. [True.] (Adults over the age of 50 should have a colonoscopy every ten years.)

Variation: Do the activity as a game with competing teams.

5. How Much Do You Remember? ★★★

a. Write the following topics on the board:

> Medications
> Allergies
> Operations
> Health Problems
> Family History
> Immunizations

b. Divide the class into pairs. Have students close their books and retell to each other what they remember about Lena Kosta's health history on student text page 110b. Then have them open their books and check to see how much they remembered.

6. Category Dictation ★★★

a. Introduce the phrase: *contagious disease* (a disease you can get from another person).

b. Have students make two columns on a piece of paper and write the following at the top of each column:

> Contagious Diseases
> Non-Contagious Diseases

c. Dictate diseases and health problems from student text page 110b and have students write them in the appropriate column. For example:

Contagious Diseases	Non-Contagious Diseases
measles	diabetes
tuberculosis	cancer
AIDS	high blood pressure
hepatitis B	asthma

d. As a class, in pairs, or in small groups, have students compare their answers.

1. Have students read the subheading *Guide to Services* and ask: "What kind of information will this article tell you?" Write students' ideas on the board.

2. Introduce the new vocabulary: *24-hour, afford, danger, drop-in-clinic, earn, emergency care, emergency room, eye care, family clinic, full range, full-service, guide, health care, health problem, interpreter, medical care, medical services, multilingual, outstanding, public health department, routine* (adj), *sliding scale, staff, translation,* and *up-to-date.* Then introduce the following medical vocabulary as necessary. Students may find looking up the words in a bilingual dictionary helpful.

   Contagious Diseases
   diphtheria—a disease that typically infects the upper respiratory tract including the throat.
   pertussis (also known as *whooping cough*)—an illness characterized by severe coughing and a noisy, "whooping" sound.
   polio—a virus that inflames the central nervous system and can result in paralysis.
   rubella (also known as *German measles*)—a virus that causes runny nose, cough, red eyes, and a skin rash. It is very dangerous for pregnant women.

3. Have students work individually to complete the comprehension exercise and then compare answers in pairs, small groups, or as a class.

MULTILEVEL VARIATION ★

Have *below-level* students work on the reading and questions in pairs to provide each other with more support.

Answers

1. C
2. B
3. D
4. A
5. C
6. D

LIFE SKILLS ENRICHMENT

Vaccination Chart

Life Skills Worksheet 32

Make copies of Life Skills Worksheet 32 and give one to each student. For homework, have students re-read the immunization information on student text page 110d and then complete the worksheet. In the next class, have students compare their answers in pairs.

First-Aid Procedures

Life Skills Worksheet 33

Make copies of Life Skills Worksheet 33 and give one to each student. Have students complete the worksheet as homework. In the next class, have students compare their answers in pairs.

1. Scrambled Words ★

a. Choose words or phrases from student text page 110d and write them on the board or on a card with the letters scrambled out of order. For example:

u f l l   g r a n e

b. Have students take turns guessing what the word or phrase is. [full range]

Variation 1: Do the activity in pairs or small groups, with students taking turns scrambling words for others to guess.

Variation 2: Do the activity as a class game with competing teams.

2. True or False? ★★

Make statements about the Guide to Services on student text page 110d and have students decide whether the statements are true or false. If a statement is false, have students correct it. For example:

The High School Health Center provides free services for students. [True.]
Vaccinations protect children from diseases such as heart disease and AIDS. [False. They protect children from diseases such as polio and measles.]
Drop-in means no appointment is necessary. [True.]
A sliding-scale fee is the same no matter how much money a person makes. [False. It changes according to how much a person makes.]

Variation: Do the activity as a game with competing teams.

3. Category Dictation ★★

a. Have students make two columns on a piece of paper and write the following at the top of each column:

Emergency Care
Routine Care

b. Dictate health care needs from student text page 110d and have students write them in the appropriate column. For example:

Emergency Care	Routine Care
a heart attack	vaccinations
an allergy to a bee sting	an earache
a dislocated shoulder	a bad cough
a severe burn	a physical examination
a broken leg	the flu

c. As a class, in pairs, or in small groups, have students compare their answers.

4. Health Center Survey ★★★

Activity Master 56

a. Make multiple copies of Activity Master 56 and give one to each student.

b. Brainstorm the names of health centers in your community. Assign one health center to each student. (There will probably be fewer health centers than students. In that case, assign one health center to more than one student.)

c. For homework, have students call or visit the website of the health center and find out the information in order to complete the chart.

d. In the next class, have students compare their notes. Which health centers offer the best services and fees?

MULTILEVEL VARIATION ★

Pair *below-level* students to investigate a health center together.

HEALTHY EATING AND A BALANCED DIET

1. Have students read the passage title *Healthy Eating and a Balanced Diet* and ask: "What do you think this article will tell you?" Write their ideas on the board.

2. Introduce the new vocabulary: *average, bean group, blood cholesterol, bones, choose, colored, consist, corn, cream, cream cheese, dairy food, dairy group, dairy products, dark green vegetables, dry beans, fat-free, fiber, food pyramid, foods, fruit group, fruit juice, grain group, grains, group, milk group, milk product, narrow, part, represent, source, staircase, starchy vegetables,* and *stripes.*

DID YOU UNDERSTAND?

Have students work individually to complete the comprehension exercise and then compare their answers in pairs, small groups, or as a class.

MULTILEVEL VARIATION ★

Have *below-level* students work on the reading and questions in pairs to provide each other with more support.

Answers
1. The five different food groups (grains, vegetables, fruit, dairy, beans and meat) plus oils.
2. Oils.
3. Because we should eat more food from this group than others.
4. Because adults should have three cups of dairy products each day.
5. Because the average adult needs less protein than other foods.
6. Because those are the healthier foods and the foods we should choose more often.

APPLYING YOUR KNOWLEDGE

Have students discuss the questions in pairs, small groups, or as a class.

LIFE SKILLS ENRICHMENT

Healthy Eating
Life Skills Worksheet 34

Make copies of Life Skills Worksheet 34 and give one to each student. Have students complete the worksheet as homework. In the next class, have students compare their answers in pairs.

A Healthy Recipe
Life Skills Worksheet 35

Make copies of Life Skills Worksheet 35 and give one to each student. Have students complete the worksheet as homework. In the next class, have students compare their answers in pairs.

1. Association Game ★

a. Write the following food groups on the board:

> vegetables
> oils
> grains
> fruit
> milk and dairy
> meat and beans

b. Divide the class into several teams. Have the students in each team work together to see how many foods they can associate with each group. For example:

> vegetables: [onions/corn/potatoes/spinach]
> oils: [cream/corn oil/butter]

c. Set a time limit for the game. When the time limit is up, call on the teams to read their list of associations to the class. The team with the most correct items wins.

Note: Some foods belong to more than one category. For example, corn belongs to the grain group as well as the vegetable group.

2. True or False? ★★

Make statements about the reading on student text page 110e and have students decide whether the statements are true or false. If a statement is false, have students correct it. For example:

> Fiber keeps blood cholesterol low. [True.]
> Fruit juice usually has a lot of fiber in it. [False. Fruit juice doesn't have fiber.]
> You should eat more dark green vegetables than starchy vegetables. [True.]
> Cream cheese is a good source of calcium. [False. Cream cheese has little or no calcium.]

Variation: Do the activity as a game with competing teams.

3. Movable Categories ★★

Activity Master 57

a. Make a copy of Activity Master 57, cut it into cards, and give each student a card.

b. Call out a category and have all the students whose words are appropriate for that category move to the right side of the room. All the other students move to the left side.

> vegetable group
> fruit group
> oils
> meat and dry beans group
> grain group
> foods with calcium
> foods high in fiber
> foods high in protein
> foods high in cholesterol
> whole grains
> starchy vegetables
> dark green vegetables
> orange vegetables

c. Those who are in the *right group* call out their words for the class to verify.

4. Healthy Eating Quiz Game ★★★

Activity Master 58

a. Make a copy of Activity Master 58, cut it into cards, and put the cards in a pile face down on a table or desk in the front of the room.

b. Divide the class into two teams. Have students from each team take turns coming up to the front of the class, picking up a card, and reading it to the team. The team must answer the question in one minute. For each correct answer the team gets one point. The team with the most points wins.

MULTILEVEL VARIATIONS

★ *Below-level* students can refer to the reading on student text page 110e to answer the questions.

★★/★★★ Challenge *at-level* and *above-level* students to close their textbooks and try to recall the information from memory.

5. Healthy Eating Poster Contest ★★★

a. Bring poster board, markers, old magazines, and glue sticks to class.

b. Divide the class into pairs. Have each pair make a poster with the most important information about healthy eating from the textbook passage on student text page 110e.

c. Have a poster contest. Award each poster with a prize. For example:

the most colorful poster
the most informative poster
the most artistic poster

d. Have students hang their posters up on classroom walls and school hallways so other students may learn about healthy eating.

CHECK-UP TEST Ⓐ Ⓑ Ⓒ Ⓓ

Have students do the check-up test and then review the answers as a class.

Answers

1. B	**6.** C
2. A	**7.** A
3. C	**8.** C
4. B	**9.** B
5. D	**10.** D

SKILLS CHECK

Words:

Explain to students that this is a list of words they have learned in the unit. Have students take turns reading each item aloud to the class. Have students put a check next to the item if they feel they have learned it. Encourage students to get a small notebook where they can write down words that are difficult for them.

I can:

Explain to students that this is a list of skills they have learned in the unit. Read each item aloud to the class. Ask individual students or pairs of students to demonstrate the skill. For example:

Teacher: I can share news.
Student A: Have you heard about the election?
Student B: No. What happened?

Teacher: I can confirm medical appointments.
Student: Hello. This is Ming Lee. I'm calling to confirm my appointment on July 6th at 9:45.

Have students put a check next to the item if they feel they have learned it. Use this information to determine which lessons you may want to review or reinforce for the entire class or for particular students.

EXPANSION ACTIVITIES

1. Listen for the Verbs ★

   a. Have students make three columns on a piece of paper and write the following at the top of each column:

      Simple Past
      Past Perfect
      Past Perfect Continuous

   b. Dictate the following sentences and have students write the verbs in the appropriate column.

      John won the marathon.
      He deserved it.
      He had been training for it every day after work.
      He hadn't gone out with friends after work in a long time.
      He had been exercising every weekend.
      He had been eating healthy food every day for months.
      He hadn't eaten junk food for months.
      He had been preparing for the marathon for a long time.
      He was happy to win it.

   c. As a class, in pairs, or in small groups, have students check their work.

2. Miming Game ★★

   Activity Master 59

   a. Make a copy of Activity Master 59, cut it into cards, and place the cards face down in a pile on a desk or table in the front of the room.

   b. Have students take turns coming to the front of the room, picking a card, and pantomiming the action on the card. The class tries to guess the action.

Variation: Do the activity as a game with teams. Make sure you have a watch or clock to time the activity. A member of each team comes to the front and pantomimes. Time how long it takes for the team to guess the correct answer. The winning team is the one that has used the fewest seconds or minutes for the game.

3. Scrambled Sentences ★★

Activity Master 60

Divide the class into pairs. Make enough copies of Activity Master 60 for half the class. Cut them into cards and distribute one set of cards to each pair of students. Have students take turns picking up a scrambled sentence prompt and then saying the sentence in the correct order.

Variation: Students can write their sentences and then compare their answers with other pairs.

4. Finish the Sentence! ★★

Begin sentences and have students add appropriate endings to the sentences using the past perfect. For example:

Teacher: He was heartbroken because . . .
Student: his girlfriend had just left him.

Teacher: She was furious because . . .
Student: her son had broken her laptop.

Other possible sentence beginnings are:

They felt foolish because . . .
He caught a cold because . . .
She lost her job because . . .
He had a tetanus vaccination because . . .
They were disappointed because . . .
He was proud because . . .

5. Board Game ★★

Activity Master 61

For this activity, you will need a die, markers, and a piece of paper. (If students use a coin as a die, the class should decide which side of the coin will indicate a move of one space and which will indicate a move of two spaces.)

a. Make multiple copies of Activity Master 61. Divide the class into small groups and give each group a copy of Activity Master 61 along with a die, markers, and a piece of paper.

b. Have students place their markers on *Start.* The group should decide who goes first. That student begins the game by rolling the die or flipping the coin and moving his or her marker. If the student responds to the question or task correctly, he or she may take one more turn. If the student doesn't respond correctly, the next student takes a turn. No one may take more than two turns at a time.

Option 1: The first person to reach *Finish* is the winner.

Option 2: The game continues until each student reaches *Finish.* This way everybody is a winner.

6. Dialog Builder! ★★★

a. Divide the class into pairs. Write a line on the board from a conversation such as the following:

That's terrible!

Other possible lines are:

I felt nostalgic because _____.
Is it true?
How did she do that?
I hope you feel better soon.
Have you heard about _____?
It's really a shame.
Yes. That would be fine.

b. Have each pair create a conversation incorporating that line. Students can begin and end their conversations any way they wish, but they must include that line in their dialogs.

c. Call on students to present their conversations to the class.

7. What's Wrong? ★★★

a. Write several sentences such as the following on the board or on a handout that you give to

(continued)

students. Some of the sentences should be correct and others incorrect. For example:

> He had been working there since a long time.
> They had never ate there before.
> She had already gone there.
> He hadn't spoken to me in a long time.
> By the time we arrived, the lecture already ended.
> She had flew on an airplane the week before.
> By the time I already got there, the store had closed.
> She enjoyed to see a movie last week.
> We had never gone fishing in a long time.
> He hadn't ridden on a bicycle since he had been a child.
> She felt nostalgic when she visited her old neighborhood.

b. Divide the class into pairs. The object of the activity is for students to identify which sentences are incorrect and then correct them. Have students compare their answers in small groups.

Variation: Do the activity as a game with competing teams. For each team's turn, write one sentence on the board and have the team decide whether the sentence is correct or not. If it isn't correct, the team must correct it. Every time a team is right, that team receives one point. The team with the greatest number of points wins.

MULTILEVEL VARIATION ★

For *below-level* students, underline the errors and have the below-level pairs focus only on correcting them.

FEATURE ARTICLE
The Jamaican Bobsled Team

PREVIEWING THE ARTICLE

1. Have students talk about the title of the article and the accompanying photographs.

2. You may choose to introduce the following new vocabulary beforehand, or have students encounter it within the context of the article:

> bobsled
> compete
> competition
> event
> fact
> fiction
> first time
> four-person
> give up
> group
> impossible (n)
> include
> Jamaican
> last time
> movie soundtrack
> Olympics
> place (v)
> reggae music
> represent
> skating (n)
> skiing (n)
> soundtrack
> strong
> Summer Olympics
> swimming (n)
> team
> track
> training center
> two-person
> weight train
> Winter Olympic Games
> Winter Olympics

> *Places Around the World*
> Calgary, Canada
> Caribbean
> Jamaica
> Lake Placid, New York
> Norway

READING THE ARTICLE

1. Have students read silently, or follow along silently as the article is read aloud by you, by one or more students, or on the audio program.

2. Ask students if they have any questions and check understanding of new vocabulary. Show the class a world map and have students identify the locations of all the place names.

3. Have students read the captions under the photos silently, or follow along silently as the captions are read aloud by you or by one or more students.

4. Ask students if they have any questions. Check understanding of new vocabulary.

5. Check students' comprehension of the article and captions by having students answer the following questions:

   Feature Article

   Why was the Jamaican Bobsled Team unusual?
   How had they trained for their first Olympic event in Calgary, Canada?
   How did they do in the 1988 Olympics?
   How did they train for the 1994 Olympic Winter Games?
   How had they become famous?
   How did they do in the 1994 Olympics?

   1st Caption

   Is the movie about the Jamaican Bobsled team true?
   What kind of music was in the movie?

   2nd Caption

   When were the first modern Olympics?
   Where were the first modern Olympics?
   What are some sports in the Summer Olympics?

What are some sports in the Winter Olympics?

EXPANSION ACTIVITIES

1. Making Inferences ★★★

a. In small groups, have students discuss the following questions:

Why do you think the Jamaican athletes decided to try bobsledding?
Why do you think their story is so popular?

b. Have the groups report back to the class.

2. Who's the Best? ★★★

a. Divide the class into small groups. Have students discuss the following questions:

What are your favorite Olympic sports?
Which countries do best in those sports?
Why are those countries so good at those sports?
What kinds of advantages do they have?

b. Have students share their ideas with the class. Write any new sports vocabulary on the board.

3. Olympic Sports Game ★★★

a. Divide the class into several teams.

b. Have the students in each team work together to make a list of all the sports that are played in the Summer Olympics.

c. Have the teams share their lists with the class. Write any new sports vocabulary on the board. The team with the longest list wins.

d. Play the game again with sports that are played in the Winter Olympics.

 AROUND THE WORLD
Children and Sports Training

1. Have students read silently or follow along silently as the text is read aloud by you, by one or more students, or on the audio program.

2. Check understanding of the expressions *distance running, sports training*.

3. Have students first work in pairs or small groups to respond to the questions. Then have students tell the class what they talked about. Write any new vocabulary on the board.

EXPANSION ACTIVITY

Dictate and Discuss ★★★

1. Divide the class into pairs or small groups.

2. Dictate sentences such as the following and then have students discuss them:

If you want to be the best, you must begin training at a very young age.
Parents often push their children too hard to win in sports.
Young children should not compete in sports.
Team sports teach children many good things.

3. Call on students to share their opinions with the rest of the class.

 INTERVIEW

1. Have students read silently, or follow along silently as the interview is read aloud by you, by one or more students, or on the audio program.

2. Ask students if they have any questions. Check understanding of the words *dream, figure-skating, level, medal, national, over and over, regional, routine*.

3. Check students' comprehension by having them answer the following questions:

How many hours a day had Olga been practicing for the Regional Competition?
How old was Olga when she began skating?
What had she done by the time she was seven?
How old was she when she found a professional coach?
What did Olga win recently?
What's the next step for her?
If she wins in the National Competition, what's the next level?

EXPANSION ACTIVITY

Student Interviews ★★★

1. Identify students in the class who are especially good at a particular sport. Have the other students form groups around these people. Then have students interview these *athletes*. Brainstorm with the class possible questions to ask. For example:

   > What's your favorite sport?
   > How long have you been doing that sport?
   > When did you begin?
   > Do you remember your first coach or teacher?
   > Have you ever thought about competing? Why or why not?
   > What's the most difficult part of your sport?
   > How often do you practice?

2. Have the groups move from speaker to speaker so they may interview all the athletes in the class.

FACT FILE
Countries in the Olympics

1. Ask students: "How many countries do you think participate in the Olympics?" Write students' estimates on the board.

2. Read the table aloud as the class follows along. Ask students: "Whose number was the closest?"

3. For a comprehension activity, state the number of countries participating in the Olympics and have students tell you what year you are describing. For example:

   > Teacher: 50 countries participated in the Olympics.
   > Student: That was in 1924.

4. As a class, in pairs, or in small groups, have students discuss the questions posed in the fact file.

LISTENING *Olympic Game Highlights*

1. Set the scene: "This is a news report about the highlights of the most recent Olympics."

   ### Culture Notes

   When covering large and complex sporting events, such as the Olympics, television reporters often report just the *highlights*, the most interesting moments.

   Three medals are awarded in an Olympic event. A *gold medal* is awarded to the first-place winner, a *silver medal* to the second-place winner, and a *bronze medal* to the third-place winner.

   ### Language Note

   The simple present tense is often used to describe an ongoing action. Sports commentators use it to narrate the actions in the sports event they are describing.

2. There is a lot of new vocabulary in the listening. Encourage students to listen for key words that will help them identify which sport is being described. For example:

   > basketball: game, team, basket
   > swimming: water
   > gymnastics: fell, graceful
   > running: run, move
   > skating: ice, move, gracefully, music

NEW VOCABULARY

Basketball basket shoot	*Running* a time of *two hours* finish line lead (n) race
Swimming even (adj) lane move through speed	*Skating* *five* point *eight* judge marks score
Gymnastics balance beam floor routine	

LISTENING SCRIPT

Listen to the Olympic Game highlights. Match the highlight and the sport.

And now, sports fans, let's finish today's program with highlights of the Olympic Games. Here are five of my favorite moments in the most recent summer and winter games:

There are three seconds left in the game. Number 38 gets ready to shoot again. His team needs this point to win the game. He shoots, and it's in the basket! [*Buzzer*] That's it! The game is over! And the United States wins 99 to 98. The U.S. gets the gold medal!

Kirshner is still in front. But wait! Look at Tanaka in the next lane! What speed! Look at him move through the water! Tanaka is even with Kirshner. Now Tanaka is ahead! And Tanaka wins the event! Japan wins the gold medal, Germany gets the silver, and Hungary gets the bronze.

Natasha knows she must do this floor routine perfectly to win the gold medal. She had problems today when she fell off the balance beam, and that's usually her best event. She's doing very well. What a strong and graceful athlete! And here's the most difficult part of her routine. Beautiful! But, oh . . . she falls! Natasha has fallen at the very end of her routine. What a shame! There will be no gold for Natasha this year.

What a race! Anderson is still in first place and Sanchez is right behind him in second place. Look at Sanchez run! He's moving ahead of Anderson. The lead has changed! Sanchez is now in front! He crosses the finish line! Sanchez wins with a time of two hours, ten minutes, and eleven seconds. So Mexico wins the gold, Canada gets the silver, and France gets the bronze.

And Tamara leaves the ice after a beautiful long program! I think that's one of the best programs I've ever seen at the Olympics. She moved so gracefully to the music. Let's see what the judges think. Look at these marks! Five-point-eight, five-point-nine, five-point-nine, five-point-eight, five-point-seven, five-point-nine, five-point-nine, six-point-oh, five-point-eight. Excellent scores! Tamara wins the gold medal! Look at all the flowers people are throwing on the ice! I'm sure this is the happiest day of Tamara's life!

Answers

1. b
2. e
3. d
4. c
5. a

EXPANSION ACTIVITIES

1. Listening Comprehension ★★★

Have students listen to the audio program again and answer the following questions:

Basketball
How many seconds were left in the game?
Who won?
By how many points did they win?

Swimming
Who was in the lead in the swimming competition?
What happened at the end of the competition?
Where is Tanaka from?

Gymnastics
How has Natasha's day been?
In what event did she fall?
Did Natasha win the gold medal?

Running
Who won the running competition?
Where is Sanchez from?
Where is Anderson from?

Ice-skating
Did Tamara skate alone?
How many judges were watching her?
Why were people throwing flowers on the ice?

2. Association Game ★★

a. Divide the class into pairs or small groups.

b. Call out a sport and tell students to write down all the words they associate with that sport. For example:

> running: lanes, sneakers, fast, finish line
> baseball: ball, uniforms, run, throw

c. Have a student from each pair or group come to the board and write their words.

Variation: Do the activity as a game in which you divide the class into teams. The team with the most number of associations is the winner.

FUN WITH IDIOMS

> Break a leg!
> Get off my back!
> Hold your tongue!
> Keep your chin up!
> Keep your eye on the ball!
> Put your best foot forward!

INTRODUCTION AND PRACTICE

For each idiom, do the following:

1. Have students look at the illustration.

2. Present the idiom. Say the expression and have the class repeat it chorally and individually. Check students' pronunciation of the words.

DO YOU KNOW THESE EXPRESSIONS?

Have students match the expressions with their meanings.

Answers

1. c
2. f
3. a
4. d
5. b
6. e

EXPANSION ACTIVITIES

1. Mystery Conversations ★★★

   a. Divide the class into pairs.

   b. Have each pair choose an idiom

   c. Write roles such as the following on word cards and give one to each pair of students:

a parent and a child
a teacher and a student
two teammates
two athletes competing against each other
a boss and an employee
a coach and an athlete
a fan and an athlete
a brother and a sister

   d. Have each pair create a short dialog that uses one of the idioms. The dialogs should be appropriate for the roles the students have on their cards.

   e. Have each pair present their dialog to the class. Then have the other students guess who the people are: Are they a parent and a child? Are they two competing athletes?

2. Idiom Challenge! ★★★

   a. Divide the class into pairs.

   b. Have each pair create a conversation in which they use as many of the idioms from text page 113 as they can.

   c. Have the pairs present their conversations to the class. Which pair used the most idioms?

 **WE'VE GOT MAIL!**

THE 1st LETTER TO *SIDE BY SIDE*

1. Have students read silently, or follow along silently as the letter is read aloud by you, by one or more students, or on the audio program.

2. Ask students if they have any questions. Check understanding of the words *gerund, infinitive, rule, verb*.

3. Check students' comprehension by having them decide whether these statements are true or false:

   The writer wants to know the rules for using gerunds and infinitive. *(True)*
   The writer uses incorrect examples of gerunds and infinitives. *(False)*

4. Ask students:

   Are you ever confused about gerunds and infinitives?
   Can you think of another example of a verb that takes a gerund?
   Can you think of another example of a verb that takes an infinitive?
   Can you think of another example of a verb that takes a gerund and an infinitive?

THE RESPONSE FROM *SIDE BY SIDE*

1. Have students read silently, or follow along silently as the letter is read aloud by you, by one or more students, or on the audio program.

2. Ask students if they have any questions. Check understanding of vocabulary.

3. Check students' comprehension by having them decide whether these statements are true or false:

   There are rules about how to use gerunds and infinitives. *(False)*
   The best way to learn how to use gerunds and infinitives is to practice using the verbs. *(True)*

4. Ask students: "How do you memorize these verbs and their forms?"

THE 2nd LETTER TO *SIDE BY SIDE*

1. Have students read silently, or follow along silently as the letter is read aloud by you, by one or more students, or on the audio program.

2. Ask students if they have any questions. Check understanding of the words *grammar, past perfect tense, present perfect, present perfect continuous*.

3. Check students' comprehension by having them decide whether these statements are true or false:

   The writer understands when to use this tense: "I have been." *(True)*
   The writer understands when to use this tense: "She has been playing." *(True)*
   The writer understands when to use this tense: "We had written." *(False)*

4. Ask students: "Have you ever had this question?"

THE RESPONSE FROM *SIDE BY SIDE*

1. Have students read silently, or follow along silently as the letter is read aloud by you, by one or more students, or on the audio program.

2. Ask students if they have any questions. Check understanding of the word *difference*.

3. Check students' comprehension by having them decide whether these statements are true or false:

   People use the present perfect to speak about an event in the past. *(True)*
   People use the present perfect to speak about an event before another event in the past. *(False)*

4. Ask students:

   Do you have a tense like the past perfect in your language?
   Can you explain how the present perfect is different from the past perfect?

EXPANSION ACTIVITY

What's Wrong? ★★★

1. Divide the class into pairs or small groups.

2. Write several sentences such as the following on the board or on a handout. Some of the sentences should be correct, and others incorrect. For example:

   > I began skating when I was three.
   > You should avoid to eat eggs.
   > By the time I was seven, I had been skiing for four years.
   > She can't stand to eat fish.
   > He practiced to do the routine for ten hours.
   > She decided become a figure skater.
   > We want to learn to speak English well.
   > He didn't stop running after he fell.
   > They had been study for it for a long time.
   > Before we left, we have already cleaned the house.
   > I had looked forward to the trip.
   > She had been swimming . . . and she had never swam before.
   > When we arrived, they had already started eating.
   > They've read the book before they saw the movie.

3. The object of the activity is for students to identify which sentences are incorrect and then correct them.

4. Have students compare their answers.

   Variation: Do the activity as a game with competing teams. The team that successfully completes the task in the shortest time is the winner.

4. Ask students if they have any questions. Check understanding of vocabulary.

5. Options for additional practice:

   - Have students write a response to Stamp4 and share their writing in pairs

   - Have students correspond with a keypal on the Internet and then share their experience with the class.

 ## WHAT ARE THEY SAYING?

FOCUS

- Preparing for an Important Event

Have students talk about the characters and the situation, and then create role plays based on the scene. Students may refer back to previous lessons as a resource, but they should not simply reuse specific conversations.

Note: You may want to assign this exercise as written homework, having students prepare their role plays, practice them the next day with other students, and then present them to the class.

 ## GLOBAL EXCHANGE

1. Set the scene: "Stamp4 is writing to a keypal."

2. Introduce the words *collect, envelope, penpal, stamp, stamp collection.*

3. Have students read silently or follow along silently as the message is read aloud by you, by one or more students, or on the audio program.

GRAMMAR

TWO-WORD VERBS: SEPARABLE

I'm going to	**put on** my boots. **put** my boots **on**. **put** them **on**.

TWO-WORD VERBS: INSEPARABLE

I	**hear from** Aunt Betty **hear from** her <s>**hear** Aunt Betty **from**</s> <s>**hear** her **from**</s>	very often.

FUNCTIONS

EXTENDING AN INVITATION

Would you like to *play tennis with me this morning*?
Would you like to *get together today*?

Are you free *after you take them back*?

DECLINING AN INVITATION

I'd like to, but I can't.
I'd really like to, but I can't.
I'm afraid I can't.

EXPRESSING INABILITY

I can't.
I'm afraid I can't.

EXPRESSING OBLIGATION

I have to *fill out my income tax form*.

I've really got to do it.

ASKING FOR AND REPORTING INFORMATION

What size do you wear?
  Size 32.

How much *does it* cost?
  The *usual* price is _____ dollars.

INQUIRING ABOUT INTENTION

Will you *take it back*?

When are you going to *call up your uncle*?

EXPRESSING INTENTION

I'm going to *call him up next week*.
I'll *call you in the morning*.
I'll *turn it off* right away.

INQUIRING ABOUT REMEMBERING

Did you remember to *turn off the oven*?

ASKING FOR ADVICE

Do you think I should *keep these old love letters*?

OFFERING ADVICE

I think you should *throw them away*.

OFFERING A SUGGESTION

Let's *get together tomorrow instead*.

Why don't you *look through all of our suits and pick out the one you like*?

OFFERING TO HELP

May I help you?

EXPRESSING WANT–DESIRE

I'm looking for a *suit*.

Do you have any *suits* that are *a little darker*?

REMEMBERING AND FORGETTING

I forgot all about it!
I completely forgot!
It slipped my mind!
It completely slipped my mind!

NEW VOCABULARY

Adjectives

baggy	plaid
concerned	plain
designer	reduced
discouraged	regular
final	select
free	single
loose	stained
missing	super
narrow	tight
organic	usual

Verbs

accept	go with
check	kiss
erase	notice
exchange	refuse
expire	save
fit	

Separable Two-Word Verbs

bring back	put away
call up	put on
clean up	take back
cross out	take down
do over	take out
drop off	think over
figure out	throw away
fill out	throw out
give back	try on
hand in	turn down
hang up	turn on
hook up	turn off
leave on	use up
look up	wake up
pick out	write down
pick up	

Inseparable Two-Word Verbs

call on	look through
feel like	look up to
get along with	pick on
get over	run into
go with	run out of
hear from	take after
leave on	

Shopping

anniversary sale
bargain
clearance
coupon
discount
discount store
dressing room
half-price
merchandise
purchase (n)
savings (n)

Clothing

button
dress shirt
running shoes
sleeve
trousers
zipper

Clothing Sizes

extra large
medium
size

Celebrations

Christmas decorations
New Year's decorations
wedding guest
wedding invitation

Places Around the US

Arizona	Denver
Colorado	Phoenix

Money

on sale
refund

Adverbs

accidentally
apparently
constantly
eventually
incorrectly
simply

Time Expressions

so far
within

Miscellaneous

accident report
alarm
answer (n)
child rearing (n)
cleaner's
college application form
definition
during the week
ex-boyfriend
ex-girlfriend
garbage
happiness
heat
hospital bill
insurance form
library book
modem
paper
portrait
selection
toy

EXPRESSIONS

I'd like to, but I can't.
in the first place
Maybe some other time.
No problem at all.
Walk home
You're in luck!

VOCABULARY PREVIEW

You may want to present these words before beginning the unit, or you may choose to wait until they first occur in a specific lesson. If you choose to introduce them at this point, here are some suggestions:

1. Have students look at the illustrations on text page 115 and identify the words they already know.

2. Present the vocabulary. Say each word and have the class repeat it chorally and individually. Check students' understanding and pronunciation of the words.

3. Practice the vocabulary as a class, in pairs, or in small groups. Have students cover the word list and look at the pictures. Practice the words in the following ways:

   • Say a word and have students tell the number of the illustration.

   • Give the number of an illustration and have students say the word.

FOCUS

- Separable Two-Word Verbs:

bring back	*pick up*
call up	*take back*
fill out	*take down*
hang up	*throw out*
hook up	*turn on*

- Separating Two-Word Verbs with Pronouns

CLOSE UP

RULE: A two-word verb consists of a main verb plus a particle. In most cases, the addition of the particle changes the meaning of the verb.

EXAMPLES: I'm going to **take** the bus.
She's going to **take back** her books.
We're going to **take down** the Christmas tree.

RULE: In some cases, the two-word verb is interchangeable with the main verb.

EXAMPLES: I'm going to **call** my uncle.
I'm going to **call up** my uncle.

RULE: Some two-word verbs are *separable*. The noun object can follow the two-word verb or the two-word verb can be separated by a noun object.

EXAMPLES: He's going to **throw out** *his old newspapers*.
He's going to **throw** *his old newspapers* **out**.

RULE: When the noun object of a two-word verb is replaced by a pronoun, the pronoun *must* be placed between the two parts of the verb.

EXAMPLES: She's going to **fill out** *her college application forms*.
She's going to **fill** *them* **out**.

I'm going to **hook up** *my new computer*.
I'm going to **hook** *it* **up**.

See text page 130 for a list of separable two-word verbs introduced in Unit 9.

INTRODUCING THE MODEL

1. Have students look at the model illustration.

2. Set the scene: "A husband and wife are talking. He's upset because a repairman has just taken the TV set from their house."

3. Present the model.

4. Full-Class Repetition.

5. Ask students if they have any questions. Check understanding of the two-word verb *bring back*.

6. Group Choral Repetition.

7. Choral Conversation.

8. Call on one or two pairs of students to present the dialog.

   (For additional practice, do Choral Conversation in small groups or by rows.)

9. Read the verbs in the box at the top of text page 116, which show how other two-word verbs can be separated by a pronoun:

   bring back the TV
   bring it back

   call up Sally
   call her up

   throw out the newspapers
   throw them out

SIDE BY SIDE EXERCISES

Examples

1. A. When are you going to call up your uncle in Ohio?
   B. I'm going to call him up sometime next week.

2. A. When is Ted going to throw out his old newspapers?
   B. He's going to throw them out sometime next week.

1. **Exercise 1:** Introduce the verb *call up*. Call on two students to present the dialog. Then do Choral Repetition and Choral Conversation practice.

2. **Exercise 2:** Introduce the verb *throw out*. Same as above.

3. **Exercises 3–9:** Either Full-Class Practice or Pair Practice.

New Vocabulary

3. fill out
   college
     application
     form
4. pick up
   cleaner's
5. take back
   library book

6. hook up
7. hang up
   portrait
8. take down
   Christmas
     decorations
9. turn on
   heat

WORKBOOK

Page 100

EXPANSION ACTIVITIES

1. Grammar Chain ★★

a. Write the following conversation model and phrases on the board:

> A. When are you going to _____?
> B. I'm going to _____ sometime tomorrow.

> pick up the groceries
> fill out the income tax form
> take back the computer
> hang up the photograph
> turn on the heat
> throw out that old couch
> call up Aunt Bertha
> hook up the computer
> take down that ugly portrait

b. Start the chain game by saying:

> Teacher (to Student A): When are you going to pick up the groceries?

c. Student A answers according to the model on the board and then asks a different question to Student B, and the chain continues. For example

> Student A: I'm going to pick them up sometime tomorrow.
> (to Student B): When are you going to throw out that old couch?
> Student B: I'm going to throw it out sometime tomorrow.
> (to Student C): When are you going to call up Aunt Bertha?
> Etc.

2. What's Missing? ★★

a. Write on the board:

> I'm going to _____ soon.

> bring back   pick up
> call up   take back
> fill out   take down
> hang up   throw out
> hook up   turn on

b. Say each of the object cues below. For each one, have students choose a two-word verb that fits that object and make a sentence using the model on the board. For example:

> Teacher: Uncle Bill
> Student: I'm going to call up Uncle Bill soon.

Object Cues:

> the college application form *(fill out)*
> some friends at the airport *(pick up)*
> these old shoes *(throw out)*
> the TV at the repair shop *(pick up)*
> my new photographs *(hang up)*
> the hammer and screwdriver you borrowed *(bring back)*
> the heat *(turn on)*
> the library books *(take back)*
> tickets at the symphony *(pick up)*
> the garbage *(throw out)*
> the new fax machine *(hook up)*
> the Christmas decorations *(take down)*
> the air conditioner *(turn on)*
> my income tax form *(fill out)*
> these old souvenirs we don't want anymore *(throw out)*
> my sister at the dentist's office *(pick up)*
> the videos *(take back)*
> this portrait of my grandmother *(hang up)*
> Mr. and Mrs. Garcia *(call up)*

3. Finish the Sentence Line-Up ★★

a. Write the following two-word verbs on the board:

(continued)

bring back	pick up
call up	take back
fill out	take down
hang up	throw out
hook up	turn on

b. Have students line up in two rows opposite each other.

c. Have the first student in the *left* row begin a sentence with one of the verbs on the board. The opposite student in the *right* row must complete the sentence. For example:

   Student 1: I turned on . . .
   Student 2: the heat.

d. Then have the next student in the *right* row begin a sentence with another verb, and the opposite student in the *left* row complete it. For example:

   Student 3: He hung up . . .
   Student 4: the picture.

e. Continue going back and forth until all the students have had an opportunity to either begin or complete a sentence.

4. Miming ★★

a. Write the following on cards:

fill out a form	turn on the heat	hang up a portrait
pick up clothes at the cleaner's	call up your girlfriend/ boyfriend	hook up a computer and a printer
take down decorations	throw out old newspapers	take back videos to the video store

b. Have students take turns picking a card from the pile and pantomiming the action on the card.

c. The class must guess what the person is doing.

Variation: Do the activity as a game with competing teams.

5. Match the Sentences ★

a. Make a set of split sentence cards such as the following:

Every Sunday we call . . .	up the family.
We have to throw . . .	out the old newspapers.
She is going to fill . . .	out the application form.
They haven't brought . . .	back the TV yet.
You can hook . . .	up the DVD player with the computer.
You should take . . .	down that horrible portrait of yourself.
Please turn . . .	on the TV.
She likes to hang . . .	up Christmas decorations around the house.
I've got to pick . . .	up my car at the repair shop.

b. Distribute a card to each student.

c. Have students memorize the sentence portion on their cards, then walk around the room trying to find their corresponding match.

d. Then have pairs of students say their completed sentences aloud to the class.

6. Sense or Nonsense? ★★

a. Divide the class into small groups.

b. Make multiple sets of cards from Activity 5, mix them up, and distribute them to each group, keeping the beginning and ending cards in different piles.

c. Have students take turns picking up one card from each pile and reading the sentence to the group. For example:

I've got to pick . . .	on the TV.

d. That group decides if the sentence makes sense or is *nonsense*.

e. After all the cards have been picked, have the groups lay out all the cards and put together all the sentence combinations that make sense.

7. Tomorrow! ★★

a. Write on the board:

> I never have the time to _____.
> I think I'll _____ tomorrow.

b. Call out a two-word verb from text page 116 and have students complete the sentence, drawing on their own experiences. For example:

Teacher: call up
Student: I never have the time to call up *my Uncle William.* I think I'll call *him* up tomorrow.

c. Have students share their sentences in groups or pairs. Ask the class: What do you avoid doing? Why?

Text Page 117: Oh, No! I Forgot!

FOCUS

- Separable Two-Word Verbs:

  hand in
  put on
  take off
  take out
  turn off

- Separating Two-Word Verbs with Pronouns and Nouns

INTRODUCING THE MODEL

This model should be presented twice: once with the object noun after the verb *(turn off the oven)* and once with the noun between the two parts of the verb *(turn the oven off)*.

1. Have students look at the model illustration.

2. Set the scene: "A husband and wife are having dinner together. They turned on the oven while they were cooking dinner, and it's still on."

3. Present the model.

4. Full-Class Repetition.

   ### Pronunciation Note

   The pronunciation focus of Unit 9 is **Linking "t" Between Vowels** (text page 130). You may wish to model this pronunciation at this point and encourage students to incorporate it into their language practice.

   I'll turn **it off** right away.

   I'll fill **it out** right away.

5. Ask students if they have any questions. Check understanding of the verb *turn off*.

6. Group Choral Repetition.

7. Choral Conversation.

8. Call on one or two pairs of students to present the dialog.

9. Expand the model with further practice. Call on pairs of students to present the model, using *the lights, the radio.*

   (For additional practice, do Choral Conversation in small groups or by rows.)

SIDE BY SIDE EXERCISES

Examples

1. A. Did you remember to take back the videos/take the videos back?
   B. Oh, no! I forgot! I'll take them back right away.

2. A. Did you remember to fill out the accident report/fill the accident report out?
   B. Oh, no! I forgot! I'll fill it out right away.

1. **Exercise 1:** Call on two students to present the dialog. Then do Choral Repetition and Choral Conversation practice.

2. **Exercise 2:** Introduce the phrase *accident report*. Same as above.

3. **Exercises 3–9:** Either Full-Class Practice or Pair Practice.

New Vocabulary	
3. alarm	7. put on
4. put away toy	8. take off
5. hand in	9. take out garbage
6. wake up	

How to Say It!

> **Remembering and Forgetting:** In spoken English there are many ways to express forgetting something.

1. Present the expressions.

2. Full-Class Repetition.

3. Ask students if they have any questions. Check understanding of the new expressions: *I forgot all about it! I completely forgot!*

It slipped my mind! It completely slipped my mind!

4. Group Choral Repetition.

5. Have students practice again the conversations in this lesson using any of these new expressions.

6. Call on pairs of students to present their conversations to the class.

WORKBOOK

Pages 101–102

EXPANSION ACTIVITIES

1. Finish the Verb! ★

Say each of the verbs below and have students add any particles they have learned to make them into two-word verbs:

Teacher	Student
bring	bring back
call	call up
fill	fill out
hand	hand in
hang	hang up
hook	hook up
pick	pick up
put	put away
	put on
throw	throw out
turn	turn on
	turn off
take	take back
	take down
	take off
	take out
wake	wake up

2. Associations ★

a. Divide the class into pairs or small groups.

b. Call out a two-word verb, and tell students to write down all the words they associate with that verb. For example:

take back: the videos/the books

fill out: the form/the application/the report
turn on: the TV/the radio/the alarm

c. Have a student from each pair or group come to the board and write their words.

Variation: Do the activity as a game in which you divide the class into teams. The team with the most number of associations is the winner.

3. What's the Word? ★★

a. Write the following verbs on the board:

bring back	take back
call up	take down
fill out	take out
hand in	take off
hang up	throw out
hook up	turn off
pick up	turn on
put away	wake up
put on	

A. Have you _____ yet?
B. Yes. I _____ yesterday.

(continued)

b. Point to a verb and call on a pair of students to create a conversation, using the model on the board. For example:

call up
A. Have you called up Uncle Marvin yet?
    or
Have you called Uncle Marvin up yet?
B. Yes. I called him up yesterday.

hand in
A. Have you handed in your English homework yet?
    or
Have you handed your English homework in yet?
B. Yes. I handed it in yesterday.

4. Scrambled Sentences ★★

a. Divide the class into teams.

b. Write individual sentences out of order on the board. For example:

it	away	off	I'll	turn	right
you	your	yesterday	in	homework
	handed				
going	off	to	his	he's	shoes
	take				

c. The first person to raise his or her hand, come to the board, and write the sentence in the correct order earns a point for that team.

d. The team with the most points wins the scrambled sentence game.

Variation: Write the words to several sentences on separate cards. Divide the class into small groups, and have students work together to put the sentences into correct order.

5. Finish the Sentence ★★

a. Write the following verbs on the board:

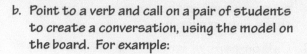

bring back	take back
call up	take down
fill out	take out
hand in	take off
hang up	throw out
hook up	turn off
pick up	turn on
put away	wake up
put on	

b. Begin the sentences below, and have students complete them with an appropriate two-word verb. For example:

Teacher: I've already read these library books, so I think I'll . . .
Student: take them back.

Questions:

My clothes are ready at the cleaner's. I think I'll . . . *(pick them up).*

I haven't spoken to Aunt Clara for a while, so I think I'll . . . *(call her up).*

I've already completed my homework, so I think I'll . . . *(hand it in).*

I love this new portrait. I'm going to . . . *(hang it up).*

Is the heat too high? I'll . . . *(turn it off).*

My new printer doesn't work. I'm having trouble . . . *(hooking it up).*

My income tax forms are on the kitchen table. It's time to . . . *(fill them out).*

I don't want these old magazines anymore. I think I'll . . . *(throw them out).*

I'm upset. It's very hot, and my air conditioner is broken. I can't . . . *(turn it on).*

I'm unhappy without my TV. When is the repairman going to . . . *(bring it back)?*

It's July, and my Christmas decorations are still in my living room. I think it's time to . . . *(take them down).*

It's late, and the children are still sleeping. It's time to . . . *(wake them up).*

The garbage is still in the kitchen. Please . . . *(take it out).*

Do you want to see my new coat? I'll . . . *(put it on).*

I've already watched all these videos. I think
  I'll . . . *(take them back)*.
Is the oven still on? You should . . . *(turn it off)*.
Billy, your toys are in the living room, and
  guests are coming for dinner. Please . . .
  (put them away).

6. Listen for the Right Answer ★★

a. Write the following on the board:

> A. Have you _____ yet?
> B. _____? Yes. I _____ a few
>   minutes ago.

b. Have pairs of students create conversations
   based on the model. Give Student A a *verb
   cue* and Student B a card with two *object
   cues*. Based on the verb he or she hears,
   Student B must choose the correct object to
   complete the dialog. For example:

Student A	Student B
turn it on	my coat the heat

A. Have you turned it on yet?
B. The heat? Yes. I turned it on a few
   minutes ago.

Cue cards:

turn it on	my coat the heat
turn it off	my jacket the stove
fill it out	the accident report a new suit
throw it out	the garbage my new raincoat
hand it in	the telephone my homework
put them away	my books my children
take it off	the oven my coat
hang them up	the portraits the magazines

READING *A Busy Saturday*

FOCUS

• Separable Two-Word Verbs

NEW VOCABULARY

during the week
feel like
modem

READING THE STORY

Optional: *Preview the story by having students talk about the story title and/or illustrations. You may choose to introduce new vocabulary beforehand, or have students encounter the new vocabulary within the context of the reading.*

1. Have students read silently, or follow along silently as the story is read aloud by you, by one or more students, or on the audio program.

2. Ask students if they have any questions. Check understanding of vocabulary.

3. Check students' comprehension, using some or all of the following questions:

> Why is everybody in the Peterson family going to be busy today?
> What does Mr. Peterson have to do? Why?
> What does Mrs. Peterson have to do? Why?
> What does Steve have to do? Why?
> What does Michael have to do? Why?
> What does Stacey have to do? Why?
> What does Abigail have to do? Why?

✓READING *CHECK-UP*

Q & A

1. Call on a pair of students to present the model.

2. Introduce the new expressions: *I'd like to, but I can't. Maybe some other time.*

3. Have students work in pairs to create new dialogs.

4. Call on pairs to present their new dialogs to the class.

READING EXTENSION

Tic Tac Question Formation

1. Draw a tic tac grid on the board and fill it with question words. For example:

Why?	Does?	What?
Which?	When?	Do?
Is?	Are?	Where?

2. Divide the class into two teams. Give each team a mark: *X* or *O.*

3. Have each team ask a question about the reading that begins with one of the question words, then provide the answer to the question. If the question and answer are correct, the team gets to put its mark in that space. For example:

> X Team: Does Abigail have to take the
> library books back?
> No, she doesn't.

Why?	X	What?
Which?	When?	Do?
Is?	Are?	Where?

4. The first team to mark out three boxes in a straight line—vertically, horizontally, or diagonally—wins.

How About You?

Have students do the activity in pairs or as a class.

Text Page 119: I Don't Think So

FOCUS

- Separable Two-Word Verbs:

cross out	think over
do over	throw away
give back	throw out
leave on	turn down
look up	write down

INTRODUCING THE MODEL

1. Have students look at the model illustration.

2. Set the scene: "Two friends are looking through some old things. One of them has found some old letters from a boyfriend. She doesn't know what to do with them."

3. Present the model.

4. Full-Class Repetition.

5. Ask students if they have any questions. Check understanding of the two-word verb *throw away*.

6. Group Choral Repetition.

7. Choral Conversation.

8. Call on one or two pairs of students to present the dialog.

   (For additional practice, do Choral Conversation in small groups or by rows.)

SIDE BY SIDE EXERCISES

Examples

1. A. Do you think I should hand in my homework?
   B. No, I don't think so. I think you should do it over.

2. A. Do you think I should use up this old milk?
   B. No, I don't think so. I think you should throw it out.

1. **Exercise 1:**

   a. Set the scene: "This person has made a lot of mistakes on his homework. He's asking what he should do."

   b. Introduce the verb *do over*.

   c. Call on two students to present the dialog. Then do Choral Repetition and Choral Conversation practice.

2. **Exercise 2:**

   a. Set the scene: "There's a little more milk in the carton. It's old, but it might be okay to drink."

   b. Introduce the verb *use up*.

   c. Same as above.

3. **Exercises 3–9:** Either Full-Class Practice or Pair Practice.

New Vocabulary	
3. erase	7. think over
cross out	8. ex-boyfriend
4. leave on	give back
5. write down	9. accept
6. definition	ex-girlfriend
look up	turn down

Language Note

Exercises 8 and 9: *Ex-boyfriend* and *ex-girlfriend*. The prefix *ex-* means *former*. Other examples of this are *ex-husband* and *ex-wife*.

As you introduce the new two-word verb in each exercise, set each of the following scenes:

3. "This person made a lot of mistakes on his homework. He isn't going to do it over, but he wants to fix the mistakes."

4. "It's very hot today. The air conditioner has been on, but now it's too cold."

5. "This person can't remember Amy's telephone number."

6. "Some students use a dictionary when they don't know the definition of a word. Other students like to ask the teacher."

7. "When you have an important decision to make, it's a good idea to think about it for a while before you make your decision."

8. "This person has broken up with her boyfriend, but she still has the ring he gave her."

9. "This person has been invited to the wedding of an old girlfriend and can't decide what to do."

WORKBOOK

Page 103

EXPANSION ACTIVITIES

1. Finish the Sentence! ★★

Read the following incomplete sentences and have students complete each with an appropriate two-word verb. For example:

Teacher: I didn't ask anyone the definition of that word. I . . .

Student: looked it up.

Sentences:

I didn't ask anyone the definition of that word. I . . .
I didn't accept the invitation. I . . .
I didn't erase my mistakes. I . . .
I didn't keep those old letters. I . . .
I didn't use up the old milk in my refrigerator. I . . .
I didn't try to remember their phone number. I . . .
I didn't leave on the air conditioner. I . . .
I didn't keep the hammer I borrowed from my neighbor. I . . .
I didn't hand in my homework. I . . .
I didn't make my decision right away. I . . .

Variation: Divide the class into teams and do the activity as a game. Say a sentence, and the first person to raise his or her hand and complete the sentence correctly gets a point for that team. The team with the most points wins the game.

2. Match the Conversations ★★

a. Make up the following matching cards:

| Don't keep those letters! | Throw them away! |

Don't drink this old milk!	Throw it out!
Don't hand in that terrible composition!	Do it over!
Don't erase your mistakes!	Cross them out!
Don't leave the heat on!	Turn it off!
Don't try to remember their address!	Write it down!
Don't ask me the definition of this word!	Look it up!
Don't make your decision right away!	Think it over!
Don't accept that invitation!	Turn it down!
Don't keep the screwdriver you borrowed!	Give it back!

b. Distribute a card to each student.

c. Have students memorize the sentences on their cards, and then have students walk around the room saying their sentences until they find their match.

d. Then have pairs of students say their matched sentences aloud to the class.

3. Concentration ★

a. Shuffle the cards from Activity 2 above and place them face down in four rows of 5 each.

b. Divide the class into two teams. The object of the game is for students to find the matching cards. Both teams should be able to see all the cards, since *concentrating* on their location is an important part of playing the game.

c. A student from Team 1 turns over two cards. If they match, the student picks up the cards, that team gets a point, and the student takes another turn. If the cards don't match, the student turns them face down, and a member of Team 2 takes a turn.

d. The game continues until all the cards have been matched. The team with the most correct matches wins the game.

Variation: This game can also be played in groups and pairs.

4. Question the Answers! ★★

a. Write the following two-word verbs on the board:

bring back	take back
call up	take down
cross out	take off
do over	take out
fill out	think over
give back	throw away
hand in	throw out
hang up	turn down
hook up	turn off
look up	turn on
pick up	wake up
put away	write down
put on	

b. Dictate answers and have students write questions for which these answers would be correct. For example:

Answer: His brother's dictionary.
Question: What did he give back?

Answer: A new recipe.
Question: What did you write down?

Answer: Her computer.
Question: What did she turn on?
What did she hook up?

c. Have students compare their questions with each other.

Answers and possible questions:

His brother's dictionary.
(What did he give back?)

A new recipe?
(What did you write down?)

Her computer.
(What did she hook up?)
(What did she turn on?)

His shoes.
(What did he put on?)

Her old letters.
(What did she throw out?)

Your homework.
(What did you do over?)
(What did you hand in?)

Their mistakes.
(What did they cross out?)

The invitation.
(What did they turn down?)

His old milk.
(What did he throw out?)

My TV.
(What did you turn on?)
(What did you turn off?)

The definition.
(What did you look up?)

The decision.
(What did she think over?)

Their photographs.
(What did they hang up?)

(continued)

Her tax forms.
(What did she fill out?)

Variation: Write the answers on cards. Divide the class into groups and give each group a set of cards.

5. Synonyms ★★

a. Write on the board:

```
call up          pick up
cross out        take back
do over          think over
fill out         throw away
give back        turn down
hand in          turn off
hang up          use up
look up          write down
```

```
Okay.  I'll _____ right away.
```

b. Read each of the statements below. Have students respond with an appropriate two-word verb synonym from the list on the board. For example:

> Teacher: Don't forget to phone her.
> Student: Okay. I'll call her up right away.

Situations:

Don't forget to phone her. *(call her up)*
Don't forget to return this book. *(take it back)*
Please complete the form. *(fill it out)*
Don't forget to find the meaning of this word.
   (look it up)

Please get off the telephone. *(hang up)*
Please write these exercises again.
   (do them over)
Don't forget to copy Mr. Franklin's address.
   (write it down)
Don't forget to get my shirt at the cleaner's.
   I need it this morning. *(pick it up)*
Please fix your mistakes. *(cross them out)*
Don't forget to give the teacher your
   homework. *(hand it in)*

6. What's Wrong? ★★★

a. Divide the class into pairs or small groups.

b. Write several sentences such as the following on the board or on a handout. Some of the sentences should be correct, and others incorrect. For example:

I think you should leave the heat on.
He's going to bring back it soon.
He should think over it.
They forgot to hand their homework in.
She'll take the old garbage out right away.
It slipped out of my mind!
I forgot all about it!
They should use up it.
We try to every address write down.
He should turn them down.

c. The object of the activity is for students to identify which sentences are incorrect and then correct them.

d. Have students compare their answers.

Variation: Do the activity as a game with competing teams. The team that successfully completes the task in the shortest time is the winner.

READING *Lucy's English Composition*

FOCUS

- Separable Two-Word Verbs

NEW VOCABULARY

accidentally
apparently
check (v)
discouraged
in the first place
incorrectly
paper
simply
throw away

READING THE STORY

Optional: Preview the story by having students talk about the story title and/or illustration. You may choose to introduce new vocabulary beforehand, or have students encounter the new vocabulary within the context of the reading.

1. Have students read silently, or follow along silently as the story is read aloud by you, by one or more students, or on the audio program.

2. Ask students if they have any questions. Check understanding of vocabulary.

3. Check students' comprehension, using some or all of the following questions:

Why is Lucy discouraged?
Why did her English teacher tell her to do her English composition over?
What had she done with her mistakes?
Why had she used several words incorrectly?
Why hadn't she written her homework on the correct paper?

✓ READING *CHECK-UP*

TRUE, FALSE, OR MAYBE?

1. True
2. False
3. Maybe
4. True
5. False
6. Maybe

WHAT'S THE WORD?

1. give it back
2. hand it in
3. do it over
4. throw it away
5. look it up
6. cross them out

READING EXTENSION

Good Study Habits

1. Have pairs of students write a list of good study habits. For example:

Look up new words in the dictionary.
Write down the new word and its definition in a special place.
Write down all homework assignments in a special place so you don't forget.

2. Have pairs of students share their lists with the class. As they talk, write their ideas on the board. According to students in the class, what are the most important study habits?

COMPLETE THE LETTERS

Before doing the activity, show students on a map the locations of *Denver, Colorado,* and *Phoenix, Arizona.*

"Discouraged Donald" Letter

1. gave it back
2. thrown them away
3. thought it over
4. turned me down
5. call her up

"Frustrated Fran" Letter

1. turns it off
2. turns it on
3. hung it up
4. took it down
5. put them away
6. took them out

For homework, have students write letters of advice to "Discouraged Donald" and "Frustrated Fran". Have students share their letters in class.

FOCUS

- Review: Separable Two-Word Verbs
- Introduction: *clean up, drop off, figure out*

INTRODUCING THE MODEL

1. Have students look at the model illustration.

2. Set the scene: "Two friends are talking on the telephone."

3. Present the model.

4. Full-Class Repetition.

5. Ask students if they have any questions. Check understanding of the words *free*, *drop off*.

   ### Language Notes

   The expression *Are you free?* means *Are you available?* or *Do you have free time?*

   In *I'd really like to*, the word *I'd* is a contraction of *I would*. The expression *I'd really like to* and similar expressions with *I'd* are often used in polite language for expressing one's wants and needs.

6. Group Choral Repetition.

7. Choral Conversation.

8. Divide the class into pairs and have students practice the model conversation.

9. Call on pairs of students to present the dialog.

   (For additional practice, do Choral Conversation in small groups or by rows.)

SIDE BY SIDE EXERCISES

Examples

1. A. Would you like to get together today?
    B. I'm afraid I can't. I have to clean up my living room.
    A. Are you free after you clean it up?
    B. I'm afraid not. I also have to throw out all my old newspapers.
    A. Would you like to get together after you throw them out?
    B. I'd really like to, but I can't. I ALSO have to pick my brother up at the train station.
    A. You're really busy today! What do you have to do after you pick him up?
    B. Nothing. But by then I'll probably be exhausted. Let's get together tomorrow instead.
    A. Fine. I'll call you in the morning.

2. A. Would you like to get together today?
    B. I'm afraid I can't. I have to figure out my hospital bill
    A. Are you free after you figure it out?
    B. I'm afraid not. I also have to fill out my insurance form.
    A. Would you like to get together after you fill it out?
    B. I'd really like to, but I can't. I ALSO have to call the doctor up.
    A. You're really busy today! What do you have to do after you call him/her up?
    B. Nothing. But by then I'll probably be exhausted. Let's get together tomorrow instead.
    A. Fine. I'll call you in the morning.

1. **Exercise 1:** Introduce the verb *clean up*. Call on two students to present the dialog. Then do Choral Repetition and Choral Conversation practice.

2. Exercise 2: Introduce the words *figure out, hospital bill, insurance form*. Same as above.

3. Exercises 3–5: Either Full-Class Practice or Pair Practice.

> **New Vocabulary**
>
> 3. New Year's decorations
> 4. pick out
>   wedding guest
>   wedding invitation

4. Exercise 6: For homework, have students write a new conversation using any two-word verbs they wish. Have students present their dialogs in the next class.

WORKBOOK

Pages 104–105

EXPANSION ACTIVITIES

1. Scrambled Dialog ★

a. Write each line of the model conversation on text page 122 or any of the exercises on text page 123 on a separate card. Scramble the cards.

b. Give the cards to 9 students. Have them unscramble the lines and put together the conversation.

2. What's the Word? ★★

a. Write on the board:

call up	look up	take off
clean up	pick out	take out
figure out	pick up	think over
hand in	put on	turn off
hang up	take down	

I'll _____ .

b. Read the sentences below and have students respond with an appropriate two-word verb from the list on the board. For example:

> Teacher: Your coat is on the floor.
> Student: I'll pick it up.

Sentences:

Your coat is on the floor. *(pick it up) (hang it up)*

Which tie should I wear with this suit? *(pick it out)*

We're supposed to write our name, address, and phone number on this form. *(fill it out)*

What does "edible" mean? *(look it up)*

How much is 2436 and 8941? *(figure it out)*

There's a lot of garbage in the kitchen. *(take it out)*

What are you going to do, stay or leave? *(think it over)*

The basement is really dirty! *(clean it up)*

Those pictures on the wall look terrible! *(take them down)*

You should wear those new gloves I gave you. *(put them on)*

That black tie doesn't look very good with your brown suit. *(take it off)*

Who's watching TV? Nobody. *(turn it off)*

I have to talk to you this weekend about something very important. *(call you up)*

3. That's a Good Idea ★★★

a. Write on the board:

> A. _____ .
> B. Why don't you _____ ?
> A. That's a good idea. I think I'll _____ _____ _____ right now.

b. Write the following on cue cards:

I'd like to hear some good music.

This coat is too warm.

My living room is so dirty, I can't stand it.

I can never remember your phone number.

I really don't need these boots during the summer.

The birthday party was a week ago. These decorations are starting to look terrible.

I'd really like to talk to my friend Bob in New York.

I'd really like to know the definition of that word.

My homework looks terrible! It has too many mistakes.

I really want to wear my blue suit, but it's at the cleaner's.

I'd really like to watch the news on TV.

I'll never be able to remember the directions to Amanda's house.

c. Divide the class into pairs and give each pair a card. Have Speaker A begin a conversation by

reading a cue. Speaker B continues the conversation using any two-word verb and the model on the board. For example:

   A. I'd like to hear some good music.
   B. Why don't you turn on the CD player?
   A. That's a good idea. I'll turn it on right now.

4. Mysteries ★★★

a. Divide the class into pairs.

b. Write the following question on the board:

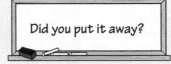

Did you put it away?

c. Have each pair create a short dialog that begins with "Did you put it away?" The dialogs should elaborate about *it* without revealing what *it* is.

d. Have each pair present their dialog to the class. Then have the other students guess what *it* is. For example:

   A. Did you put it away?
   B. Yes. I put it in the closet, under some shoes. I don't think she can find it.
   A. I hope she likes it.
   B. We'll give it to her after we have the cake tomorrow.

   [a birthday gift]

5. Chain Story ★★

a. Tell students they're going to construct a story about preparing for a party, using two-word verbs. Ask: "What two-word verbs have you learned?" Make a list of the verbs on the board as they name them.

b. Begin the story by saying: "Today is a busy day. First, I have to clean up my apartment."

c. Have each student take a turn in which he or she repeats or rewords the last sentence of the previous person and then adds a new line using one of the two-word verbs. For example:

Student 1: First I have to clean up my apartment. After I clean it up, I have to put up some decorations.

(continued)

Student 2: After I put them up, I have to pick up some flowers.

Student 3: After I pick them up, I have to hang up some decorations.

Etc.

6. Student Lists ★★

a. Write the following events on the board:

> a job interview
> a play performance
> a wedding
> a marriage proposal
> a New Year's Eve party
> a vacation in Tahiti

b. Divide the class into pairs.

c. Have each pair choose one of the events on the board and make up a list of all the things to do before that event. Encourage students to use their newly learned two-word verbs.

d. Have students share their lists with the class.

Variation: ★★★ Have students read their lists, but not say what the event is, and the class has to guess the event based on the list.

7. Group Story Game ★★★

a. Divide the class into small groups.

b. Have each group write a story in which they use as many two-word verbs as they can.

c. The group that includes the most number of two-word verbs is the winner of the *story game.*

FOCUS

- Inseparable Two-Word Verbs

call on	*look up to*
get along with	*pick on*
get over	*run into*
hear from	*run out of*
look through	*take after*

CLOSE UP

RULE: Some two-word verbs are inseparable. The noun or pronoun object must always follow the two-word verb.

EXAMPLES: I **heard from** *Aunt Betty* last week.
I **heard from** *her* last week.

See text page 130 for a list of inseparable two-word verbs introduced in Unit 9.

INTRODUCING THE MODEL

1. Have students look at the model illustration.

2. Set the scene: "A brother and a sister are talking. They usually get a letter from their aunt every month."

3. Present the model.

4. Full-Class Repetition.

5. Ask students if they have any questions. Check understanding of the verb *hear from*.

6. Group Choral Repetition.

7. Choral Conversation.

8. Call on one or two pairs of students to present the dialog.

   (For additional practice, do Choral Conversation in small groups or by rows.)

SIDE BY SIDE EXERCISES

Examples

1. A. Have you run into Mr. Clark recently?
   B. Yes, I have. I ran into him just last week.

2. A. Have you run out of paper recently?
   B. Yes, I have. I ran out of it just last week.

1. **Exercise 1:** Introduce the verb *run into*. Call on two students to present the dialog. Then do Choral Repetition and Choral Conversation practice.

2. **Exercise 2:** Introduce the verb *run out of*. Same as above.

3. Exercises 3–6: Either Full-Class Practice or Pair Practice.

New Vocabulary

3. get over
4. call on
5. look through
6. pick on

How About You?

Introduce the new expressions *get along with, take after, look up to.* Write these new expressions on the board. Then point to each one as you tell the following situations:

"Mary *gets along with* her sister very well. They never argue, and they like each other very much. They enjoy spending time together."

"John *takes after* his father. John's father is good at mathematics. John does very well in math, too. His father can sing very well, and John sings well, too."

"Mr. and Mrs. Smith have a son named Mark. Mark really *looks up to* his parents. He thinks they're wonderful people, and he hopes he'll be like them when he grows up."

Have students answer the questions in pairs or as a class.

WORKBOOK

Pages 106–107

EXPANSION ACTIVITIES

1. Scrambled Sentences ★

a. Divide the class into teams.

b. Write individual sentences out of order on the board. For example:

week	last	over	got	it	she
looked	we	yesterday		them	
	through				
our	into	yesterday	ran	neighbor	
we					

c. The first person to raise his or her hand, come to the board, and write the sentence in the correct order earns a point for that team.

d. The team with the most points wins the scrambled sentence game.

Variation: Write the words to several sentences on separate cards. Divide the class into small groups, and have students work together to put the sentences into the correct order.

2. Finish the Sentence Line-Up ★★

a. Write the following two-word verbs on the board:

hear from
pick on
take after
run into
call on
get along with
look through
get over
look up to

b. Have students line up in two rows opposite each other.

c. Have the first student in the *left* row begin a sentence with one of the verbs on the board. The opposite student in the *right* row must complete the sentence. For example:

Student 1: I heard from . . .
Student 2: my grandmother.

d. Then have the next student in the *right* row begin a sentence with another verb, and the opposite student in the *left* row complete it. For example:

Student 3: He called on . . .
Student 4: the student.

e. Continue going back and forth until all the students have had an opportunity to either begin or complete a sentence.

3. Match the Sentences ★★

a. Make a set of split sentence cards such as the following:

We don't have enough flour to make bread. We ran . . .	out of it.
I see my neighbor all the time. Every day I run . . .	into her.
My house is very messy. I'm going to clean . . .	it up.
I'm confused by my insurance form. I can't figure . . .	it out.
Every morning I take my son to school. I drop . . .	him off.

I don't like this new chair. I'm going to take . . .	it back.
My daughter fights with my son. She always picks . . .	on him.
They were very sick. I hope they got . . .	over it.
He's just like his mother. He takes . . .	after her.
I miss my Aunt Clara. I'd like to hear . . .	from her.
Sam usually gives the correct answer. Teachers like to call . . .	on him.

b. Distribute a card to each student.

c. Have students memorize the sentence portion on their cards, then walk around the room trying to find their corresponding match.

d. Then have pairs of students say their completed sentences aloud to the class.

(continued)

4. Sense or Nonsense? ★★

Use the cards from Activity 3.

a. Mix up the cards and distribute sets of cards to each group, keeping the beginning and ending cards in different piles.

b. Have students take turns picking up one card from each pile and reading the sentence to the group. For example:

I miss my Aunt Clara. I'd like to hear . . .	after her.

c. That group decides if the sentence makes sense or is *nonsense*.

d. After all the cards have been picked, have the groups lay out all the cards and put together all the sentence combinations that make sense.

5. Category Dictation ★★

a. Have students draw two columns on a piece of paper. At the top of one column, have students write <u>Separable</u>, and at the top of the other column, have them write <u>Inseparable</u>.

b. Dictate various two-word verbs from the chapter and have students write them in the appropriate column. For example:

<u>Separable</u>	<u>Inseparable</u>
hang up	hear from
look up	look through
pick out	pick on
take out	take after

6. Synonyms: Guess Who? ★★

a. Write the following two-word verbs on the board:

call on	look up to
get along with	pick on
get over	run into
hear from	run out of
look through	take after

I don't know. Who _____?

b. Read the sentences below and have students respond with an appropriate two-word verb from the list on the board. For example:

Teacher: Guess who I met downtown!
Student: I don't know. Who did you run into?

Sentences:

Guess who I met downtown! *(run into)*
Guess who my little brother was fighting with! *(pick on)*
Guess who wrote me a letter! *(hear from)*
Guess which student Ms. Thomas asked about two-word verbs *(call on)*
Guess who I admire! *(look up to)*
Guess who doesn't have any more paper! *(run out of)*
Guess which of my parents I'm similar to! *(look like/take after)*
Guess who my favorite friends are! *(get along with)*
Guess who doesn't have the flu any more! *(get over)*

7. Create a Story ★★★

a. Put the following on the board:

Julie

b. Set the scene: "Julie is twelve years old. She's a healthy, happy young girl."

c. Ask the following questions about *Julie*. Have students use their imaginations to make up answers.

1. Julie has two younger brothers. Does she pick on them? (When? Why?)
2. Julie is the best student in her class. Does she get embarrassed when the teacher calls on her?

3. How does she get along with the other students in her class?

4. Julie likes to get letters and phone calls. Who does she like to hear from?

5. Who does Julie look up to? Who looks up to Julie?

6. After school Julie likes to go to the drug store and buy a soda. Who does she hope she runs into there?

7. Last year Julie had a boyfriend, but they broke up. Has she gotten over it yet?

8. What's Wrong? ★★★

a. Divide the class into pairs or small groups.

b. Write several sentences such as the following on the board or on a handout. Some of the sentences should be correct, and others incorrect. For example:

I ran into Herbert yesterday.
I ran them into yesterday.
She'll drop them off at 2:00.
I'll fill out it at home.
He doesn't get along with them.
You should write down it.
She doesn't take him after,
The teacher always calls me on.
She got over the flu.
They did their homework over.

c. The object of the activity is for students to identify which sentences are incorrect and then correct them.

d. Have students compare their answers.

Variation: Do the activity as a game with competing teams. The team that successfully completes the task in the shortest time is the winner.

READING *A Child-Rearing Problem*

FOCUS

- Inseparable Two-Word Verbs

NEW VOCABULARY

answer (n)
child rearing (n)
concerned
constantly
eventually
so far

READING THE STORY

Optional: *Preview the story by having students talk about the story title and/or illustration. You may choose to introduce new vocabulary beforehand, or have students encounter the new vocabulary within the context of the reading.*

1. Have students read silently, or follow along silently as the story is read aloud by you, by one or more students, or on the audio program.

2. Ask students if they have any questions. Check understanding of vocabulary.

3. Check students' comprehension, using some or all of the following questions:

    How do Timmy and his little sister Patty get along with each other?
    What do they constantly do?
    When does he pick on her?
    When does she pick on him?

Why are their parents concerned?
How have they looked for an answer to their problem?
Have they been successful so far?
What are they hoping?

READING EXTENSION

Child-Rearing Advice

1. Divide the class into pairs and ask them to write a list of advice for the parents.

2. Have the pairs share their lists with the class. As they talk, write their ideas on the board and discuss them as a class.

✓ READING *CHECK-UP*

TRUE, FALSE, OR MAYBE?

1. False

2. True

3. True

4. False

5. Maybe

CHOOSE

Before doing the exercise, introduce the word *kiss*.

1. a

2. a

3. b

4. b

5. a

6. b

7. a

8. b

ROLE PLAY *May I Help You?*

FOCUS

- Review: Separable and Inseparable Two-Word Verbs

ROLE PLAY

1. Set the scene: "A salesman in a department store is talking to a customer."

2. Go over the conversational model. Introduce the following new vocabulary:

baggy	regular
dressing room	selection
extra large	size
fit	tight
loose	try on
medium	usual
narrow	within
No problem at all.	You're in luck.
plain	

Language Note

May I help you?, *I think I'll take (it/them)*, and *Thanks for your help* are expressions that are typically used in shopping situations.

3. Present Exercise 1 at the bottom of text page 127 with a student. Then do Choral Repetition practice.

4. Divide the class into pairs, and have students practice Exercises 1–3.

5. Call on pairs of students to present their role plays.

Example

1. A. May I help you?
   B. Yes, please. I'm looking for a suit.
   A. What size do you wear?
   B. *(Size 40.)*
   A. Here. How do you like this one?
   B. Hmm. I think it's a little too *(dark)*. Do have any suits that are a little *(lighter)*?
   A. Yes. We have a wide selection. Why don't you look through all of our suits on your own and pick out the one you like?
   A. Can I try it on?
   B. Of course. You can try it on in the dressing room over there.

[5 minutes later]

   A. Well, how does it fit?
   B. I'm afraid it's a little too *(short)*. Do you have any suits that are a little *(longer)*?
   A. Yes, we do. I think you'll like THIS suit. It's a little *(longer)* than the one you just tried on.
   B. Will you take it back if I decide to return it?
   A. Of course. No problem at all. Just bring it back within *(10)* days, and we'll give you your money back.
   B. Fine. I think I'll take it. How much does it cost?
   A. The usual price is *(200)* dollars. But you're in luck! We're having a sale this week, and all of our suits are *(20)* percent off the regular price.
   B. That's a real bargain! I'm glad I decided to buy a suit this week. Thanks for your help.

6. **Exercise 4:** For homework, have students write a new role play with any article of clothing they wish. Encourage students to use dictionaries to find new words they wish to use. Have students act out their role plays in the next class.

WORKBOOK

Page 108

READING *On Sale*

FOCUS

- Separable and Inseparable Two-Word Verbs

NEW VOCABULARY

button	notice	trousers
final	on sale	walk home
go with	plaid	zipper
happiness	refund (n)	
men's clothing store	refuse (v)	

READING THE STORY

Optional: *Preview the story by having students talk about the story title and/or illustrations. You may choose to introduce new vocabulary beforehand, or have students encounter the new vocabulary within the context of the reading.*

1. Have students read silently, or follow along silently as the story is read aloud by you, by one or more students, or on the audio program

2. Ask students if they have any questions. Check understanding of vocabulary.

3. Check students' comprehension, using some or all of the following questions:

> Why did Gary go to a men's clothing store yesterday?
> What did he look through?
> What did he pick out first?
> How did it fit?
> What did he pick out next?

How did it fit?
Finally, what did he pick out?
How did it fit?
Then what did he decide to buy?
What did he look through?
What did he pick out first?
How did they fit?
What did he pick out next?
How did they fit?
Finally, what did he pick out?
How did they fit?
Why was Gary especially happy?
Why didn't Gary's happiness last very long?
What did he do the next day?
Why did the people at the store refuse to give him his money back?
What will Gary do the next time he buys something on sale?

✓ READING *CHECK-UP*

WHAT'S THE SEQUENCE?

1. Gary went shopping for clothes yesterday.

2. Gary picked out a few jackets he really liked.

3. The brown jacket seemed to fit perfectly.

4. He picked out several pairs of trousers.

5. A pair of plaid pants fit very well.

6. He paid only half of the regular price.

7. He walked home feeling very happy.

8. But then, Gary noticed problems with the jacket and the pants.

9. Gary went back and asked for a refund.

10. The store refused to give him back his money.

11. He walked home feeling very upset and angry.

READING EXTENSION

Consumer Advice

1. Have pairs of students write a list of advice for Gary (or any other consumer). For example:

   > Always read the signs next to the cashier.
   > Always ask about the store's return policy.
   > Look for holes in the clothes.
   > Keep your receipt.

2. Have pairs of students share their lists with the class. As they talk, write their ideas on the board.

How About You?

Have students do the activity in pairs or as a class.

 LISTENING

Listen and choose what the people are talking about.

1. A. Where can I try them on?
   B. The dressing room is over there.

2. A. Now remember, you can't bring them back!
   B. I understand.

3. A. Have you filled it out yet?
   B. No. I'm having some trouble. Can you help me?

4. A. Please drop them off at the school by eight o'clock.
   B. By eight o'clock? Okay.

5. A. Where should I hang them?
   B. What about over the fireplace?

6. A. Have you thought it over?
   B. Yes, I have.

7. A. It's cold in here.
   B. You're right. I'll turn it on.

8. A. Should we use it up?
   B. No. Let's throw it out.

9. A. What are you going to do?
   B. I'm going to turn it down.

Answers

1. a
2. a
3. a
4. b
5. a
6. b
7. b
8. a
9. b

PRONUNCIATION *Linking "t" Between Vowels*

> The consonant "t" is pronounced with a flapped [d] sound when it occurs between vowels.

Focus on Listening

Practice the sentences in the left column. Say each sentence or play the audio one or more times. Have students listen carefully and repeat.

Focus on Pronunciation

Practice the sentences in the right column. Have students say each sentence and then listen carefully as you say it or play the audio.

If you wish, have students continue practicing the sentences to improve their pronunciation.

JOURNAL

Have students write their journal entries at home or in class. Encourage students to use a dictionary to look up words they would like to use. Students can share their written work with other students if appropriate. Have students discuss what they have written as a class, in pairs, or in small groups

GRAMMAR FOCUS

Answers

1. throw them out
2. heard from them
3. hook it up
4. fill it out
5. calls on me
6. get over it
7. took it out
8. put them away
9. ran into him
10. get along with them
11. take them back

CONVERSATION

1 *Identifying Sale Prices & Bargains*

1. Have students look at the photo. Ask: "Where are they?" (They're in a store.) "What's the customer doing?" (She's pointing to a sign.) Have students look at each sign. Model the pronunciation and have students repeat. Introduce the words *bargain, clearance, exchange* (v), *half-price,* and *reduced.*

2. Model Conversation 1 with a student volunteer.

   A. Excuse me. I think that price is wrong.
   B. It is?
   A. Yes. The sign on the rack says "20% off."
   B. Okay. Let me check.

3. In pairs, have students practice the conversations as you circulate around the classroom.

4. Call on pairs of students to present their conversations to the class.

CONVERSATION

2 *Returning & Exchanging Defective Products*

1. Ask the class: "What do you do when you buy something and then realize that it's defective (broken)?" Write students' ideas on the board. Introduce the words *missing* (adj), *sleeve,* and *stained.*

2. Model Conversation 1 with a student volunteer.

   A. I'd like to return this coat.
   B. What's the matter with it?
   A. Two buttons are missing.
   B. Would you like to exchange it?
   A. No, thank you. I'd like a refund, please. Here's my receipt.

3. In pairs, have students practice the conversations as you circulate around the classroom.

4. Call on pairs of students to present their conversations to the class.

TEAMWORK

Call on a student volunteer to read the directions aloud. Have students work in pairs to write down their ideas and then practice conversations about returning items. Have each pair present an original conversation to the class.

LIFE SKILLS ENRICHMENT

Speaking with a Cashier

Life Skills Worksheet 36

Make copies of Life Skills Worksheet 36 and give one to each student. Have students complete the worksheet as homework. In the next class, have students compare their answers in pairs.

EXPANSION ACTIVITIES

1. Scrambled Dialogs: Speaking with a Cashier ★

Activity Master 62

Divide the class into pairs. Make multiple copies of Activity Master 62, cut them into cards, and give one set of cards to each pair. Tell students that there are two conversations on this Activity Master. Have the partners sort and reorder the conversations. Then call on two different pairs of students to read a conversation aloud while the others listen to check for accuracy.

2. Disappearing Dialog ★★

Write one of the model conversations on the board and ask for two student volunteers to read the conversation. Erase a few of the words from the dialog and have two different students read the conversation. Erase more words and call on two more students to read the conversation. Continue erasing words and calling on pairs of students until everyone has had a turn and the dialog has *disappeared*.

3. Pair Interviews ★★

Write the following questions on the board. Have students interview each other in pairs and then report back to the class. Make a list on the board of the names of students' favorite stores and the times of the best sales.

What's your favorite clothing store?
What stores have good clothing sales?
What time of year are there good clothing sales?
Have you ever had a problem returning an item? What happened?

4. Role Play ★★★

Activity Master 63

a. Make multiple copies of Activity Master 63. Cut the role-play cards into A cards and B cards and clip each role play (1 or 2) together.

b. Divide the class into pairs. Give each partner one set of role-play cards—A or B. Tell students they have five minutes to act out the role play.

c. As students are acting out their role plays, circulate to help as necessary.

d. After five minutes, call on a few pairs to perform their role plays for the class.

MULTILEVEL VARIATION ★★/★★★

If *at-level* or *above-level* students finish their role plays quickly, give them the other set of role-play cards.

5. Dictate and Discuss ★★★

Divide the class into pairs. Dictate sentences such as the following and have students discuss whether they agree or disagree with the statements.

February and August are the best months for clothing sales.
Clothing on sale is usually *defective*.
Buy one, get one free is the same as 50% off.
Stores have to accept returns.

1. Point to the advertisements on student text page 130b. Ask: "What are these?" (Advertisements for clothing stores.) Introduce the new words: *anniversary sale, designer* (adj), *discount, discount store, dress shirt, half price, merchandise, running shoes, save, savings* (n), *select* (adj), and *super* (adj).

2. Have students work individually to complete the comprehension exercise and then compare answers in pairs, small groups, or as a class.

MULTILEVEL VARIATION ★

Have *below-level* students work on the reading and questions in pairs to provide each other with more support.

Answers

1. B	**4.** C
2. D	**5.** A
3. A	**6.** D

TEAMWORK

For homework, have students cut out clothing sale ads from the newspaper and bring them to class. In pairs, have students compare prices of products on sale. Ask students to identify the best prices and sales and then share their findings with the class.

LIFE SKILLS ENRICHMENT

Sale Prices

Life Skills Worksheet 37

Make copies of Life Skills Worksheet 37 and give one to each student. Have students complete the worksheet as homework. In the next class, have students compare their answers in pairs.

1. Scrambled Words ★

a. Choose words or phrases from the advertisement on student text page 130b and write them on the board or on a card with the letters scrambled out of order. For example:

b. Have students take turns guessing what the word or phrase is. [reduced]

Variation 1: Do the activity in pairs or small groups, with students taking turns scrambling words for others to guess.

Variation 2: Do the activity as a class game with competing teams.

2. True or False Sale Prices ★★

Make statements about the advertisements on student text page 130b and have students decide whether the statements are true or false. If a statement is false, have students correct it. For example:

The sale price on the Rockwell running shoes is better at Watson's. [False. It's better at Perry's.]
Men's dress shirts are 33.3% off at Watson's. [True.]
You save $1.98 if you buy two Ellen Clare tee shirts at Perry's. [True.]
Perry's has better prices on men's dress shirts. [True.]
You save $8 on women's tee shirts at Watson's. [False. You save $7.]

Variation: Do the activity as a game with competing teams.

3. How Much Do You Remember? ★★

a. Write the following clothing types on the board:

Skirts
Dress Shirts
Running Shoes
Tee Shirts
Jeans

b. Divide the class into pairs. Have students close their books and retell to each other what they remember about the prices at Watson's and Perry's department stores on student text page 130b. Then have them open their books and check to see how much they remembered.

4. Telephone ★★

Divide the class into large groups. Have each group sit in a circle. Whisper a short message to one student in each group. For example:

"There's a big sale at Tyler's Department Store. Clearance items are 75% off. Shoes are 'buy one, get one free.' And all jackets are 'buy one, get one half price!'"

The first student whispers the message to the second student, who whispers it to the third student, and so forth around the circle. When the story gets to the last person, that student says it aloud. Is it the same message you started with? The group with the most accurate message wins.

5. Information Gap ★★★

Activity Master 64

a. Make multiple copies of Activity Master 64 and cut them in half (Ad A and Ad B).

b. Divide the class into pairs. Give each partner a different Activity Master—A or B. Have students share their information and fill in their ads. For example:

A. What's the discount on men's pants?

B. 30% off.

c. When the pairs have finished completing their ads, have them look at their partner's Activity Master to make sure they have written the information correctly.

MULTILEVEL VARIATION ★★★

If *above-level* students finish early, have them decide what they could buy at Lucy's Department Store for $75.

1. Point to the coupons on student text page 130c. Ask: "What are these?" (Coupons.) "What kind of store are they for?" (A supermarket.)   Then ask questions such as the following to get students oriented to the information on the coupons. "What's the expiration date of the coupon on Pollyanna Jam?" "How much do you save on a dozen eggs with the coupon?"

2. Introduce the new words: *coupon, expire, organic, purchase* (n), and *single.*

3. Have students work individually to complete the comprehension exercise and then compare answers in pairs, small groups, or as a class.

MULTILEVEL VARIATION ★

Have *below-level* students work on the reading and questions in pairs to provide each other with more support.

Answers

1. B	**5.** D
2. D	**6.** C
3. C	**7.** A
4. B	**8.** C

TEAMWORK

For homework, have students find food product coupons and bring them to class. In pairs, have students compare their coupons for similar products. Ask students to identify the best coupon values and then share their findings with the class. (Be sure to encourage students to actually use the coupons the next time they go to the supermarket!)

LIFE SKILLS ENRICHMENT

Coupon Math

Life Skills Worksheet 38

Make copies of Life Skills Worksheet 38 and give one to each student. Have students complete the worksheet as homework. In the next class, have students compare their answers in pairs.

EXPANSION ACTIVITIES

1. Brainstorming: Where to Find Coupons ★

Have the class brainstorm where they can find coupons. Write students' ideas on the board. Then have students rank these coupon sources from one to four, with one being the most common. For example:

1. newspaper
2. supermarket circulars in stores
3. Internet
4. mail

2. True or False? ★★

Make statements about the coupons on student text page 130c and have students decide whether the statements are true or false. If a statement is false, have students correct it. For example:

The Pollyanna Jam coupon is valid until September 18, 2012. [True.]
The coupon for Bob & Joe's Ice Cream expires on August 10, 2012.
    [False. It expires October 8, 2012.]
You save 50 cents on each pint of ice cream if you buy two pints of Bob & Joe's Ice Cream with the coupon. [True.]
You can save 70 cents when you buy two jars of jam. [False. The coupon is for only one jar of jam.]

Variation: Do the activity as a game with competing teams.

3. Food Shopping Survey ★★★

Activity Master 65

a. Make multiple copies of Activity Master 65 and give one to each student.

b. Have students interview their classmates. The interviewer should record the answers and write the additional comments on the Activity Master.

c. When students have completed their interviews, have them work in small groups to tally up the responses. Have them report their findings to the class.

d. Follow up with a class discussion of the following questions:

What are the most common ways to save money on food?
Are money-saving strategies different for people with large families than for people who live alone? How are they different?
Who does the food shopping more often—men or women?

4. Advantages and Disadvantages ★★★

Activity Master 66

a. Divide the class into groups of three. Make multiple copies of Activity Master 66 and distribute one to each group.

b. Have students talk about the advantages and disadvantages of using food coupons. Have one student in each group take notes on the Activity Master. For example:

Using Food Coupons	
Advantages (+)	Disadvantages (−)
Save money on brand names.	Coupons are easy to lose.

c. Have students tell the class their ideas.

CHECK-UP TEST

Have students do the check-up test and then review the answers as a class.

Answers

1. C	**6.** D
2. B	**7.** C
3. A	**8.** B
4. C	**9.** A
5. D	**10.** C

SKILLS CHECK

Words:

Explain to students that this is a list of two-word verbs and words they have learned in the unit. Have students take turns reading each item aloud to the class. Have students put a check next to the item if they feel they have learned it. Encourage students to get a small notebook where they can write down words that are difficult for them.

I can:

Explain to students that this is a list of skills they have learned in the unit. Read each item aloud to the class. Ask individual students or pairs of students to demonstrate the skill. For example:

    Teacher: I can ask and answer: How do they fit?
Student A: How do they fit?
Student B: They're too short.

    Teacher: I can return defective products.
Student A: I'd like to return this shirt.
Student B: What's the matter with it?
Student A: It's stained.
Student B: Would you like to exchange it?
Student A: No, thank you. I'd like a refund, please. Here's my receipt.

Have students put a check next to the item if they feel they have learned it. Use this information to determine which lessons you may want to review or reinforce for the entire class or for particular students.

EXPANSION ACTIVITIES

1. Do You Remember the Verbs? ★

Check students' retention of the vocabulary depicted on the opening page of Unit 9 by doing the following activity:

a. Have students open their books to page 115 and cover the list of verbs.

b. Either call out a number and have students tell you the verb, or say a verb and have students tell you the number.

Variation: You can also do this activity as a game with competing teams.

2. Category Dictation ★★

a. Have students make two columns on a piece of paper and write the following at the top of each column:

    Separable
    Inseparable

b. Dictate two-word verbs from the unit and have students write them in the appropriate column. For example:

Separable	Inseparable
pick out	call on
try on	look through
take back	run into
hook up	get over
throw away	pick on
take off	hear from
turn off	look for

c. As a class, in pairs, or in small groups, have students check their work.

3. Miming Game ★★

Activity Master 67

a. Make a copy of Activity Master 67, cut it into cards, and place the cards face down in a pile on a desk or table in the front of the room.

b. Have pairs of students take turns coming to the front of the room, picking a card from the pile, and pantomiming the action on the card. The class must guess the action.

Variation: Do the activity as a game with competing teams.

4. Scrambled Sentences ★★

Activity Master 68

Divide the class into pairs. Make enough copies of Activity Master 68 for half the class. Cut them into cards and distribute one set of cards to each pair of students. Have students take turns picking up a scrambled sentence prompt and then saying the sentence in the correct order.

Variation: Students can write their sentences and then compare their answers with other pairs.

5. Finish the Sentence! ★★

Begin a sentence using a two-word verb from Unit 9 and have students repeat what you said and add appropriate endings. For example:

Teacher: He's going to pick . . .
Student 1: He's going to pick up the kids.
Student 2: He's going to pick out a new color
for the dining room.

6. Board Game ★★

Activity Master 69

For this activity, you will need a die, markers, and a piece of paper. (If students use a coin as a die, the class should decide which side of the coin will indicate a move of one space and which will indicate a move of two spaces.)

a. Make multiple copies of Activity Master 69. Divide the class into small groups and give each group a copy of Activity Master 69 along with a die, markers, and a piece of paper.

b. Have students place their markers on *Start*. The group should decide who goes first. That student begins the game by rolling the die or flipping the coin and moving his or her marker. If the student responds to the question or task correctly, he or she may take one more turn. If the student doesn't respond correctly, the next student takes a turn. No one may take more than two turns at a time.

Option 1: The first person to reach *Finish* is the winner.

Option 2: The game continues until each student reaches *Finish*. This way everybody is a winner.

7. Dialog Builder! ★★★

a. Divide the class into pairs. Write a line on the board from a conversation such as the following:

It completely slipped my mind!

Other possible lines are:

I'm afraid I can't.
No, I don't think so.
Oh, no! I forgot!
May I help you?
I think the price is wrong.
What's the matter with it?

b. Have each pair create a conversation incorporating that line. Students can begin and end their conversations any way they wish, but they must include that line in their dialogs.

c. Call on students to present their conversations to the class.

(continued)

8. What's Wrong? ★★★

a. Write several sentences such as the following on the board or on a handout that you give to students. Some of the sentences should be correct and others incorrect. For example:

I have to take back them to the library.
I have to pick up my car at the repair shop.
She's going to bring back it sometime
   next week.
I'm going to hook it up later.
Did you remember to turn on the alarm?
I'll turn on it right away.
I think you should think over it.
They heard her from last week.
She ran it out of last week.
I like to return this coat.
What's the problem with it?
Would you like exchange it?

b. Divide the class into pairs. The object of the activity is for students to identify which sentences are incorrect and then correct them. Have students compare their answers in small groups.

Variation: Do the activity as a game with competing teams. For each team's turn, write one sentence on the board and have the team decide whether the sentence is correct or not. If it isn't correct, the team must correct it. Every time a team is right, that team receives one point. The team with the greatest number of points wins.

MULTILEVEL VARIATION ★

For *below-level* students, underline the errors and have the below-level pairs focus only on correcting them.

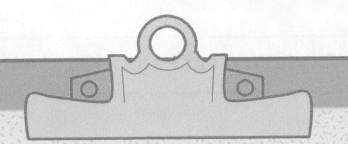

Teacher's Notes

GRAMMAR

CONNECTORS:

Too/So

I'm hungry.	I am, too. So am I.
I can swim.	I can, too. So can I.
I've seen that movie.	I have, too. So have I.
I have a car.	I do, too. So do I.
I worked yesterday.	I did, too. So did I.

EITHER/NEITHER

I'm not hungry.	I'm not either. Neither am I.
I can't swim.	I can't either. Neither can I.
I've haven't seen that movie.	I haven't either. Neither have I.
I don't have a car.	I don't either. Neither do I.
I didn't work.	I didn't either. Neither did I.

BUT

I don't sing, **but** my sister does.	
She didn't know the answer, **but** I did.	
He can play chess, **but** I can't.	
We're ready, **but** they aren't.	

I'm tired,	and he is, too. and so is he.
He'll be busy,	and she will, too. and so will she.
She's been sick,	and he has, too. and so has he.
They sing,	and she does, too. and so does she.
She studied,	and I did, too. and so did I.

I'm not tired,	and he isn't either. and neither is he.
He won't be busy,	and she won't either. and neither will she.
She hasn't been sick,	and he hasn't either. and neither has he.
They don't sing,	and she doesn't either. and neither does she.
She didn't study,	and I didn't either. and neither did I.

FUNCTIONS

ASKING FOR AND REPORTING INFORMATION

How do you know *Mr. and Mrs. Randall*?

Have you heard *tomorrow's weather forecast*?

Where were you when *the accident happened*?
  I was *standing on the corner*.

Tell me about *your skills*.
Have you had any *special vocational training*?
When can you *start*?

SHARING NEWS ABOUT SOMEONE

Have you heard about *Harry*?
Have you heard the news about *Harry*?
Have you heard what happened to *Harry*?

EXPRESSING LIKES

I like *peppermint ice cream*.

He enjoys *sports*.

EXPRESSING DISLIKES

I don't like *macaroni and cheese*.
I don't like *fairy tales* very much.

INQUIRING ABOUT WANT–DESIRE

Why do *you and your husband* want to *enroll in my dance class*?

What *do you and Greg* want to *talk to me about*?

Why don't *you and your friends* want to *come to the game*?

EXPRESSING WANT–DESIRE

He wants *this parking space*.

She doesn't want to *take the garbage out*.

INQUIRING ABOUT ABILITY

Can you *baby-sit for us tomorrow night*?

EXPRESSING ABILITY

I can *speak four languages fluently*.

EXPRESSING INABILITY

I can't *skate* very well.

I won't be able to *go bowling next Saturday*.

INQUIRING ABOUT INTENTION

What *are you and your brother* going to do *when you grow up*?

EXPRESSING INTENTION

I'm going to *start an Internet company*.

EXTENDING AN INVITATION

Are you interested in *seeing a movie tonight*?

DESCRIBING

My sister and I are exactly the same.
My sister and I are very different.

I'm *tall and thin*.
I have *brown eyes and black curly hair*.

She's very *outgoing and popular*.

INQUIRING ABOUT FEELINGS–EMOTIONS

Why *do you and your sister* look so frightened?

Why were *you and your wife* so nervous?

EXPRESSING APPRECIATION

I appreciate that.
That's very kind of you.
That's very nice of you.

NEW VOCABULARY

Verbs

accomplish
afford
allow
analyze
balance
beat (v)
behave
calculate
care about
commute
compare
deserve
develop
discuss
expect
explain
find out
help (someone) with
hide
interest
lay off
lift up
lose interest
major (in)
move ahead
offer
organize
pay attention
prefer
press
put down
research
respect
search
speak up
support
tend (to)
think ahead
walk *their* dog

Adjectives

academic
advanced
allergic (to)
appropriate
available
basic
certain
compatible
concise
conservative
creative
cultural
entry-level
equal
familiar
frightened
hands-on
hardworking
hopeful
ironed
lenient
liberal
main
opposed to
pessimistic
philosophical
professional
professional-looking
similar
strict
vocational
willing

Adverbs

clearly
creatively
differently
far
fluently
lately
safely

Performing Arts

dance class
theater group

Politics

defense
energy
equal rights
government
minorities
nuclear energy
rights

Business/ Employment

business English
business letter
business office
business plan
business procedures
business trip
business world
business writing
entrepreneurship
evaluation
Internet company
job opening
job performance
  evaluation
layoff (n)
meeting
memo
payroll
skill
time management
training program
typing skills
wages

(continued)

want ad
yearly evaluation

Schooling

adult education course
assignment
background
catalog
educational
evening class
homework assignment
prerequisite
training
vocational training

Computers

computer class
computer skills
electronic mail
Excel spreadsheet
keyboarding skills
Microsoft Outlook
Microsoft Word
PowerPoint
software
spreadsheet
Word
word processing software

Health/Medical

cardiopulmonary resuscitation
cut (n)
emergency care procedure
first aid
health regulation
health science
poison
Red Cross certification

People

salesman
school nurse
food and beverage specialist

Performing Arts

dance class
theater group

Politics

defense
energy
equal rights
government
minorities
nuclear energy
rights

Food

culinary arts
macaroni and cheese
peppermint ice cream

Miscellaneous

ability
act (n)
alarm system
appearance
attitude
background
basics
checkbook
code
coincidence
collection
conference
despite
fairy tale
features
feedback
filter
fingernails
flyer
glass
graph
grooming
group
ice skating (n)
introduction
lid
lighting

neither
newsletter
on button
opportunity
original
outlook
overseas
parking space
personality
point of view
procedure
profession
project
public speaking
quality
reason
shock
situation
speech
start button
success
surprise (n)
telephone skills
thunder
travel reservation
turn (n)
use (n)
variety
whatever
winter sport
worksheet

EXPRESSIONS

an hour a day
as the days go by
by any chance
for the past few days
go through some difficult times
have a lot in common
"made for each other"
on the weekend
out of town
outlook on life
"touchy subject"
What a coincidence!
you can see why

VOCABULARY PREVIEW

You may want to introduce these words before beginning the unit, or you may choose to wait until they first occur in a specific lesson. If you choose to introduce them at this point, here are some suggestions:

1. Have students look at the illustrations on text page 131 and identify the words they already know.

2. Present the vocabulary. Say each word and have the class repeat it chorally and individually. Check students' understanding and pronunciation of the words.

3. Practice the vocabulary as a class, in pairs, or in small groups. Have students cover the word list and look at the pictures. Practice the words in the following ways:

   • Say a word and have students tell the number of the illustration.

   • Give the number of an illustration and have students say the word.

FOCUS

• *So, Too* in 1st person Expressions:

$$I \left\{ \begin{array}{l} am \\ can \\ have \\ do \\ did \end{array} \right\}, too.$$

$$So \left\{ \begin{array}{l} am \\ can \\ have \\ do \\ did \end{array} \right\} I.$$

CLOSE UP

RULE:	The expressions *so* and *too* are interchangeable in meaning, but they require different word orders. *Too* comes at the end of the sentence and is preceded by a comma. *So* reverses the word order, with the verb preceding the subject.
EXAMPLES:	I'm tired. **I am, too.** **So am I.**

RULE:	The auxiliary verb replaces and agrees with the initial verb phrase.

EXAMPLES:	*(To Be)*	I **am** happy.	So **am** I.	I **am**, too.
	(Past Continuous)	I **was** watching.	So **was** I.	I **was**, too.
	(Future: Will)	I'**ll be** busy.	So **will** I.	I **will**, too.
	(Present Perfect)	I'**ve been** sick.	So **have** I.	I **have**, too.
	(Simple Present)	I **have** an exam	So **do** I.	I **do**, too.
	(Simple Past)	I **missed** the bus.	So **did** I.	I **did**, too.

INTRODUCING THE MODEL

1. Have students look at the model illustration.

2. Set the scene: "Two friends are talking about a problem they both have."

3. Present the model twice, once with each expression in the brackets.

4. Full-Class Repetition.

5. Ask students if they have any questions.

Check understanding of the expressions *allergic (to), What a coincidence!*

6. Group Choral Repetition.

7. Choral Conversation.

8. Call on one or two pairs of students to present the dialog. Have students practice both of the expressions with the model.

(For additional practice, do Choral Conversation in small groups or by rows.)

9. Practice the expressions in the boxes at the top of the page. There are five short dialogs (each with a statement and a response). For each:

a. Present the dialog, and have students repeat chorally. Then call on pairs of students to present the dialog.

b. Write on the board:

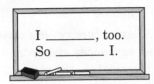

I _____, too.
So _____ I.

Have students close their books. Read each statement. Then, point to the expressions on the board and call on students to form correct responses. For example:

Teacher: I'm hungry.
Student: I am, too.

Teacher: I'm hungry.
Student: So am I.

SIDE BY SIDE EXERCISES

Examples

1. A. I'm a vegetarian.
   B. What a coincidence!
      I am, too./So am I.

2. A. I like peppermint ice cream.
   B. What a coincidence!
      I do, too./So do I.

1. Exercise 1: Call on two pairs of students to present the dialog. Have each pair use a different expression of agreement.

2. Exercise 2: Introduce the expression *peppermint ice cream*. Same as above.

3. Exercises 3–8: Either Full-Class Practice or Pair Practice. Have students practice both possible expressions for each exercise.

New Vocabulary

3. fluently
5. business trip
6. lately

4. Exercise 9: Have students use the model as a guide to create their own conversations, using vocabulary of their choice. Encourage students to use dictionaries to find new words they want to use. This exercise can be done orally in class or for written homework. If you assign it for homework, do one example in class to make sure students understand what's expected. Have students present their conversations in class the next day.

WORKBOOK

Pages 109–110

EXPANSION ACTIVITIES

1. Match the Sentences ★★

a. Make a set of split sentence cards such as the following:

I went to the ballgame.	So did I.
I'll be on vacation next week.	I will, too.
I had already done that.	I had, too.
I can play tennis very well.	I can, too.
I've got to leave now.	So do I.
I'm going to see the play.	I am, too.
I was at a play last night.	So was I.
I've worked hard this week.	So have I.

b. Distribute a card to each student.

c. Have students memorize the sentences on their cards, then walk around the room trying to find their corresponding match.

d. Then have pairs of students say their matching sentences aloud to the class.

2. Concentration ★

a. Using the cards from Activity 1, place the first sentences face down in two rows of 4 each. In a different area, place the second sentences face down in two rows of 4 each.

b. Divide the class into two teams. The object of the game is for students to find the matching cards. Both teams should be able to see all the cards, since *concentrating* on their location is an important part of playing the game.

c. A student from Team 1 turns over a card from each group (first sentences and second sentences). If they match, the student picks up the cards, that team gets a point, and the student takes another turn. If the cards don't match, the student turns them face down, and a member of Team 2 takes a turn.

d. The game continues until all the cards have been matched. The team with the most correct matches wins the game.

Variation: This game can also be played in groups and pairs.

3. Grammar Chain ★★

a. Write the following conversation model on the board:

A. I _____.
B. What a coincidence! So _____ I.

b. Start the chain game by saying:

Teacher (to Student A): I like to watch scary movies.

c. Student A answers according to the model on the board and then makes a different statement to Student B, and the chain continues. For example

Student A: What a coincidence! So do I.
(to Student B): I've studied the guitar for two years.

Student B: What a coincidence! So have I.
(to Student C): I went to the Baxter Boys concert last night.

Etc.

4. So Do I! ★★

a. Have each student write one sentence about a favorite weekend activity beginning with *I like*...

b. Have students take turns reading their sentences aloud to the class—for example, "I like to go camping." Any other students in the class who genuinely like to do the same thing on the weekend respond by saying "I do, too."

c. Count the number of students who agree with each statement. What are the most popular weekend activities in the class?

Text Page 133: What a Coincidence!

FOCUS

- *Either, Neither* in 1st Person Expressions:

$$\left.\begin{array}{l} I'm\ not \\ I\ can't \\ I\ haven't \\ I\ don't \\ I\ didn't \end{array}\right\} either. \qquad Neither \left\{\begin{array}{l} am \\ can \\ have \\ do \\ did \end{array}\right\} I.$$

CLOSE UP

RULE:	The expressions *either* and *neither* are interchangeable in meaning, but they require different word orders. *Either* comes at the end of the sentence. *Neither* reverses the word order, with the verb preceding the subject.
EXAMPLES:	I'm not hungry. **I'm not either.** **Neither am I.**
RULE:	A negative verb is used with *either*, and an affirmative verb is used with *neither*.
EXAMPLES:	I didn't work. I did**n't either.** **Neither** did I.

PRESENTING THE MODEL

1. Have students look at the model illustration.

2. Set the scene: "Two people are dancing."

3. Present the model twice, once with each expression in the brackets.

4. Full-Class Repetition.

5. Ask students if they have any questions. Check understanding of vocabulary.

6. Group Choral Repetition.

7. Choral Conversation.

8. Call on one or two pairs of students to present the dialog. Have students practice both of the expressions with the model.

(For additional practice, do Choral Conversation in small groups or by rows.)

9. Practice the expressions in the boxes at the top of the page. There are five short dialogs (each with a statement and a response). For each:

a. Present the dialog, and have students repeat chorally. Then call on pairs of students to present the dialog.

b. Write on the board:

> I _____ either.
> Neither _____ I.

Have students close their books. Read each statement. Then, point to the expressions on the board and call on students to form correct responses. For example:

Teacher: I'm not hungry.
Student: I'm not either.

Teacher: I'm not hungry.
Student: Neither am I.

SIDE BY SIDE EXERCISES

Examples

1. A. I don't like macaroni and cheese.
   B. What a coincidence!
      I don't either./Neither do I.

2. A. I didn't see the stop sign.
   B. What a coincidence!
      I didn't either./Neither did I.

1. **Exercise 1:** Introduce the expression *macaroni and cheese*. Call on two students to present the dialog. Then do Choral Repetition and Choral Conversation practice.

Culture Note

Macaroni and cheese is a common food served to children in school cafeterias.

2. **Exercise 2:** Same as above.

3. **Exercises 3–8:** Either Full Class Practice or Pair Practice. Have students practice both possible expressions for each exercise.

4. **Exercise 9:** Have students use the model as a guide to create their own conversations, using vocabulary of their choice. Encourage students to use dictionaries to find new words they want to use. This exercise can be done orally in class or for written homework. If you assign it for homework, do one example in class to make sure students understand what's expected. Have students present their conversations in class the next day.

WORKBOOK

Pages 111–112

EXPANSION ACTIVITIES

1. Match the Sentences ★★

a. Make a set of split sentence cards such as the following:

I didn't like the movie.	Neither did I.
I won't be in class tomorrow.	Neither will I.
I had never done that.	I hadn't either.
I wasn't feeling well yesterday.	I wasn't either.
I can't ski very well.	Neither can I.

I'm not going to get there on time.	Neither am I.
I don't have to work tonight.	I don't either.
I haven't been to Moscow.	I haven't either.

b. Distribute a card to each student.

c. Have students memorize the sentences on their cards, then walk around the room trying to find their corresponding match.

d. Then have pairs of students say their matching sentences aloud to the class.

(continued)

2. Concentration ★

a. Using the cards from Activity 1, place the first sentences face down in two rows of 4 each. In a different area, place the second sentences face down in two rows of 4 each.

b. Divide the class into two teams. The object of the game is for students to find the matching cards. Both teams should be able to see all the cards, since *concentrating* on their location is an important part of playing the game.

c. A student from Team 1 turns over a card from each group (first sentences and second sentences). If they match, the student picks up the cards, that team gets a point, and the student takes another turn. If the cards don't match, the student turns them face down, and a member of Team 2 takes a turn.

d. The game continues until all the cards have been matched. The team with the most correct matches wins the game.

Variation: This game can also be played in groups and pairs.

3. Grammar Chain ★★

a. Write the following conversation model on the board:

> A. I _____.
> B. What a coincidence!
>   Neither _____ I.
>   *or*
>   So _____ I.

b. Start the chain game by saying:

> Teacher (*to Student A*): I *didn't sleep well last night.*

c. Student A answers according to the model on the board and then makes a different statement (either positive or negative) to Student B, and the chain continues. For example:

> Student A: What a coincidence! Neither did I.
> (*to Student B*): I've been studying very hard.
>
> Student B: What a coincidence! So have I.
> (*to Student C*): I didn't eat a big breakfast this morning.
>
>   Etc.

4. Neither Do I! ★★

a. Choose a category (for example: foods, celebrities, household chores) and have each student write one negative sentence beginning with *I don't like . . .*

b. Have students take turns reading their sentences aloud to the class—for example, "I don't like eggs." Any other students in the class who genuinely agree with that statement respond by saying: "Neither do I."

c. Count the number of students who agree with each statement. What are the least popular (*foods/celebrities/household chores*) in the class?

FOCUS

- Expressions with *So* and *Too* with All Pronouns

GETTING READY

Practice the 3rd person singular with a variety of tenses.

1. Write on the board:

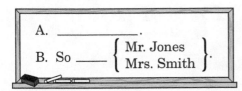

2. Set the scene: "A school needs to hire a new language teacher. Two people want the job: Mr. Jones and Mrs. Smith. Let's talk about them."

3. Read the statements below and have students respond, using line *B* of the model on the board.

> Mrs. Smith *studied* Spanish in Madrid and French in Paris. *(So did Mr. Jones.)*

> Mr. Jones *has studied* in many countries around the world. *(So has Mrs. Smith.)*

> By the time Mr. Jones was sixteen, he *had already studied* many languages. *(So had Mrs. Smith.)*

> Mrs. Smith *is teaching* in England now. *(So is Mr. Jones.)*

> Mr. Jones *teaches* there every summer. *(So does Mrs. Smith.)*

> Mrs. Smith *is going to write* a book soon. *(So is Mr. Jones.)*

> Mr. Jones *will send* us his new book as soon as it's ready. *(So will Mrs. Smith.)*

> Mrs. Smith *will be coming* for a job interview next week. *(So will Mr. Jones.)*

INTRODUCING THE MODEL

1. Have students look at the model illustration.

2. Set the scene: "This family has just finished eating dinner, and the father is starting to wash the dishes."

3. Present the model twice, once with each expression in the brackets.

4. Full-Class Repetition.

5. Ask students if they have any questions. Check understanding of the expression *help me with*.

6. Group Choral Repetition.

7. Choral Conversation.

8. Call on one or two pairs of students to present the dialog. Have students practice both of the expressions.

   (For additional practice, do Choral Conversation in small groups or by rows.)

SIDE BY SIDE EXERCISES

Examples

1. A. Why weren't you and Bob at the meeting this morning?
   B. I missed the bus, and he did too/and so did he.

2. A. Why are you and Vanessa so nervous today?
   B. I have two final exams tomorrow, and she does too/and so does she.

1. **Exercise 1:** Call on two students to present the dialog. Then do Choral Repetition and Choral Conversation practice.

2. **Exercise 2:** Same as above.

3. **Exercises 3–13:** Either Full Class Practice or Pair Practice. Have students practice both possible expressions for each exercise.

New Vocabulary

3. Internet Company
5. walk their dog
6. out of town
7. for the past few days
10. parking space
12. act (of a play)
13. hide thunder and lightning

---

4. **Exercise 14:** Have students use the model as a guide to create their own conversations, using vocabulary of their choice. Encourage students to use dictionaries to find new words they want to use. This exercise can be done orally in class or for written homework. If you assign it for homework, do one example in class to make sure students understand what's expected. Have students present their conversations in class the next day.

WORKBOOK

Page 113

EXPANSION ACTIVITIES

1. Same and Different ★★★

a. Write the following categories on the board:

sports   school
music   home
food   family
clothes   travel

b. Divide the class into pairs.

c. The object is for pairs of students to find one thing in each of the categories that they have in common and then report back to the class. For example:

sports: She can play tennis, and so can I.
music: I like classical music, and she does, too.
food: She ate cereal for breakfast, and so did I.
clothes: I have a yellow raincoat, and she does, too.
school: She enjoys science, and so do I.
home: My apartment building has six floors, and hers does, too.
family: I have a cat and a dog, and so does she.
travel: She's been to New York City, and so have I.

2. What's Wrong? ★★★

a. Divide the class into pairs or small groups.

b. Write several sentences such as the following on the board or on a handout. Some of the sentences should be correct, and others incorrect. For example:

I've already seen that play, and so have she.
He's afraid of dogs, and so they are.
They'll be back by 9:00, and we will, too.
She's going to see it tomorrow, and are we, too.
They missed the train, and so did he.
I'm eating dinner right now, and she is, so.
He'll be working overtime tonight, and will I, too.
They've heard her sing before, and I have so.
You were very sleepy, and too was I.

c. The object of the activity is for students to identify which sentences are incorrect and then correct them.

d. Have students compare their answers.

Variation: Do the activity as a game with competing teams. The team that successfully completes the task in the shortest time is the winner.

3. Class Story ★★★

a. Write the following on the board:

    is
    has
    went
    can
    will
    is going to
    has _____ed

b. Begin by saying: "Jean and her sister Joan are very similar."

c. Student 1 adds another sentence, using any verb on the board. For example: "Jean is tall and thin, and so is Joan."

d. Continue around the room in this fashion, with each student adding another sentence.

For example:

Student 2: Jean has a new job, and so does Joan.

Student 3: Jean went to college in Boston, and so did Joan.

Student 4: Jean can swim very fast, and Joan can, too.

Student 5: Jean will be a doctor someday, and so will Joan.

Student 6: Jean is going to move to Miami, and Joan is, too.

Student 7: Jean has been to San Francisco, and so has Joan.

e. You can do the activity again, beginning and ending with different students.

If the class is large, you may want to divide students into groups to give students more practice.

Option: Have students tell a story about "Ned and his brother Ted."

READING *"Made For Each Other"*

FOCUS

- Connectors:
  and . . . too
  so

NEW VOCABULARY

academic	minorities
art museum	nuclear energy
background	offer (v)
collection	opposed to
compatible	outlook on life
cultural	personality
equal rights	similar
group	support
have a lot in common	tend (to)
ice skating (n)	theater group
"made for each other"	use (n)
major in (v)	

READING THE STORY

Optional: *Preview the story by having students talk about the story title and/or illustrations. You may choose to introduce new vocabulary beforehand, or have students encounter the new vocabulary within the context of the reading.*

1. Have students read silently, or follow along silently as the story is read aloud by you, by one or more students, or on the audio program.

2. Ask students if they have any questions. Check understanding of vocabulary.

3. Check students' comprehension, using some or all of the following questions:

Why are Louise and Brian very compatible people?
How are their backgrounds similar?
How are their academic interests similar?
How are their athletic interests similar?
How are their cultural interests similar?
How are their personalities similar?
How are their outlooks on life similar?
What does everybody say about Louise and Brian?

✓ READING *CHECK-UP*

TRUE, FALSE, OR MAYBE?

1. True
2. False
3. True
4. Maybe
5. False
6. False
7. False

READING EXTENSION

1. ***Same and Different***

   a. Write the following categories on the board:

   > background
   > cultural interests
   > sports
   > academic interests
   > personalities
   > outlooks on life

   b. Divide the class into pairs.

   c. The object is for pairs of students to find one thing in each of the categories that they have in common and then report back to the class.

2. A Close Friend

a. Have students write about a close friend and ways in which they are similar to their close friend. Have students consider the categories mentioned in the above activity.

b. Have students share their writing in small groups.

 LISTENING

Before you do the exercise, check understanding of the word *scientific*.

Listen and choose what people are talking about.

1. A. To tell the truth, I'm a little shy.
   B. What a coincidence! I am, too.

2. A. I enjoy going to plays and concerts.
   B. We're very compatible. So do I.

3. A. I'm enjoying this course.
   B. I am, too.

4. A. I'm from Minnesota.
   B. That's interesting. So am I.

5. A. I go swimming three times a week.
   B. What a coincidence! I do, too.

6. A. I'm opposed to using animals in scientific experiments.
   B. I am, too.

Answers

1. a
2. b
3. a
4. b
5. a
6. b

FOCUS

- Expressions with *Either* and *Neither* with All Pronouns

GETTING READY

Practice expressions with *either* and *neither*.

1. Write on the board:

Tim _____.
Tom _____ either.
Neither _____ Ted.

2. Set the scene: "Tim, Tom, and Ted are triplets.* May 27th is Tim's birthday. It's Tom and Ted's birthday, too."

3. Read the following statements about *Tim*. Have students make statements about *Tom* and *Ted*, using the model on the board. For example:

> Teacher: Tim isn't a very good student.
> Student: Tom isn't either, and neither is Ted.

Statements about Tim:

Tim hadn't studied Spanish before this year.
Tim won't be finishing high school next year.
Tim isn't going to go to college.
Tim can't dance very well.
Tim doesn't like Italian food.
Tim didn't like sports when he was young.
Tim couldn't come to meet us today.

*Triplets are three children born at a single birth.

INTRODUCING THE MODEL

1. Have students look at the model illustration.
2. Set the scene: "Someone is talking to a brother and sister on a roller coaster."
3. Present the model.
4. Full Class Repetition.
5. Ask students of they have any questions. Check understanding of the word *frightened*.
6. Group Choral Repetition.
7. Choral Conversation.
8. Call on one or two pairs of students to present the dialog.

   (For additional practice, do Choral Conversation in small groups or by rows.)

SIDE BY SIDE EXERCISES

Examples

1. A. Why haven't you and your roommate hooked up your new DVD player?
   B. I don't understand the instructions, and he doesn't either/neither does he.

2. A. Why didn't you or your parents answer the telephone all weekend?
   B. I wasn't home, and they weren't either/neither were they.

1. **Exercise 1:** Call on two students to present the dialog. Then do Choral Repetition and Choral Conversation practice.

2. **Exercise 2:** Same as above.

3. **Exercises 3–13:** Either Full Class Practice or Pair Practice. Have students practice both possible expressions for each exercise.

New Vocabulary

  5. dance class
  6. school nurse
12. afford
13. fairy tale

Language Note

Exercise 13: *Fairy tales* are short stories about magical creatures that are told to young children.

4. Exercise 14: Have students use the model as a guide to create their own conversations, using vocabulary of their choice. Encourage students to use dictionaries to find new words they want to use. This exercise can be done orally in class or for written homework. If you assign it for homework, do one

example in class to make sure students understand what's expected. Have students present their conversations in class the next day.

WORKBOOK

Pages 114–115

EXPANSION ACTIVITIES

1. Same and Different ★★★

a. Write the following categories on the board:

sports	school
music	home
food	family
clothes	travel

b. Divide the class into pairs.

c. The object is for pairs of students to find one *negative* thing in each of the categories that they have in common and then report back to the class. For example:

sports: He can't play golf, and neither can I.
music: I don't like classical music, and he doesn't either.
food: He didn't have eggs for breakfast, and neither did I.
clothes: I don't own a tuxedo, and he doesn't either.

school: He doesn't like mathematics, and neither do I.
home: I don't live on the first floor, and neither does he.
family: I don't have a sister, and he doesn't either.
travel: He's never been on a boat, and I haven't either.

2. What's Wrong? ★★★

a. Divide the class into pairs or small groups.

b. Write several sentences such as the following on the board or on a handout. Some of the sentences should be correct, and others incorrect. For example:

I've never gone on a safari, and neither he has.
She isn't going to the party, and I'm not neither.
They won't arrive soon, and she won't either.
I'm not going to call them, and they are neither.

(continued)

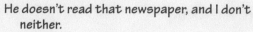

He doesn't read that newspaper, and I don't neither.

She can't figure skate very well, and either can't I.

He won't do that, and neither will they.

They've never heard her sing before, and I haven't neither.

You weren't very tired, and neither I was.

c. The object of the activity is for students to identify which sentences are incorrect and then correct them.

d. Have students compare their answers.

Variation: Do the activity as a game with competing teams. The team that successfully completes the task in the shortest time is the winner.

3. Class Story ★★★

a. Write the following on the board:

```
isn't
doesn't like
didn't
can't
won't
isn't going to
hasn't _____ed
```

b. Begin by saying, "Ned and his brother Ted are very similar."

c. Student 1 adds another sentence, using any verb on the board. For example: "Ned isn't a very good athlete, and neither is Ted."

d. Continue around the room in this fashion, with each student adding another sentence. For example:

Student 2: Ned doesn't like to cook, and Ted doesn't either.

Student 3: Ned didn't do well in school, and neither did Ted.

Student 4: Ned can't type, and Ted can't either.

Student 5: Ned won't be able to help you, and neither will Ted.

Student 6: Ned isn't going to be very successful, and Ted isn't either.

Student 7: Ned hasn't taken many vacations, and neither has Ted.

e. You can do the activity again, beginning and ending with different students.

If the class is large, you may want to divide students into groups to give students more practice.

Option: Have students tell a story about "Jean and her sister Joan."

READING *Laid Off*

FOCUS

- Connectors:
  and ... either
  neither

NEW VOCABULARY

as the day goes by	layoff (n)
at the same time	main
available	on the weekend
certain	pessimistic
commute	prefer
despite	skill
expect	surprise (n)
far (adv)	training
go through some	typing skills
difficult times	vocational
hopeful	want ad
job opening	willing
lay-off (v)	

READING THE STORY

Optional: Preview the story by having students talk about the story title and/or illustrations. You may choose to introduce new vocabulary beforehand, or have students encounter the new vocabulary within the context of the reading.

1. Have students read silently, or follow along silently as the story is read aloud by you, by one or more students, or on the audio program.

2. Ask students if they have any questions. Check understanding of vocabulary.

   Culture Note

   Companies lay off people when there are too many employees and too little work for them. Workers who are laid off can collect a part of their salary while they are waiting to be called back to work or until they find a new job.

3. Check students' comprehension, using some or all of the following questions:

   Why are Jack and Betty Williams going through some difficult times?
   Why are they becoming more and more concerned about their futures?
   Were the layoffs a surprise?
   Why not?
   What hadn't they expected?
   What have they been doing ever since they were laid off?
   Have they been successful?
   What's the main reason they're having trouble finding work?
   Have the want ads been helpful?
   Have there been many job openings?
   Have their friends been helpful?
   What's another reason they're having trouble finding work?
   What do Jack and Betty know about computers?
   How are their typing skills?
   Have they had any special vocational training?
   What's a third reason they're having trouble finding work?
   What do they think about working at night?
   What do they think about working on weekends?
   What do they think about commuting far to work?
   Are Jack and Betty completely discouraged? Why not?

✓ READING *CHECK-UP*

TRUE, FALSE, OR MAYBE?

1. False
2. False
3. Maybe
4. True
5. Maybe

READING EXTENSION

What Can They Do?

1. Have the class discuss the following questions:

   What is one problem Jack and Betty Williams have?
   (They don't have any vocational skills.)

   What is one possible solution?
   (Betty can take a typing class.)

   What will happen if she does that?
   (Betty will get some good job skills, but she might have to wait to find a job.)

2. Write students' ideas on the board. Be sure to discuss several different problems and several different solutions.

3. Have students write two or three paragraphs in which they give advice to Jack and Betty, using the ideas generated from this class discussion.

A JOB INTERVIEW

1. Check understanding of the expression *educational background*.

2. Have students role-play a job interview using the questions suggested on text page 140. One student is the job interviewer. The other is the job applicant. Have pairs of students practice their role plays and then present them to the class.

Text Page 141: You Should Ask Them

FOCUS

• Contrasting Statements with *But*

INTRODUCING THE MODEL

1. Have students look at the model illustration.

2. Set the scene: "A woman is talking to the girl who lives next-door."

3. Present the model.

4. Full-Class Choral Repetition.

   ### Pronunciation Note

   The pronunciation focus of Unit 10 is **Contrastive Stress** (text page 144). Model this pronunciation at this point and encourage students to incorporate it into their language practice.

   > I can't, but my SISTER can.
   > You should ask HER.

5. Ask students if they have any questions. Check understanding of the word *baby-sit*.

6. Group Choral Repetition.

7. Choral Conversation.

8. Call on one or two pairs of students to present the dialog.

   (For additional practice, do Choral Conversation in small groups or by rows.)

9. Read the statements in the box at the top of the page, and have students repeat chorally.

SIDE BY SIDE EXERCISES

Examples

1. A. Have you heard the weather forecast?
   B. No, I haven't, but my FATHER has. You should ask HIM.

2. A. Do you have a hammer?
   B. No, I don't, but my upstairs NEIGHBORS do. You should ask THEM.

1. **Exercise 1:** Call on two students to present the dialog. Then do Choral Repetition and Choral Conversation practice.

2. **Exercise 2:** Same as above.

3. **Exercises 3–6:** Either Full-Class Practice or Pair Practice.

> ### New Vocabulary
>
> 4. homework assignment
> 5. by any chance
> 6. pay attention
>   salesman

How to Say It!

> **Offering a Suggestion:** There are many ways to offer a suggestion. "You should ask HER," "Why don't you ask HER?" and "How about asking HER?" are equally polite. *How about* is followed by a gerund.

1. Present the expressions.

2. Full-Class Repetition.

3. Ask students if they have any questions. Check understanding of the expressions: *Why don't you . . .? How about . . . ?*

4. Group Choral Repetition.

5. Have students practice again the conversations in this lesson using any of these new expressions.

6. Call on pairs to present their conversations to the class.

WORKBOOK

Pages 116–117

1. Places Around the World ★★★

a. Write on the board:

> How are they similar?
> How are they different?

b. Divide the class into small groups of 3 to 5 students. Have each group choose two cities (either local cities or world cities). Have the students work together to write five ways these cities are similar and five ways they're different. Encourage students to use dictionaries if they need to.

c. Have one student from each group present the findings to the class. For example:

London and Rome
(similar)
London isn't a small city, and neither is Rome.
Rome has some very old buildings, and London does, too.

(different)
People in London speak English, but in Rome people speak Italian.
The weather in London is very cold in the winter, but the weather in Rome isn't.

2. Our Differences ★★★

a. Write the following categories on the board:

> sports   school
> music   home
> food   family
> clothes   travel

b. Divide the class into pairs.

c. The object is for pairs of students to find one thing in each of the categories that they *don't* have in common and then report back to the class. For example:

sports: She can't play soccer, but I can.
music: I like rock music, but she doesn't.
food: She enjoys Italian food, but I don't.
clothes: Her shoes are red, but mine aren't.

school: I'm taking history this year, but she isn't.
home: My apartment has a jacuzzi, but hers doesn't.
family: Her sister is in college, but mine isn't.
travel: She's never flown in an airplane, but I have.

3. Telephone ★

a. Divide the class into large groups. Have each group sit in a circle.

b. Set the scene: "A couple is in a restaurant. They're ordering spaghetti and meatballs, but they have very special instructions!"

c. Whisper the food order to one student. For example:

"They both want spaghetti and meatballs. She wants spaghetti with butter, and he does, too. She doesn't want tomato sauce, but he does. She wants the meatballs on the spaghetti, but he doesn't. He wants them on a different plate."

d. The first student whispers the food order to the second student, and so forth around the circle.

e. When the message gets to the last student, that person says it aloud. Is it the same message you started with? The group with the most accurate message wins.

4. Comparison Shopping ★★

a. Bring to class several shopping catalogs.

b. Divide the class into pairs or small groups and give each group two catalogs selling similar merchandise.

c. Have students compare the selections and prices in their catalogs. For example:

This catalog sells clothes and shoes, but that one doesn't. That one only sells shoes.
This catalog sells shoes for men and women, and that one does, too.
This catalog has good quality shoes, and so does that one.

d. Have students report back to the class and discuss which catalogs are the best for shopping.

5. Matchmaker ★★★

a. Divide the class into groups of four. Give each student in the group one of the following cards.

> - John grew up in a big family in a big city.
> - John doesn't like to play golf, but he likes to play tennis.
> - John is a Spanish teacher.
> - John is a vegetarian.
> - John enjoys going to movies, but he doesn't like to dance.

> - Mary grew up in a small family in a small town.
> - Mary doesn't like to play golf, and she doesn't like to play tennis.
> - Mary is a lawyer.
> - Mary is a vegetarian.
> - Mary enjoys going to movies, and she likes to dance.

> - Louise grew up in a small family in a big city.
> - Louise likes to play golf, and she likes to play tennis.
> - Louise is a French teacher.
> - Louise likes to eat meat.
> - Louise enjoys going to movies, but she doesn't like to dance.

> - Carla grew up in a big family in a small town.
> - Carla doesn't like to play golf, but she likes to play tennis.
> - Carla is a science teacher.
> - Carla is a vegetarian.
> - Carla doesn't enjoy going to movies, but she likes to dance.

b. The student holding the *John* card begins by reading aloud the first sentence. Students then take turns reading aloud the corresponding sentences for *Carla, Mary,* and *Louise.* After each round, have students compare their characters. For example:

Student 1: John grew up in a big family.
Student 2: Carla did, too.
Student 3: But John is from a big city, and so is Louise.

c. Have students continue comparing people and then decide on the best match for John.

d. Have students report back to the class and give reasons for their conclusions.

READING *"Touchy Subjects"*

FOCUS

- But

NEW VOCABULARY

allow	defense	strict
an hour a day	government	"touchy subject"
behave	lenient	whatever
conservative	liberal	you can see why

READING THE STORY

Optional: *Preview the story by having students talk about the story title and/or illustrations. You may choose to introduce new vocabulary beforehand, or have students encounter the new vocabulary within the context of the reading.*

1. Have students read silently, or follow along silently as the story is read aloud by you, by one or more students, or on the audio program.

2. Ask students if they have any questions. Check understanding of vocabulary.

3. Check students' comprehension, using some or all of the following questions:

    Do Larry and his parents agree when they talk about politics?
    What are their political philosophies?
    What do Larry and his parents think about the president?
    What do Larry and his parents think about money for defense?

    Do the Greens and their next-door neighbors, the Harrisons, agree when they talk about child rearing?

What are their philosophies of child rearing?
When do the Greens and the Harrisons let their children watch television?
What do the Greens and the Harrisons think about table manners?

✓ READING CHECK-UP

TRUE, FALSE, OR MAYBE?

1. True
2. Maybe
3. False
4. Maybe
5. False

READING EXTENSION

"Touchy Subject" Role Play

1. Brainstorm with the class what they think some *touchy subjects* are. Write their ideas on the board.

2. Have students think of good responses to people who begin to talk about a touchy subject. Write their ideas on the board.

3. Have students practice and then present brief role plays in which one student introduces a touchy subject and the other responds appropriately.

How About You?

1. Present the questions.

2. Have the students do the activity as written homework, using a dictionary for any new words they wish to use.

3. Have students present and discuss what they have written in pairs or as a class.

ON YOUR OWN *Same and Different*

FOCUS

- Review: *So / Too / Either / Neither*

ON YOUR OWN ACTIVITY

1. Have students look at the illustration and cover the text with a piece of paper.

2. Have students listen as you read or play the audio about the sisters.

3. Have students look at the text and listen as you read or play the audio once more.

4. Check understanding of the words *overseas, philosophical, respect (v)*.

5. Write on the board:

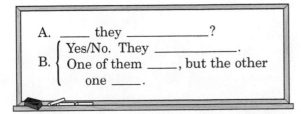

Call on pairs of students to ask and answer questions about the sisters, using the model on the board. For example:

A. Do they have black hair?
B. Yes. They both have black hair.

A. Are they married?
B. No. They aren't married.

A. Do they like classical music?
B. One of them does, but the other one doesn't.

A. Have they been to New York?
B. One of them has, but the other one hasn't.

WORKBOOK

Pages 118–119

 JOURNAL

Have students write their journal entries at home or in class. Encourage students to use a dictionary to look up words they would like to use. Students can share their written work with other students if appropriate. Have students discuss what they have written as a class, in pairs, or in small groups

PRONUNCIATION
Contrastive Stress

GRAMMAR FOCUS

Contrastive Stress: When making a contrast to something previously said, the words with new information are stressed and pronounced at a higher pitch.

Focus on Listening

Practice the sentences in the left column. Say each sentence or play the audio one or more times. Have students listen carefully and repeat.

Focus on Pronunciation

Practice the sentences in the right column. Have students say each sentence and then listen carefully as you say it or play the audio.

If you wish, have students continue practicing the sentences to improve their pronunciation.

Answers

1. so did
2. neither have
3. can't either
4. do, too
5. so are
6. don't either
7. I'm not, is
8. are, too
9. hadn't either
10. neither will
11. does, too
12. so has
13. neither am
14. don't, does

MULTILEVEL VARIATION ★★★

Challenge *above-level* students to cover the grammar boxes as they complete the grammar exercises.

CONVERSATION
1 *Requesting Help;*
Sequences of Instructions

1. Have students look at the photo. Ask: "Where are they?" (They're in a workplace kitchen.) "What's the woman doing?" (She's explaining how to use the coffee machine.) Have students look at the instructions for how to make coffee. Model the pronunciation and have students repeat. Introduce the words *filter, on button,* and *press.* Have two students read the first conversation aloud for the rest of the class.

2. Introduce the rest of the new vocabulary: *alarm system, code, glass, lid, lift up, original, start button,* and *put down.*

3. In pairs, have students practice the conversations as you circulate around the classroom.

4. Call on pairs of students to present their conversations to the class.

TEAMWORK *Instructions*
2 *for Operating Equipment*

Call on a student volunteer to read the directions aloud. Have students brainstorm procedures they can explain as you write their ideas on the board. Then have students work in pairs to choose a procedure and write down the instructions. Have them practice the conversation before they present it to the class.

LIFE SKILLS ENRICHMENT

Giving Instructions

Life Skills Worksheet 39

Make copies of Life Skills Worksheet 39 and give one to each student. Have students complete the worksheet as homework. In the next class, have students compare their answers in pairs.

EXPANSION ACTIVITIES

1. Scrambled Instructions ★

Activity Master 70

Divide the class into pairs. Make multiple copies of Activity Master 70 and cut them into cards. Give each pair one set of cards, and have the partners sort and reorder the three sets of instructions. Have pairs then practice giving and following the sequence of instructions.

2. Class Survey: Do You Know How to...? ★★

Activity Master 71

a. Make multiple copies of Activity Master 71 and give one copy to each student.

b. Practice the question on the questionnaire. For example:

   A. Do you know how to drive a truck?
   B. Yes, I do.

c. Have students walk around the classroom interviewing other students. When a student gets a yes answer to the question, the student writes in the person's name and then continues interviewing until getting a yes answer to the second question . . . and so on.

d. After ten minutes have students tell the class what they learned. For example:

   Student 1: Lina and Jong know how to hook up a computer.
   Student 2: So do Kim and Pamela.
   Student 3: Sam and Raul know how to hook up a computer, too.

3. Dictate and Discuss ★★★

Divide the class into pairs. Dictate sentences such as the following and have students discuss whether they agree or disagree with the statements.

   It's okay to ask questions at work.
   You should never ask your supervisor for help.
   It isn't polite to repeat what someone else says.
   When I'm silent, it means I understand the instructions.
   When I repeat instructions, I show I understand them.
   When someone helps you, you should say thank you.

GETTING A PROMOTION

1. Read the article title aloud. Ask: "What can you do to get the promotion you've been waiting for?" Write students' ideas on the board. Introduce the new words: *accomplish, appearance, appropriate, attitude, business English, care about, clearly, compare, computer class, computer skills, creative, creatively, deserve, develop, differently, discuss, evaluation, evening class, feedback, find out, fingernails, grooming, hardworking, ironed* (adj), *job performance evaluation, lose interest, meeting, move ahead, opportunity, point of view, professional, project, quality, speak up, success, think ahead, training program, turn* (n), and *yearly evaluation.*

2. Have students work individually to complete the comprehension exercise on student text page 144c and then compare answers in pairs, small groups, or as a class.

MULTILEVEL VARIATION ★

Have *below-level* students work on the reading and questions in pairs to provide each other with more support.

Answers

1.	C	**5.**	C
2.	B	**6.**	D
3.	A	**7.**	A
4.	B	**8.**	D

3. Have students individually complete the Test Yourself! self-evaluation on student text page 144c and then compare their answers in pairs. Follow up with a class discussion of the following questions: "Are there some qualities that don't matter in your work?" (For example, if you work on a shift in a factory, it doesn't matter whether or not you arrive early.) "Are there qualities that are important for your job?" (For example, a secretary must be very organized, and a server in a restaurant must be able to remember details.)

LIFE SKILLS ENRICHMENT

Job Performance Evaluation

Life Skills Worksheet 40

Make copies of Life Skills Worksheet 40 and give one to each student. Have students complete the evaluation form as they think about their own job performance. If students don't currently have a job, ask them to consider their performance in a previous job. In the next class, have students hand in their evaluations to you.

1. Scrambled Words ★

a. Choose words or phrases from the article on student text page 144b and write them on the board or on a card with the letters scrambled out of order. For example:

j b o   p r r e o f n c m e a

b. Have students take turns guessing what the word or phrase is. [job performance]

Variation 1: Do the activity in pairs or small groups, with students taking turns scrambling words or phrases for others to guess.

Variation 2: Do the activity as a class game with competing teams.

2. Job Performance Matching Game ★★

Activity Master 72

a. Make a copy of Activity Master 72 and cut it into cards. Distribute the cards randomly, one to each student.

Note: The cards with the borders are topic headings and the others are sentences that belong under each topic heading.

b. Have students walk around the room telling each other the lines on their cards until they find their topic group. Make sure students don't show their cards to their classmates since this is a listening and speaking exercise.

c. Call on students to read their topic headings and sentences to the class.

3. True or False? ★★

Make statements about the article on student text page 144b and have students decide whether the statements are true or false. If a statement is false, have students correct it. For example:

Dependable and hardworking are good qualities in an employee. [True.]
Grooming is another word for cleaning your office. [False. Grooming is another word for staying clean and keeping a good appearance.]
Everyone has a different point of view. [True.]
It's good to gossip at work. [False. It's never good to gossip.]

Variation: Do the activity as a game with competing teams.

4. How Much Do You Remember? ★★

a. Write the following topics from the article on the board:

Your Appearance
How Well You Get Along with People
Your Attitude at Work
Your Skills
Your Job Performance

b. Divide the class into pairs. Have students close their books and retell to each other what they remember about each topic from the article on student text page 144b. Then have them open their books and check to see how much they remembered.

5. Describe Yourself! ★★

Activity Master 73

Make a copy of Activity Master 73 and give one to each student. Have students circle the words and phrases that best describe themselves and then write a paragraph about themselves using the circled vocabulary. Have students submit their writing to you for feedback.

6. Ranking ★★★

a. Have students look at the qualities in the self-test on student text page 144c and choose the six most important items for getting promoted in their own job. For example:

> *Sales Assistant*
> get along with customers
> communicate clearly
> dress appropriately
> be helpful
> have a positive attitude
> be dependable and hardworking

b. In pairs, have students compare their lists.

1. Have students look at the adult education course catalog on student text page 144d. Ask: "What's this a catalog for?" (Classes at an adult education center.) Then ask questions such as the following to get students oriented to the information in the catalog. "How many business courses are there?" (Six.) "What's the course number for the *Business Procedures* class?" (BUS 101)

2. Introduce the new catalog vocabulary: *ability, adult education course, advanced, analyze, basic, basics, catalog, concise, familiar, features, hands-on, interest* (v), *introduction, safely, prerequisite,* and *variety*.

   Then introduce the following specialized field vocabulary.

   Culinary Arts
   entry-level position
   food and beverage specialist
   health regulation

   Business
   balance (v)   payroll
   bookkeeping   profession
   business plan   professional-looking
   calculate   public speaking
   checkbook   telephone skills
   conference   time management
   entrepreneurship   travel reservation
   memo   wages
   organize

   Computers
   electronic mail   research (v)
   Excel spreadsheet   search (v)
   flyer   software
   graph   speech
   keyboarding skills   spreadsheet
   Microsoft Outlook   Word
   Microsoft Word   word processing
   newsletter   software
   PowerPoint   worksheet

   Health Science
   beat (v)   poison
   cardiopulmonary   procedure
     resuscitation   Red Cross
   cut (n)   certification
   emergency care   shock
     procedure   situation
   first aid

3. Have students work individually to complete the comprehension exercise and then compare answers in pairs, small groups, or as a class.

MULTILEVEL VARIATION ★

Have *below-level* students work on the reading and questions in pairs to provide each other with more support.

Answers

1.	C	**6.**	D
2.	D	**7.**	B
3.	B	**8.**	C
4.	C	**9.**	B
5.	A	**10.**	D

YOUR EDUCATION PLAN

Have students discuss their ideas for their future education in pairs or small groups. Then have students take five minutes to individually complete the plan.

CLASS DISCUSSION

Call on a student volunteer to read the questions aloud. Have students discuss their ideas as you write them on the board.

LIFE SKILLS ENRICHMENT

Your Education Plan

Life Skills Worksheet 41

Make copies of Life Skills Worksheet 41 and give one to each student. Have students complete the education plan as homework. In the next class, have students compare their plans in pairs.

EXPANSION ACTIVITIES

1. Brainstorming: Adult Education Courses ★

Have the class brainstorm what schools in their area offer adult education courses such as the ones on student text page 144d. Write students' ideas on the board.

2. Association Game ★

a. Write the fields of study from the course catalog on student text page 144d on the board:

Business
Computers
Culinary Arts
Health Science

b. Divide the class into several teams. Have the students in each team work together to see how many words they can associate with each field. For example:

Business:	[bookkeeping/memo/ profession/time management]
Computers:	[keyboarding/PowerPoint/ spreadsheet/graph]
Culinary Arts:	[beverages/recipes/ menus/health regulations]
Health Science:	[first aid/emergencies/ poison/Red Cross]

c. Set a time limit for the game. When the time limit is up, call on the teams to read their list of associations to the class. The team with the most correct items wins.

3. True or False? ★★

Make statements about the adult education courses on student text page 144d and have students decide whether the statements are true or false. If a statement is false, have students correct it. For example:

Bookkeeping is about paying wages and reporting. [True.]

PowerPoint is a software program. [True.]
Students have to know how to keyboard before they take COM 101. [False. This is an introductory class.]
Entrepreneurship is about how to work in emergency care. [False. It is about how to start your own business.]

Variation: Do the activity as a game with competing teams.

4. Ranking ★★★

a. Have students look at the adult education courses on student text page 144d and circle the five courses they would most like to take. Have students rank these items from one to five, with one being the one they would like to take the most. For example:

1. BUS 105 Business Writing
2. BUS 106 Public Speaking
3. COM 101 Microsoft Word
4. COM 102 Microsoft Outlook
5. COM 106 Excel Spreadsheets

b. Have students share their lists in small groups and talk about the classes they would like to take.

c. Have students tell the class what they learned about their classmates. For example:

Student 1: Elena would like to take COM 103 and so would I.
Student 2: Pablo wants to learn about Food Preparation, and Anna does, too.

5. Mystery Course Conversations ★★★

a. Have pairs of students choose an adult education course from the catalog on student text page 144d and create a conversation about that course. Tell students they *can't* use the name of the course they chose in their conversations.

(continued)

b. Call on the pairs to present their conversations and have the class guess what the *mystery course* is. For example:

  A. Oh! This course looks interesting. I want to learn more about how to use the computer.
  B. Don't you already know how to use Microsoft Word?

  A. Yes, but this course is about advanced features. There's still a lot for me to learn!

[Answer: COM 201 Microsoft Word II]

CHECK-UP TEST

Have students do the check-up test and then review the answers as a class.

Answers

1. B	**6.** A
2. A	**7.** B
3. C	**8.** D
4. D	**9.** B
5. C	**10.** C

SKILLS CHECK

Words:

Explain to students that this is a list of words they have learned in the unit. Have students take turns reading each item aloud to the class. Have students put a check next to the item if they feel they have learned it. Encourage students to get a small notebook where they can write down words that are difficult for them.

I can:

Explain to students that this is a list of skills they have learned in the unit. Read each item aloud to the class. Ask individual students or pairs of students to demonstrate the skill. For example:

    Teacher: I can offer suggestions.
Student A: You should ask them.

    Teacher: I can request help at work.
Student A: Excuse me. Can you help me?
Student B: Sure. How can I help?
Student A: Can you show me how to make a copy?
Student B: Sure. I'll be happy to.

Have students put a check next to the item if they feel they have learned it. Use this information to determine which lessons you may want to review or reinforce for the entire class or for particular students.

EXPANSION ACTIVITIES

1. Do You Remember the Verbs? ★

Check students' retention of the vocabulary depicted on the opening page of Unit 10 by doing the following activity:

a. Have students open their books to page 131 and cover the list of words.

b. Either call out a number and have students tell you the word, or say a word and have students tell you the number.

Variation: You can also do this activity as a game with competing teams.

2. Scrambled Sentences ★★

Activity Master 74

Divide the class into pairs. Make enough copies of Activity Master 74 for half the class. Cut them into cards and distribute one set of cards to each pair of students. Have students take turns picking up a scrambled sentence prompt and then saying the sentence in the correct order.

Variation: Students can write their sentences and then compare their answers with other pairs.

3. Match Game ★★

Activity Master 75

a. Make a copy of Activity Master 75 and cut it into cards. Distribute the cards randomly, one to each student.

Note: The longer cards are sentence beginnings and the shorter cards are sentence endings.

b. Have students memorize the lines on their cards. Then have students circulate around the room saying their lines until they find their match. Make sure students don't show their cards to their classmates since this is a listening and speaking exercise.

(continued)

c. When students have found their match, have them compare their cards and then come show you.

d. Continue until students have found all the matches.

MULTILEVEL VARIATION ★

Below-level students can look at the cards as they do the activity.

4. Concentration ★★

Activity Master 75

a. Divide the class into pairs. Make multiple copies of Activity Master 75, cut them into cards, and distribute one set to each pair.

b. Have students shuffle the cards and place the longer cards in two rows face down and the shorter cards in two rows face down.

c. The object of the game is for students to match sentence beginnings and endings. Both students should be able to see the cards, since *concentrating* on their location is an important part of playing the game.

d. Student A turns over a long card and a short card, and if they match the student keeps the cards. If the cards don't match, the student turns them face down and Student B takes a turn.

The game continues until all the sentences have been completed. The student with the most correct *matches* wins the game.

MULTILEVEL VARIATION ★

Below-level students can read through the sentence beginnings and endings all at once and then match the cards face up.

5. Mix and Match Words ★★

Activity Master 76

a. Divide the class into groups of three. Make a copy of Activity Master 76 for each group. Cut the Activity Masters into cards and

place them in two piles face down.

Note: The small cards are adjectives words and the large cards are nouns.

b. Distribute the two sets of cards to each group. Have students take turns picking up one card from each pile and reading the word combination to the group. For example:

athletic	feedback

The group decides if the adjective can describe the noun. If it can, they write it down on a piece of paper.

c. After all the cards have been chosen, have the group lay out all the cards and write out all the word combinations they saw in Unit 10.

MULTILEVEL VARIATION ★

Below-level students can read through the two sets of cards all at once and then pair up adjectives and nouns.

6. Board Game ★★

Activity Master 77

You will need a die and markers for this activity. (If students use a coin as a die, the class should decide which side of the coin will indicate a move of one space and which will indicate a move of two spaces.)

a. Make multiple copies of Activity Master 77. Divide the class into small groups and give each group a copy of Activity Master 77 along with a die and markers.

b. Have students place their markers on *Start*. The group should decide who goes first. That student begins the game by rolling the die or flipping the coin and moving his or her marker. If the student responds to the question or task correctly, he or she may take one more turn. If the student doesn't respond correctly, the next student takes a turn. No one may take more than two turns at a time.

Option 1: The first person to reach *Finish* is the winner.

Option 2: The game continues until each student reaches *Finish*. This way everybody is a winner.

7. Dialog Builder! ★★★

a. Divide the class into pairs. Write a line on the board from a conversation such as the following:

What a coincidence!

Other possible lines are:

Why can't you _____?
Why don't you _____?
So do I.
Neither will he.
I'll be happy to.

b. Have each pair create a conversation incorporating that line. Students can begin and end their conversations any way they wish, but they must include that line in their dialogs.

c. Call on students to present their conversations to the class.

8. What's Wrong? ★★★

a. Write several sentences such as the following on the board or on a handout that you give to students. Some of the sentences should be correct and others incorrect. For example:

I'm not hungry, but so is he.
She didn't like it, and neither did he.
He's been studying for years, and she is, too.
She got a promotion, and I got one either.
We'll go shopping together, and so will she.
They eat out every night, and so did I.
You've been to Spain, but neither have I.
She couldn't stand the noise, but I could.
They'll be busy, and I will so.
He hasn't had an evaluation, and either have I.

b. Divide the class into pairs. The object of the activity is for students to identify which sentences are incorrect and then correct them. Have students compare their answers in small groups.

Variation: Do the activity as a game with competing teams. For each team's turn, write one sentence on the board and have the team decide whether the sentence is correct or not. If it isn't correct, the team must correct it. Every time a team is right, that team receives one point. The team with the greatest number of points wins.

MULTILEVEL VARIATION ★

For *below-level* students, underline the errors and have the below-level pairs focus only on correcting them.

FEATURE ARTICLE *From Matchmakers to Dating Services*

PREVIEWING THE ARTICLE

1. Have students talk about the title of the article and the accompanying photograph.

2. You may choose to introduce the following new vocabulary beforehand, or have students encounter it within the context of the article:

> agreement
> approve
> arrange
> arrangement
> astrologer
> astrological
> birth
> choose
> custom
> dating service
> education
> freedom
> horoscope
> information
> marriage
> match (n)
> matchmaker
> matchmaking service
> modern-day
> newlywed
> occupation
> partner
> personal ad
> questionnaire
> rural
> tradition
> traditionally
> valuable
> version

READING THE ARTICLE

1. Have students read silently, or follow along silently as the article is read aloud by you, by

one or more students, or on the audio program.

2. Ask students if they have any questions. Check understanding of vocabulary.

3. Check students' comprehension by having them answer these questions:

> How do families in India traditionally arrange a marriage?
> What does a matchmaker do?
> How are marriage traditions and customs changing in modern cities?
> What is the modern-day version of a matchmaker?

EXPANSION ACTIVITIES

1. Dictate and Discuss ★★★

   a. Divide the class into pairs or small groups.

   b. Dictate sentences such as the following and then have students discuss them:

   > A husband and wife in an arranged marriage can learn to love each other.
   > Parents know best who their child should have as a husband or wife.
   > An astrologer can help people decide if they are a good match.

   c. Call on students to share their opinions with the rest of the class.

2. How People Meet ★★

   a. Divide the class into several groups. Have students brainstorm different ways people meet marriage partners in their culture.

   b. Have the groups report back to the class.

3. Advantages and Disadvantages ★★★

   a. Have students draw two columns on a piece of paper. At the top of one column, have students write Advantages. At the top of the other column, have them write Disadvantages.

   b. Have students brainstorm the advantages and disadvantages of having an arranged marriage.

Write their ideas in the columns and have students copy the list on their papers.

c. Have students repeat the exercise, naming the advantages and disadvantages of choosing one's own partner.

4. Interviews ★★★

In this activity, students interview their elders to find out how they met their marriage partners.

a. Have students brainstorm questions they would like to ask in their interviews.

b. Have students conduct their interviews outside the classroom and then write a report of the interview to share in class.

FACT FILE
When People Get Married

1. Before reading the Fact File, show the class a world map. Have students identify the locations of the following place names:

Australia
Brazil
Greece
India
Japan
Korea
Mexico
Russia
Saudi Arabia
Swaziland
Sweden

2. Ask students: "In which of these countries do you think people marry at a young age?" Have students rank the countries according to what they believe. Write students' ideas on the board. Then have students read the table on student text page 145 to check their predictions.

3. Read the table aloud as the class follows along. Ask: "Is this list different from your list? How is your list different?"

EXPANSION ACTIVITY

Making Inferences ★★★

1. In small groups, have students discuss the following questions:

   Why do you think people marry younger in some countries?
   Why do you think they marry older in other countries?
   This fact file gives the average age of the woman (the bride). Do you think the age of the man (the groom) is older or younger? Why?

2. Have groups report back to the class.

AROUND THE WORLD
Wedding Customs and Traditions

1. Before reading the text, show the class a world map. Have students identify the locations of the following places:

Colombia	Korea
Cyprus	Romania
India	the Slovak Republic
Japan	the United States

2. Have students read silently, or follow along silently as the text is read aloud by you, by one or more students, or on the audio program.

3. Ask students if they have any questions. Check understanding of new vocabulary.

bouquet	light (v)
bride	pin (v)
candle	private
catch	reception hall
confetti	throw
couple	veil
crown	wedding procession
flower petal	wish
groom	worship
involve	

4. Have students first work in pairs or small groups to respond to the question. Then have students tell the class what they talked about. Write any new vocabulary on the board.

EXPANSION ACTIVITIES

1. Categorization ★★

a. Write the following categories on the board: <u>Clothes</u>, <u>Places</u>, <u>Special Customs</u>, <u>Throwing Things</u>.

b. Have students read the text and captions again, and have them put the information into the appropriate categories on the board. For example:

<u>Clothes</u>
silver crown
veil

<u>Places</u>
in a church
in homes
outdoors

<u>Special Customs</u>
pinning money
lighting candles
cutting the cake

<u>Throwing Things</u>
confetti
flower petals
rice

c. Have the class then brainstorm other traditions they know and add them to the categories on the board (or if necessary, create new categories).

2. Wedding Pictures ★★★

If possible, have students bring in pictures of a wedding they attended. Have students share their pictures in small groups. Have students tell the following:

What did the bride wear? How about the groom?
What special food was there at the wedding?
Where was the wedding ceremony?
What did the guests do to bring good luck to the bride and groom?
Tell about the music and dancing.
How did the bride and groom arrive? How did they leave?

INTERVIEW

1. Have students read silently, or follow along silently as the interview is read aloud by you, by one or more students, or on the audio program.

2. Ask students if they have any questions. Check understanding of the expression *blind date.*

EXPANSION ACTIVITIES

1. Ranking ★★★

a. Have the class brainstorm several different places to meet a marriage partner. Write their ideas on the board.

b. Have students rank these place from the *best* to the *worst* places to meet a marriage partner.

c. As a class, in pairs, or in small groups, have students compare their lists and explain their reasoning.

2. Student Interviews ★★★

a. Have students interview each other about ways they have met a boyfriend or a girlfriend, and perhaps even their marriage partners.

b. Have the class compile its results. Ask: "What is the most common way to meet a partner? Which of these ways is more successful? Which ways resulted in marriage?"

FUN WITH IDIOMS

to be nuts about (someone)
to fall for (someone)
to give (someone) the cold shoulder
to stand (someone) up

INTRODUCTION AND PRACTICE

For each idiom do the following:

1. Have students look at the illustration.

2. Present the idiom. Say the expression and have the class repeat it chorally and individually. Check students' pronunciation of the words.

DO YOU KNOW THESE EXPRESSIONS?

Have students match the expressions with their meanings.

Answers

1.	b	**3.**	a
2.	d	**4.**	c

EXPANSION ACTIVITIES

1. Idiom Challenge! ★★★

a. Divide the class into pairs.

b. Have each pair create a conversation in which they use as many of the idioms from text page 147 as they can.

c. Have the pairs present their conversations to the class. Which pair used the most idioms?

2. Dialog Builder ★★★

a. Divide the class into pairs.

b. Write several idioms and other new vocabulary words from this Gazette on the board. For example:

```
to be nuts about someone
to stand someone up
to fall for someone
to give someone the cold shoulder

matchmaker
partner
background
bouquet of flowers
choose
```

c. Have each pair create a conversation incorporating at least six of the items. Students can begin and end their conversations any way they wish, but they must include at least six items in their dialogs.

d. Call on students to present their conversations to the class.

 WE'VE GOT MAIL!

THE 1ST LETTER TO *SIDE BY SIDE*

1. Have students read silently, or follow along silently as the letter is read aloud by you, by one or more students, or on the audio program.

2. Ask students if they have any questions. Check understanding of the words *inseparable, separable, two-word verb*.

3. To check students' comprehension, have students answer the following question:

   What does the writer want to know?

4. Ask students:

   Did you ever have this question?
   Can you think of an example of a separable two-word verb?
   Can you think of an example of an inseparable two-word verb?

THE RESPONSE FROM *SIDE BY SIDE*

1. Have students read silently, or follow along silently as the letter is read aloud by you, by one or more students, or on the audio program.

2. Ask students if they have any questions. Check understanding of the words *circle, sentence, separately, suggestion*.

3. Check students' comprehension by having them decide whether these statements are true or false:

   There's a rule that explains which two-word verbs are separable and which two-word verbs are inseparable. *(False)*

The best way to learn about two-word verbs is to memorize them all. *(True)*

It's correct to say "Hear you from soon." *(False)*

4. Ask students: How do *you* remember which two-word verbs are separable and which are inseparable?

EXPANSION ACTIVITIES

1. Class Game ★★

a. Divide the class into teams.

b. Give the teams five minutes to make a list of the two different types of two-word verbs: separable and inseparable.

c. Have the teams share their lists. The team with the longest list of correct verbs wins.

2. What's Wrong? ★★★

a. Divide the class into pairs or small groups.

b. Write several sentences such as the following on the board or on a handout. Some of the sentences should be correct, and others incorrect. For example:

She will bring back it next week.
He didn't cross out his mistakes.
The teacher always calls me on in class.
They never hear her from.
We almost ran out milk of yesterday.
He has hooked the computer up.
She has taken off it.
They wrote down all their notes.
My big brother always picks on me.
They don't take their father after.
We plan to look through our books tonight.
He can't figure out it.

c. The object of the activity is for students to identify which sentences are incorrect and then correct them.

d. Have students compare their answers.

Variation: Do the activity as a game with competing teams. The team that successfully completes the task in the shortest time is the winner.

THE 2ND LETTER TO *SIDE BY SIDE*

1. Have students read silently, or follow along silently as the letter is read aloud by you, by one or more students, or on the audio program.

2. Ask students if they have any questions. Check understanding of the word *expressions*.

3. Check students' comprehension by having them decide whether these statements are true or false:

"Turn on" has a similar meaning to "turn down." *(False)*

The meaning of two-word verbs is different from the meaning of each verb separately. *(True)*

The writer doesn't understand why English uses the same verbs again and again. *(True)*

4. Ask students:

Did you ever have this question?

Can you think of other verbs that change their meaning when they are part of a two-word verb?

THE RESPONSE FROM *SIDE BY SIDE*

1. Have students read silently, or follow along silently as the letter is read aloud by you, by one or more students, or on the audio program.

2. Ask students if they have any questions. Check understanding of the words *decline, formal, informal, resemble, speaker, unhappy.*

3. Check students' comprehension by having them decide whether these statements are true or false:

When people want to speak formally, they use two-word verbs. *(False)*

There are many verbs that have the same meaning as many two-word verbs. *(True)*

"Decline" means the same as "turn on." *(False)*

"Resemble" means the same as "take after." *(True)*

GLOBAL EXCHANGE

1. Set the scene: "PedroJ is writing to a keypal."

2. Have students read silently or follow along silently as the message is read aloud by you, by one or more students, or on the audio program.

3. Ask students if they have any questions. Check understanding of the words *alike*, *originally*.

4. Options for additional practice:

   • Have students write a response to PedroJ and share their writing in pairs

   • Have students correspond with a keypal on the Internet and then share their experience with the class.

 LISTENING *"Telephone Tag"*
True or False?

1. Set the scene: "Jim and Mary are trying to make plans for the weekend. They keep missing each other's calls, and they leave messages for each other."

2. Introduce the expression *telephone tag*.

LISTENING SCRIPT

Listen to the messages on Mary and Jim's answering machines. Answer true or false.

[Monday, 6:15 P.M.]
Hi, Mary. It's Jim. Are you by any chance interested in going to a jazz concert this Friday night? Please call me and let me know. Talk to you later.

[Monday, 9:13 P.M.]
Hi, Jim. It's Mary. I'm returning your call. Thanks for the invitation. I know you like jazz, and I do, too. And I'd really like to go to the concert with you, but I have to work this Friday night. Do you want to play tennis on Saturday afternoon? Let me know. 'Bye.

[Tuesday, 3:40 P.M.]
Hi, Mary. It's Jim. I'm sorry I missed your call last night. I was at the laundromat, and I got home very late. I'm free on Saturday, but unfortunately, I really don't like to play tennis. Actually, I'm a very bad tennis player. Do you want to go to the ballet with me on Saturday night? Let me know and I'll order tickets. Talk to you soon.

[Wednesday, 5:50 P.M.]
Hi, Jim. It's Mary. I got your message. Believe it or not, I've already gone to the ballet this week. I went with my sister last night. I have an idea! Let's see the new Steven Steelberg movie. I hear that it's great. Call and let me know.

[Thursday, 6:30 P.M.]
Hi, Mary. It's Jim. Sorry I missed your call again. I guess we're playing "telephone tag!" The movie sounds great. I haven't seen it yet. Do you want to have dinner before the movie? There's a wonderful new Italian restaurant downtown. Let me know. 'Bye.

[Friday, 5:17 P.M.]
Hi, Jim. Guess who! You won't believe it! I just found out that I have to work this Saturday night. It's a shame because I really wanted to see that movie. I'm not busy on Sunday. Are you free on Sunday afternoon? Let me know. By the way, I don't really like Italian food very much. There's a very good Greek restaurant in my neighborhood. Maybe we can have dinner there after the movie. What do you think? Talk to you later.

Answers

1. True
2. False
3. True
4. True
5. False

 **WHAT ARE THEY SAYING?**

FOCUS

- Things People Have (or Don't Have) in Common

Have students talk about the people and the situation, and then create role plays based on the scene. Students may refer back to previous lessons as a resource, but they should not simply reuse specific conversations.

Note: You may want to assign this exercise as written homework, having students prepare their role plays, practice them the next day with other students, and then present them to the class.

UNIT 1

WORKBOOK PAGE 2

A. What's Happening?

1. What's, reading, She's reading
2. Where's, going, He's going
3. What's, watching, She's watching
4. What are, cooking, I'm cooking
5. Where are, moving, We're moving
6. Where are, sitting, They're sitting
7. What's, composing, He's composing
8. What are, baking, I'm baking

WORKBOOK PAGE 3

B. On the Phone

1. are
   I'm watching
   Is
   she is, She's taking
2. Are
   They're
   are they
   is doing
   is playing
   What are you
   I'm cooking
3. Is
   he isn't, He's exercising
   She's, She's fixing

WORKBOOK PAGE 4

C. You Decide: *Why Is Today Different?*

1. clean, I'm cleaning, . . .
2. irons, he's ironing, . . .
3. argue, we're arguing, . . .
4. worry, I'm worrying, . . .
5. watches, she's watching, . . .
6. writes, he's writing, . . .
7. take, I'm taking, . . .
8. combs, he's combing, . . .
9. gets up, she's getting up, . . .
10. smiles, he's smiling, . . .
11. bark, they're barking, . . .
12. wears, she's wearing, . . .

WORKBOOK PAGE 5

D. What Are They Saying?

1. Do you recommend
2. Does, bake
3. Does, get up
4. Do, complain
5. Does, speak
6. Does, live
7. Do you watch
8. Does she play

9. Does he practice
10. Do you plant
11. Does he add
12. Do you wear
13. Does she ride
14. Does he jog
15. Do we need
16. Does he iron
17. Do they have

WORKBOOK PAGE 6

E. Puzzle

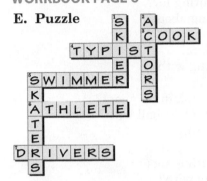

F. What's the Answer?

1. b
2. c
3. b
4. c
5. b
6. c
7. a
8. b

WORKBOOK PAGE 7

G. What Are They Saying?

1. don't, doesn't
   isn't, cook
2. don't, I'm
   drive
3. Do you
   don't, I'm
   You're, type
4. composes, he's
5. isn't, doesn't
   swimmer
6. don't
   speak, speaker

H. Listening

Listen to each question and then complete the answer.

1. Does Jim like to play soccer?
2. Is Alice working today?
3. Are those students staying after school today?
4. Do Mr. and Mrs. Jackson work hard?
5. Does your wife still write poetry?
6. Is it raining?
7. Is he busy?
8. Do you have to leave?
9. Does your sister play the violin?
10. Is your brother studying in the library?
11. Are you wearing a necklace today?
12. Do you and your husband go camping very often?
13. Is your niece doing her homework?
14. Are they still chatting online?
15. Do you and your friends play Scrabble very often?

Answers

1. he does
2. she isn't
3. they are
4. they do
5. she doesn't
6. it is
7. he isn't
8. I do
9. she doesn't
10. he is
11. I'm not
12. we do
13. she is
14. they aren't
15. we don't

13. typed
14. made
15. fixed
16. finished
17. put
18. spilled
19. went
20. ordered
21. felt
22. forgot
23. crashed
24. fell
25. broke
26. hurt
27. left
28. took
29. went

J. What's the Question?

1. What are you waiting for?
2. Who is he thinking about?
3. What are they ironing?
4. Who are you calling?
5. Who is she dancing with?
6. What's he watching?
7. What are they complaining about?
8. Who is she playing baseball with?
9. Who are they visiting?
10. What are you looking at?
11. What are you writing about?
12. Who is he arguing with?
13. Who is she knitting a sweater for?
14. What are you making?
15. Who are you sending an e-mail to?
16. What are they worrying about?
17. Who is she talking to?
18. Who is he skating with?

K. What Are They Saying?

1. your
   We're, them
2. his
   He, them, his
3. they, me
4. her
   She, them
5. your
   I, my
6. your
   I'm, her
7. They, them
8. us, it
9. he, it
10. your
    She, my

L. What's the Word?

1. with
2. —
3. at
4. to
5. about
6. —
7. —, with
8. for
9. —

UNIT 2

A. Herbert's Terrible Day!

1. had
2. got up
3. ate
4. rushed
5. ran
6. missed
7. waited
8. decided
9. arrived
10. sat
11. began
12. called

B. Listening

Listen and circle the correct answer.

1. They work.
2. They worked.
3. We study English.
4. I waited for the bus.
5. We visit our friends.
6. She met important people.
7. He taught Chinese.
8. She delivers the mail.
9. I wrote letters to my friends.
10. I ride my bicycle to work.
11. He sleeps very well.
12. I had a terrible headache.

Answers

1. every day
2. yesterday
3. every day
4. yesterday
5. every day
6. yesterday
7. yesterday
8. every day
9. yesterday
10. every day
11. every day
12. yesterday

C. What's the Word?

1. wanted
2. lifted
3. painted
4. roller-bladed
5. planted
6. needed
7. waited
8. decided

D. Puzzle: *What Did They Do?*

E. What's the Question?

1. Did you buy
2. Did they take
3. Did she see
4. Did he speak
5. Did you break
6. Did it begin
7. Did she fly
8. Did you have
9. Did they go
10. Did I sing
11. Did he meet
12. Did you lose

F. What's the Answer?

1. they were bored
2. I wasn't hungry
3. they were tired
4. she wasn't prepared
5. he was angry
6. I wasn't on time
7. she wasn't thirsty
8. I was scared
9. they were sad

G. Something Different

1. didn't drive, drove
2. didn't come, came
3. didn't take, took
4. didn't go, went
5. didn't forget, forgot
6. didn't wear, wore
7. didn't teach, taught
8. didn't eat, ate
9. didn't give, gave
10. didn't sit, sat
11. didn't have, had
12. didn't sing, sang

H. What Are They Saying?

1. Did you
   didn't, was
2. Did you
   didn't
   met
3. Did
   did
   wasn't
4. Did
   she didn't
   weren't
5. Did, fall
   he didn't
   fell
   was
6. Did
   I didn't, rode
   was
   was
7. Did you
   did, was
   didn't
   was

8. Was
   was, Were
   I wasn't, didn't
9. Did
   did
   didn't
   were
10. Did
    they didn't
    danced
    were
11. did
    I did, bought
    Did you
    didn't
    wasn't
12. were
    were
    I was, was
    was
    wasn't

I. How Did It Happen?

1. He sprained his ankle while he was playing tennis.
2. She ripped her pants while she was exercising.
3. I broke my arm while I was playing volleyball.
4. He poked himself in the eye while he was fixing his sink.
5. We hurt ourselves while we were skateboarding.
6. They tripped and fell while they were dancing.

7. He burned himself while he was cooking french fries.
8. She got a black eye while she was fighting with the kid across the street.
9. I cut myself while I was chopping carrots.
10. He lost his cell phone while he was jogging in the park.

L. What's the Question?

1. Who did you meet?
2. What did she lose?
3. Where did you do your exercises?
4. When did they leave?
5. How did she get here?
6. Where did he sing?
7. How long did they stay?
8. What kind of movie did you see?
9. Why did he cry?
10. Who did she write a letter to?
11. What did they complain about?
12. How many grapes did you eat?
13. Where did he speak?
14. How long did they lift weights?
15. Who did she give a present to?
16. What kind of pie did you order?
17. How many videos did you rent?
18. Who did they send an e-mail to?
19. When did he fall asleep?
20. When did you lose your hat?

M. Our Vacation

1. we didn't
   did you go
   We went
2. we didn't
   did you get there
   We got there by plane.
3. it didn't
   did it leave
   It left
4. we didn't
   weather did you have
   We had
5. we didn't
   hotel did you stay in
   We stayed in a small hotel.
6. we didn't
   food did you eat
   We ate Japanese food.
7. we didn't
   did you take (with you)
   We took

8. we didn't
did you get around the city
We got around the city by taxi.

9. we didn't
did you meet
We met

10. we didn't
did you buy
We bought

11. we didn't
did you speak
We spoke English.

12. we did
money did you spend
We spent . . .

N. Sound It Out!

1. these	**10.** his
2. did	**11.** Richard
3. Rita	**12.** every
4. big	**13.** speaks
5. green	**14.** with
6. mittens	**15.** week
7. knit	**16.** sister
8. Did Rita knit these big green mittens?	**17.** Richard speaks Greek with his sister every week.
9. Greek	

UNIT 3

A. What Are They Saying?

1. No, I didn't.
rode
I'm going to ride

2. No, he didn't.
wore
He's going to wear

3. No, she didn't.
gave
She's going to give

4. No, they didn't.
drove
They're going to drive

5. No, we didn't.
had
We're going to have

6. No, I didn't.
went
I'm going to go

7. No, he didn't.
wrote
He's going to write

8. No, she didn't.
left
She's going to leave

B. Bad Connections!

1. your dentist going to do
2. are you going to go
3. is she going to move to Alaska
4. What are they going to give you?
5. What are you going to do?
6. When are you going to get married?
7. Who are you going to meet?

8. What are you going to name your new puppy?
9. Why are they going to sell your house?
10. Where are you going to go?
11. Who do you have to call?
12. Why are you going to fire me?

C. Listening

Listen and choose the time of the action.

1. My daughter is going to sing Broadway show tunes in her high school show.
2. Janet bought a new dress for her friend's party.
3. Are you going to go out with George?
4. I went shopping at the new mall.
5. How did you poke yourself in the eye?
6. Who's going to prepare dinner?
7. Did the baby sleep well?
8. I'm really looking forward to Saturday night.
9. Is your son going to play games on his computer?
10. We're going to complain to the landlord about the heat in our apartment.
11. We bought a dozen donuts.
12. I'm going to take astronomy.

Answers

1. b	**3.** a	**5.** a	**7.** b	**9.** a	**11.** b
2. a	**4.** b	**6.** b	**8.** a	**10.** b	**12.** a

D. The Pessimist and the Optimists

1. won't have	you will, You'll
2. will hurt	he won't, He won't
3. won't	she will, She'll
4. will be	she won't, She won't
5. won't lose	you will, You'll
6. will forget	they won't, They won't
7. won't fix	he will, He'll
8. won't	they will, They'll like
9. I'll	you won't, You won't

E. What Will Be Happening?

1. she will, She'll be doing
2. I will, I'll be filling out
3. he won't, He'll be working out
4. they will, They'll be cleaning
5. he will, He'll be browsing
6. we will, We'll be watching
7. she won't, She'll be attending
8. it won't, It'll be raining

G. What Are They Saying?

1. giving, will you be giving
2. will you be doing, be doing
3. talk, talk, studying
4. having/eating, will you be having/eating

I. Whose Is It?

1. yours	**3.** his	**5.** theirs	**7.** hers
2. mine	**4.** hers	**6.** ours	**8.** hers

WORKBOOK PAGES 32–33

K. What Does It Mean?

1. b	**6.** a	**11.** a	**16.** b	**21.** c
2. c	**7.** c	**12.** c	**17.** a	**22.** a
3. b	**8.** b	**13.** a	**18.** b	**23.** b
4. b	**9.** a	**14.** b	**19.** c	**24.** c
5. a	**10.** c	**15.** a	**20.** a	

L. Listening: *Looking Forward*

Listen to each story. Then answer the questions.

What Are Mr. and Mrs. Miller Looking Forward to?

Mr. and Mrs. Miller moved into their new house in Los Angeles last week. They're happy because the house has a large, bright living room and a big, beautiful yard. They're looking forward to life in their new home. Every weekend they'll be able to relax in their living room and enjoy the beautiful California weather in their big, beautiful yard. But this weekend Mr. and Mrs. Miller won't be relaxing. They're going to be very busy. First, they're going to repaint the living room. Then, they're going to assemble their new computer and VCR. And finally, they're going to plant some flowers in their yard. They'll finally be able to relax NEXT weekend.

Answers **1.** a **2.** c **3.** b

What's Jonathan Looking Forward to?

I'm so excited! I'm sitting at my computer in my office, but I'm not thinking about my work today. I'm thinking about next weekend because next Saturday is the day I'll be getting married. After the wedding, my wife and I will be going to Hawaii for a week. I can't wait! For one week, we won't be working, we won't be cooking, we won't be cleaning, and we won't be paying bills. We'll be swimming in the ocean, relaxing on the beach, and eating in fantastic restaurants.

Answers **4.** b **5.** c **6.** b

What's Mrs. Grant Looking Forward to?

Mrs. Grant is going to retire this year, and she's really looking forward to her new life. She won't be getting up early every morning and taking the bus to work. She'll be able to sleep late every day of the week. She'll read books, she'll work in her garden, and she'll go to museums with her friends. And she's very happy that she'll be able to spend more time with her grandchildren. She'll take them to the park to feed the birds, she'll take them to the

zoo to see the animals, and she'll baby-sit when her son and daughter-in-law go out on Saturday nights.

Answers **7.** b **8.** a **9.** c

WORKBOOK PAGES 34–35

CHECK-UP TEST: Units 1–3

A.

1. are
   dance
2. drives
3. you're
   swimmers
4. I'm
   typist
5. aren't, skiers

B.

1. didn't, was
   spoke
2. didn't
   bought
3. Did
   didn't, got
4. didn't, taught
   was
5. Did
   didn't, talked
   wasn't

C.

1. What are you writing about?
2. What are they going to fix?
3. Where did he hike?
4. When will she be ready?
5. How did they arrive?
6. How long will you be staying?
7. How many people is she going to hire?

D.

1. She's adjusting her satellite dish.
2. He chats online.
3. I'm going to visit my mother-in-law.
4. They delivered groceries.
5. He was baking a cake.
6. I'll take the bus.
7. We'll be watching TV.
8. I was chopping carrots.

E.

Listen to each question and then complete the answer.

Ex. Does your brother like to swim?
1. Are you going to buy donuts tomorrow?
2. Will Jennifer and John see each other again soon?
3. Doctor, did I sprain my ankle?
4. Does Tommy have a black eye?
5. Is your daughter practicing the violin?
6. Do you and your husband go to the movies very often?
7. Does Diane go out with her boyfriend every Saturday evening?
8. Will you and your wife be visiting us tonight?

Answers

1. I am	**4.** he does	**7.** she doesn't
2. they won't	**5.** she isn't	**8.** we will
3. you did	**6.** we do	

UNIT 4

A. For Many Years

1. I've ridden
2. I've flown
3. I've given
4. I've spoken
5. I've taken
6. I've done
7. I've drawn
8. I've written
9. I've driven

B. Listening

Listen and choose the word you hear.

1. I've ridden them for many years.
2. Yes. I've taken French.
3. I'm giving injections.
4. I've driven one for many years.
5. Yes. I've written it.
6. I'm drawing it right now.
7. I've spoken it for many years.
8. Yes. I've drawn that.

Answers

1. a	3. a	5. b	7. a
2. b	4. b	6. a	8. b

C. I've Never

1. I've never flown
2. I've never gotten
3. I've never ridden
4. I've never drawn
5. I've never written
6. I've never taken
7. I've never sung
8. I've never swum
9. I've never been
10. I've never gone
11. I've never given
12. I've never seen

D. Listening

Is Speaker B answering Yes *or* No? *Listen to each conversation and circle the correct answer.*

1. A. Do you know how to drive a bus?
   B. I've driven a bus for many years.

2. A. I usually take the train to work. Do you also take the train?
   B. Actually, I've never taken the train to work.

3. A. Are you a good swimmer?
   B. To tell the truth, I've never swum very well.

4. A. Did you get up early this morning?
   B. I've gotten up early every morning this week.

5. A. I'm going to give my dog a bath today. Do you have any advice?
   B. Sorry. I don't. I've never given my dog a bath.

6. A. Do you like to eat sushi?
   B. Of course! I've eaten sushi for many years.

7. A. I just got a big raise! Did you also get one?
   B. Actually, I've never gotten a raise.

8. A. I did very well on the math exam. How about you?
   B. I've never done well on a math exam.

Answers

1. Yes	3. No	5. No	7. No
2. No	4. Yes	6. Yes	8. No

E. What Are They Saying?

1. Have you ever gotten
   I got
2. Have you ever ridden
   I rode
3. Have you ever worn
   I wore
4. Have you ever gone
   I went
5. Have you ever given
   I gave
6. Have you ever fallen
   I fell

G. What Are They Saying?

1. Have, eaten
   they have, They ate
2. Has, driven
   he has, He drove
3. Has, gone
   she has, She went
4. Have, seen
   we have, We saw
5. Have, taken
   they have, They took
6. Have, spoken
   I have, I spoke
7. Have, written
   you have, You wrote
8. Have, met
   we have, We met

H. Not Today

1. They've, eaten
   They ate
2. She's, gone
   She went
3. He's, worn
   He wore
4. We've, done
   We did
5. He's, given
   He gave
6. I've, seen
   I saw
7. We've, bought
   We bought
8. She's, visited
   She visited
9. He's, taken
   He took

I. What's the Word?

1. go	7. ate	13. wear	19. driven
2. went	8. eaten	14. worn	20. drive
3. gone	9. eat	15. wore	21. drove
4. seen	10. write	16. spoke	22. do
5. saw	11. written	17. speak	23. did
6. see	12. wrote	18. spoken	24. done

J. What Are They Saying?

1. I've, done
   I did
   have, written
   I have
2. I've, swum
   I swam
3. I've, taken
   I took

   Have, taken
   I have, took
4. He's, gotten
   He got
5. We've, eaten
   We ate
   eaten
6. I've, spoken
   I spoke

L. In a Long Time

1. I haven't ridden
2. haven't bought
3. I haven't flown
4. I haven't taken
5. I haven't swum
6. hasn't eaten
7. hasn't cleaned
8. He hasn't read
9. I haven't studied
10. haven't seen
11. I haven't given
12. He hasn't made
13. haven't gone
14. I haven't danced

M. Puzzle: *What Have They Already Done?*

N. A Lot of Things to Do

1. He's already gone to the supermarket.
2. He hasn't cleaned his apartment yet.
3. He's already gotten a haircut.
4. He hasn't baked a cake yet.
5. He's already fixed his CD player.
6. She's already taken a shower.
7. She hasn't done her exercises yet.
8. She hasn't fed the cat yet.
9. She's already walked the dog.
10. She hasn't eaten breakfast yet.
11. They haven't done their laundry yet.
12. They've already gotten their paychecks.
13. They've already paid their bills.
14. They haven't packed their suitcases yet.
15. They haven't said good-bye to their friends yet.
16. She's already written to Mrs. Lane.
17. She's already called Mr. Sanchez.
18. She hasn't met with Ms. Wong yet.
19. She hasn't read her e-mail yet.
20. She's already sent a fax to the Ace Company.

O. Listening

What things have these people done? What haven't they done? Listen and check Yes *or* No.

1. A. Carla, have you done your homework yet?
   B. Yes, I have. I did my homework this morning.
   A. And have you practiced the violin?
   B. No, I haven't practiced yet. I promise I'll practice this afternoon.

2. A. Kevin?
   B. Yes, Mrs. Blackwell?
   A. Have you written your report yet?
   B. No, I haven't. I'll write it immediately.
   A. And have you sent a fax to the Crane Company?
   B. No, I haven't. I promise I'll send them a fax after I write the report.

3. A. Have you fed the dog yet?
   B. Yes, I have. I fed him a few minutes ago.
   A. Good. Well, I guess we can leave for work now.
   B. But we haven't eaten breakfast yet!

4. A. I'm leaving now, Mr. Green.
   B. Have you fixed the pipes in the basement, Charlie?
   A. Yes, I have.
   B. And have you repaired the washing machine?
   A. Yes, I have. It's working again.
   B. That's great! Thank you, Charlie.
   A. I'll send you a bill, Mr. Green.

5. A. You know, we haven't done the laundry all week.
   B. I know. We should do it today.
   A. We also haven't vacuumed the rugs!
   B. We haven't?
   A. No, we haven't.
   B. Oh. I guess we should vacuum them today.

6. A. Are we ready for the party?
   B. I think so. We've gotten all the food at the supermarket, and we've cleaned the house from top to bottom!
   A. Well, I guess we're ready for the party!

7. A. Have you spoken to the landlord about our broken light?
   B. Yes, I have. I spoke to him this morning.
   A. What did he say?
   B. He said we should call an electrician.
   A. Okay. Let's call Ajax Electric.
   B. Don't worry. I've already called them, and they're coming this afternoon.

8. A. Have you hooked up the new VCR yet?
   B. I can't do it. It's really difficult.
   A. Have you read the instructions?
   B. Yes, I have. I've read them ten times, and I still can't understand them!

Answers

	Yes	No			Yes	No
1.	✔	___	5.		___	✔
	___	✔			___	✔
2.	___	✔	6.		✔	___
	___	✔			✔	___
3.	✔	___	7.		✔	___
	___	✔			✔	___
4.	✔	___	8.		___	✔
	✔	___			✔	___

WORKBOOK PAGES 48–49

P. What Are They Saying?

1. have, spoke
   did
   flown
2. Have
   haven't, saw
   see
   seen
3. taken
   took
   Have, sent
   sent
   Have, given
4. Have
   have, went

Have, gone/been
have, I went/was
5. did
   gave
   are you going to buy
   spent
   did you
   bought
   listen
6. I'm not, taken
   got
   Have
   I have, ate
   washed/done

WORKBOOK PAGE 50

R. Julia's Broken Keyboard

1.
> Judy,
>
> Have you seen my blue and yellow jacket at your house? I think I left it there yesterday after the jazz concert. I've looked everywhere, and I just can't find it anywhere.
>
> Julia

2.
> Dear Jennifer,
>
> We're sorry you haven't been able to visit us this year. Do you think you could come in June or July? We really enjoyed your visit last year. We really want to see you again.
>
> Julia

3.
> Jeff,
>
> Jack and I have gone out jogging, but we'll be back in just a few minutes. Make yourself comfortable. You can wait for us in the yard. We haven't eaten lunch yet. We'll have some yogurt and orange juice when we get back.
>
> Julia

4.
> Dear Jane,
>
> We just received the beautiful pajamas you sent to Jimmy. Thank you very much. Jimmy is too young to write to you himself, but he says "Thank you." He's already worn the pajamas, and he's enjoying them a lot.
>
> Julia

5.
> Dear Janet,
>
> Jack and I are coming to visit you and John in New York. We've been to New York before, but we haven't visited the Statue of Liberty or the Empire State Building yet. See you in January or maybe in June.
>
> Julia

6.
> Dear Joe,
>
> We got a letter from James last week. He has enjoyed college a lot this year. His favorite subjects are German and Japanese. He's looking for a job as a journalist in Japan, but he hasn't found one yet.
>
> Julia

WORKBOOK PAGE 51

S. Is or Has?

1. has	8. is	15. has
2. is	9. is	16. is
3. is	10. has	17. has
4. has	11. is	18. is
5. is	12. has	19. is
6. is	13. is	20. has
7. has	14. has	

UNIT 5

WORKBOOK PAGE 52

A. How Long?

1. I've had a headache since
2. They've been married for
3. He's owned a motorcycle since
4. She's been interested in astronomy for
5. I've had a cell phone since
6. We've known each other since
7. They've had a dog for
8. I've had problems with my upstairs neighbor for
9. She's been a computer programmer since
10. He's played in the school orchestra since
11. There have been mice in our attic for

WORKBOOK PAGE 53

B. What's the Question?

1. How long has, wanted to be an engineer
2. How long has, owned his own house
3. How long have, been married
4. How long have, been interested in photography
5. How long has, worn glasses
6. How long have, known how to snowboard
7. How long has, had a girlfriend
8. How long has, been a pizza shop in town

WORKBOOK PAGE 55

D. Since When?

1. I'm
   I've been sick
2. has
   She's had
3. knows
   He's known
4. They're
   They've been
5. We're
   We've been
6. have
   I've had
7. It's
   It's been
8. plays
   She's
9. is
   He's been
10. I'm
    I've been

WORKBOOK PAGE 56

E. Listening

Listen and choose the correct answer.

1. Bob has been engaged since he got out of the army.
2. My sister Carol has been a professional musician since she finished music school.
3. Michael has been home since he fell and hurt himself last week.
4. My wife has gotten up early every morning since she started her new job.
5. Richard has eaten breakfast in the school cafeteria every morning since he started college.
6. Nancy and Tom have known each other for five and a half years.
7. My friend Charlie and I have played soccer every weekend since we were eight years old.
8. Patty has had short hair since she was a teenager.
9. Ron has owned his own business since he moved to Chicago nine years ago.
10. I've been interested in astronomy for the past eleven years.
11. I use my personal computer all the time. I've had it since I was in high school.
12. Alan has had problems with his house since he bought it fifteen years ago.

Answers

1. b	4. b	7. a	10. a
2. b	5. a	8. b	11. b
3. a	6. a	9. b	12. a

F. Crossword

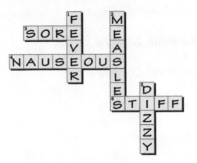

WORKBOOK PAGE 57

G. Scrambled Sentences

1. Julie has liked jazz since she was a teenager.
2. He's known how to play the piano since he was a little boy.
3. I've been interested in astronomy since I was young.
4. They've been engaged since they finished college.
5. He's been a chef since he graduated from cooking school.
6. She's wanted to be a teacher since she was eighteen years old.
7. They've owned their own business since they moved here a year ago.

WORKBOOK PAGE 58

I. Then and Now

1. walk
   They've walked
   they
   walked
2. speaks
   He's spoken
   he spoke
3. is
   She's been
   she was
4. taught
   he teaches
   He's taught
5. has
   visited
   visited
   visit
6. has
   She's had
   had

WORKBOOK PAGE 59

J. Looking Back

1. has Victor been
   He's been a musician, 1990
2. was he
   He was a photographer, 7 years
3. has Mrs. Sanchez taught
   She's taught science, 1995
4. did she teach
   She taught math, 9 years
5. did your grandparents have
   They had a cat, 11 years
6. have they had
   They've had a dog, 1998

7. has Betty worked
She's worked at the bank, 2000

8. did she work
She worked at the mall, 2 years

9. did your parents live
They lived in New York, 20 years

10. have they lived
They've lived in Miami, 2001

WORKBOOK PAGE 61

L. Listening

Listen and choose the correct answer.

1. A. Have you always been a salesperson?
B. No. I've been a salesperson for the past four years. Before that, I was a cashier.

2. A. How long has your daughter been in medical school?
B. She's been in medical school for the past two years.

3. A. Have your parents always lived in a house?
B. No. They've lived in a house for the past ten years. Before that, they lived in an apartment.

4. A. How long have you wanted to be an actor?
B. I've wanted to be an actor since I was in college. Before that, I wanted to be a musician.

5. A. Do you and your husband still exercise at your health club every day?
B. No. We haven't done that for a year.

6. A. Has James been a bachelor all his life?
B. No, he hasn't. He was married for ten years.

7. A. Has your sister Jane always wanted to be a writer?
B. Yes, she has. She's wanted to be a writer all her life.

8. A. Have you ever broken your ankle?
B. No. I've sprained it a few times, but I've never broken it.

9. A. Have you always liked classical music?
B. No. I've liked classical music for the past few years. Before that, I liked rock music.

10. A. Has Billy had a sore throat for a long time?
B. He's had a sore throat for the past two days. Before that, he had a fever.

11. A. Jennifer has been the store manager since last fall.
B. What did she do before that?
A. She was a salesperson.

12. A. Have you always been interested in modern art?
B. No. I've been interested in modern art since I moved to Paris a few years ago. Before that, I was only interested in sports.

Answers

1. b	**3.** a	**5.** b	**7.** b	**9.** b	**11.** b
2. b	**4.** b	**6.** a	**8.** a	**10.** b	**12.** a

UNIT 6

WORKBOOK PAGE 62

A. What's the Word?

1. since	**4.** since	**7.** since
2. for	**5.** since	**8.** for
3. for	**6.** for	

B. Choose

1. a	**3.** b	**5.** b
2. b	**4.** a	**6.** b

WORKBOOK PAGE 63

C. How Long?

1. I've been studying since
2. She's been feeling sick for
3. He's been having problems with his car for
4. They've been arguing since
5. We've been waiting for
6. It's been ringing since
7. He's been talking for
8. They've been dating since
9. I've been teaching since
10. You've been chatting online for

WORKBOOK PAGE 64

D. What Are They Doing?

1. is looking
He's been looking

2. is jogging
She's been jogging

3. is barking
It's been barking

4. are planting
They've been planting

5. is doing
He's been doing

6. is browsing
She's been browsing

7. are assembling
They've been assembling

8. baking
I've been baking

9. are making
You've been making

E. Listening

Listen and choose the correct time expressions to complete the sentences.

1. A. How long have you been living there?
   B. I've been living there since . . .
2. A. How long has your daughter been practicing the piano?
   B. She's been practicing for . . .
3. A. How long have I been running?
   B. You've been running since . . .
4. A. How long have you been feeling bad?
   B. I've been feeling bad for . . .
5. A. How long have they been waiting?
   B. They've been waiting for . . .
6. A. How long has your son been studying?
   B. He's been studying since . . .
7. A. How long have your sister and her boyfriend been dating?
   B. They've been dating since . . .
8. A. Dad, how long have we been driving?
   B. Hmm. I think we've been driving for . . .
9. A. How long has your little girl been crying?
   B. She's been crying for . . .

Answers

1. a	**3.** a	**5.** b	**7.** b	**9.** b
2. b	**4.** b	**6.** a	**8.** a	

WORKBOOK PAGES 66–67

G. What Are They Saying?

1. Have you been waiting
   have
   I've been waiting
2. Has it been snowing
   it has
   It's been snowing
3. Has he been taking
   he has
   He's been taking
4. Have you been working
   I haven't
   been working
5. Has, been making
   it has
   It's been making
6. Have you been vacuuming
   I have
   I've been vacuuming
7. Have they been studying
   they have
   They've been studying

8. Have we been running
   have
   We've been running
9. Have you been wearing
   I haven't
   I've been wearing
10. Have you been playing
    I haven't
    I've been playing

H. Listening

Listen and choose what the people are talking about.

1. She's been directing it for an hour.
2. We've been rearranging it all morning.
3. I've been paying them on time.
4. He's been playing them for years.
5. Have you been bathing them for a long time?
6. They've been rebuilding it for a year.
7. She's been writing it for a week.
8. He's been translating them for many years.
9. I've been reading it all afternoon.
10. She's been knitting them for a few weeks.
11. We've been listening to them all afternoon.
12. I've been recommending it for years.
13. They've been repairing it all day.
14. She's been taking it all morning.
15. I've been solving them all my life.

Answers

1. a	**4.** a	**7.** a	**10.** a	**13.** b
2. b	**5.** b	**8.** a	**11.** b	**14.** a
3. b	**6.** b	**9.** b	**12.** a	**15.** b

WORKBOOK PAGE 68

I. Sound It Out!

1. interested
2. is
3. Steve's
4. in
5. history
6. sister
7. very
8. Chinese
9. Steve's sister is very interested in Chinese history.
10. receive
11. this
12. any
13. Peter
14. week
15. didn't
16. e-mail
17. Peter didn't receive any e-mail this week.

K. What's Happening?

1. We've been eating
   We've, eaten
   We haven't eaten
2. She's been seeing
   She's, seen
   She hasn't seen
3. He's been swimming
   He's, swum
4. She's been going
   She's, gone
5. He's been talking
   He's, talked
   he hasn't talked
6. They've been writing
   They've, written
   they haven't written
7. he's been making
   He's, made
   He hasn't made
8. She's been studying
   She's, studied
   she hasn't studied
9. He's been reading
   He's, read
   he hasn't read
10. They've been
    complaining
    They've, complained
    haven't complained

L. Listening

Listen and decide where the conversation is taking place.

1. A. I'm really tired.
   B. No wonder! You've been chopping tomatoes for the past hour.

2. A. Mark! I'm surprised. You've been falling asleep in class all morning, and you've never fallen asleep in class before.
   B. I'm sorry, Mrs. Applebee. It won't happen again.

3. A. I've been washing these shirts for the past half hour, and they still aren't clean.
   B. Here. Try this Presto Soap.

4. A. We've been standing in line for an hour and forty-five minutes.
   B. I know. I hope the movie is good. I've never stood in line for such a long time.

5. A. What seems to be the problem, Mr. Jones?
   B. My back has been hurting me for the past few days.
   A. I'm sorry to hear that.

6. A. You know, we've been reading here for more than two hours.
   B. You're right. I think it's time to go now.

7. A. Do you want to leave?
   B. I think so. We've seen all the paintings here.

8. A. How long have you been exercising?
   B. For an hour and a half.

9. A. We've been waiting for an hour, and it still isn't here.
   B. I know. I'm going to be late for work.

10. A. I think we've seen them all. Which one do you want to buy?
    B. I like that black one over there.

11. A. We've been watching this movie for the past hour, and it's terrible!
    B. You're right. Let's change the channel.

12. A. I've got a terrible headache.
    B. Why?
    A. Customers have been complaining all morning.
    B. What have they been complaining about?
    A. Some people have complained about our terrible products, but most people have complained about our high prices.

Answers

1. a	4. a	7. b	10. b
2. b	5. a	8. a	11. a
3. b	6. b	9. b	12. b

M. Which Word?

1. leaking
2. flying
3. run
4. made
5. have you been
6. seen
7. given
8. taken
9. gone
10. has been ringing
11. singing

O. A New Life

1. He's never lived in a big city
2. He's never taken English lessons
3. He's never taken the subway
4. He's never shopped in American supermarkets
5. He's never eaten American food
6. He's never played American football

8. They've been living in a big city
9. They've been taking English lessons
10. They've been taking the subway
11. They've been shopping in American supermarkets
12. They've been eating American food
13. They've been playing American football

CHECK-UP TEST: Units 4–6

A.

1. have, eaten
2. hasn't taken
3. haven't written
4. has, gone
5. haven't paid
6. has, had

B.

1. Have you spoken
2. Has he ridden
3. Have they gotten
4. Has he, flown
5. Has she, been
6. Have you met

C.

1. It's been sunny
2. We've been browsing
3. She's had
4. He's been studying
5. They've been arguing
6. I've known
7. She's been
8. We've been cleaning

D.

1. She's been working at the bank since
2. They've been barking for
3. It's been snowing for
4. I've wanted to be an astronaut since

E.

1. He's owned
   he owned
2. I've been
   I was
3. She's liked
   she liked

F.

Listen and choose the correct answer.

1. A. How long has Janet been an actress?
   B. She's been an actress since she graduated from acting school.

2. A. Have you watched the news yet?
   B. Yes. I saw the president, and I heard his speech.

3. A. Have you always lived in Denver?
   B. No. We've lived in Denver since 1995. Before that, we lived in New York.

4. A. Has Dad made dinner yet?
   B. Not yet. He still has to make it.

5. A. How long has your ceiling been leaking?
   B. It's been leaking for more than a week.
   A. Have you called the superintendent?
   B. Yes, I have. I've called him several times.

6. A. Billy is having trouble with his homework.
   B. Has he asked anyone to help him?
   A. No, he hasn't.

Answers

1. b	3. b	5. a
2. a	4. a	6. b

UNIT 7

WORKBOOK PAGE 78

A. What Do They {Enjoy Doing / Like to Do}?

1. enjoy
2. likes to, Talking
3. enjoy
4. like to, Knitting
5. enjoy
6. likes to, delivering
7. enjoy, being
8. likes to, planting
9. enjoys, chatting
10. like to, playing
11. enjoy
12. likes to, going
13. enjoy

WORKBOOK PAGE 80

C. What's the Word?

1. complain
2. sitting
3. eat
4. clean
5. wear
6. cleaning
7. go
8. going
9. sit
10. complaining
11. eating
12. wearing

WORKBOOK PAGE 82

F. My Energetic Grandfather

1. to play/playing
2. to play
3. play

WORKBOOK PAGE 83

H. Choose

1. to buy
2. moving
3. going
4. changing
5. get
6. retiring

WORKBOOK PAGE 85

K. What's the Word?

1. rearranging
2. eating
3. worrying
4. to get/getting
5. to exercise/
   exercising
6. to ask/asking
7. arguing
8. to take/taking
9. paying, to pay/
   paying
10. to fall/falling

L. Good Decisions

1. biting
2. to do/doing
3. to cook
4. to cook/cooking
5. paying
6. cleaning
7. gossiping
8. interrupting

M. Problems!

1. falling
   falling
2. to lift/lifting
   to lift/lifting
   lifting
3. to tease/teasing
   teasing
   crying
   teasing

4. driving
   to drive/driving
   to drive/driving
5. dressing
   to dress/dressing
   dressing
6. stepping
   to dance/dancing
   going

N. Listening

Listen and choose the correct answer.

1. Dr. Gomez really enjoys . . .
2. Whenever possible, my wife and I try to avoid . . .
3. Next summer I'm going to learn . . .
4. Every day Rita practices . . .
5. My parents have decided . . .
6. I've considered . . .
7. Are you thinking about . . .
8. I'm going to quit . . .
9. Why do you keep on . . .
10. My doctor says I should stop . . .
11. David can't stand . . .
12. Are you going to continue to . . .
13. James doesn't want to start . . .
14. Next semester Kathy is going to begin . . .
15. You know, you can't keep on . . .

Answers

1. a	5. a	9. a	13. a
2. a	6. a	10. b	14. a
3. b	7. b	11. b	15. b
4. b	8. b	12. b	

O. What Does It Mean?

1. b	4. b	7. b	10. b
2. c	5. c	8. a	11. b
3. a	6. a	9. c	12. c

UNIT 8

A. Before

1. had eaten
2. had, gotten
3. had, visited
4. had driven
5. had, cut
6. had spent
7. had, gone

8. had made
9. had seen
10. had, left
11. had had
12. had, given
13. had lost

C. Late for Everything

1. had, left
2. had, begun
3. had, gone---
4. had, closed

5. had, started
6. had, left
7. had, arrived

D. In a Long Time

1. hadn't listened
2. hadn't seen
3. hadn't had
4. hadn't gone
5. hadn't remembered
6. hadn't ironed, hadn't shaved
7. hadn't lost
8. hadn't skied
9. hadn't gotten
10. hadn't taken off
11. hadn't studied
12. hadn't ridden

E. Working Hard

1. She was studying for her science test.
2. She had already written an English composition.
3. She hadn't practiced the trombone yet.
4. She hadn't read the next history chapter yet.
5. She hadn't memorized her lines for the school play yet.
6. He was hooking up the new printer.
7. He had already sent an e-mail to the boss.
8. He had already given the employees their paychecks.
9. He hadn't written to the Bentley Company yet.
10. He hadn't taken two packages to the post office yet.
11. They were cleaning the garage.
12. They had already assembled Billy's new bicycle.
13. They had already fixed the fence.
14. They hadn't repaired the roof yet.
15. They hadn't started to build a tree house yet.
16. She was playing squash.
17. She had already done yoga.
18. She had already gone jogging.
19. She hadn't lifted weights yet.
20. She hadn't swum across the pool 10 times yet.

F. What Had They Been Doing?

1. had been talking
2. had been living

3. had been working
4. had been going out

5. had been planning
6. had been thinking about
7. had been getting
8. had been borrowing
9. had been eating
10. had been rehearsing
11. had been looking forward
12. had been training
13. had been arriving

WORKBOOK PAGE 96

I. Marylou's Broken Keyboard

1.

Roger,

I'm afraid there's something wrong with the fireplace in the living room. Also, the refrigerator is broken. I've been calling the landlord for three days on his cell phone, but he hasn't called back. I hope he calls me tomorrow.

Marylou

2.

Louise,

I'm terribly worried about my brother Larry's health. He hurt his leg while he was playing baseball. He had already dislocated his shoulder while he was surfing last Friday. According to his doctor, he is also having problems with his blood pressure and with his right wrist. He really should try to relax and take life a little easier.

Marylou

3.

Arnold,

Can you possibly recommend a good restaurant in your neighborhood? I'm planning on taking my relatives to lunch tomorrow, but I'm not sure where.

We ate at a very nice Greek restaurant near your apartment building last month, but I haven't been able to remember the name. Do you know the place?

Your friend,
Marylou

4.

Rosa,

I have been planning a trip to Florida. I'll be flying to Orlando on Friday, and I'll be returning three days later. Have you ever been there? I remember you had family members who lived in Florida several years ago.

Please write back.

All my love,
Marylou

WORKBOOK PAGE 97

J. Listening

Listen and choose the correct answer.

1. Steve lost his voice.
2. Is Beverly one of your relatives?
3. We just canceled our trip to South America.
4. Ricky has been failing all of his tests this year.
5. Francine dislocated her shoulder.
6. What did you and your students discuss in class?
7. My girlfriend and I rode on the roller coaster yesterday.
8. Grandma can't chew this piece of steak very well.
9. Jimmy loves my homemade food.
10. Did you see the motorcycles go by?
11. Do you think Mr. Montero will take a day off soon?
12. Amy wanted to ask her boss for a raise, but she got cold feet.
13. Have you heard that Margaret sprained her wrist?
14. I have to make an important decision.
15. I envy you.
16. I feel terrible. Debbie and Dan broke up last week.
17. My ankle hurts a lot.
18. I was heartbroken when I heard what happened.
19. Michael was furious with his neighbors.
20. We went to a recital last night.
21. Tom, don't forget to shine your shoes!
22. My friend Carla is extremely athletic.
23. My husband and I have been writing invitations all afternoon.
24. Charles rented a beautiful tuxedo for his niece's wedding.

Answers

1. c	6. b	11. a	16. c	21. b
2. b	7. a	12. c	17. b	22. c
3. c	8. b	13. b	18. c	23. a
4. b	9. c	14. a	19. b	24. c
5. c	10. b	15. c	20. a	

WORKBOOK PAGES 98–99

CHECK-UP TEST: Units 7–8

A.

1. eating
2. wrestling
3. to stop
4. boxing
5. Swimming
6. to skate
7. talking
8. doing

B.

1. hadn't spoken	**5.** hadn't had
2. had, done	**6.** hadn't taken
3. had, left	**7.** hadn't eaten
4. hadn't written	**8.** hadn't gone

C.

1. had been working	**3.** had been arguing
2. had been training	**4.** had been planning

D.

Listen and choose the correct answer.

Ex. My grandfather likes to . . .
1. Susan says she's going to stop . . .
2. My wife and I are thinking about . . .
3. David is considering . . .
4. I can't stand to . . .
5. You should definitely keep on . . .

Answers

1. b   **2.** a   **3.** b   **4.** b   **5.** a

UNIT 9

WORKBOOK PAGE 100

A. What Are They Saying?

1. pick him up	**6.** hook it up
2. turned it on	**7.** throw them out
3. take them back	**8.** took it back
4. fill them out	**9.** took them down
5. hang it up	**10.** call her up

WORKBOOK PAGE 101

B. What Are They Saying?

1. turn on	**5.** take off
turn it on	take them off
2. hand, in	**6.** put, away
hand it in	put them away
3. wake up	**7.** Put, on
wake them up	put them on
4. turn, off	**8.** bring, back
turn it off	bring her back

WORKBOOK PAGE 103

D. What Are They Saying?

1. do it over	**6.** turn him down
2. gave it back	**7.** throw them away
3. hook it up	**8.** written it down
4. think it over	**9.** cross them out
5. look it up	**10.** turned it off

WORKBOOK PAGE 104

E. What's the Word?

1. put away	**5.** call up	**9.** throw out
2. hook up	**6.** write down	**10.** hang up
3. take back	**7.** clean up	
4. wake up	**8.** put away	

WORKBOOK PAGE 105

F. What Should They Do?

1. think it over	**5.** figure it out
2. give it back	**6.** wake them up
3. used it up	**7.** turn it off
4. look it up	**8.** throw them out

G. Listening

Listen and choose the correct answer.

1. A. I looked in the refrigerator, and I can't find the orange juice.
    B. That's because we . . .

2. A. I'm frustrated! My computer isn't working today.
    B. I think you forgot to . . .

3. A. What should I do with the Christmas decorations?
    B. I think it's time to . . .

4. A. Should I take these clothes to the cleaner's?
    B. Yes. You should definitely . . .

5. A. Hmm. What does this word mean?
    B. You should . . .

6. A. I have to return this skateboard to my cousin.
    B. When are you going to . . .

7. A. This math problem is very difficult.
    B. Maybe I can . . .

8. A. I'll never remember their new telephone number.
    B. You should . . .

9. A. I just spilled milk on the kitchen floor!
    B. Don't worry. I'll . . .

Answers

1. b	**3.** a	**5.** b	**7.** b	**9.** b
2. b	**4.** b	**6.** a	**8.** a	

WORKBOOK PAGE 106

H. Come Up With the Right Answer

1. take after
   take after him
2. heard from
   hear from him
3. called on
   call on me
4. looking through
   looked through them
5. got over
   got over it
6. look up to
   look up to me
7. ran into
   ran into her
8. get along with
   get along with her
9. picks on
   picks on them

WORKBOOK PAGE 107

J. Choose

1. b	4. b	7. b	10. b	13. b
2. a	5. a	8. a	11. a	14. b
3. b	6. b	9. a	12. a	

WORKBOOK PAGE 108

K. What Does It Mean?

1. b	3. b	5. a	7. b
2. c	4. c	6. a	8. c

L. Listening

Listen and choose the correct answer.

1. I really look up to my father.
2. My brother picks on me all the time.
3. Did you throw away the last can of paint?
4. I still haven't gotten over the flu.
5. Have you heard from your cousin Sam recently?
6. Why did you turn him down?
7. Did your French teacher call on you today?
8. George picked out a new suit for his wedding.
9. I have to drop my sister off at the airport.
10. Everything in the store is 20 percent off this week.
11. This jacket fits you.
12. Did you try on a lot of shoes?

Answers

1. c	4. a	7. a	10. b
2. b	5. b	8. c	11. a
3. c	6. c	9. c	12. b

UNIT 10

WORKBOOK PAGE 109

A. Not the Only One

1. did I	5. I will	9. I did
2. I do	6. was I	10. will I
3. can I	7. am I	11. do I
4. I am	8. I have	

WORKBOOK PAGE 110

B. What a Coincidence!

1. do I	5. I will	9. I am
2. I do	6. did I	10. do I
3. I did	7. I was	11. am I
4. have I	8. I did	

WORKBOOK PAGE 111

C. Not the Only One

1. did I	5. I won't	9. I didn't
2. I'm not	6. have I	10. do I
3. was I	7. I can't	11. will I
4. I can't	8. am I	

WORKBOOK PAGE 112

D. Listening

Listen and complete the sentences.

1. I missed the bus this morning.
2. I'm allergic to nuts.
3. I'll be on vacation next week.
4. I've never flown in a helicopter.
5. I can speak Chinese.
6. I like to go sailing.
7. I'm not going to the company picnic this weekend.
8. I saw a very good movie last night.
9. I don't go on many business trips.
10. I've been to London several times.
11. I'm not a vegetarian.
12. I should lose a little weight.
13. I can't stop worrying about my health.
14. I hate to drive downtown.
15. I won't be able to go to Nancy's party this Saturday night.

Answers

1. did I	6. I do	11. I'm not
2. I am	7. am I	12. I should
3. will I	8. I did	13. can I
4. I haven't	9. do I	14. do I
5. I can	10. have I	15. I won't

WORKBOOK PAGE 113

G. What Are They Saying?

1. did he	5. you should	9. I do
2. will she	6. they were	10. . . ., so has
3. he was	7. so can	
4. has she	8. did he	

WORKBOOK PAGE 114

H. What Are They Saying?

1. can I	5. were they	9. neither has
2. they didn't	6. she hasn't	10. she hadn't
3. is he	7. will they	
4. she doesn't	8. aren't either	

WORKBOOK PAGE 115

I. What Are They Saying?

1. so did she
   she did, too
2. neither could he
   he couldn't either
3. so does he
   he does, too
4. neither does she
   she doesn't either
5. neither had she
   she hadn't either
6. so is he
   he is, too

WORKBOOK PAGE 116

J. Our Family

1. aren't, been
2. is, playing, doing
3. can, drawing, was
4. doesn't, going
5. isn't, has been taking
6. haven't, lived, for, lived
7. doesn't, hasn't spoken
8. won't, hasn't
9. does, sung, since
10. aren't, up, away
11. doesn't, for
12. aren't, skating, had, skated

WORKBOOK PAGE 117

K. Listening

Listen and complete the sentences.

1. I missed the bus today, . . .
2. I'm allergic to cats, . . .
3. I'll be on vacation next week, . . .
4. You've never seen a rainbow, . . .
5. I can speak Italian, . . .
6. I like to go sailing, . . .
7. I've been on television several times, . . .
8. I saw an exciting movie last weekend, . . .
9. I won't be in the office tomorrow, . . .
10. We were late, . . .
11. I'm not a vegetarian, . . .
12. I saw the stop sign, . . .
13. I can't swim very well, . . .
14. They have to work overtime this weekend, . . .
15. I won't be able to go to Sam's party this Friday night, . . .
16. I'm not afraid of flying, . . .
17. I haven't eaten breakfast yet, . . .
18. The other students weren't bored, . . .

Answers

1. didn't
2. isn't
3. won't
4. have
5. can't
6. doesn't
7. haven't
8. didn't
9. will
10. wasn't
11. is
12. didn't
13. can
14. don't
15. will
16. is
17. have
18. was

WORKBOOK PAGE 118

M. Sound It Out!

1. cooks
2. too
3. shouldn't
4. put
5. cookies
6. good
7. sugar
8. Good cooks shouldn't put too much sugar in their cookies.
9. two
10. books
11. bookcase
12. who
13. took
14. afternoon
15. Susan's
16. Who took two books from Susan's bookcase this afternoon?

WORKBOOK PAGE 119

N. What Does It Mean?

1. j
2. c
3. q
4. s
5. n
6. h
7. i
8. x
9. m
10. v
11. w
12. y
13. b
14. a
15. u
16. l
17. p
18. e
19. o
20. k
21. f
22. t
23. z
24. g
25. d
26. r

WORKBOOK PAGES 120–121

CHECK-UP TEST: Units 9–10

A.

1. it in
2. up to him
3. from her
4. it over
5. it up
6. out of it
7. for it
8. them up
9. them out
10. it down
11. over it

B.

1. so is
2. neither will
3. were, too
4. can't either
5. so have
6. did, too
7. neither has
8. so do
9. neither is

C.

Listen and complete the sentences.

Ex. Nancy knows how to type, . . .
1. I'm interested in science, . . .
2. I won't be home this evening, . . .
3. I own my own business, . . .
4. I've never hooked up a computer, . . .
5. You just got a raise, . . .

Answers

1. isn't
2. will
3. doesn't
4. has
5. didn't

UNIT 1 TEST

WORKBOOK PAGES T1–T4

A–E.

1. D	11. A	21. A	31. C
2. B	12. D	22. D	32. D
3. C	13. A	23. B	33. B
4. A	14. B	24. A	34. A
5. D	15. C	25. B	35. B
6. C	16. A	26. A	36. D
7. B	17. D	27. C	37. C
8. B	18. B	28. C	38. A
9. C	19. C	29. A	39. C
10. D	20. B	30. B	40. D

E. Listening Assessment

Read and listen to the questions.

35. How can you listen to the information in Spanish?

36. How can you listen to the information in Arabic?

37. How many days a week is the program open?

38. When can you take a placement test for fall English classes?

39. On what date do fall classes begin?

40. How can you listen to the information again?

Now listen to the automated telephone message, and answer the questions.

Thank you for calling the Plainfield Adult Education Program. To hear this message in Spanish, press two. In Chinese, press three. In Korean, press four. In Vietnamese, press five. In Haitian Kreyol, press six. In Arabic, press seven. To continue this message in English, press one. At this time, the office is closed. The adult education program is open Monday through Friday from eight thirty A.M. to nine thirty P.M. Registration for fall classes begins on September third. Placement testing for fall English classes begins on August twenty-sixth and ends on September second. All classes in the fall session of the adult education program begin on September tenth. To repeat this message, please press the star key. Thank you for calling the Plainfield Adult Education Program. Have a nice day.

UNIT 2 TEST

WORKBOOK PAGES T5–T10

A–F.

1. C	11. A	21. A	31. B
2. D	12. C	22. D	32. B
3. B	13. B	23. C	33. C
4. C	14. A	24. C	34. B
5. A	15. D	25. A	35. A
6. B	16. D	26. B	36. A
7. D	17. A	27. D	37. C
8. C	18. B	28. D	38. B
9. B	19. C	29. C	39. D
10. D	20. B	30. A	40. D

F. Listening Assessment

Read and listen to the questions.

38. What is Rosa's address?

39. Where is David during this conversation?

40. Why did David get lost?

Now listen to the telephone conversation and answer the questions.

A. Hello.

B. Hi, Rosa. This is David. I'm on my way to your party, but I'm afraid I'm lost.

A. Where are you?

B. I'm at the corner of Madison Street and Central Avenue. I think I followed your directions. I took the Number 5 bus and got off at Main Street. Then I walked up Main Street to the post office and turned right on Madison Street. And I walked along Madison Street four blocks, but I can't find Lake Street.

A. Okay. I know what happened. You had to turn left at the post office, not right. So you walked the wrong way on Madison Street.

B. I see. What should I do?

A. Walk four blocks back down Madison Street to Main Street, and then keep walking straight another four blocks to Lake Street.

B. Okay.

A. Then turn right on Lake Street. My apartment building is number fourteen thirty (1430).

B. Okay, thanks. See you soon.

G. LEARNING SKILL: Listing Events in Chronological Order

3

6

5

1

4

2

UNIT 3 TEST

WORKBOOK PAGES T11–T14

A–E.

1. B	11. D	21. A	31. C
2. D	12. B	22. D	32. A
3. C	13. A	23. C	33. B
4. A	14. C	24. D	34. C
5. C	15. D	25. A	35. B
6. B	16. A	26. D	36. B
7. B	17. C	27. A	37. A
8. A	18. D	28. B	38. A
9. D	19. B	29. C	39. D
10. C	20. A	30. C	40. D

E. Listening Assessment

Read and listen to the questions.

38. Who is sick?

39. Where is the student now?

40. Where should the mother go?

Now listen to the telephone conversation and answer the questions.

A. Hello. May I speak to Mrs. Vacano, please?

B. This is Mrs. Vacano.

A. Hello. This is Ms. Harper, the school nurse, calling. I have your son, Raymond, here in my office.

B. What's the matter? Is he okay?

A. It isn't anything serious. Raymond didn't feel well during gym class this morning, so the gym teacher sent him to me. He has a stomachache, and he has a low fever.

B. I see. Should I come and pick him up? I'm at work now, but I can come over in about thirty minutes, since my lunch hour will begin at twelve noon.

A. I think that's a good idea. He'll be resting here in the meantime. Please go to the main office when you arrive.

B. Okay. Thank you very much for calling. I'll be there as soon as I can.

UNIT 4 TEST

WORKBOOK PAGES T15–T18

A–F.

1. A	11. C	21. A	31. B
2. D	12. A	22. D	32. A
3. B	13. D	23. B	33. C
4. C	14. B	24. C	34. B
5. B	15. A	25. A	35. A
6. D	16. D	26. C	36. B
7. A	17. B	27. C	37. C
8. C	18. A	28. A	38. D
9. B	19. C	29. B	39. A
10. D	20. C	30. C	40. C

F. Listening Assessment

Read and listen to the questions.

38. Where is the job interview probably taking place?

39. When CAN'T the job applicant work?

40. How often are the employees paid?

Now listen to the job interview and answer the questions.

A. Do you know how to take inventory?

B. Yes. I've taken inventory for many years in my current job.

A. And do you know how to speak with customers?

B. Yes. I speak with customers every day in the Women's Clothing Department of our store.

A. Are you able to work evenings?

B. Yes. I'm available afternoons and evenings. In the morning I go to school.

A. And are you able to work weekends?

B. Yes. What are the hours on weekends?

A. On Saturdays we're open from 9 A.M. to 9 P.M. On Sundays we're open from noon to 6 P.M. Do you have any other questions?

B. Yes. When do employees receive their paychecks?

A. Every Friday afternoon.

B. And are there health benefits with this job?

A. Yes. We pay for your health insurance. And there's another benefit. Employees receive a 30 percent discount on all items in the store.

B. That's very good.

A–G.

1. B	11. C	21. C	31. C
2. C	12. D	22. A	32. A
3. A	13. A	23. D	33. A
4. B	14. B	24. C	34. B
5. D	15. C	25. D	35. D
6. A	16. A	26. B	36. D
7. C	17. D	27. A	37. A
8. C	18. C	28. C	38. B
9. A	19. B	29. B	39. D
10. D	20. B	30. D	40. C

G. Listening Assessment

Read and listen to the questions.

38. Which abbreviation describes the hours for this position?

39. Which statement describes the experience this job requires?

40. Which sentence is probably in the ad for this job?

Now listen to the conversation and answer the questions.

A. Hello. Furniture Systems International. This is Pat.

B. Hello. I'm calling about the ad in today's paper. Is the position still available?

A. Yes, it is. What information can I give you about the position?

B. What are the hours?

A. It's an eight-hour workday, Monday through Friday, from nine to five.

B. I see. And what experience is required?

A. Excellent typing skills are required. And we prefer an applicant with previous office experience.

B. I understand. I'd like to set up an interview.

A. All right. Can you come in next Tuesday at 10 A.M.?

B. Yes, I can.

A. All right. Hold on a moment, and my assistant will take your name and phone number and give you directions to our building.

B. Thank you.

A–F.

1. B	11. D	21. D	31. B
2. A	12. C	22. A	32. C
3. C	13. A	23. C	33. B
4. D	14. B	24. B	34. A
5. A	15. C	25. A	35. B
6. B	16. D	26. D	36. A
7. C	17. D	27. B	37. C
8. C	18. A	28. B	38. D
9. D	19. B	29. C	39. B
10. B	20. C	30. A	40. A

F. Listening Assessment

Read and listen to the questions.

38. Which pets are NOT allowed in the building?

39. Which utility is included in the rent?

40. Where can tenants park a second car?

Now listen to the conversation and answer the questions.

A. Do you have any more questions about the apartment or the apartment building?

B. Yes. Are pets allowed in the building?

A. Cats, birds, and small dogs are permitted. Large dogs are not permitted.

B. And are utilities included in the rent?

A. Water and heat are included. Tenants pay the utility companies directly for electricity, telephone service, and cable TV service.

B. I have another question. We have two cars. Can we park them in the parking garage under the building?

A. Each apartment has one parking space in the garage. You can park your other car in the outside parking lot behind the building. When you move in, you can go to the rental office and get a parking sticker to put on the windshield of each car.

B. When someone comes to visit us, where can they park?

A. They can park in the visitor parking spaces in the parking lot. Do you have any other questions?

B. No. That's everything.

G. WRITING ASSESSMENT: Bank Transactions

WITHDRAWAL APPLICATION	Date _(date filled in)_	
	CASH WITHDRAWAL	$200
83219745	CHECK WITHDRAWAL	
Account number		
	TOTAL WITHDRAWAL	$200

(student's signature)
Signature

DEPOSIT SLIP	Date _(date filled in)_

CURRENCY	
COIN	
CHECKS	$575.25
LESS CASH	$100.00
TOTAL	$475.25

42439182
Account number

(student's name printed)
Name

(student's signature)
Sign here ONLY if cash received from deposit

1024

(date filled in)

Pay to the order of ____ E-Star Energy ____ $ 37.92

Thirty-seven dollars and 92/100 ____ Dollars

For _____ _(student's signature)_

057009345 200042534 1024

Number	Date	Description	Amount of Debit (−)	Amount of Credit (+)	Balance
1022	1/14	Metrovision Cable TV	49.50		1,461.50
1023	1/16	Telecom	32.51		1,428.99
1024	(date)	E-Star Energy	37.92		1,391.07

UNIT 7 TEST

WORKBOOK PAGES T31–T36

A–F.

1. C	11. A	21. B	31. C
2. B	12. D	22. D	32. A
3. D	13. C	23. A	33. A
4. C	14. C	24. D	34. B
5. A	15. D	25. B	35. A
6. B	16. B	26. C	36. C
7. D	17. D	27. D	37. D
8. B	18. A	28. C	38. B
9. A	19. C	29. C	39. D
10. B	20. C	30. B	40. C

F. Listening Assessment

Read and listen to the questions.

38. Who just had a baby?
39. What are Tonya and Barry thinking about doing?
40. How did Ken go to Tampa?

Now listen to the conversation and answer the questions.

A. Hi, Ken. The weather is terrible today, isn't it?
B. It's awful, Tonya. And I forgot to bring an umbrella.
A. Too bad. How was your weekend, Ken?
B. It was great. I went to Tampa to visit my sister and her husband. They just had a baby,

and this was my first time to see my new niece.

A. What's her name?
B. Leona.
A. That's a pretty name.
B. And how was YOUR weekend?
A. It was okay. On Saturday, Barry and I continued looking for a new apartment. We have to move from our apartment building in two more months.
B. Did you find anything?
A. No. We keep on looking for apartments in town, but the rents are very high. So now we're considering looking for a place outside the city. Sunday was more fun. A lot of our friends came over to watch the football game on our new TV. Did you watch the game?
B. No. I couldn't. But I listened to it on the radio while I was driving back home from Tampa. What a great game!
A. Definitely!

UNIT 8 TEST

WORKBOOK PAGES T37–T42

A–F.

1. C	11. C	21. D	31. B
2. B	12. A	22. C	32. A
3. D	13. B	23. A	33. C
4. A	14. D	24. C	34. A
5. D	15. B	25. B	35. B
6. C	16. C	26. D	36. C
7. A	17. D	27. B	37. B
8. C	18. A	28. C	38. C
9. B	19. B	29. A	39. D
10. D	20. A	30. C	40. B

F. Listening Assessment

Read and listen to the questions.

38. Why is Victoria calling the doctor's office?

39. When was she scheduled to come in?

40. When is her new appointment?

Now listen to the conversation and answer the questions.

A. Midtown Medical Clinic.
B. Hello. This is Victoria Carson. I need to reschedule an appointment.
A. All right, Ms. Carson. When are you scheduled to come in?
B. I have an appointment with Dr. Martin on Tuesday, April thirteenth, at ten o'clock.
A. On Tuesday, April thirteenth, at ten o'clock?
B. Yes. That's right.

A. Okay. Let me see. We have an opening on Thursday, April fifteenth, at four o'clock. Is that a convenient time?
B. No, I'm afraid not. Mornings are better for me. My daughter isn't in preschool in the afternoon so I have to stay home and take care of her.
A. All right. Let's see. We don't have any more openings for morning appointments that week. Can you come in the following Tuesday, April twentieth, at eleven o'clock?
B. Did you say Tuesday the twentieth at eleven o'clock?
A. Yes.
B. Okay. That would be fine.
A. Then we'll see you Tuesday, April twentieth, at eleven o'clock.
B. Thanks very much.

UNIT 9 TEST

WORKBOOK PAGES T43–T48

A–F.

1. C	11. C	21. D	31. B
2. D	12. B	22. A	32. C
3. B	13. C	23. B	33. B
4. C	14. D	24. C	34. A
5. D	15. B	25. C	35. B
6. A	16. C	26. B	36. C
7. B	17. A	27. D	37. A
8. C	18. D	28. D	38. B
9. A	19. B	29. A	39. C
10. A	20. D	30. B	40. D

F. Listening Assessment

Read and listen to the questions.

38. How many items is the customer returning to the store?

39. What's the matter with the blouse?

40. Why can't the customer receive a refund?

Now listen to the conversation and answer the questions.

A. May I help you?
B. Yes, please. I'd like to return this coat and this blouse.
A. What's the matter with them?
B. A button is missing on the coat, and one sleeve of the blouse is stained.
A. All right. Do you have your receipt?
B. No, I'm afraid not. I can't find it.
A. Well, I can't give you a refund without a receipt. You can exchange the items, or I can give you a store gift card for the amount of your purchase.

B. I don't think I want to exchange them. I'll take the store gift card.

A. All right.

UNIT 10 TEST

A–F.

1. D	11. B	21. C	31. B
2. B	12. B	22. D	32. C
3. C	13. D	23. D	33. A
4. B	14. C	24. A	34. B
5. A	15. A	25. C	35. A
6. D	16. D	26. B	36. B
7. C	17. C	27. C	37. C
8. B	18. B	28. A	38. D
9. D	19. C	29. B	39. A
10. C	20. A	30. C	40. C

F. Listening Assessment

Read and listen to the questions.

38. When is the copy machine ready to print?

39. What does the employee need to copy?

40. How can someone copy a large map on this machine?

Now listen to the conversation and answer the questions.

A. Excuse me. Can you show me how to use this copy machine?

B. Sure. I'll be happy to. How many pages do you need to copy?

A. Just one page.

B. And is it a regular-size piece of paper?

A. Yes. It's this letter.

B. Okay. Then you can use the copy machine's automatic document feeder. If the paper is larger than regular size, you have to lift up the lid and put the document on the glass.

A. I see.

B. So first, check to make sure the machine is on and ready to print. If this green light here is on, the machine is ready.

A. Okay. I see the green light. What should I do if the green light isn't on?

B. Flip this switch here on the side of the machine to turn on the power.

A. I see.

B. Put the original document here in the automatic document feeder. It should be face up.

A. Face up?

B. Yes. Face up, so you are looking at the printed side of the document.

A. Okay.

B. Then press the Start button here. Any questions?

A. Yes. If I have to lift up the lid and put a larger document on the glass, should it be face up?

B. No. It should be face down.

A. I understand. And how many pieces of paper can I put in the automatic document feeder?

B. It can hold fifty pages.

A. Fifty?

B. Yes.

A. Okay. Thanks very much.

B. You're welcome.

SIDE BY SIDE PICTURE CARDS

Numerical List

1. pen
2. book
3. pencil
4. notebook
5. bookshelf
6. globe
7. map
8. board
9. wall
10. clock
11. bulletin board
12. computer
13. table
14. chair
15. ruler
16. desk
17. dictionary
18. living room
19. dining room
20. kitchen
21. bedroom
22. bathroom
23. attic
24. yard
25. garage
26. basement
27. restaurant
28. bank
29. supermarket
30. library
31. park
32. movie theater
33. post office
34. zoo
35. hospital
36. read
37. cook
38. study
39. eat
40. watch TV
41. sleep
42. play the piano
43. play the guitar
44. play cards
45. play baseball
46. drink
47. teach
48. sing
49. listen to music
50. plant
51. listen to the radio
52. swim
53. fix ___ sink
54. fix ___ car
55. fix ___ TV

56. fix ___ bicycle
57. clean ___ apartment
58. clean ___ yard
59. feed ___ cat
60. feed ___ dog
61. paint
62. do ___ exercises
63. wash ___ clothes
64. wash ___ windows
65. wash ___ car
66. brush ___ teeth
67. wash ___ hair
68. tall – short
69. young – old
70. heavy/fat – thin
71. new – old
72. married – single
73. handsome – ugly
74. beautiful/pretty – ugly
75. large/big – small/little
76. noisy – quiet
77. expensive – cheap
78. easy – difficult
79. rich – poor
80. sunny
81. cloudy
82. raining
83. snowing
84. hot
85. warm
86. cool
87. cold
88. ride ___ bicycle
89. bake
90. dance
91. school
92. hotel
93. gas station
94. bus station
95. clinic
96. fire station
97. bakery
98. video store
99. barber shop
100. laundromat
101. drug store
102. church
103. department store
104. police station
105. hair salon
106. book store
107. health club
108. cafeteria

109. train station
110. sad
111. happy
112. angry
113. nervous
114. thirsty
115. hungry
116. hot
117. cold
118. sick
119. embarrassed
120. tired
121. scared
122. cry
123. smile
124. shout
125. bite ___ nails
126. perspire
127. shiver
128. blush
129. yawn
130. cover ___ eyes
131. mechanic
132. secretary
133. teacher
134. baker
135. truck driver
136. chef
137. singer
138. dancer
139. actor
140. actress
141. have lunch
142. have dinner
143. go swimming
144. go shopping
145. go dancing
146. go skating
147. go skiing
148. go bowling
149. headache
150. stomachache
151. toothache
152. backache
153. earache
154. cold
155. fever
156. cough
157. sore throat
158. work
159. type
160. shave
161. wait for the bus
162. sit
163. apples

164. bananas
165. bread
166. cake
167. carrots
168. cheese
169. chicken
170. eggs
171. fish
172. grapes
173. ketchup
174. lemons
175. lettuce
176. mayonnaise
177. meat
178. mustard
179. onions
180. oranges
181. pears
182. pepper
183. potatoes
184. salt
185. soy sauce
186. tomatoes
187. butter
188. coffee
189. cookies
190. flour
191. ice cream
192. milk
193. orange juice
194. rice
195. soda
196. sugar
197. tea
198. yogurt
199. airport
200. baseball stadium
201. concert hall
202. courthouse
203. flower shop
204. hardware store
205. ice cream shop
206. motel
207. museum
208. parking garage
209. pet shop
210. playground
211. shoe store
212. toy store
213. university
214. high school

Alphabetical List

actor **139**
actress **140**
airport **199**
angry **112**
apples **163**
attic **23**

backache **152**
bake **89**
baker **134**
bakery **97**
bananas **164**
bank **28**
barber shop **99**
baseball stadium **200**
basement **26**
bathroom **22**
beautiful **74**
bedroom **21**
big **75**
bite ___ nails **125**
blush **128**
board **8**
book **2**
book store **106**
bookshelf **5**
bread **165**
brush ___ teeth **66**
bulletin board **11**
bus station **94**
butter **187**

cafeteria **108**
cake **166**
carrots **167**
chair **14**
cheap **77**
cheese **168**
chef **136**
chicken **169**
church **102**
clean ___ apartment **57**
clean ___ yard **58**
clinic **95**
clock **10**
cloudy **81**
coffee **188**
cold **117**
cold **154**
cold **87**
computer **12**
concert hall **201**
cook **37**
cookies **189**
cool **86**
cough **156**
courthouse **202**
cover ___ eyes **130**
cry **122**

dance **90**
dancer **138**

department store **103**
desk **16**
dictionary **17**
difficult **78**
dining room **19**
do ___ exercises **62**
drink **46**
drug store **101**

earache **153**
easy **78**
eat **39**
eggs **170**
embarrassed **119**
expensive **77**

fat **70**
feed ___ cat **59**
feed ___ dog **60**
fever **155**
fire station **96**
fish **171**
fix ___ bicycle **56**
fix ___ car **54**
fix ___ sink **53**
fix ___ TV **55**
flour **190**
flower shop **203**

garage **25**
gas station **93**
globe **6**
go bowling **148**
go dancing **145**
go shopping **144**
go skating **146**
go skiing **147**
go swimming **143**
grapes **172**

hair salon **105**
handsome **73**
happy **111**
hardware store **204**
have dinner **142**
have lunch **141**
headache **149**
health club **107**
heavy **70**
high school **214**
hospital **35**
hot **116**
hot **84**
hotel **92**
hungry **115**

ice cream **191**
ice cream shop **205**

ketchup **173**
kitchen **20**

large **75**

laundromat **100**
lemons **174**
lettuce **175**
library **30**
listen to music **49**
listen to the radio **51**
little **75**
living room **18**

map **7**
married **72**
mayonnaise **176**
meat **177**
mechanic **131**
milk **192**
motel **206**
movie theater **32**
museum **207**
mustard **178**

nervous **113**
new **71**
noisy **76**
notebook **4**

old **69, 71**
onions **179**
orange juice **193**
oranges **180**

paint **61**
park **31**
parking garage **208**
pears **181**
pen **1**
pencil **3**
pepper **182**
perspire **126**
pet shop **209**
plant **50**
play baseball **45**
play cards **44**
play the guitar **43**
play the piano **42**
playground **210**
police station **104**
poor **79**
post office **33**
potatoes **183**
pretty **74**

quiet **76**

raining **82**
read **36**
restaurant **27**
rice **194**
rich **79**
ride ___ bicycle **88**
ruler **15**

sad **110**
salt **184**

scared **121**
school **91**
secretary **132**
shave **160**
shiver **127**
shoe store **211**
short **68**
shout **124**
sick **118**
sing **48**
singer **137**
single **72**
sit **162**
sleep **41**
small **75**
smile **123**
snowing **83**
soda **195**
sore throat **157**
soy sauce **185**
stomachache **150**
study **38**
sugar **196**
sunny **80**
supermarket **29**
swim **52**

table **13**
tall **68**
tea **197**
teach **47**
teacher **133**
thin **70**
thirsty **114**
tired **120**
tomatoes **186**
toothache **151**
toy store **212**
train station **109**
truck driver **135**
type **159**

ugly **73, 74**
university **213**

video store **98**

wait for the bus **161**
wall **9**
warm **85**
wash ___ car **65**
wash ___ clothes **63**
wash ___ hair **67**
wash ___ windows **64**
watch TV **40**
work **158**

yard **24**
yawn **129**
yogurt **198**
young **69**

zoo **34**

Categories

Adjectives

angry **112**
beautiful **74**
big **75**
cheap **77**
cold **117**
difficult **78**
easy **78**
embarrassed **119**
expensive **77**
fat **70**
handsome **73**
happy **111**
heavy **70**
hot **116**
hungry **115**
large **75**
little **75**
married **72**
nervous **113**
new **71**
noisy **76**
old **69, 71**
poor **79**
pretty **74**
quiet **76**
rich **79**
sad **110**
scared **121**
short **68**
sick **118**
single **72**
small **75**
tall **68**
thin **70**
thirsty **114**
tired **120**
ugly **73, 74**
young **69**

Ailments

backache **152**
cold **154**
cough **156**
earache **153**
fever **155**
headache **149**
sore throat **157**
stomachache **150**
toothache **151**

Classroom

board **8**
book **2**
bookshelf **5**
bulletin board **11**
chair **14**
clock **10**
computer **12**
desk **16**
dictionary **17**
globe **6**
map **7**
notebook **4**
pen **1**
pencil **3**
ruler **15**
table **13**
wall **9**

Community

airport **199**
bakery **97**
bank **28**
barber shop **99**
baseball stadium **200**
book store **106**
bus station **94**
cafeteria **108**
church **102**
clinic **95**
concert hall **201**
courthouse **202**
department store **103**
drug store **101**
fire station **96**
flower shop **203**
gas station **93**
hair salon **105**
hardware store **204**
health club **107**
high school **214**
hospital **35**
hotel **92**
ice cream shop **205**
laundromat **100**
library **30**
motel **206**
movie theater **32**
museum **207**
park **31**
parking garage **208**
pet shop **209**
playground **210**
police station **104**
post office **33**
restaurant **27**
school **91**
shoe store **211**
supermarket **29**
toy store **212**
train station **109**
university **213**
video store **98**
zoo **34**

Foods

apples **163**
bananas **164**
bread **165**
butter **187**
cake **166**
carrots **167**
cheese **168**
chicken **169**
coffee **188**
cookies **189**
eggs **170**
fish **171**
flour **190**
grapes **172**
ice cream **191**
ketchup **173**
lemons **174**
lettuce **175**
mayonnaise **176**
meat **177**
milk **192**
mustard **178**
onions **179**
orange juice **193**
oranges **180**
pears **181**
pepper **182**
potatoes **183**
rice **194**
salt **184**
soda **195**
soy sauce **185**
sugar **196**
tea **197**
tomatoes **186**
yogurt **198**

Home

attic **23**
basement **26**
bathroom **22**
bedroom **21**
dining room **19**
garage **25**
kitchen **20**
living room **18**
yard **24**

Occupations

actor **139**
actress **140**
baker **134**
chef **136**
dancer **138**
mechanic **131**
secretary **132**
singer **137**
teacher **133**
truck driver **135**

Verbs

bake **89**
bite ___ nails **125**
blush **128**
brush ___ teeth **66**
clean ___ apartment **57**
clean ___ yard **58**
cook **37**
cover ___ eyes **130**
cry **122**
dance **90**
do ___ exercises **62**
drink **46**
eat **39**
feed ___ cat **59**
feed ___ dog **60**
fix ___ bicycle **56**
fix ___ car **54**
fix ___ sink **53**
fix ___ TV **55**
go bowling **148**
go dancing **145**
go shopping **144**
go skating **146**
go skiing **147**
go swimming **143**
have dinner **142**
have lunch **141**
listen to music **49**
listen to the radio **51**
paint **61**
perspire **126**
plant **50**
play baseball **45**
play cards **44**
play the guitar **43**
play the piano **42**
read **36**
ride ___ bicycle **88**
shave **160**
shiver **127**
shout **124**
sing **48**
sit **162**
sleep **41**
smile **123**
study **38**
swim **52**
teach **47**
type **159**
wait for the bus **161**
wash ___ car **65**
wash ___ clothes **63**
wash ___ hair **67**
wash ___ windows **64**
watch TV **40**
work **158**
yawn **129**

Weather

cloudy **81**
cold **87**
cool **86**
hot **84**
raining **82**
snowing **83**
sunny **80**
warm **85**

GLOSSARY

The number after each word indicates the page where the word first appears in the text.
(adj) = adjective, (adv) = adverb, (n) = noun, (v) = verb.

"24/7" **65**
"9 to 5" **65**
24-hour **110d**
a few years ago **88**
a little later **27**
a little while ago **41**
a long time **27**
ability **144d**
Abraham Lincoln **20d**
absence **32e**
absent **32b**
academic **136**
accent **59**
accept **119**
accident **20a**
accident report **117**
accidentally **120**
accomplish **144b**
account number **10b**
act (n) **135**
act (v) **4**
actor **1**
actually **145**
ad **145**
add **94b**
address **10a**
adjust **29**
adjustments **80b**
administration building
   32e
adult **110c**
adult education course
   144d
advance notice **110a**
advanced **144d**
advertisement **64b**
advice **10c**
afford **110d**
afraid **50c**
Africa **33**
after midnight **35**
afternoon **7**
after-school **32b**
age **65**
agree **144b**
agreement **145**
ahead of time **98**
AIDS **110b**
air conditioner **119**
airplane **38**
airport **30**
alarm **117**
alarm clock **131**
alarm system **144a**
Albania **33**
Alcatraz prison **49**

alike **148**
all right **73**
all the time **7**
all weekend **35**
allergic **131**
allergy **110c**
allow **142**
already **42**
always **58**
amazing **75**
American **20c**
amount **67**
an hour a day **142**
analyze **144d**
angry **13**
animal **80a**
ankle **14**
anniversary **94c**
anniversary sale **130b**
annual **94b**
another **32b**
answer (n) **94c**
answer (v) **35**
answer the telephone **50b**
apartment **12**
apartment building **73**
apologize **144b**
apparently **120**
appearance **144b**
appetite **110b**
apple **69**
application **50a**
application form **129**
apply **20e**
apply for **50a**
appoint **10c**
appointment **66**
appreciate **78**
appropriate **144d**
approve **10c**
April **7**
area **65**
argue **8**
arm **54**
armed forces **10c**
army **8**
arrange **64b**
arrangement **145**
arrive **10b**
art **32b**
art museum **32c**
as soon as **73**
ashamed **17**
Asia **33**
ask **29**
ask for a raise **67**

asleep **66**
aspect **110c**
aspirin **44**
assemble **29**
assembly line **94b**
assistant **61**
assistant manager **61**
asthma **110b**
astrologer **145**
astrological **145**
astronaut **51**
astronomy **23**
at 7:30 **25**
at night **34**
at once **80d**
at the last minute **108**
at the same time **140**
at this point **44**
athlete **4**
athletic **131**
attend **26**
attendance **64c**
attitude **144b**
attractive **128**
audience **16**
August **7**
aunt **9**
Austria **33**
Austria-Hungary **33**
available **94b**
avenue **10a**
average **110e**
avoid **80b**
awake **66**
aware **59**
awesome **48**

baby **75**
baby son **71**
baby-sit **141**
baby-sitter **79**
bachelor **60**
back **54**
back problem **110b**
backache **60**
background **136**
bad **14**
badly **16**
baggy **127**
bake **2**
balance (n) **80b**
balance (v) **144d**
balance beam **113**
balance information **80b**
balanced diet **110e**
balcony **80a**

ball **113**
ballet dancer **5**
ballet instructor **5**
banana **43**
bank **37**
bank account **10b**
bank account number **10b**
barber **62**
bargain **127**
bark **70**
baseball **3**
basement **80d**
basics **144d**
basket **113**
basketball **112**
bath **27**
bathroom **49**
bathtub **83**
Batman **23**
be located **103**
beach **35**
bean group **110e**
beat **144d**
beautiful **35**
become **10c**
bed **44**
bedroom **73**
bee sting **110b**
been **52**
Beethoven **2**
before today **139**
beforehand **108**
begin **20c**
beginning (n) **44**
behave **142**
believe **50c**
belong **10c**
best **43**
best friend **43**
bet **17**
better **5**
between 1892 and 1954
   33
bicycle **12**
big **18**
bill (household) **8**
bill (legislative) **10c**
billing **80b**
billing date **80b**
billing period **80b**
billing summary **80b**
bills **26**
Bingo **43**
biology **23**
bird **80a**
birth **145**

computer lab **35**
computer programmer **51**
computer programming **109**
concerned **125**
concert tickets **72**
concise **144d**
Confederacy **20d**
conference **144d**
confetti **146**
confidently **144d**
confirm **110a**
confused **68**
conservative **142**
consider **81**
consist **110e**
constantly **125**
contact **80d**
contain **32b**
continue **81**
contract **80a**
convenient **110a**
conversation **94c**
cook (n) **4**
cook (v) **2**
cookbook **98**
cookies **2**
copy (n) **144a**
copy (v) **94a**
copy machine **94b**
corn **110e**
corner **134**
correct **35**
cost **127**
costume **99**
cotton **20d**
cotton candy **40**
couch **67**
cough (n) **110d**
count **57**
country **20c**
couple **146**
coupon **130c**
course **35**
cousin **9**
cover (v) **13**
cover letter **64b**
co-worker **31**
CPR (cardiopulmonary resuscitation) **144d**
crash **111**
cream **110e**
cream cheese **110e**
create **50c**
creative **144b**
creatively **144b**
credit card account **10b**
credit information **10b**
credit rating **80c**
credits **80b**
crime **10b**
critical **85**
cross **113**
cross out **115**

crown **146**
cruise **39**
cry **13**
Cuban **34**
culinary arts **144d**
cultural **136**
culture **145**
cup **130c**
curly **143**
current **50a**
current charges **80b**
curtain **99**
custodian **47**
custom **145**
customer **10b**
customer assistance line **80b**
customer service **64b**
cut (n) **144d**
cut (v) **10b**
cut himself **14**
Cyprus **146**

daily **15**
dairy food **110e**
dairy group **110e**
dairy product **110e**
Dallas **61**
dance **4**
dance class **139**
dance lesson **37**
dancer **1**
danger **110d**
dark **126**
dark green vegetables **110e**
date (n) **77**
date (v) **69**
date of birth **10a**
date of employment **50a**
dating service **145**
daughter **3**
dawn **20b**
day **5**
day care **66**
day off **31**
day shift **66**
daylight **20b**
daytime **65**
dear **32a**
December **7**
decide **20c**
decision **10c**
Declaration of Independence **20c**
declare **10c**
decline **148**
decorations **123**
dedicated **54**
defense **142**
definite **35**
definition **119**
deli counter **64b**
deliver **12**

deliver a baby **75**
demonstration **20e**
demonstrator **16**
Denmark **67**
dental appointment **32b**
dental examination **110c**
dentist **79**
dentist's appointment **94b**
Denver **49**
department **61**
department store **61**
depend **10c**
dependable **144b**
deposit (v) **64e**
depression **110b**
describe **20c**
deserve **109**
designer **130b**
desk **47**
despite **140**
dessert **23**
develop **144b**
diabetes **110b**
dictionary **29**
die **10c**
diet **89**
difference **114**
different **5**
differently **144b**
difficult **15**
dining room **64b**
dinner **2**
dinner party **98**
dinner table **97**
diphtheria **110d**
direct deposit **64c**
direct traffic **69**
disagree **142**
disappointed **24**
discount **130b**
discount store **64a**
discouraged **120**
discover **80d**
discrimination **20d**
discuss **95**
dishes **134**
dislocate **105**
dislocate *her* shoulder **105**
distance running **112**
divorced **10a**
dizzy **54**
do **3**
do business **65**
do card tricks **97**
do gymnastics **105**
do homework **27**
do lab tests **50b**
do over **119**
do poorly **107**
do research **26**
do sit-ups **69**
do the tango **105**
do yoga **38**

doctor **20a**
doctor's appointment **94b**
document **10b**
dog **80a**
dog day-care worker **66**
dollar **127**
donut **22**
doorbell **98**
dose **110d**
downtown **76**
dozen **130c**
draw **38**
dream **112**
dress (v) **144b**
dress shirt **130b**
dressing room **126**
drink **13**
drive **4**
driver **1**
driver's test **106**
driveway **98**
driving school **109**
drop off **122**
drop-in-clinic **110d**
drug **110b**
dry **20b**
dry beans **110e**
due date **80b**
dumpster **80d**
during the past few months **121**
during the week **118**
dusk **20b**
dust **110b**
DVD player **138**

earache **110d**
early **35**
early Saturday morning **35**
earn **109**
earthquake **33**
easy **36**
eat **2**
eat out **96**
economic **33**
education **32b**
education history **50a**
educational background **140**
efficient **144b**
eggs **96**
elect **10c**
electric bill **46**
electrician **24**
electronic mail **144d**
elevator **40**
e-mail **8**
Emancipation Proclamation **20d**
embarrassed **16**
emergency **144d**
emergency care procedure **110d**

emergency maintenance number **80d**
emergency procedure **144d**
emergency room **110d**
emotional **30**
Empire State Building **49**
employee **8**
employer **50a**
employment **64c**
employment history **50b**
employment website **50c**
empty (adj) **30**
empty (v) **80d**
end (n) **64c**
end (v) **20c**
energy **80b**
enforce **10c**
engaged **56**
engineer **58**
engineering **92**
English **2**
enjoy **31**
enough **98**
enroll **92**
enter **20b**
enthusiastically **144b**
entire **128**
entrepreneurship **144d**
entry-level **144d**
envelope **114**
envy **86**
equal rights **137**
equipment **111**
erase **119**
especially **128**
Esquilino **33**
Europe **23**
evaluation **144b**
even **113**
evening **7**
evening class **144d**
event **35**
event (Olympic) **113**
eventually **125**
ever **40**
ever since **86**
every day **5**
every morning **50c**
every Sunday morning **7**
every time **121**
everyday **148**
exact **68**
exactly **94b**
exam **13**
examination **110c**
examine **145**
example **33**
ex-boyfriend **119**
Excel spreadsheet **144d**
excellent **5**
exchange **130c**
excited **30**
exciting **32b**

excuse **83**
executive branch **10c**
exercise **3**
exercise bike **37**
ex-girlfriend **119**
exhausted **79**
exist **66**
expect **140**
expensive **66**
experience **15**
experiment **76**
expire **130d**
explain **10c**
express **68**
expression **148**
extra **109**
extra large **126**
extremely **44**
eye **13**
eye care **110d**
eye examination **110c**

fact **111**
factory **20e**
factory worker **65**
facts of life **57**
fail **106**
fairy tale **139**
fall **11**
fall asleep **13**
fall for **147**
fall off **113**
fall through **108**
fall/autumn **22**
familiar **144d**
family **9**
family clinic **110d**
family history **110b**
family restaurant **64b**
family reunion **35**
famous **60**
fan **111**
fancy **18**
fantastic **48**
far **140**
farm **20d**
fast-food restaurant **84**
fat-free **110e**
father **9**
favor **28**
favorite **8**
fax **65**
features **144d**
February **7**
federal court **10c**
feed **46**
feedback **144b**
feel **17**
feel better **104**
feel dizzy **54**
feel like **118**
fence **49**
fever **20a**
fiber **110e**

fiction **102**
fight (n) **15**
figure out **123**
figure skate **87**
figure skating **112**
file **144d**
fill in **50a**
fill out **26**
filter **144a**
final **129**
final exam **35**
finally **92**
find **30**
find out **144b**
fine **62**
fingernail **144b**
finish **13**
finish line **113**
fire **108**
fire hazard **80d**
firefighter **65**
first **102**
first aid **144d**
first name **10a**
first-aid course **40**
fish **64b**
Fisherman's Wharf **49**
fit **127**
fix **28**
flat tire **20a**
flavor **130c**
flight **139**
flood **33**
floor routine **113**
flow **33**
flower petal **146**
flowers **75**
flu **124**
flu shot **110c**
fluently **132**
fly **30**
fly a kite **95**
flyer **144d**
fog **20b**
folk song **23**
follow **44**
following **110c**
food **34**
food and beverage specialist **144d**
food pyramid **110e**
foods **110e**
foolish **98**
foot **113**
football **6**
for a few years **25**
for a long time **25**
for a minute **27**
for about an hour **71**
for many years **38**
for more than a week **54**
for several days **10b**
for several hours **25**
for the past 24 hours **54**

for years **66**
foreign **33**
foreign born **33**
forever **66**
forget **13**
form (n) **64c**
form (v) **20d**
formal **148**
former **33**
fortunate **60**
four times a year **32b**
four-person **111**
free (adj) **122**
free (v) **20d**
free time **9**
freedom **20d**
frequent **110b**
freshman **32b**
Friday **7**
friend **3**
friendly **94c**
frightened **131**
from 7:00 A.M. until 3:00 P.M. **66**
front (adj) **105**
front (n) **20b**
front steps **29**
front teeth **105**
fruit **80d**
fruit juice **110e**
frustrated **44**
full **54**
full payment **80b**
full range **110d**
full-service **110d**
funny **67**
furious **73**
furniture **20d**
future **30**
future tense **35**

garbage **117**
Georgia **59**
Germany **33**
gerund **114**
get a promotion **109**
get a raise **39**
get along with **124**
get around **19**
get over **124**
get ready (for) **108**
get rid of **44**
get stuck **40**
get to **100**
give a party **97**
give back **119**
give blood **42**
give piano lessons **75**
give the kids a bath **27**
give up **111**
go back **89**
go by **100**
go canoeing **95**
go kayaking **45**

go scuba diving **40**
go to bed **46**
go together **106**
go water-skiing **24**
go window-shopping **95**
go with **128**
gold **113**
Golden Gate Bridge **49**
gossip **85**
government **142**
graduate **56**
grammar **114**
groom **146**
group **111**
growl **17**
guess **88**
guidance counselor **51**
guitarist **51**
gymnastics **105**

habit **85**
hair **53**
half-price **130a**
Halloween **23**
hallway **73**
ham **67**
hammer **29**
hand in **115**
handle (v) **64b**
hands-on **144b**
hang **80a**
hang up **115**
happen **17**
happily **60**
happiness **128**
happy **17**
harbor (n) **33**
harbor (v) **80a**
hard **34**
hardware **50b**
hardwood floor **80a**
hardworking **144b**
hate **81**
have **19**
have the time **45**
have to **35**
head **146**
headache **54**
health **91**
health care **110d**
health center **110a**
health club **26**
health food **109**
health plan **110c**
health problem **110d**
health regulation **144d**
health science **144d**
healthy **110c**
hear **10c**
hear from **124**
hearing test **110c**
heart **110e**
heart attack **107**
heart disease **110b**

heartbroken **98**
heat **116**
heating system **73**
height **10a**
helicopter **39**
help (n) **127**
help (v) **32b**
help with **134**
help-wanted sign **50c**
hepatitis **110b**
hide **131**
high **54**
high blood pressure **110b**
high fever **54**
high school **32b**
highlight **113**
highway **110a**
hike **14**
Hindu **146**
hire **50c**
historic **33**
history **57**
hobby **94c**
hockey **112**
hold **10c**
Holland **66**
home **19**
home town **102**
homemade **102**
homework **27**
homework assignment
    141
honor roll **32b**
hook up **115**
hope **32b**
hopeful **140**
horoscope **145**
horse **38**
hospital **25**
hospital bill **123**
hot-air balloon **39**
hotel **18**
hours of work **64c**
house **32b**
House of Representatives
    10c
household **10a**
housework **66**
Hungary **33**
hungry **13**
hurt **11**
hurt himself **14**
husband **9**

ice cream **23**
ice cream shop **102**
ice skate **26**
ice skating **136**
icy **20b**
idea **44**
identify theft **10b**
illness **32b**
imagine **30**
immediately **80d**

immigrant **20e**
immigrate **34**
immigration **33**
Immigration Act **20e**
immunization **110b**
important **12**
imported **98**
impossible **111**
in ____ minutes **27**
in 1983 **34**
in a few minutes **25**
in a little while **25**
in a long time **45**
in advance **99**
in love **55**
in one day **79**
in the morning **35**
in the past **65**
in the past 24 hours **55**
in years **62**
incarcerated **64a**
include **32b**
income tax form **26**
incorrectly **120**
incredible **75**
independence **20c**
Independence Day **20c**
Independence Hall **20c**
independent **20c**
independently **32b**
India **145**
inexpensive **10b**
infect **64c**
infinitive **114**
influenza **110b**
informal **148**
information **10b**
ingredients **64b**
injection **38**
injure **104**
injure *her* knee **104**
inn **64a**
inseparable **148**
instant **65**
instead **122**
instruction **138**
instructor **1**
insulin **110b**
insurance form **123**
intelligent **67**
interest (v) **144d**
interested (in) **53**
interesting **9**
interests **9**
international **65**
Internet **50c**
Internet company **134**
Internet service **50c**
interpret **10c**
interpreter **110d**
interrupt **85**
intersection **20b**
interview (n) **64b**
interview (v) **112**

introduction **144d**
inventory **41**
invitation **98**
invite **108**
involve **146**
Ireland **33**
iron **2**
ironed **144b**
island **33**
item **110b**

jack **28**
jacket **128**
jail **25**
jam **130c**
Jamaica **111**
Jamaican **111**
jammed **80d**
January **7**
jar **130c**
jazz **57**
jealous **39**
jeans **127**
job **30**
job application form **50a**
job bank **50c**
job fair **50c**
job listing **50c**
job opening **50c**
job opportunity **50c**
job performance
    evaluation **144d**
job posting **50c**
job search **50c**
jog **17**
journalist **51**
joy **17**
judge (court) **10c**
judge (Olympic) **113**
judicial branch **10c**
July **7**
jump **17**
June **7**
junior **32b**
junk food **85**
just **35**

karate **77**
keep **17**
keep clear **80d**
keep on **81**
Kenya **112**
key **72**
keyboarding skills **144d**
kid (n) **15**
kid (v) **74**
kidney disease **110b**
kids **27**
kill **20d**
kilowatt hour **80b**
kimono **40**
kind **145**
kindergarten **110d**
kindly **110a**

kiss 131
kitchen 2
kitchen cabinet 80d
kite 96
knee 55
knit 2
know 34
know how 94b

ladder 29
lake 35
Lake Placid 111
land 10c
landfill 80d
landlord 8
lane 113
language 18
laps 109
laptop 98
large 33
last (adj) 59
last (v) 66
last January 22
last name 10a
last night 13
last spring 22
last Sunday 22
last time 111
last week/month/year 22
latch-key children 32b
late 20a
late payment 80c
lately 132
late payment charge 80b
late-night 65
Latin America 33
laundromat 50c
laundry 37
lay off (v) 140
layoff (n) 140
lazy 67
lead (n) 113
lead (v) 20d
leader 20d
leaf 17
leak (n) 135
leak (v) 69
learn 32b
learner 68
learning 32b
lease 80a
leased (adj) 80a
leave 30
leave for school 46
leave on 119
lecture 100
left turn 20b
leg 104
legal 80a
legislative branch 10c
lend 28
lenient 131
lesson 75
letter 2

level 112
liberal 142
library 26
library book 116
lid 144a
life 30
lift up 144a
light (adj) 126
light (n) 20b
light (v) 146
lightning 131
like 4
limousine 39
lines 13
list (n) 67
list (v) 50a
listen 9
listening (n) 94c
little 54
Little Red Riding Hood 8
live 9
liver disease 110b
living conditions 33
living room 49
loaf 130c
local 65
local services 80c
located 103
lonely 30
long 58
long distance 80c
look 16
look for 50c
look forward to 31
look through 50c
look up 119
look up to 124
loose 127
lose 11
lose *his* voice 105
loss 110b
lost interest 144b
lottery 59
love 55
love letter 101
low 110e
low-fat 110e
luck 35
lunch 37
lunch break 64c
lunch tray 94a

macaroni and cheese 133
Madagascar 9
magazine 31
magic trick 15
magician 15
mail (n) 10b
mail (v) 94b
mail room 47
mailbox 10b
main 140
maintenance 80d
maintenance request 80d

major (in) 136
make 10c
make a decision 88
make a list 67
make conversation 94c
make noises 72
make sure 110d
mall 26
man 35
manage 32b
management 64b
manager 50c
manufacturing company
    65
marathon 76
March 7
March on Washington
    20e
margarine 110e
marital status 10a
marks 113
marriage 145
married 9
marry 33
Martin Luther King Jr. 20e
match 145
matchmaker 145
matchmaking service 145
math 123
math problem 129
mathematics 34
May 7
may 68
mean 64a
meaning 32b
measles 53
measure height and
    weight 50b
meat 110e
mechanic 24
medal 112
medical 33
medical appointment 32b
medical assistant 50b
medical care 110d
medical clinic 110a
medical examination 33
medical history 110b
medical problem 110c
medical reason 64c
medical records 50b
medical school 60
medical services 110d
medication 110b
medicine 46
Mediterranean 19
medium 126
meet 11
meeting 20c
Melbourne 34
member 10c
memories 102
memorize 95
men's clothing store 128

mend 69
menu 64b
merchandise 130b
merry-go-round 102
message 32b
metal 80d
meter number 80b
meter reading 80b
Microsoft Word 144d
Microsoft Outlook 144d
Middle East 33
middle name 50b
mile 31
milk 13
milk group 110e
milk product 110e
million 10b
mind 117
minerals 110e
minimum 80a
minorities 137
miss 20a
missing (adj) 130a
mistake 35
modem 118
modern 111
modern art 57
modern-day 145
Moldova 33
moment 147
Monday 7
Monday morning 35
money 10b
Monopoly 45
month 7
more than a week 54
morning 7
mother 9
motorcycle 68
mountain 24
move 30
move ahead 144b
move out 102
move through 113
movie hero 102
movie soundtrack 111
movie star 94c
movie theater 79
movies 94c
Mozart 97
muffin 22
multilingual 110d
multivitamin 110e
mumps 110b
museum 49
music building 32c
music school 56
music teacher 5
musician 51
must 114

nails 91
name 9
narrow 110e

nation **20d**
national **112**
national government **20c**
national holiday **20c**
native **33**
natural **33**
natural disaster **33**
natural-born **10c**
nauseous **55**
necessary **64c**
neck **54**
need **20c**
needle **17**
neighbor **50c**
neighborhood **33**
neither **133**
nervous **13**
network (v) **50c**
network programming **93**
never **39**
new **14**
New Year's decorations **123**
newlywed **145**
news **3**
news program **23**
newsletter **144d**
newspaper **2**
next (adj) **110c**
next (adv) **146**
next January **22**
next spring **22**
next Sunday **22**
next week **22**
nice **18**
night **7**
night shift **65**
noises **72**
non-prescription drug **110b**
normally **66**
North **20d**
North Africa **33**
Northern states **20d**
Norway **111**
nostalgic **102**
note **66**
notebook **120**
notice (v) **128**
notification **110a**
November **7**
now **46**
nuclear **137**
nuclear energy **137**
number **32b**
nurse **65**
nutrient **110e**
nuts **110e**
nuts about **147**

occupation **145**
occur **20e**
ocean **101**
October **7**

offer **136**
office **35**
office assistant **50b**
office clerk **47**
office party **67**
office worker **65**
officer **79**
official **33**
often **3**
oil **94a**
oils **110e**
old **45**
Olympics **111**
on button **144a**
on sale **128**
on time **64c**
once **7**
once a day **7**
onion soup **23**
online **50c**
open (v) **10b**
open (adj) **17**
open house **32b**
opening (n) **110a**
opera **97**
operate **65**
operation **110b**
opinion **65**
opportunity **34**
opposed to **137**
opposite **121**
orange **110e**
orange juice **44**
order **64b**
organic **130c**
organize **144d**
original **144a**
originally **148**
Orlando **8**
others **64c**
outdoors **146**
outgoing **143**
outlook on life **137**
outside **35**
outskirts **102**
outstanding **110d**
oven **98**
over **54**
over and over **112**
overseas **143**
overtime **26**
own (v) **53**
owner **20d**

P.O. Box **80b**
pack **35**
package (n) **67**
package (v) **64b**
pain **54**
paint **2**
painter **50**
painting **121**
pair **128**
pants **128**

paper **120**
parade **100**
parents **2**
parent-teacher association **32b**
park **17**
parking lot **80a**
parking space **131**
parking ticket **79**
part **32b**
part fact **111**
part fiction **111**
participant **113**
participate **32b**
partner **145**
party **31**
pass **33**
pass a test **109**
pass by **102**
past (adj) **33**
past due **80b**
past participle **68**
past perfect tense **114**
patient (n) **50b**
patient information form **10a**
pay (n) **64c**
pay (v) **10b**
pay attention **113**
pay stub **10b**
paycheck **41**
payment **80b**
payment due **80b**
payment received **80b**
payment schedule **64c**
payroll **144d**
payroll office **64c**
pea soup **23**
peach **67**
peel **64b**
pen **67**
pencil **67**
penpal **114**
people **12**
peppermint ice cream **132**
percent **32b**
perfect **114**
perfectly **68**
perform **95**
perhaps **30**
permanently **30**
person **10c**
personal **57**
personal ad **145**
personal computer **57**
personal possessions **80d**
personality **137**
pertussis **110d**
pessimistic **140**
pest control company **80d**
pet **80a**
phenomenal **48**

philosophical **143**
phone **71**
photo album **124**
photocopy center **65**
photograph **75**
photography **32b**
physical exam **110d**
physical examination **110c**
physician **51**
piano recital **107**
Picasso **57**
pick **69**
pick on **124**
pick out **115**
pick up **66**
picnic **24**
picture **18**
piece **10b**
pin (n) **17**
pin (v) **146**
pint **130c**
pit **80d**
pizza **12**
place (n) **35**
place (v) **80a**
place of birth **10a**
plaid **128**
plain **126**
plan (v) **64b**
plan (n) **24**
plane **13**
plane ticket **98**
plans **24**
plant (n) **98**
plant (v) **75**
plantation **20d**
play **3**
play baseball **3**
play Bingo **43**
play cards **23**
play chess **141**
play golf **82**
play hide and seek **101**
play Monopoly **45**
play Scrabble **3**
play sports **4**
play squash **105**
play tennis **24**
player **1**
pleasure **78**
plumber **35**
pneumonia **110b**
pneumonia vaccination **110c**
point **113**
point of view **144b**
poison **144d**
poke **14**
police **10b**
police officer **51**
polio **110d**
politely **144b**
political **33**

politics **83**
polka dot **97**
pool **19**
poor **111**
poorly **107**
popcorn **102**
popular **111**
population **10c**
portrait **116**
position **50a**
positive **144b**
possible **145**
possibly **28**
post office **10b**
potato **67**
power **10c**
power and light **80b**
power outage **80b**
Powerpolnt **144d**
practice (n) **94c**
practice (v) **3**
prefer **140**
premises **80a**
preparation **80d**
prepare **14**
prepare for **144b**
prepared **13**
prescription drug **110c**
present (adj) **33**
present (n) **50b**
present (v) **144d**
present perfect continuous
    tense **114**
present perfect tense **41**
present tense **35**
presentation **41**
president **10c**
press **144a**
prevent **10b**
preventive care **110b**
previous **64c**
price **127**
principal **16**
prison **49**
private **146**
probably **122**
problem **31**
procedure **144d**
product **38**
profession **144d**
professional **5**
professional-looking **144d**
program **112**
progress **94b**
prom **133**
promise **73**
promotion **109**
property **80a**
protect **110d**
protein **110e**
protest (n) **20e**
proud **60**
provide **80d**
psychology **97**

public **33**
public building **50c**
public health department
    110d
public library **50c**
public school **33**
public speaking **144d**
punch in **64c**
punch out **64c**
purchase (n) **130c**
purchase (v) **95**
purple **43**
put **80a**
put away **115**
put down **144a**
put on **99**
put to bed **66**

quart **130c**
question **35**
questionnaire **145**
quick **94b**
quickly **128**
quiet **30**
quietly **142**
quit **81**

race **113**
rack **94a**
radio **24**
rain (n) **20b**
rain (v) **24**
rainbow **40**
raincoat **117**
raise (n) **39**
rash **32a**
read **2**
ready **108**
real **67**
realize **16**
really **35**
reason **32a**
receipt **10b**
receive **32b**
recent **65**
recently **34**
reception hall **146**
receptionist **50b**
recipe **98**
recognize **10c**
recommend **112**
recommendation **110b**
record (v) **64c**
recycle **80d**
recycling bin **50c**
recycling collection site
    50c
recycling program **80d**
red **17**
Red Cross certification
    144d
red light **20b**
red spots **54**
reduced **130a**

reduced waste **50c**
reference **50a**
refrigerator **73**
refund **129**
refuse **80a**
reggae music **111**
regional **112**
register **144b**
registration hall **33**
regular **35**
rehearse **95**
reindeer **66**
reindeer herder **66**
relatives **30**
relax **31**
reliable **80d**
religion **94c**
remaining balance **80c**
remember **20d**
rent (n) **80a**
rent (v) **48**
rental agreement **80a**
rental office **80d**
repair (n) **80a**
repair (v) **49**
repair shop **122**
repairman **116**
report (n) **38**
report (v) **10b**
report card **32b**
reporter **84**
represent **110e**
representative **20c**
republic **33**
request (n) **80d**
require **144b**
reschedule **110a**
research (v) **144d**
resemble **148**
resident **110d**
respect **143**
respond **80d**
responsibility **144b**
rest (n) **90**
rest (v) **44**
restaurant **10b**
result **33**
resume **64b**
retire **10c**
retirement **31**
return **10b**
Revolutionary War **20c**
rice **98**
ride (n) **39**
ride (v) **11**
right (adj) **55**
right (n) **20c**
right away **28**
right now **27**
ring (n) **119**
ring (v) **69**
rinse out **50d**
rip **15**
risk **110c**

road **62**
road surface **20b**
robbery **55**
roller coaster **101**
roller-skate **104**
room **16**
roommate **99**
routine (adj) **80d**
routine (n) **112**
rubella **110d**
rude **85**
rug **49**
rule **114**
rules of the road **109**
run **20a**
run away **99**
run into **124**
run out of **124**
running shoes **130b**
rural **145**

sad **13**
safari **66**
safari guide **66**
safe **80d**
safely **144d**
safety **32b**
sail away **100**
salad plate **64b**
salary **49**
sale **127**
salesman **141**
salesperson **51**
same **34**
sandwich **64b**
satellite **53**
satellite dish **29**
satisfaction **48**
satisfactory **32b**
satisfied **120**
Saturday **7**
Saudi Arabia **33**
save **130c**
save up **64c**
savings **130b**
saxophone **62**
say **20c**
say good-bye **30**
say hello **102**
schedule (n) **66**
schedule (v) **50b**
schedule appointments
    50b
scheduled **110a**
school **5**
school attendance line
    32a
school event **32b**
school nurse **139**
school play **13**
school year **32b**
science **102**
science center **32c**
science fiction **13**

science teacher 102
score 113
Scrabble 3
screening test 110c
screwdriver 29
scuba dive 40
seafood 64b
search 144d
second 144a
secretary 47
see 17
seem 114
select 130b
selection 126
sell 20d
semester 23
Senate 10c
senator 10c
send 8
senior 32b
senior citizen 110c
sentence 148
separable 148
separately 148
September 7
serious 94c
serve 10c
service (n) 80d
service address 80b
service balance 80b
set up 94a
seven days a week 34
seven years later 34
several times a week 136
severe 110b
shake 17
share 94c
shave 14
shift 65
shine 95
shirt 2
shock 144d
shoes 98
shoot 113
shop 26
shopper 65
shopping mall 102
short 58
shorts 129
shoulder 16
shout 8
shovel 98
show 94b
show tune 23
shower 73
shred 10b
shredder 10b
shy 137
Siberia 66
siblings 110b
sick 44
sick day 64c
sick leave 64c
sign (n) 65

sign (v) 10c
sign up 64c
signature 10b
silver 113
similar 136
simple 121
simply 120
since last Friday 52
sincerely 32a
sing 4
Singapore 60
singer 1
single 9
sink 45
sister 5
sit 16
situation 144d
size 126
skate 4
skater 1
skating 111
ski 4
skier 1
skiing 111
skills 50a
skin 144b
skirt 130b
slave 20d
sleep 12
sleeve 130a
slice 64b
sliding scale 110d
slip 117
slippery 20b
Slovak Republic 146
small 18
small talk 94c
smart 67
smile 94c
smoke detector 80d
smoothly 80d
snow (n) 20b
snow (v) 71
snowboard 14
so far 125
soccer 5
social security number
    10a
socks 75
software 144d
soldier 20c
solve 144b
some other time 118
sometime next week 116
son 8
son-in-law 91
soon 25
sophomore 32b
sorry 68
soundtrack 111
soup 130c
source 110e
South 20d
Southern states 20d

souvenir 19
Soviet republic 33
space 53
spaghetti 43
speak 11
speak up 144b
speaker 148
special 35
specialist 144d
speech 40
speed 113
spend 34
sports 4
sports car 59
sports fan 113
sports jacket 92
sports training 112
sprain 14
sprain *her* ankle 14
sprain *her* wrist 105
sprain *his* back 105
spring 22
square 49
squash 105
staff 64b
stained 130a
staircase 110e
stamp 114
stamp collection 114
stand 16
stand in line 69
stand up 147
starchy vegetable 110e
start 58
start button 144a
state (n) 10a
state (v) 50a
state government 20c
statement 80b
statement date 80b
statue 49
Statue of Liberty 49
stay 5
stay home 35
stay open 65
stay up 99
stay with 30
steak bone 105
steal 10b
stereo system 121
stiff 54
stiff neck 55
still 44
stomach problems 110b
stomachache 32a
stop 20b
stop sign 133
storage area 80d
store (n) 10b
store (v) 80d
store manager 58
story 35
straight 17
strange 72

strawberry 110b
strawberry shortcake 101
street 10a
street festival 110c
strict 131
strictly 80a
stripe 110e
strong 110e
stuck 40
student 8
student center 32c
study 2
subject 142
submit 145
suburbs 34
subway 66
subway pusher 66
success 144b
successful 60
suggestion 148
suit 23
suitcase 98
summary 80c
summer 22
Summer Olympics 111
summer vacation 31
sun 84
Sunday 7
super 130b
Superman 23
supermarket 24
supervise 32b
supervisor 16
supplies 64b
support 137
Supreme Court 10c
Supreme Court justice
    10c
sure 28
surf 87
surprise 140
surprised 47
Swahili 38
Swaziland 145
sweater 2
Sweden 67
sweetheart 147
swim 3
swimmer 1
swimming 111
switch 65
swollen 54
swollen knee 54
Sydney 34
system 80d

table 94a
take 13
take a course 97
take a ride 39
take a shower 66
take a tour 49
take a trip 102
take a walk 37

take after **124**
take back **116**
take blood pressure **50b**
take care **34**
take down **115**
take home **109**
take inventory **50b**
take messages **50b**
take off **100**
take out **121**
take time **54**
take your medicine **46**
takeout food **64b**
talent **50c**
talk **7**
talk show **8**
tall **143**
tango **105**
tap dance **87**
tardiness **64c**
tax **144d**
taxi **19**
taxi driver **50**
teach **11**
teacher **1**
team (sports) **111**
team (work) **64b**
team player **94c**
tease **91**
technical school **93**
tee shirt **130b**
teenager **57**
teeth **105**
telephone **65**
telephone bill **8**
telephone number **10a**
telephone skills **144d**
tell **5**
tenant **80d**
tend to **137**
tennis **5**
tennis coach **5**
tense (adj) **35**
tense (n) **35**
tenth-grade **102**
term **10c**
term paper **46**
terminated **64a**
termites **57**
terrible **104**
terrific **48**
test **36**
tetanus **110d**
tetanus shot **110c**
Texas **57**
thank **35**
thank-you note **75**
the day after **121**
the next day **129**
the other day **109**
the rest of **90**
the weekend before **96**
theater **32b**
theater group **136**

Therm **80b**
thief **10b**
thin **143**
thing **5**
think **20d**
think about **81**
think ahead **144b**
think over **119**
thirsty **13**
this Friday night **23**
this January **22**
this morning **16**
this spring **22**
this Sunday **22**
this weekend **24**
Thomas Jefferson **20c**
thousands **50c**
three times a day **7**
three years ago **34**
throw **10b**
throw away **115**
throw out **116**
thunder **135**
Thursday **7**
ticket **72**
tie **43**
tied up **36**
tight **127**
time **32b**
time clock **64c**
time management **144d**
time sheet **64c**
time zone **65**
timeline **20e**
tip **50c**
tired **12**
today **16**
tomato **130c**
tomorrow **32a**
tomorrow morning **21**
tone **32a**
tongue **113**
tonight **21**
tool **50b**
toothache **32a**
top (n) **49**
top (adj) **67**
topic **94c**
Toronto **30**
total (adj) **33**
total (n) **64c**
total amount due **80b**
total balance **80c**
touchy **142**
tour **49**
tourist **19**
town **102**
toy **117**
track **111**
tradition **145**
traditional **65**
traditionally **145**
traffic **20a**
train (n) **20a**

train (v) **64b**
train station **123**
training **111**
training center **111**
training program **144b**
training session **94b**
trash **10b**
travel **35**
travel reservation **144d**
traveler's check **98**
tree house **24**
trip (n) **102**
trip (v) **14**
trouble **94b**
trousers **128**
truck **38**
truth **83**
try **44**
try on **115**
tuberculosis **110b**
tuberculosis test **110b**
Tuesday **7**
tulip **66**
tulip farmer **66**
Turkish **34**
turn (n) **144b**
turn down **119**
turn off **35**
turn on **80d**
tuxedo **29**
TV program **35**
twenty-four hours a day **65**
twice **7**
twice a day **7**
twist **104**
twist *his* ankle **104**
two hours later **121**
two-person **111**
two-word verb **148**
type (n) **146**
type (v) **4**
typical **47**
typist **1**

Ukraine **33**
umbrella **132**
unbelievable **75**
uncle **9**
uncomfortable **94c**
understand **64a**
unfortunately **24**
unfriendly **94c**
unhappy **148**
unhealthy **85**
unique **66**
United Nations **49**
unpaid balance **80b**
unsatisfactory **32b**
until 8:00 **25**
until next year **25**
unused **64c**
unusual **111**
upset **16**

upstairs (adj) **141**
upstairs (adv) **135**
up-to-date **110d**
urban **33**
usage **80b**
use (n) **137**
use (v) **35**
use up **119**
used **76**
usual **127**
usually **16**

vacation **18**
vacation day **64c**
vaccination **110b**
vacuum **49**
valuable **77**
van **41**
varicella **110d**
variety **144d**
Vatican **19**
vegetable dish **64b**
vegetable group **110e**
vegetables **98**
vegetarian **89**
vehicle **20a**
veil **146**
verb **114**
version **145**
vice-president **10c**
victim **10b**
village **146**
violinist **1**
visit (n) **102**
visit (v) **8**
vitamins **109**
vocational center **32c**
vocational school **50a**
vocational training **140**
voice **105**
voice mail **67**
volleyball **14**
volunteer (v) **32b**
voter **10c**

wages **144d**
wait **47**
waiting room **54**
wake up **20a**
walk (n) **37**
walk (v) **102**
walk home **128**
walk the dog **131**
wallet **10b**
want **5**
want ad **131**
war **10c**
wash **12**
watch **3**
watch TV **9**
water (n) **80d**
water (v) **95**
water heater **73**
water-ski **24**